MOON HANDBOOKS®

FOUR CORNERS

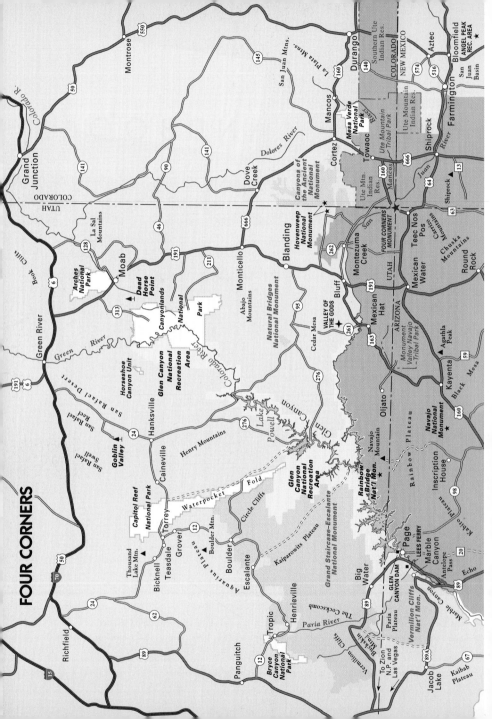

FOUR CORNERS

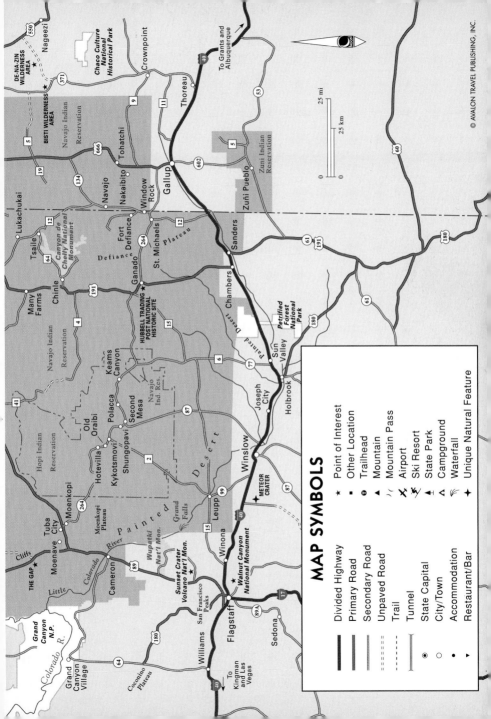

near Cow Canyon Trading Post, Bluff, Utah

© JULIAN SMITH

MOON HANDBOOKS®

FOUR CORNERS

INCLUDING NAVAJO AND HOPI COUNTRY, MOAB, AND LAKE POWELL

FIRST EDITION

JULIAN SMITH

AVALON
TRAVEL

MAPS

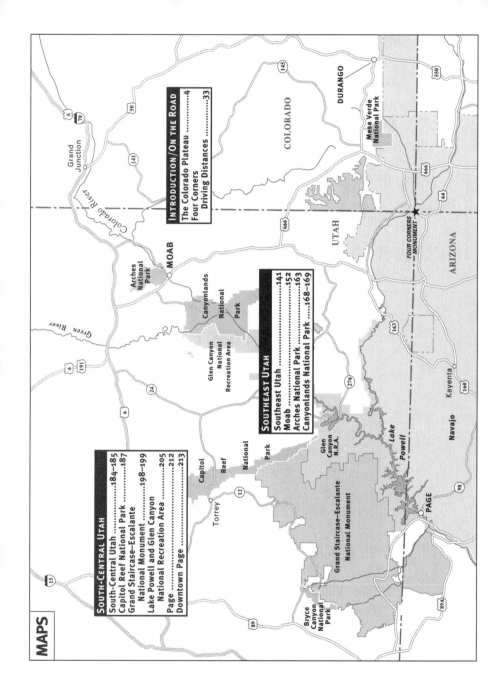

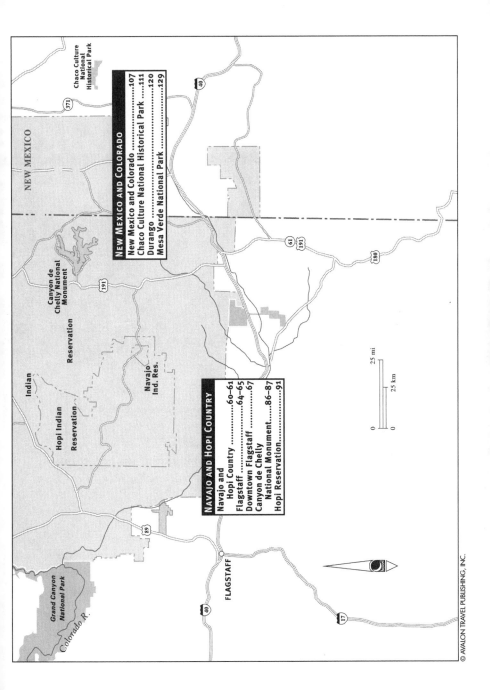

NEW MEXICO AND COLORADO

NAVAJO AND HOPI COUNTRY

NEW MEXICO

Chaco Culture
National
Historical Park

Canyon de
Chelly National
Monument

Reservation

Indian

Hopi Indian
Reservation

Navajo
Ind. Res.

Grand Canyon
National Park

Colorado R.

FLAGSTAFF

25 mi

25 km

© AVALON TRAVEL PUBLISHING, INC.

Contents

© JULIAN SMITH

Introduction 1

This is the windswept, sun-punished heart of the Southwest, where you'll encounter valleys strewn with thousand-foot mesas, the thundering rapids of the Colorado River, the living heart of the Navajo and Hopi nations, and the ruins of peoples even more ancient. This unforgiving landscape offers many rewards— not the least of which is seeing yourself through the lens of another culture.

On the Road 31

Whether you build your travels around exploring Anasazi ruins, driving your dusty van down the farthest dirt road, or vanishing for weeks on foot, bike, or raft, arm yourself with the right information and you'll find firsthand that the Four Corners is truly like no other place on earth.

Navajo and Hopi Country

At the edge of the loneliest yet most extraordinary acreage of the Colorado Plateau you'll find Flagstaff, the region's most vibrant city. But indigenous cultures truly define the Four Corners: Anasazi cliff dwellings are scattered throughout, and the Navajo and Hopi tribes have emerged into the 21st century with their pride and many of their traditions intact.

New Mexico and Colorado

Slashed by arroyos and backed by pine-covered peaks, these rolling plains and tablelands are rich in oil. But true riches are rooted deep in the past—the archaeological sites of Mesa Verde and Chaco Canyon. The lively mountain city of Durango offers more contemporary diversions: skiing, hiking, biking, and college-town ambience.

Southeast Utah

Snowcapped mountains plunging into river canyons, hot-air balloons soaring over desert towers, mountain bikes tumbling down the Slickrock Trail, white water raging along the Colorado and Green Rivers . . . these are just a few of the reasons to come to Southeast Utah. Moab is the pulsing epicenter of this land of extremes, which also offers national parks, a national monument, and vistas that will leave you weak in the knees.

South-Central Utah

Big, beautiful, remote, and nearly empty, South-Central Utah features some of the wildest geography on the continent. The steps of the Grand Staircase march across the region's western reaches, while the Escalante River winds its way through tortuous canyons before draining into Lake Powell. At the southern end of this water-sports Mecca, just over the border in Arizona, the tourist town of Page offers respite from all of the activity.

ABOUT THE AUTHOR
Julian Smith

A life has to move or it stagnates.
—Beryl Markham

Julian Smith has been writing since he learned to read, and traveling since his first family trip to Cape Cod as a toddler. A pre-college summer in Brazil sparked a love affair with (and in) Latin America, fueled by a stint studying the cloud forests of Costa Rica. Days after wrangling a degree in biology from the University of Virginia, he found himself hopelessly entangled in a self-publishing venture that resulted nine months later in the one-pound, eight-ounce *On Your Own in El Salvador,* the first in-depth guide to that country. *Moon Handbooks Ecuador* came two years later.

Julian returned to Virginia, where there was much rejoicing, although everyone kept saying the same thing: "Didn't you graduate?" Since completing *Moon Handbooks Virginia,* he has contributed to *Road Trip USA, Online Travel Planning for Dummies, National Geographic Traveler,* and other publications. He has somehow earned a Masters' degree in Wildlife Ecology in the meantime, while eating smoked salmon and studying grizzly bears on the coast of British Columbia.

As far as normal jobs go, Julian has done pretty well. He's worked as a Canyonlands National Park ranger, guided tourists through the Central American rainforest, and tried (in vain) to protect the vegetable garden of one of the richest men in the world from marauding rodents. Along the way he's found himself freezing atop Kilimanjaro, meditating in a Japanese Zen temple, doused with rum in a Cuban santería ceremony, and, through absolutely no fault of his own, fleeing from Ugandan pygmies.

He is currently editing a journal for the Ecological Society of America in Washington, DC. Snowboarding, mountain biking, and rock climbing still keep things interesting back east, and the rest of his time goes toward reruns of *The Simpsons* and plotting his eventual return to the Southwest. For more travel writing, photography, updates, and assorted oddities, stop by his website, www.juliansmith.com.

Benedicto:

May your trails be crooked, winding, lonesome, dangerous, leading to the most amazing view. May your mountains rise into and above the clouds. May your rivers flow without end, meandering through pastoral valleys tinkling with bells, past temples and castles and poets' towers into a dark primeval forest where tigers belch and monkeys howl, through miasmal and mysterious swamps and down into a desert of red rock, blue mesas, domes and pinnacles and grottos of endless stone, and down again into a deep vast ancient unknown chasm where bars of sunlight blaze on profiled cliffs, where deer walk across the white sand beaches, where storms come and go as lightning clangs upon the high crags, where something strange and more beautiful and more full of wonder than your deepest dreams waits for you—beyond that next turning of the canyon walls.

Edward Abbey

Introduction

I'm not sure when or where I realized the Four Corners is my favorite place on earth. It might have been during that summer monsoon in the canyon country, dark anvil clouds opening in a Biblical torrent that vanished into the sand within an hour. Or maybe it was while watching a sunset from Muley Point, sparks from my juniper campfire leaping into the deepening darkness. The crazy thrill of paddling a dime-store raft across the Colorado River, rapids thundering just around the bend, probably had something to do with it too. Awareness may also have dawned in that slot canyon in the Escalante, camera and pants held high as I waded through the muddy, ice-cold water. Or maybe my realization is all thanks to

Romeo, the old Navajo man I picked up hitch-hiking near Page, who told me about his herds of horses and then just smiled and said, "I am happy."

In any case, no place I've ever been bears even remote resemblance to the high, windswept, sun-punished heart of the Southwest. It is a landscape that exhausts the vocabulary, has you reaching for the thesaurus and then tossing it aside in frustration. Wallace Stegner called it "a country that calls for wings"—watch ravens play above a valley strewn with thousand-foot mesas and you will ache to join them. Over it all stretches the endless, indescribable bowl of sky, the "brilliant blue world of stinging air and moving cloud" that Willa Cather described in *Death Comes for the Archbishop*:

© JULIAN SMITH

Muley Point, on the edge of Cedar Mesa, near Mexican Hat

*Everywhere the sky is the roof of the world;
but here the earth was the floor of the sky.
The landscape one longed for when one was
far away, the thing all about one, the world
one actually lived in, was the sky, the sky!*

The Four Corners is a region steeped in history,
with villages centuries older than the country they
eventually became part of. A crossroads of Indian,
Spanish, and American cultures, this area lets you
interact with tribes on two of the country's largest
reservations and explore the ruins
of peoples even more ancient. Gaze
up at huge, wraithlike figures
painted in Old Testament times
and it's hard not to marvel at a culture that prospered in this merciless
setting yet evaporated in less than a
century, leaving behind countless
artifacts and ruins. The Navajo,
Hopi, and Ute tribes all weathered
the influx of Anglo settlers to
emerge with their pride and many
of their traditions intact. This is
the region where in one day you
can eat a taco next to a Navajo ma-
tron dressed in her best turquoise
and silver, watch a feathered god
dance in a Hopi village plaza, and
enjoy a good-humored bargaining session over a rug
that took months to hand-weave. Adjusting to this
world within a world is sometimes a shock, but
the reward—seeing your own culture through the
lens of another—is well worth it.

If you're never happier than when you are careening down singletrack on a mountain bike, negotiating white water, loping through an aspen
meadow on horseback, or sleeping under the
stars, you're in luck in this region. As outdoor
recreation goes, the only thing the Four Corners
lacks is a good surfing beach—though Moab
does have a waterpark and Lake Powell has plenty
of shoreline. Pick a sport for each season—hike in
the spring, raft in the summer, bike in the fall, ski
in the winter—and you'll still have plenty to
spare, from llama packing and hot-air ballooning
to rock climbing and trout fishing. Activities
special to the area include riding the narrow-

gauge rail line out of Durango and exploring
slot canyons so narrow you have to scoot through
sideways. For those addicted to solitude, it's possible to get good and truly lost out here, and
have a heck of a lot of fun doing it. There is
nowhere else in the Lower 48 where it's so easy to
lose the crowds—or anyone else, for that matter.

The enchantment of the place, though, is impossible to put into words, although many have
tried. "I am drunk with the fiery elixir of beauty,"
wrote Everett Ruess, the vagabond artist who disappeared into a Utah canyon at the
age of 20. "I have seen almost more
beauty than I can bear." Edward
Abbey, one of the most famous
voices of the western deserts, told of
the "huge vibration of light and
stillness and solitude" that "shapes
itself in the form of hovering wings
spread out across the sky from the
world's rim to the world's end."

Yet in the end description is futile. The spirit of the Southwest,
cliché as the term has become, is
ineffable; it must be experienced
in person. "It is a mystery," said
Steinbeck in *Travels with Charlie,*
"something concealed and waiting." With that, though, comes
the possibility of discovery, and the fact that you're
reading this far is a good start.

When you take the next step, you'll come to
understand how extraordinary this place is and
why it inspires such reverence among residents
and even casual visitors. Spend some time here
and you too will appreciate the words of the
Blessing Way, a ceremonial chant the Navajo use
to restore *hozho,* the sacred harmony that gives
focus and purpose to life:

*In beauty I walk
With beauty before me I walk
With beauty behind me I walk
With beauty above me I walk
With beauty around me I walk
It has become beauty again
It has become beauty again
It has become beauty again
It has become beauty again.*

> *It is a landscape that
> exhausts the vocabu-
> lary, has you reaching
> for the thesaurus and
> then tossing it aside in
> frustration. Wallace
> Stegner called it "a
> country that calls for
> wings"—watch ravens
> play above a valley
> strewn with thousand-
> foot mesas and you
> will ache to join them.*

The Land

The Four Corners is part of the larger **Colorado Plateau**, one of the major physiographic provinces of the western United States. Expand the (admittedly arbitrary) boundaries of the Four Corners outward and you have the Colorado Plateau: 130,000 square miles (337,000 square kilometers) of southern Utah, northern Arizona, northwestern New Mexico, and southwestern Colorado. Bounded by the Rocky Mountains to the north and east, the Sonoran Desert to the south, and Nevada's Great Basin to the west, the Colorado Plateau consists of relatively flat country sliced by rivers and punctuated by buttes and mountains.

GEOLOGY

Geologic History

The combined forces of weather, gravity, and plate tectonics have filled this region with an amazing variety of topography. If you remember nothing else about the complex surface of the Four Corners (and there is a lot), keep these three words in mind: deposition, uplift, and erosion. At its simplest, the Four Corners' stupendous scenery can be summed up in three steps. First, layers of sediment were laid down like Navajo blankets on a bed. Next, these were bent, abused, and generally lifted toward the sky by huge energies below ground. Finally, wind, rain, ice, and, above all, flowing water molded these layers into the mesas and canyons and endless other landforms that fill the region today.

In all, some 300 million years of geologic history are visible in the Four Corners, a display with few equals in the world. The oldest rocks in the region, at the bottom of the Grand Canyon, date to the middle of the Precambrian Era (4.6 billion–570 million years ago). During the Cambrian, Devonian, Mississippian, and Permian Periods, (570–320 million years ago), the region was much closer to the equator, and warm tropical seas left behind layers of early marine fossils. A series of mountain ranges called the Ancestral Rockies rose during the Pennsylvanian Period (320–286 million years ago), including the Uncompahgre Uplift in what is now eastern Utah and western Colorado. Probably as high as today's Rockies, these mountains shed sediments into lower-elevation depressions such as the Paradox Basin, which filled and emptied of water as deep geologic faults shifted well into the Permian Period (286–245 million years ago).

During the Triassic Period (245–208 million years ago), continental drift carried the land north into warmer climates. Increased rainfall fed lakes, streams, marshes, and early forests, some of which were buried and turned to stone, to be uncovered much later. Ferns and early conifers, along with primitive amphibians and reptiles, were also covered in silt, mud, and sand. Dinosaur fossils were added to the mix during the Jurassic Period (208–144 million years ago), when the local climate cooled somewhat as the continent moved even further north. By this time the Uncompahgre Uplift had been mostly worn away, and seas flowing in from the west and north created muddy tidal flats whose petrified ripples turn up near sand dunes also frozen by the forces of time.

More marine fossils are found in layers dating to the Cretaceous Period (104–66 million years ago), when waters spread across North America from Alaska to Mexico. The modern Rocky Mountains rose during this period as well, taking 20–30 million years and plenty of distorting of the earth's crust to reach their current heights. More uplift followed during the Tertiary Period (66–2 million years ago), starting with the formation of the laccolithic mountains that rise above the plateau today. The La Sals, the Abajos, the Henry Mountains, and Navajo Mountain are all formed over huge blisters of magma that pushed upward without breaking through to the surface.

Beginning about 15 million years ago, the entire plateau, which until then had existed close to sea level, was lifted up about 3,000 feet. Steeper slopes made rivers flow faster, increasing erosion, and rapid downcutting occurred along the course of the Colorado and Green Rivers. About 10,000 feet of sedimentary deposits have eroded in the last 10–15 million years, exposing millions of

INTRODUCTION

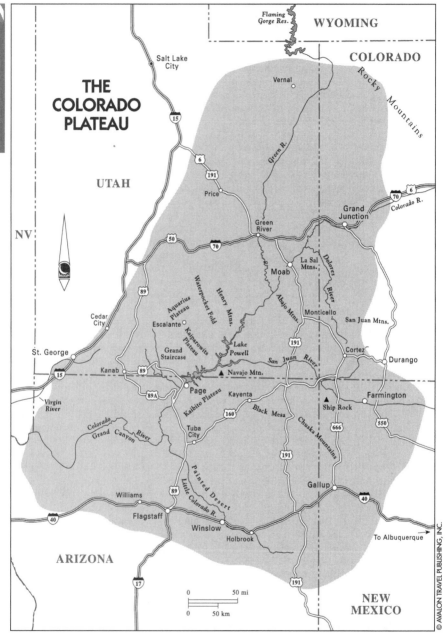

THE COLORADO PLATEAU

WYOMING

COLORADO

Flaming Gorge Res.

Salt Lake City

Vernal

Rocky Mountains

UTAH

Green R.

Price

Grand Junction

Colorado R.

NV

Green River

50

70

89

Moab

La Sal Mtns.

Dolores River

Waterpocket Fold

Aquarius Plateau

Henry Mtns.

Abajo Mtns.

Monticello

San Juan Mtns.

Cedar City

Escalante

Kaiparowits Plateau

Lake Powell

191

Cortez

Durango

St. George

Grand Staircase

San Juan River

15

Kanab

89

Navajo Mtn.

Page

Kaibito Plateau

Kayenta

Ship Rock

Farmington

Virgin River

89A

160

Black Mesa

666

550

Colorado River

Grand Canyon

Tuba City

Chuska Mountains

191

Painted Desert

Gallup

Williams

89

Little Colorado R.

40

Flagstaff

ARIZONA

Winslow

Holbrook

To Albuquerque

17

191

0   50 mi

0   50 km

NEW MEXICO

© AVALON TRAVEL PUBLISHING, INC.

CANYON COUNTRY ROCK LAYERS

More than 300 million years of layering and erosion are visible in the canyon country of the Four Corners. Over the eons sandstones, limestone, shales, and mudstones were laid down beneath rivers, swamps, deserts, and shallow oceans. With so much geology on display, it can be a chore to remember which layer is which—let alone when it was laid down.

Some layers, like the distinctive sheer walls of Wingate Sandstone near Moab, are easy to recognize. Others are not, especially when they change from place to place, like the ubiquitous Navajo Sandstone, deposited as dunes during the Jurassic Period. In Canyonlands and Capitol Reef National Parks, its distinctive rounded contours are the color of chalk and cream. It starts turning pink in the lower reaches of Zion Canyon, and the walls of Glen Canyon are still salmon-colored somewhere beneath the silty waters of Lake Powell to the south.

A few mnemonic devices can help with the names of rock layers. Heading up the Colorado River from Lees Ferry, remember the phrase "Many Canyon Walls Know No Capitalist Exploitation" to recall the layers visible from bottom (oldest) to top: Moenkopi, Chinle, Wingate, Kayenta, Navajo, Carmel, and Entrada. Another saying takes you from top to bottom: "Every New Kangaroo Wants Chocolate Milk" (Entrada, Navajo, Kayenta, Wingate, Chinle, Moenkopi). The three most visible layers in southeast Utah are the Kayenta, Navajo, and Entrada.

work—hopefully from a safe distance. Well into the 20th century towers collapsed and chunks fell from arches; rocks tumble from cliffs almost every day.

Major Features

Elevations in the Four Corners range from 2,000 feet (600 meters) at the bottom of the Grand Canyon to 12,700 feet (3,870 meters) in the La Sal Mountains near Moab, but they average 3,000–5,000 feet. The tension between lifting up and tearing down shows in the contrast between huge, shallow basins such as northern New Mexico's oil-rich San Juan Basin and smaller uplifted areas with names like Defiance, Monument, Zuñi, and the Circle Cliffs.

Dark green forests cover the largest ranges: the **La Sal Mountains** east of Moab, the **Abajo Mountains** west of Monticello, and the **Henry Mountains** east of Capitol Reef National Park. On the Navajo Reservation, **Navajo Mountain** rises south of Lake Powell, and the **Chuska** and **Carrizo Mountains** follow the Arizona-New Mexico border. Boulder and Thousand-Lake Mountain form the bulk of the **Aquarius Plateau,** in south-central Utah near the colorfully named cliffs that make up the **Grand Staircase** to the west. Other dramatic features include stair-step **monoclines** stretching for dozens of miles; the Waterpocket Fold is the largest of these, but the list includes Comb Ridge on Cedar Mesa and The Cockscomb in the southern Escalante. Black Mesa, rich in coal, underlies most of the Hopi Reservation and the central Navajo Reservation.

The list goes on: buttes and mesas, looming cliffs, and volcanic necks and dikes dot the terrain by the hundreds. Long, brown rivers meander for miles before exploding into white water in deep, shaded canyons. The **Colorado River,** creator of the Grand Canyon, is the unquestioned champion, even though dams and reservoirs punctuate much of its length, and more often than not it trickles to nothing in the desert of northern Mexico instead of reaching the Gulf of California. Born in the Colorado Rockies, it follows a major fault zone running northeast to southwest from Utah into Arizona, and is joined in the heart of Canyonlands National Park by the **Green River,** which flows south from Wyoming. The **San Juan**

years of older rock layers. About 5.5 million years ago, the San Andreas Fault opened the Gulf of California, freeing the Colorado River to flow into the ocean to the southwest.

The forces of erosion continued through the Quaternary period (2 million years ago–present), and the youngest geologic features are still in the process of being created and destroyed. The forces of weather, gravity, and chance shape arches, spires, natural bridges, and hoodoos; volcanic necks and dikes are exposed as their softer outer layers wear away. The time scale involved is immense, but if you're lucky you might see the geologic process at

GEOLOGIC TERMS

anticline: arch-shaped upfold in rock layers

arch: freestanding stone curve formed by erosion

butte: flat-topped hill with sloping sides, higher than it is wide

concretion: rounded mineral mass found in sedimentary rock

cross-bedding: linear patterns in sandstone created by shifting wind directions (also called cross stratification)

desert varnish: dark rock coating formed by water and microbes

diatreme: solidified neck of an explosive volcano, later exposed by erosion

dike: "sheet" of igneous rock formed by fissures filling and cooling

fault: fracture or break in a rock mass that has moved

graben: straight-walled canyon formed by down-shifted fault blocks (German for "ditch" or "grave")

horst: uplifted block remaining between grabens

joint: fracture or break in a rock mass that has not moved

mesa: flat-topped hill with steeply sloping sides, wider than it is high

monocline: step-like fold in rock layers

natural bridge: freestanding stone curve formed by flowing water

pothole: shallow, water-collecting depression created by erosion

slickrock: smooth, bare sandstone

syncline: trough-shaped downfold in rock layers

talus: rock fragments that accumulate at the bottom of eroding slopes or cliffs

River runs west across northern New Mexico and Arizona before joining **Lake Powell,** a huge reservoir in southern Utah formed by the Colorado River backing up behind Glen Canyon Dam. The Little Colorado River drains the southern Navajo Reservation before it joins the Colorado in the Grand Canyon. Verdant valleys line some sections of riverbank. These are fed by countless streams and washes, many of which flow only a few days out of the year.

CLIMATE

The Colorado Plateau is classified as arid to semi-arid, receiving an average of 11.8 inches (300 mm) of rain per year—a little too much to qualify as desert, but close enough. This, along with the fact that the plateau sits an average of 5,000 feet (1,500 m) above sea level, means that **extreme temperatures** are the norm. Summer heat over 100°F drops to a winter chill below 0°F.

With little cloud cover or vegetation to get in the way, up to 90 percent of sunlight typically reaches the ground, compared to less than 50 percent in other temperate regions. Ground temperatures skyrocket by day, particularly during the sweltering summer months, June–Sept. At night, however, the dry air lets the heat escape just as quickly, and temperatures plummet. **Daily temperature fluctuations** can be tremendous; a drop of 40°F between noon and night is not unusual.

Deserts are characterized as much by **seasonal rainfall** as by low rainfall. When it does come, most **precipitation** falls during **summer monsoons** ("male rain" to the Navajo) and winter snows. Cloudbursts are usually heralded by black clouds and anvil-shaped thunderheads visible for miles. Occasionally the rain actually evaporates before it hits the ground, a phenomenon called virga which happens most often in winter, when low-level air is very dry. Lightning is a danger on high-altitude plateaus; seek shelter if you're caught out in the open. These downpours can dump inches of water in just a few minutes, and the topography has a tendency to channel the rain over a wide area into narrow gullies. (The ground is also usually too dry to absorb that much moisture that quickly.) This results in rivers that suddenly rise, dry washes that abruptly flow, or the most extreme example, **flash floods** that can scour a narrow canyon with little or no warning. Moisture that falls as snow is useless to plants until it melts in the spring, when the occasional showers are gentler (the Navajo's nourishing "female rain") than summer rainstorms.

Flora and Fauna

The Colorado Plateau's tortured topography blesses it with a wide range of biological diversity, from bare rock to lush riverbanks, sweltering lowlands to snowy alpine tundra. Most of it is high and dry, averaging about 4,000 feet above sea level and receiving only 12 inches of rain per year. The result is an arid landscape whose inhabitants are well adapted to life where water is a precious commodity. Numerous microclimates give rise to special mini-ecosystems, including hanging gardens, potholes, and cryptobiotic soil crusts. It helps that this region is one of the largest roadless areas (some say *the* largest) in the Lower 48, but human encroachment has taken a toll even so.

A good source of information on the ecosystems of the Southwest is *The Southwestern Naturalist,* www.emporia.edu/swan/joureng.htm, a journal published by the **Southwestern Association of Naturalists,** based at Emporia State University in Kansas.

FLORA

The arid reaches of the Colorado Plateau favor sparse, scrubby vegetation spread widely across the lowlands. More than 2,500 species of vascular plants grow in the region, over 200 of them endemic. Species from the Great Basin to the west mix with those from the Rocky Mountains to the east. Forests cover the mountains, with different tree communities occurring at different heights. The banks of streams and rivers are lined with lush vegetation, some native, some not.

Dealing with Drought

A desert (or near-desert) calls for special adaptations to collect water and hold onto it. Even when rain does fall, moisture doesn't stick around for long:

heavy rains tend to run off hard, dry soils rather than soak in. Between soil evaporation and plant transpiration (water loss during photosynthesis), collectively termed "evapotranspiration," water loss can approach the ridiculous: regions that receive less than five inches of rain a year may lose 120 inches! (In Moab, for example, potential evapotranspiration is over 80 inches per year.) Plants, which are unable to move on when things get tough, have to do the best with what's available.

Most plants in this region are able to wait for the right time to throw energy into making flowers or seeds. After a summer thundershower, a barren plateau can erupt with color as desiccated plants put out blossoms almost overnight. Some grass and flower seeds can lie dormant in the soil for years, waiting to germinate until just the right amount of precipitation falls. Some plants flower only at night to avoid losing water to the daytime heat. Many perennial plants resist drought by getting rid of a plant's biggest water-wasters: its leaves. Thorns on cacti minimize water loss, and small, hairy or scale-like leaves and waxy coverings on other plants cut down on moisture lost to moving air.

Other plants take a more direct route by growing only near constant water supplies, such as in streamside areas or in the unique, fragile **hanging gardens** found at springs and seeps, which are full of ferns, monkey-flowers, and other species that are rare elsewhere. Willows and cottonwoods send roots deep to reach the water table along rivers and sporadic streams. When rain falls, the best plan is to gather as much as possible, as quickly as possible. With this in mind (evolutionarily speaking), the lethal leaves of the narrowleaf yucca channel moisture into the plant's center just as the wide, shallow roots of the

CRYPTOBIOTIC SOIL

The dark, rough covering that grows on undisturbed sandy soil takes its name from the Greek words for "hidden" and "life," and for a long time it was a mystery to biologists. It turns out this crust—a mix of mosses, lichens, algae, and fungi—is crucial to the ecology of the desert. The ground-level equivalent of an old-growth forest, "crypto" starts as a dark scattering across the sand and can take centuries to grow just three or four inches. Frost buckling cracks the spongy covering and lifts it into tiny waves that solidify and help trap moisture and windblown seeds and spores. In addition to absorbing and holding water, crypto helps prevent soil erosion and provides nutrients such as nitrogen that plants need for growth. Without it, plant communities would take much longer to develop, or they might not at all. Cryptobiotic crust is very fragile; it can take years to recover from a boot print or tire track. Sometime it's impossible to dodge while in the backcountry, but do your best to avoid crunching the crypto during your travels.

prickly pear cactus absorb water dropped during brief rain showers.

Trees and Shrubs

The woody plants of the Colorado Plateau are usually small, widely spaced, and long-lived; some can live up to a century. They're tough too—their roots can split rocks. One of the most common shrubs is **Mormon tea,** an odd-looking broom-like plant that contains pseudoephedrine, a drug used in nasal decongestants. Early settlers boiled this relative of pines and junipers into a bitter but effective medicinal tea. **Blackbrush** is also ubiquitous, and although it's full of thorns, that doesn't keep desert bighorn sheep from eating it. The leaves of **four-winged saltbush,** which grows in soils too salty for other plants, have a distinctively saline taste many creatures find savory.

Fremont's cottonwood is unmistakable anywhere there is water, with its huge, gnarled trunks and delicate green leaves. Named for the downy, highly flammable cotton produced by the female trees, it can grow up to 90 feet tall. Other common plants in riparian areas include **netleaf hackberry,** and the invasive **Russian olive** and **tamarisk,** which can crowd out native vegetation. One of the most interesting partnerships in the Colorado Plateau involves the **narrowleaf yucca,** which looks like a collection of green swords all pointing outward. Unlike its relative the agave, or century plant, which flowers only once before dying, the narrowleaf yucca sends up a towering flower stalk every spring. After mating, the female yucca moth

gathers yucca pollen into a ball and spreads it to other yucca plants, so the larvae that hatch from the eggs she lays will have something to eat. In the process the moth pollinates the plant. Each would be lost without the other: yucca moth larvae feed only on yucca pollen, and the moths are the plant's only pollinators.

Between 4,500 and 5,500 feet, the most common plants are the **Utah juniper** and the **piñon pine.** This plant community covers an estimated 75,000 square miles of the dry, rocky West, making it one of the region's most common forest types. The juniper, whose leaves look like broccoli from a distance, is covered with shaggy bark that indigenous tribes used as kindling and to line baby cradleboards. Not a true cedar but rather a cypress, the juniper can stop circulation to its twisted outer branches during a drought to keep the rest of the tree alive. The scientific name of the **piñon pine,** *pinus edulis,* hints at its seasonal treasure: the delicious, protein-rich seeds inside its compact cones, produced in huge crops every 3–7 years. Roasted or eaten raw, they boast 5,000 calories per pound, making them an important food source for prehistoric people and animals alike. (Some birds breed late or not at all between pine nut crops.) The smallest member of the pine family smells sweet in a campfire, and its pitch was used to make baskets, mend pottery, and dress wounds.

Other common plants in this zone include the **cliffrose,** with its fragrant yellow blossoms; **mountain mahogany,** which resembles blackbrush

juniper

(mahogany branches alternate while those of blackbrush sprout opposite); and **big sagebrush,** one of the classic plants of the West. Mark Twain called it the "fag-end of vegetable creation," but it shelters smaller plants and animals, and has been eliminated from half of its historic acreage.

Between 6,500 and 8,000 feet, the most common tree is the **ponderosa pine,** with long needles grouped into threes and puzzle-like bark that smells like vanilla or butterscotch. Northern Arizona is home to the largest ponderosa pine forest in the world, with members averaging about 100 feet tall and three feet in diameter. Ponderosas are resistant to the fires that periodically clear the undergrowth, leaving pine forests wide open at eye level. The **Gambrel oak, bigtooth maple,** and **Utah serviceberry** are also found in the pine-oak belt.

Higher up the isolated mountain ranges, between 8,000 and 9,500 feet, is the domain of the **Douglas fir** and the **quaking aspen.** The fir (which is not really a fir, but a separate species altogether) has distinctive "mouse tails" called brachts poking out from between its cone scales. In its first two decades, it can grow two feet per year—a good thing since it's one of the most

valuable timber trees in the world. The white bark and shimmering green leaves of the aspen are unmistakable, and the seedlings are often one of the first things to grow in land cleared by humans or fire. This zone includes the **white fir** and **berry bushes** such as raspberry, gooseberry, and thimbleberry. The highest plant zone, from 9,500 feet to tree line at 11,500 feet, is home to the **Englemann spruce, blue spruce, subalpine fir, limber pine,** and **lodgepole pine.**

Flowers

Desert flowers, also a hardy bunch, are easy to underestimate—many visitors are amazed to see the plateau's color potential fully realized after a long-awaited downpour. Red blooms of the **Eaton's penstemon, common globemallow,** and **Indian paintbrush** are easy to spot, as are yellow flowers like the **sunflower, rough mule's ear,** and **newberry's twinpod.** I still have trouble telling the purplish **milkvetch** and **locoweed** apart, so it's good I'm not a cow; the latter contains an alkaloid that can drive grazers crazy or even kill them if they eat too much. The **dwarf lupine** and **showy four-o'clock** have bluish-purple flowers that are more easily distinguishable.

White flowers like the **Apache plume** and the delicate **sego lily** often serve a dual purpose; not only are they alluring, they're easier for pollinators to spot at night. That's why both the **sacred datura** and the **dwarf evening primrose** have white blossoms, as well as distinctive scents. The bell-like blooms of the datura, the largest flowers in canyon country, are pollinated by moths the size of small birds. The flower's toxic psychotropic compounds have long been used to induce spiritual visions. Moths aren't the only pollinators out there; butterflies, bees, wasps, birds, flies, and beetles are also hard at work, doing good simply by indulging their own selfish interests.

Cacti

Cacti are desert plants *par excellence*—the Ferraris of drought resistance. Succulent stems and pads store moisture and expand to hold more, while letting very little leak out through their waxy coatings. Spines protect the plant, and stomata open only at night to collect carbon dioxide for photosynthesis, conserving even more moisture. The cacti you're most likely to see include the **prickly pear,** with flattened, palm-sized pads and yellow or red blooms that appear

for only a few days. The fleshy interior of its red fruit, called *tuna* in Spanish, is eaten by animals and people (just make sure you get all those tiny little spines out—trust me). The **claret cup cactus,** which is pollinated by hummingbirds, produces crimson blooms in April and May on densely packed stems.

Invaders

It's hard to believe, but even in this inhospitable land some late-arriving plants have taken root and spread like wildfire. **Tamarisk,** imported from the Mediterranean in the 19th century, was planted as an ornamental and to control streamside erosion. The water-loving shrub took off at 12 miles per year until it established itself in nearly every tributary of the Colorado River. Tamarisks reproduce well in salty soils, and suck up twice as much water as any native species—a single plant can absorb 300 gallons per day through a taproot up to 50 feet long, and it's estimated that together tamarisks soak up 2–4.5 million gallons of water per day in the West, as much in a year as 20 million people.

Dense stands crowd out other plants, including cottonwoods, whose seeds can't sprout in the

© JULIAN SMITH

prickly pear cactus

shade. They also provide little food for other wildlife, burn very easily, and are hard to eradicate. To prevent new shoots from sprouting, stumps much be treated with herbicides and other species planted nearby. Luckily, tamarisk control efforts have begun, starting with the Tamarisk Research and Control Act of 2003. Rangers in the Maze district of Canyonlands National Park spray choked waterways with herbicides, and have already cleared some canyons of the intruder.

Shipments of wheat from Europe in the late 1800s brought the first seeds of **cheatgrass,** which now covers some 100 million acres across the West. Since it germinates in the fall and spends the winter storing energy and growing roots (as native plants lie dormant), it gets the jump when spring comes. It's also more efficient at using underground water and colonizing areas disturbed by cultivation, overgrazing, or fire. Animals don't like to eat it, and its seed heads are really annoying when they latch on to your socks. In all, cheatgrass is a formidable competitor, having replaced native grasslands on a scale seldom seen in botanical history.

FAUNA

Though the largest living things you see out here (aside from other hikers) are mostly birds and the occasional fleeing cottontail, a wide variety of critters call the Colorado Plateau home. Most wisely avoid the triple threats of heat, drought, and other animals by venturing into the open only at certain times of day or season.

Desert Adaptations

Many animals avoid the stress of daytime temperatures by coming out only at dawn and dusk (crepuscular) or at night (nocturnal). Fields of sagebrush start hopping near sunset as cottontails and jackrabbits emerge from their burrows, unwittingly calling their eager predators the coyotes. Porcupines, mule deer, and many birds also favor the cooler, dimmer in-between times, while many rodents, bobcats, mountain lions, and foxes wait until full darkness. Bats and owls, of course, are nocturnal.

Those that do come out by day (diurnal) have other strategies for surviving the heat. Some animals alter their activity patterns depending on the temperature. Mosquitoes, for example, come out at different times of day, or not at all, depending on how hot it is. Lizards and snakes are crepuscular in summer, diurnal in the spring and fall, and go into a state of semi-hibernation (torpor) in winter. If the moisture content of their plant food is over 75 percent, pronghorns can survive without drinking any water, as can the nocturnal Ord's kangaroo rat, which can extract all the liquids it needs from the seeds it eats.

Mammals

Desert bighorn sheep, driven close to extinction by livestock diseases and hunting, have been reintroduced into southeast Utah by the National Park Service. If you venture into the backcountry, you may spot one of the sure-footed ungulates, often in bands of females and young. During the fall and winter rut, males charge each other with a crash of their large curved horns. Herds of **pronghorns** roam the flats, where they can leap up to eight feet high and run up to 65 miles per hour. **Mule deer** thrive throughout the plateau now that most of their predators have been eliminated. They migrate to high ground in the summer, and males sport large racks of antlers. Their odd, bounding leap is called "stotting."

You can tell **desert cottontails** and **black-tailed jackrabbits** apart by size; jackrabbits are larger and more gangly, with long black-tipped ears useful for getting rid of excess heat. Similarly, a **gray fox** is larger than a **kit fox** and not nearly as cute—the latter's large ears and big bushy tail make it one of the most adorable desert creatures. Like these others, **coyotes** blend in well with the scenery in their buff and gray pelts. As big as medium-sized dogs, they flourish everywhere from the Escalante to backyards in Phoenix. A pack of coyotes yipping at the stars is one of the most hauntingly distinctive sounds in the Four Corners.

Ringtails are related to raccoons and have the striped, bushy tails to prove it. Daredevils of the cracks and ledges of canyon country, their incredible agility, balance, and daring (not to mention hind feet that can rotate 180° for a better

INTRODUCTION

POTHOLES OF LIFE

The sandstone depressions that pepper the Four Corners sit bone-dry and lifeless for much of the year. After a good-sized rain, however, the eruption of activity that follows is as astounding as it is rapid. Eggs, larvae, and small organisms that have survived temperatures from freezing to 140°F burst into life, which may be compressed into only a few weeks or even days until the pothole dries up again. Algae are present even in the smallest pools, providing a bottom rung to the abbreviated food chain. In bigger pools, tadpoles and fairy shrimp larvae squiggle in the muddy depths, backswimmer insects dive for the bottom, and predaceous diving beetles pursue the newly hatched. Take a closer look the next time you're gulping down a mouthful, and try not to disturb potholes any more than necessary. Whether they're full or empty, these amazing ecosystems are tenacious but delicate.

grip) let them climb places nobody else can. A host of chipmunks, squirrels, rats, and mice keeps these larger animals well fed. **Deer mice** are infamous for harboring the horrific hantavirus, which killed a number of people in the area in 1993. You'll probably see the conglomerated nests (middens) of four species of **woodrats** beneath rock overhangs. These are useful to scientists trying to reconstruct the ancient ecology of the Four Corners since their nests contain a little bit of just about everything under the sun—hence their common name, pack rat. The nighttime skies are the domain of nearly two dozen types of bats, from the **big brown bat** to the **western pipistrelle,** the smallest bat in the United States.

Beavers and grizzly bears, once both native to the area, have been exterminated. On the other hand, the black-footed ferret has been reintroduced, and it's only a matter of time before reintroduced gray wolves work their way up from southern Arizona or down from northern Utah.

Birds

Those far-off silhouettes soaring on the thermals are hard to distinguish. If it holds its wings in a "V" and wobbles as it glides, it's a **turkey vulture,** helping to keep the desert clean of carrion with its excellent eyesight and keen sense of smell. A large bird with flat wings and an even flight could be a **golden eagle,** boasting a six-foot wingspan, or a **red-tailed hawk,** the most common large bird of prey in the country. The red-tail's screeching call has added atmosphere to so many classic Westerns it's become an auditory cliché. Other raptors you might spot include the **sharp-shinned hawk** and **Cooper's hawk,** which look very similar (Cooper's are bigger). **Peregrine falcons,** the poster children of successful wildlife conservation, dive after prey at 180 mph, making them the world's fastest animal.

The **common raven** is one of the smartest animals, let alone birds, in the world. It can learn to speak, count to at least 10, and outperform graduate students in tests of memory. You'll often see these playful, jet-black birds cavorting in midair, doing barrel rolls or playing tag or catch. The black-and-white **black-billed magpies,** also in the crow family, are quite bright as well. Like ravens, they mate for life and have a wide range of vocalizations. Speaking of bird calls, the liquid descending notes of the seldom-seen **canyon wren** could be the theme song of the Colorado Plateau. The high desert scrub is the domain of the **piñon jay** and the **western scrub jay,** while the **mountain bluebird** sticks out like a sore (but beautiful) thumb.

Other common birds of the Colorado Plateau include **hummingbirds** (black-chinned and broad-tailed), **woodpeckers** (hairy and downy), and various **chickadees, warblers, flycatchers,** and the occasional **spotted towhee** rustling in the underbrush. After dark the **great horned owl** soars silently after rabbits, skunks, and even other birds.

Reptiles and Amphibians

The yellow and green **collared lizard,** perching prominently on rocks and stumps, seems enamored of its own beauty, but actually it's the male defending its territory. Like other Four Corners lizards, such as the **plateau lizard** and various kinds of **whiptail lizards,** they do pushups to display their markings and sprint after insects, spiders, and small arthropods. **Gopher** and **racer snakes** kill their prey through constriction, while garter snakes lie in wait near potholes for frogs and tadpoles. Despite the number of characters zapped in movies, there probably aren't as many poisonous snakes out here as you think. The **midget-faded rattlesnake** packs a potent wallop for its size, however, while the **prarie rattler** migrates miles in search of deer mice to swallow.

Aside from the months of waiting for the rain to fall, the life of a **Great Basin spadefoot toad** doesn't sound so bad: find water, drink to bursting, eat up to half your weight in a single night, and mate like crazy—then burrow back into the mud and do it again next year. Potholes are often full of their eggs and tadpoles in early summer. The **canyon treefrog** often sit immobile near water, hoping their excellent camouflage will keep them safe. Like the spadefoot, this frog can survive desiccation and heat that would kill a non-desert amphibian.

Insects and Arachnids

Contrary to popular myth, the sting of the **tarantula** is no more dangerous than that of the bee. Tarantulas grow up to six inches across, and their hairy legs and giant fangs are enough to give arachniphobes the screaming fits. Be glad you're not one of them, however, when the **tarantula hawk** comes calling. These wasps paralyze tarantulas and lay their eggs on the living body, which provides food for the hatching larvae. **Scorpions** are incredibly ancient creatures, evolutionarily speaking. Fantastically, they glow under ultraviolet light. If you have a chance to shine one after dark, you'll be amazed at how many scorpions are out there. Beware: their sting can be fatal to small children and dogs, and highly toxic to adults.

Female **black widow spiders** are also highly poisonous—steer clear of a black spider with a red hourglass on its abdomen. **Velvet ants** are also no fun to play with. They look like colorful, hairy ants, but have a bite toxic enough to earn the nickname "cow-killer." Shiny black **darkling beetles** spray a noxious liquid from the end of their abdomen. These inch-long beetles are very common. They don't fool the grasshopper mouse with their threat posture, rear end raised: it simply sticks the spraying end in the ground and chomps the other one.

ENVIRONMENTAL ISSUES

Most conservation conflicts in the Four Corners area concern public land use. These have reached their most heated peak in southern Utah. Once you strip away the details, most of the debate boils down to the fact that many residents resent outside influences—whether it's the federal government, recent arrivals, or environmental groups based elsewhere—telling them how to manage the vast surrounding federal lands, which locals feel they have more stake in, and experience with, than anyone else. The other groups point out that generations of land leasing and use don't ensure the land is being used sustainably; in many cases, they argue, it's being mined, logged, or grazed to death. Old ways of life die hard as the economy shifts, and the most beautiful acres on earth cause some of the most apoplectic arguments you've ever seen.

Monuments and Wilderness Areas

President Clinton ruffled many feathers nationwide when he created 15 national monuments, including in the Four Corners the Canyons of the Ancients, the Vermilion Cliffs, the Grand Canyon–Parashant in northern Arizona, and the gigantic Grand Staircase–Escalante in southern Utah. A lawsuit by a coalition including the Utah Association of Counties, the Colorado-based Mountain States Legal Foundation, and the Blue Ribbon Coalition, an off-road vehicle (ORV) advocacy group, was defeated in 2002 when a federal court ruled that the president acted within his authority under the 1906 Antiquities Act in authorizing the monuments. (Even land use within monuments remains controversial; local ranchers refused to remove their livestock from the Grand Staircase–Escalante for years after the monument was set aside.)

Still up in the air is the fate of millions of acres of desert that environmental groups are hoping to protect under **America's Red Rock Wilderness Act.** This legislation would designate over nine million acres of southern Utah (85 percent of which is within two miles of a road) as off-limits to development and mechanical access. The Sierra Club and the Southern Utah Wilderness Alliance

(SUWA) have gained 163 sponsors of the bill in the House and 17 in the Senate, but the House Resources Committee, controlled by conservative Utah politicians, has kept it stalled.

An area can be set aside as wilderness only if it has few or no roads, and here the legal wrangling starts to get esoteric. A one-sentence statute known as **R.S. 2477** is invoked by local landowners and counties to prevent the creation of wilderness areas, even though it was passed in 1866. Originally intended to give Civil War–era prospectors easy access to claims, the provision says simply that the "right of way for the construction of highways across public lands not otherwise reserved for public purposes is hereby granted"—in this case, to the state and country legislatures. It was repealed by the 1976 Federal Lands Policy and Management Act, but a grandfather clause continues to honor valid existing rights.

The result is endless, deadly serious arguments over what is and isn't a road. Areas being considered for wilderness protection are marbled with thousands of dirt trails, sandy washes, ORV tracks, seismic exploration lies, and cow paths. In Utah alone, about 15,000 road claims are being debated. The more of these unmaintained tracks can be declared "roads," the smaller the chance a given acre can be declared wilderness. Passions run high and there is little middle ground. County officials send out bulldozers to improve rights-of-way, and environmental groups sue to stop them.

In 2002 the drama played out on the side of the environmental groups when the National Park Service decided to permanently prohibit vehicular access to Salt Creek Canyon in the Needles district of Canyonlands National Park. San Juan County had invoked R.S. 2477 in its claim over the popular route up the creek bed, but the Park Service's own studies found that motor vehicles were harming vegetation and water quality. A federal judge ruled that the county had to show evidence—beyond aerial photos and affidavits from cowboys who rode the route decades before—that the road was actually built and led somewhere; the Park Service followed suit. Two years later, the second Bush administration delighted ORV enthusiasts by pledging to finalize a rule making it easier for Western states, counties, and cities to enforce R.S. 2477 claims.

Off-Road Vehicles

A key issue in the argument over roads is ORVs, including motorcycles and four-wheel all-terrain vehicles (ATVs). (The easily tipped three-wheeled ATVs have been gradually phased out.) With 80,000 registered ORVs, Utah is second only to California in popularity of the sport, so it's lucky for ORV buffs that 94 percent of BLM land in the state is open to their use. Popular areas like the San Rafael Swell, however, are still being fought over by ORV groups, who question the worth of wilderness that few people ever see, and their opponents, who cringe at the spiraling tracks and noise. Those favoring ORV control also cite surveys that suggest most public lands visitors prefer non-motorized access, and they claim that ATVs disturb six acres of topsoil for every 20 miles of travel. With only one BLM ranger to patrol 2.5 million acres in the Swell, any ORV ban would likely depend on the honor system regardless.

Mining and Drilling

The high desert plateaus of the Four Corners hide substantial reserves of uranium, coal, oil, gas, and other things that take much more than a pick and shovel to unearth. The BLM, nicknamed the "Bureau of Logging and Mining" by its detractors, leases its immense holdings to oil and gas companies to search for new deposits, raising the ire of conservation groups, tribal members, and some local residents. The dispute has reached a peak under the second Bush administration, which has directed the BLM to consider opening more public lands in the Rocky Mountains and the Southwest to oil and gas drilling as part of its push to expand national energy reserves.

In 2001, the Department of the Interior authorized the use of "thumper trucks" around Canyonlands and Arches National Parks near Moab. These vehicles send seismic waves deep into the earth to map underground structures and leave huge gouges in the desert as they go. A year later, a federal judge temporarily blocked this activity in the 25,000-acre Dome Plateau region east of Arches, accusing the BLM of failing to accurately predict the effects on the ecosystem. The parks remain safe, for now, but areas near the Needles such as Lockhart Basin and Hatch Point were left open for exploration.

Overgrazing

It may be hard to believe, but much of the Colorado Plateau was once covered by lush grasslands. As bison and other ungulates migrated through the plateau, they not only mowed the shoots but also churned up the earth and fertilized it with their dung. The native ungulates have long since been replaced by cows and sheep, which are kept in much smaller areas year-round. In their search for water, livestock tear up delicate riparian areas and graze anything green and edible down to the ground. Fast-growing invaders such as cheatgrass move in, drastically changing the delicate ecosystems.

This process was already well underway by the turn of the 19th century, when overgrazing had stopped forest regeneration in the highlands and trampled lowland soils to a bare crust. With improved range management techniques, things have improved over the decades, but only to a limited extent. The effect of livestock on the environment is far-reaching; for example, some 85–90 percent of Colorado River water goes to farms to grow feed, including water-guzzling plants like alfalfa. Ranching has always been a marginal enterprise in the West, where alkaline soils and low rainfall add up to a losing equation. Indeed, Western beef makes up only a small fraction of the country's supply. Many visitors find it astounding that anyone ever thought this area would be a good place to raise livestock, yet the grip of the cowboy mythos on the national identity is a tight one. That's part of the reason why the ranching industry, aided by inexpensive grazing permits for federal land, holds political clout far out of proportion to its social and economic impact.

History

PREHISTORY

Early Cultures

The history of the Four Corners is largely the history of the Southwest itself, a region that generally includes all of Arizona and New Mexico and parts of Texas, Oklahoma, Colorado, Utah, and Nevada. Some of the oldest records of human occupation in the New World have been found here, dating as far back as 25,000 years. As early at 10,000 B.C., small groups of humans lived in the basin of prehistoric Lake Bonneville, an inland sea that covered much of modern-day Utah before it shrunk to leave behind the Great Salt Lake. During the **desert archaic** cultural period, starting about 6000 B.C., nomadic hunters and gatherers spread throughout the region in search of game and edible plants, living in caves or temporary brush shelters and leaving little trace of their passing.

Agriculture spread north from Mexico between 2000 and 500 B.C., allowing larger, more permanent settlements to supplement wild forage with a more nutritious diet of squash, corn, and beans. People made crude pottery to cook and store food and water. Farming techniques improved in the first millennium A.D., and the construction of partially underground pithouses became widespread.

The Basketmakers

Between about A.D. 100 and 700, the **Basketmaker** culture concentrated on crop cultivation and domestication of animals such as dogs and turkeys, which provided companionship, meat, bones for tools, and feathers for clothing. The Basketmaker peoples wove yucca fibers into cord and sandals, and wore ornaments of stones and shells traded from the south. Crops were grown in small garden plots, and large game like deer and elk was taken down with spears thrown using a device called the atlatl. Their baskets were true works of art, elaborately decorated and woven tightly enough that, lined with pitch, they could be used for cooking by dropping in red-hot stones. Around A.D. 500, villages grew in size to contain many food storage bins and the first **kivas,** round ceremonial chambers built partly underground. Lined with benches, these were centered around fire pits and a *sipapu,* a small hole symbolizing the one through which they believed their ancestors had emerged from the underworld.

Rise of the Anasazi

Basketmaker peoples gradually developed into the tribes known today as the **Anasazi,** an Athapascan (Navajo) word which translates roughly as "ancient enemies" or "enemies of my ancestors." (This term has come under fire recently from the group's Pueblo descendants, who claim it is derogatory and prefer the less offensive "Ancestral Puebloans." You'll hear both, but "Anasazi" is still more widely used.) In the **Developmental period** (A.D. 700–1050), Pueblo culture centered on planned villages frequently built on a north-south axis. Often home to several hundred people, these villages contained pithouse structures as well as hundreds of rooms built of stone masonry. They were surrounded by tilled fields where cotton may have been grown. Infants were carried in hard cradleboards that flattened their skulls (perhaps purposely). Anasazi

pottery was finer and more elaborately decorated than that of the Basketmaker peoples.

Anasazi settlements expanded into the **Classic Pueblo** period (A.D. 1050–1300), which saw the construction of the great cliff houses that today draw thousands of visitors each year. Built in large natural alcoves in canyon walls, these freestanding structures resembled apartment blocks made of stone, with up to four stories designed so that the roof on one would be the porch for the one above. This period also brought what has been called the **Chaco Phenomenon,** referring to the massive constructions at Chaco Canyon in northwest New Mexico. Perhaps influenced by Central American cultures, the Puebloans built a series of "great houses" at Chaco unlike anything the Southwest had ever seen. Huge timbers were carried from the Chuska and San Mateo Mountains to serve as floor and roof beams in structures with up to one thousand rooms. A radiating network of roads made Chaco the Rome of the ancient Southwest, concentrating the religious, cultural, and political energies of communities spread over 40,000 square miles. The Chacoans built many "great kivas" up to 16 feet deep and 70 feet in diameter; their pottery skills reached new heights.

© JULIAN SMITH

Anasazi mortar, Aztec Ruins National Monument

End of an Era

After its peak around A.D. 1300, Chaco and the entire Pueblo culture experienced a startlingly rapid decline that left cliff houses and Great Houses abandoned. It was as if their inhabitants simply picked up one day and walked off. This decline was probably due to a combination of factors including overpopulation, resource depletion, raids by new tribes arriving from the north, widespread droughts (around A.D. 1130–1180 and A.D. 1276–1299), and ill-fated changes in religious and political leadership. It may also have been a time of hunger and terror. Archaeologists have turned up evidence of violence around this time, including some recent, controversial finds indicating cannibalism. This is very touchy subject among descendants of the Anasazi, who believe the dead are not to be discussed and who consider the suggestion of cannibalism the worst sort of insult. Even so, stop for a moment at the next cliff house and imagine frenzied raiders approaching across withered fields as you madly call for your children and scramble to pull up the ladders in time. Whatever happened here, it's hard to visit some of these remote ruins and not feel a touch of paranoia.

During the **Regressive Pueblo** period (1300–1700), a civilization that once numbered in the hundreds of thousands was scattered to the winds. Anasazi offshoots rose briefly in this tail-end time, including the **Kayenta Anasazi** of northeastern Arizona who left the ruins in Canyon de Chelly and Navajo National Monument. The **Mesa Verde Anasazi** of southwest Colorado and southeastern Utah reached their peak as Chaco faded, but suffered the same fate soon after. On the whole, however, the descendants of the Anasazi merged with other groups on the more fertile lands to the south and east, along the Rio Grande and the Hopi mesas.

North of the Anasazi, a separate group known as the **Fremont** flourished in the western Colorado Plateau and the eastern Great Basin of Nevada from about A.D. 750–1250. Originally thought to be a primitive branch of the Anasazi, the Fremont have been accepted as a distinct culture, although a much less cohesive one. They settled in villages, grew similar crops, and made baskets and pottery like their neighbors, but left fewer artifacts and nothing approaching the grandeur of the cliff palaces. The groups did seem to mingle somewhat in south-central Utah, but like the Anasazi, and probably for many of the same reasons, the Fremont went into decline and vanished by A.D. 1500.

More Recent Tribes

As the Anasazi and the Fremont faded, new cultural groups moved in from the north. These more aggressive, nomadic peoples spoke dialects of the Athapascan languages of western Canada; they would eventually evolve into the **Navajo** and **Apache** tribes. The exact timing of the immigration is unclear, but it was definitely underway by the time the Spanish arrived in the 16th century. These groups would become some of the most feared raiders in the history of the Southwest as the cultures of the Old and New Worlds clashed. The Apache moved south of the Colorado Plateau, but the Navajo stayed in the area around the Four Corners. They adopted many Pueblo customs, including farming, weaving, livestock herding, a matrilineal society, and the clan system. Their traditional log hogans have been traced to Asian origins, and they kept up the habit of adopting from other cultures—horses from the Spanish, for example, and the art of silversmithing from the Mexicans.

The **Hopi** are descendants of the Anasazi, more or less, but the origins of the **Ute** tribe are less clear; it is known their ancestors came from the north and west, but when is unclear.

THE EUROPEANS ARRIVE

Spanish missionaries and explorers were the first Europeans to traverse the American Southwest. They came in search of souls and gold, respectively, and were spurred in their often miserable and deadly travels by the thousands of "heathens" waiting to be converted and legends of golden cities in the sand. Historically leading the way were the conquistadors who had already met with success: Hernán Cortés, who in 1521 defeated the entire Aztec empire of central Mexico with only 500 men, and Francisco Pizarro, who helped topple the fabulously wealthy Andean kingdom of the Inca in the 1530s. The legends of El Dorado ("The Golden One") and the Seven Golden Cities of Cibola got a boost from the tales of **Alvar Nuñez Cabeza de Vaca,** who, after being shipwrecked off the Florida coast in 1528, spent eight years wandering across the Southwest with a small group of survivors until he eventually reached the Spanish colonies in Mexico.

Early Explorers

In 1540, **Francisco Vázquez de Coronado** led a party of 300 into Arizona in search of the cities of gold and to claim the region for Spain. Finding no treasure in the Zuñi pueblos, the heavily armed group advanced north, where a side expedition led by García López de Cárdenas became the first Europeans to gaze into the Grand Canyon. Indigenous groups, including the Hopi, kept using the legend of the golden cities to urge the Spaniards onwards ("Cibola? Uh, yeah—it's just a few days that way. Keep going, you can't miss it!"). The party forged through northern New Mexico and Texas, not realizing until they reached Kansas that the only gold in sight was the setting sun on the walls of the adobe pueblos. Only 100 men made it back to Mexico City, where Coronado died in 1554 after being found guilty of corruption and atrocities against the Indians.

Half a century later, **Juan de Oñate** established the colony of New Mexico for Spain. Married to a granddaughter of Cortés, Oñate led 400 settlers across the Rio Grande and sent scouting parties in search of treasure in Quivira (central Kansas). He quickly earned a reputation for brutality among the settlers, which served as a warm-up for his retribution for a brief uprising among the residents of the pueblo of Acoma, high atop a mesa in what is now western New Mexico. When 11 Spaniards, including one of Oñate's nephews, were killed in 1598, the furious conquistador laid siege to the sheer-walled mesa and burned the pueblo. About 800 Indians were killed, and every adult male survivor had one foot cut off. In 1601, Oñate returned from an unsuccessful treasure hunt to find his colony mostly deserted. Further quests to the Colorado River and the Gulf of California were also failures, and he resigned his post in 1607.

SPANISH NEW MEXICO

These early expeditions soured relations between Europeans and native tribes for centuries. The Spanish gradually assumed control over much of the Southwest in the 18th century from their capital city of La Villa Real de la Santa Fe de San Francisco de Asis (known today, thankfully, simply as Santa Fe), founded in 1610. Subsistence agriculture in river valleys, trade with Mexico, and the raising of sheep and horses formed the basis of the economy, despite regular attacks by Apache, Comanche, and Navajo warriors. The effects of missionaries varied: while some served as intermediaries, speaking out for Indians' rights in the face of European settlement, others did their best to supplant native cultural traditions with Christianity.

By the late 17th century, things came to a head. Continued persecution, punishment, and executions for "witchcraft" and "idolatry" had pushed native tribes to the edge. Abortive revolts in the Zuñi, Hopi, and Rio Grande Pueblos served as prelude to a massive uprising in 1680 known as the **Pueblo Revolt.** Led by a Tewa medicine man named Pope, the insurrection was organized by runners carrying knotted strings encoding the fateful date. On August 10, some 17,000 Puebloans, including 6,000 warriors in battle paint, rose against 3,000 Spanish colonists. The furious tribes burned churches and their holy icons, threw friars from cliffs, and massacred entire communities as the Spanish survivors retreated to Santa Fe. After a six-day siege, a ragged column was allowed to march south down the Rio Grande valley, leaving some 400 dead amid the ruins.

Even as they retreated, however, the Spanish were already planning their return, and by 1700 they had reconquered much of the Southwest, extending their New World empire from Panama to California and Santa Fe. Albuquerque was founded in 1706, and during the 1700s the Spanish population of New Mexico increased to as much as 25,000, many times the size of the Texas and California colonies. Priests once again visited tribes to try to convert them to Christianity, but these efforts met with mixed success. They did discover more about the geography of the region,

STATE FAST FACTS

State	Total Area, Square Miles (rank)	Percent Owned by Federal Government (rank)	Nickname	Capital
Arizona	114,006 (6th)	44.3% (8th)	Grand Canyon State	Phoenix
Colorado	104,100 (8th)	38.9% (9th)	Centennial State	Denver
New Mexico	121,598 (5th)	36.2% (10th)	Land of Enchantment	Santa Fe
Utah	84,904 (13th)	67.9% (2nd)	Beehive State	Salt Lake City

State	Population (2000)	Population Density per Square Mile (rank, 1990)	Per Capita Income (2000)
Arizona	5,130,632	45.2 (37th)	$24,988
Colorado	4,301,261	41.5 (38th)	$32,434
New Mexico	1,819,046	15 (46th)	$21,931
Utah	2,233,169	27.2 (42nd)	$23,436

Largest Cities	Population (2000)
Flagstaff, AZ	52,894
Farmington, NM	37,844
Gallup, NM	20,209
Durango, CO	13,922
Winslow, AZ	9,520
Cortez, CO	7,977
Page, AZ	6,809
Aztec, NM	6,378
Holbrook, AZ	4,917
Moab, UT	4,779

however, particularly during the **Dominguez-Escalante Expedition** led by Fathers Francisco Atanasio Dominquez and Silvestre Velez de Escalante. In 1776, as a new nation was declaring its independence across the continent, 14 men set out to find a northern route between the missions of Santa Fe and Monterey, California.

They made their way through western Colorado, crossing the Green River and going as far north as what is now Cedar City, Utah, before heading west, becoming the first Europeans to venture into Nevada's Great Basin Desert. Bludgeoned by blizzards and starvation, they survived on the kindness of groups of Utes and Paiutes

before drawing lots to see if they should press on or turn back. The result—turn back—probably saved their lives. The fathers crossed northern Arizona along the Vermilion Cliffs and the Paria River before fording the Colorado River at Marble Canyon, at a spot still known as the Crossing of the Fathers. In six months and 2,000 miles, they had failed in their goal but added much to European knowledge of the intermountain West.

The colony of New Mexico continued to limp along, far from the resources and attention of Mexico City, the center of Spanish authority in the New World. The opening of the **Old Spanish Trail** in the early 19th century allowed the transport of livestock and slaves from Santa Fe to central Utah and, eventually, Los Angeles. Slave raids were only one of a long list of reasons the Navajo had become the colony's most dangerous enemies. They raided settlements from horseback along with Comanche and Ute warriors. (The Canyon del Muerto in Canyon de Chelly was named after a slave raid that left hundreds of Navajo women and children dead in 1805.)

THE UNITED STATES TAKES OVER

Taking advantage of the Spanish colony's relative weakness, explorers, surveyors, and adventurers pushed west from the young United States. Zebulon Pike, John Frémont, and John Gunnison all led parties exploring the intermountain West. A vast territory had been added to the country's borders by the 1803 Louisiana Purchase, and in 1821 the Republic of Mexico's independence from Spain transferred much of the Southwest to new ownership. Anglo settlers continued to trickle in, including Mormons led by Brigham Young, whose wagons entered the Great Salt Lake valley in 1847. Fleeing religious persecution, the Latter-Day Saints busily set about establishing a highly regulated, self-sufficient colony that stretched from the Sierra Nevada to the Rockies and from Oregon to Arizona. Colonists were organized by skill and leadership and sent out to settle the farthest corners of the territory to strengthen the church's hold on the land. The unforgiving land made settlement a grueling experience, wrote Wallace Stegner in *Mormon Country:*

> *Its destiny was plain on its face, its contempt of man and his history and his theological immortality, his Millennium, his Heaven on Earth, was monumentally obvious. Its distances were terrifying, its cloudbursts catastrophic, its beauty flamboyant and bizarre and allied with death.*

In 1846, Brig. Gen. Stephen Watts Kearny arrived in Santa Fe to proclaim the beginning of American dominion over the Southwest. The one-sided **Mexican-America War** (1846-48) made good on this promise, resulting in the transfer of the northern half of Mexico—what is today most of California, Nevada, Arizona, New Mexico, and Utah—to American hands. The

Mormon wagon on display at the Nations of the Four Corners Cultural Center in Bluff

$10 million **Gadsden Purchase** in 1853 shifted another 30,000 square miles of southern Arizona and New Mexico from Mexico to the United States. Americans now owned the Southwest, but by the end of the 19th century, only a handful of explorers, trappers, soldiers, miners, and missionaries had ventured onto the Colorado Plateau. The government began to build Army posts to protect immigrants and settlers from Indians, and the frontier territories were dominated by cabals that made fortunes off the livestock industry and the newly laid railroads, while mostly ignoring the needs of native groups.

Utah, however, was off and running. By 1860, over 150 communities totaling 40,000 inhabitants had sprouted. Despite raids by local tribes, the desert bloomed with crops grown using ingenious irrigation techniques. The Mormons' autonomy (and their penchant for polygamy) rankled the federal government, and in 1857, President James Buchanan sent 2,500 soldiers to the territory to replace Young as governor. Mormon leaders saw this as more religious persecution, declared martial law, and prepared to defend themselves. The **"Utah War"** ended without bloodshed when the two sides eventually reached a diplomatic solution.

RAILROADS AND STATEHOOD

The latter half of the 19th century brought the American Civil War, which had relatively little effect in the Southwest, and the completion of the **transcontinental railroad.** On May 10, 1869, a symbolic golden spike was driven at Promontory, Utah, and the linking of rail lines to both coasts officially closed the American frontier. The impact was far-reaching and immediate as immigrants poured in and products such as timber, minerals, and livestock were transported across the vast distances. Where the rail lines went, so did life: along the tracks cities sprang up almost overnight (many named after railroad engineers), bringing jobs and radically altering lives in long-isolated areas. If a town refused to grant privileges to the railroads, settlers simply built another town down the line. The Atchison, Topeka and Santa Fe Railway from St. Louis reached Albuquerque in 1880, northern Arizona in 1883, and Los Angeles in 1885, the same year the Northern Pacific Railway reached Seattle. Another golden-spike moment occurred in Tucson in 1880, when the Southern Pacific Railroad connected California with New Orleans.

The arrival of the "Iron Horse" also signaled the end of the freedom enjoyed by native tribes, who found themselves being crowded off and ousted from their homelands by European immigrants. Though they didn't take this displacement lying down, they never really stood a chance; by sheer force of numbers and technology, Americans rolled over the West and its indigenous peoples in a steady, unstoppable tide. In 1863, the famous frontiersman and Civil War veteran Kit Carson was ordered to end the problem of Navajo raids once and for all. Once considered a good friend by native tribes, Carson began a brutal military campaign that ended with a futile last stand by the Navajo in Canyon de Chelly. Some 8,000 men, women, and children were then marched 300 miles to Bosque Redondo (later called Fort Sumner), on the Pecos River in eastern New Mexico. Many did not survive the infamous "Long Walk," and those that did may have wished they hadn't. The poorly planned site was called a reservation but in reality was a gulag. Sicknesses and disease compounded the cold and misery resulting from a meager wood supply, and worms destroyed the corn crops. Four years of suffering ended when Navajo leader Barboncito negotiated the return of his people to their ancestral lands in Arizona and New Mexico in 1868. In return, the Navajo had to agree never to raise arms against the United States or her citizens and to send their children to American schools. The Navajo Reservation was later expanded to its current boundaries, and in 1882, 4,000 square miles out of its center of was set aside for the Hopi. (Land disputes between the traditionally distrustful tribes continue to this day.) The Apache were forced onto reservations in the 1880s, despite fierce resistance from bands led by chiefs Geronimo, Cochise, and Victorio.

The "Wild West"

The last decades of the 1800s encompassed that mythic intersection of time and place the images of which have spread around the world. It was in the West, and it was wild, but this historical moment bore little resemblance to the operatic, fresh-scrubbed version promulgated by dime novels and the silver screen. Lawmen like legendary Pat Garrett and Wyatt Earp were tough as nails but few and far between, and lawlessness most often took the form of cattle rustling and various forms of shady land dealings. Alcohol, prostitution, and gambling dulled the growing pains of a frontier that was no longer really a frontier, but in many ways still felt like one. Homesteaders, including many Mormons, eked out a living by farming along streams and rivers. Ranchers grazed thousands of sheep, cows, and horses on the seemingly endless acres of the Colorado Plateau, even though much of it offered substandard forage, and moved their herds from the lowlands to the mountains as the seasons changed. Much of the rural economy centered on the trading post, an institution that came to serve as combination bank, store, and social club.

Powell's Expeditions

The age of exploration was not over yet. Much of the Four Corners was still terra incognita, the last blank spot on the map of the continental United States. To remedy this, the professor and one-armed Civil War hero **Major John Wesley Powell** led two survey trips down the Colorado River through the Grand Canyon in 1869 and 1871. Braving terrifying rapids in sluggish wooden boats, Powell's expeditions had little idea what they were getting into, particularly the first time through. They still managed to collect specimens, take photographs, and complete a topographic map of the previously unknown Grand Canyon region, and had the honor of naming the last river (the Escalante) and mountain range (the Henrys) to be added to the U.S. map. Powell described the experience in his classic knucklebiter *Exploration of the Colorado River of the West and Its Tributaries*. The explorer went on to direct the U.S. Geological Survey, plead for justice for native tribes as special commissioner to the Indians in Utah and Nevada, and argue futilely for the wise use of the West's scant water.

Colorado achieved statehood in 1876, followed by Utah in 1896. Mormon settlers, who had already applied to join the Union numerous times, were forced to discontinue polygamy and the church's political activities before they were finally admitted.

INTO THE 20TH CENTURY

In 1912, New Mexico and Arizona became the 47th and 48th states, respectively. Both remained very undeveloped, sparsely populated areas where stagecoaches still carried passengers and mules delivered mail to isolated settlements. The region's stark beauty was starting to gain national attention, though, and the first few decades of the 20th century brought an influx of tourists, retirees, and winter residents ("snowbirds") and the construction of motor courts and "dude ranches" to house them. Native Americans became U.S. citizens with the passage of the Indian Citizenship Act in 1924—just in time for the Great Depression, which brought drought, rural emigration, and the relief programs of the New Deal. Many emigrants moved to California in search of work along the new Route 66, the "Mother Road" stretching from Chicago to Los Angeles which ran through Albuquerque and Flagstaff.

Relations with native tribes in the early days of the reservations remained tense. Things weren't helped by the government's plan of livestock reduction among the Navajo, implemented in the 1930s out of concern over soil erosion and overgrazing. Thousands of sheep, goats, and horses were slaughtered in front of their horrified owners, who considered the animals to be almost members of the family. Along with the Long Walk, this set in place a legacy of distrust of the federal government that still lingers.

The Hollywood Version

By now the legend of the Old West was firmly entrenched in the national consciousness, largely as a result of the **"Westerns"** Hollywood churned out at an increasing rate. With roots in the radio dramas of the 1930s and 1940s, early Westerns often involved singing by the likes of Dale Autry and Roy Rogers. It was the epic films of director John Ford, however, that defined the genre for decades to come. Larger-than-life characters played by actors like John Wayne were shown in rugged struggles of good versus evil set against sweeping backdrops such as Monument Valley. Ford and Wayne collaborated on the classics *Stagecoach* (1939), *Rio Grande* (1950), *The Searchers* (1956), and *How the West Was Won* (1962). *Cheyenne Autumn* (1964) was Ford's final tribute to the tribes he had often depicted in a less than positive light. When they weren't the bad guys, native characters were mostly interchangeable and played by dark-skinned Europeans or Navajo, regardless of their supposed tribe. (In some of the films, Navajo actors apparently said some pretty racy things in their own language, which had reservation audiences privately snickering when they were first shown.)

The turn of the century also saw the beginnings of a serious Southwest **tourism industry.** Instrumental in opening the region were the restaurants and lodges operated by the **Fred Harvey Company** along the Atchison, Topeka and Santa Fe Railway. Huge log structures in Zion, Bryce, and the North Rim of the Grand Canyon, as well as places like Winslow's La Posada, catered to the moneyed crowd who came for the views, the service, and the "Harvey Girls," a famously smart and pretty bunch of waitresses. Harvey's hotels operated from the 1880s to the 1950s, proof that the rugged wonders of the Southwest could be enjoyed in comfort.

Fruits of the Land

The pace of change quickened during World War II, when many rural young men—Anglo, Indian, and Hispanic alike—were drafted into the military or found jobs with the government. During WWII, a handful of Navajo served as code talkers for the Marines in the Pacific, helping ensure victory for the United States. By the middle of the century, the Colorado Plateau's **resource-based economy** was firmly entrenched, dependent on the extraction and/or processing of natural products such as lumber, minerals, gas, oil, and grass (through grazing). Those activities that required water or power, including agriculture, grazing, and mining, were supported by major public works projects which began with the 1902 Reclamation Act and led to the construc-

tion of the Roosevelt Dam (1911), the Hoover Dam (1936), and the Glen Canyon Dam (1966). Much of this region would still be barren desert without the federal government's concerted effort to transform it into a tamed, productive landscape—an important point to remember in the midst of frequent cries for local autonomy and freedom from federal tyranny. Crops such as cotton, grain, fruit, and alfalfa (for cattle) helped support the rural economies, along with cattle and sheep ranching.

Mining had been important in the Southwest for centuries, particularly in Arizona, whose copper reserves were exposed in massive open-pit excavations. The discovery of natural gas and petroleum in Texas and Oklahoma in the early 1900s was only the beginning; oil was discovered on the Navajo Reservation in 1922, suspicions about coal beneath Black Mesa were proved true, and major oil and natural-gas fields were discovered in the San Juan Basin of northwestern New Mexico and southwestern Colorado in the 1940s. In the 1950s, the Cold War brought a sharp demand for the element **uranium,** a key ingredient in the atomic bomb. Prospectors armed with Geiger counters combed the Colorado Plateau in Army-surplus Jeeps, opening new roads and occasionally even striking it rich—just discovering a new lodge of high-grade ore snagged a $10,000 reward. By 1955, about 800 uranium mines were spread across the plateau, but when the Atomic Energy Commission stopped buying uranium ore in 1970, the market collapsed and mining stopped.

RECENT HISTORY

Rachel Carson's book *Silent Spring,* published in 1962, is usually credited with sparking the modern **environmental movement.** Its account of the effects of pesticides on birds struck a nerve with readers around the world and motivated the passage of several environmental laws in the United States, including the Wilderness Act (1964), the National Environmental Policy Act (1969), which created the Environmental Protection Agency, and the Clean Air Act (1970). In 1966, three years after the gates of Glen Canyon

Dam were closed, the Sierra Club fought the Bureau of Reclamation's plans to dam the Grand Canyon. In response to the Bureau's claim that a dammed river would let tourists get closer to the canyon walls, the Sierra Club ran full-page ads in the *New York Times* and the **Washington Post** asking, "Should we flood the Sistine Chapel so tourists can get closer to the ceiling?" The bold move cost the group its tax-exempt status, but boosted membership and helped defeat the plan three years later.

Published in 1968, Edward Abbey's *Desert Solitaire* would do for the Southwest deserts what *Silent Spring* did for birds and forests. The pithy account of two seasons as a ranger at Arches National Park, liberally laced with calls to protect the Four Corners' natural wonders from the forces of development and tourism, has become an environmental classic. The first Earth Day was held on April 22, 1970, followed in 1980 by the "Sagebrush Rebellion" near Moab. During a July 4 Earth First! rally, the local county commission responded by sending a flag-flying bulldozer to carve a road into what the BLM had identified as a potential wilderness study area.

Winds of Change

The resource economy is struggling, but even as "sustainability" becomes the new buzzword, old ways die hard. The long-term value of the coal deposits beneath Black Mesa on the Navajo and Hopi lands has been estimated as high as $100 billion, but the effects of draining a billion gallons per year from the underground aquifer (to carry coal slurry to power plants) is hotly debated. Recent controversies over land use in the San Juan Basin have pitted oil and gas drillers against an unlikely alliance of environmentalists and sixth-generation ranchers. More than 10,000 head of cattle graze in the basin, and ranchers say that oil

Outdoor recreation is becoming the Four Corners' modern gold mine. Mountain bikers, hikers, river-runners, and families in vans and RVs have discovered the scenic and cultural wonders of the Colorado Plateau.

drilling—which produced $2.4 billion in oil and gas income in 2001—has contaminated water and led to erosion and the death of livestock. Instead of turning local communities into ghost towns by cutting off access to minerals, the creation of new parks and monuments has brought a new economic boom: **tourism.**

Outdoor recreation is becoming the Four Corners' modern gold mine. Mountain bikers, hikers, river-runners, and families in vans and RVs have discovered the scenic and cultural wonders of the Colorado Plateau. Visitors support growing numbers of hotels, restaurants, tour companies, and other businesses. Retirees are drawn to the scenery and climate, particularly of Arizona. As populations rise, however, the already meager water supply is stretched even thinner. Southwestern states fight over the allocation of diverted water flows, especially from the Colorado River, which no longer even reaches the Gulf of California.

To make things worse, starting in the late 1990s, the region entered the worst drought in over a century; by some estimates, it compares to the most severe droughts of the past 1,400 years. Reservoirs sit at record lows, farms have shriveled, and bone-dry forests ignite at the slightest spark. As of 2002, soil moisture levels were barely registering, and a plague of bark beetles had decimated pines trees weakened by the drought, 2 million in northern Arizona alone.

On the bright side, New Mexico passed a law requiring utilities to get 10 percent of their electricity supply from renewable energy sources, such as solar, by the year 2011. The future of this amazing, austere, but still fragile region depends on whether we can find the right balance between leaving it alone, living on its terms, and loving it fervently.

The People

Over a third of all Native Americans live in the Southwest, mostly in Arizona and New Mexico. The tribes you'll encounter in the Four Corners are the Navajo, the Hopi, and the Ute, but other Pueblo tribes, as well as the Apache, have reservations nearby. With their high unemployment rate, low per capita income, widespread alcohol abuse, and impoverished living conditions, Indian reservations can be disheartening places (*Slate* magazine described Kayenta as "almost poetically depressing"). The United States has always had a schizophrenic relationship with native cultures, alternately idealizing and scorning them, all the while conveniently ignoring the nation's culpability for their near-total destruction during European settlement. Though old ways are fading in the face of modern technological civilization, many Native Americans are determined to preserve their traditional cultures, arts, and ceremonies no matter what. A visit to a reservation can be like a cold bucket of water in the face, replacing hazy romantic notions with harsh, Third-World reality. But it can also be an incredibly enjoyable and enlightening experience, offering a glimpse into a fascinating way of life that has endured despite all odds.

Cultural issues associated with visiting reservations are discussed under "Tips for Travelers," and native crafts get a fuller treatment under "Shopping," both in the On the Road chapter.

NAVAJO
Demography
The *Diné*, as the Navajo call themselves, are the second-largest tribe in the United States after the Cherokee, with 282,000 members. About 165,000 of them live on the country's largest reservation, 25,000 square miles comprising about a quarter of the state of Arizona and sections of New Mexico and Utah. This traditional territory is called *Dinetah,* meaning "among the People," or *Din'e Bike'yah,* "the land between the sacred mountains," referring to the tribe's traditional territorial boundaries. To the

north is *Sisnaajinii* (Blanca Peak) near Alamosa, Colorado, representing dawn; *Tsoodzil* (Mt. Taylor) rises near Grants, New Mexico, and symbolizes the daytime sky; *Dook'o'oosliid* (the San Francisco Peaks) near Flagstaff signifies twilight; and *Dibe Nitsaa* (Mt. Hesperus) near Durango represents night.

Despite significant natural resources, including massive reserves of coal, natural gas, and oil, "the Rez" is still a very poor place. According to the 1990 census, over half of its residents lived below the poverty line, with an average income of just over $14,000 per year (vs. the national average of $39,000) and unemployment as high as 50 percent. Only two-thirds of houses have electricity and half lack running water. One cause of the poverty is a booming population; the tribe grew almost 80 percent from 1980 to 2000.

Gambling on the reservations has twice been voted down, in part because it is seen as a sickness in traditional Navajo teachings, so you won't find any casinos. Tribe members support themselves through industry, farming, and raising livestock such as goats, sheep, and horses. Tourism and the sale of traditional crafts, including weaving, pottery, and silverwork—mostly to *belagaana* (Anglos)—are also important sources of income.

Organization
The Navajo Nation (this term is also used to refer to the reservation itself) is a sovereign entity within the United States, with its own government and courts. Navajo land is held in trust by the federal government, which under the original treaties assumed responsibility for the tribe members' health and welfare. The Navajo Nation is divided into about 110 political divisions called chapters, roughly corresponding to counties. Elected leaders address local community problems and select delegates for the overall Tribal Council based in Window Rock, Arizona. The Navajo Police have jurisdiction over the reservation, but they share duties with the state and federal law enforcement agencies as well, including the FBI and the Bureau of Indian Affairs. The

BIA still has some administrative and maintenance duties on the reservation, but these are gradually being turned over to the tribe.

Language

The Navajo speak an Athapascan language similar to that of the Apache, their cultural cousins who arrived with them from the north around the 1400s. Navajo is a colorful, descriptive language, full of subtle nuance and puns, and it incorporates words from other languages, such as *beeso* for "money" from the Spanish *peso.* Navajo is also incredibly difficult to learn well, so it was perfect for a WWII code that remained unbroken through the Pacific theater. (It is ironic that before and after WWII, Navajo children were punished for speaking their own language in government-run boarding schools that were trying to "take the Indian out of the Indian.")

Arts

Experts at borrowing useful skills from other cultures, the Navajo adopted weaving from their Pueblo neighbors and silversmithing from Mexican artisans during the Spanish occupation of the Southwest. Hand-woven wool rugs have reached an exquisite level of artistry, although fewer and fewer young women are learning the skills and patience to weave like their grandmothers. Navajo silverwork is equally impressive. Other crafts include baskets, pottery, sand paintings, and kachina dolls copied from the Hopi.

Traditional Culture

Traditional Navajo beliefs revolve around the idea that the proper state of the universe is one of order, balance, and happiness called *hozho,* often translated as "beauty." When *hozho* is present, all is well; when it is lost through violence or the breaking of cultural taboos, things swing out of kilter and evil witches called Skinwalkers roam at night. Particularly stringent rules surround incest and death. A contagion called *chindi* following the loss of a life can pollute a dwelling if it happens indoors. Disharmony must be put right through rituals called "sings," which have been handed down through generations. Days of chanting, drumming, and ceremonial purification are supervised by a medicine man. Sings include the Blessing Way and the Enemy Way for cleansing after battle,

Native American pottery

© JULIAN SMITH

NAVAJO CODE TALKERS

During World War II, the obscurity of the Navajo language helped win the battle for the Pacific. The idea came from engineer Philip Johnston, who had grown up on the Navajo Reservation as the son of a Protestant missionary. Knowing that only a few dozen people outside the reservation spoke the tribe's language, Johnston convinced the Marine Corps that spoken Navajo would make an excellent code. Thirty tribal members were recruited as "code talkers."

Native American languages, including Choctaw, had been used as codes in World War I, but the pilot program took things a step farther. Navajo is an extremely complex language, full of dialect and nuance, and at the time was still unwritten. Johnston had the idea to use ordinary Navajo words for military terms to add an extra layer of encoding. *Cha* ("beaver") became "minesweeper," *gini* ("chicken hawk") meant "dive bomber," and *besh-lo* ("iron fish") meant "submarine." Some 411 words were encoded, and multiple Navajo words were assigned to 12 commonly used letters. For example, *be-la-sana* ("apple") and *tse-nil* ("axe") both stood for "A."

The code talkers, many of whom had never been off the reservation, were drilled repeatedly. There was no room for error; transmissions had to be fast and accurate—a single mistake could cost lives. Twenty-seven code talkers were sent to Guadalcanal; two stayed behind to train others. One dropped out of training.

The brass were skeptical, but the code talkers quickly proved their value. From 1942 to 1945, the Navajo participated in every Marine assault in the Pacific, including Guadalcanal, Peliliu, Tarawa, and Iwo Jima. They transmitted from trenches, foxholes, and jungle redoubts, reporting on battlefield conditions and calling in air support and supplies. The Indians were often mistaken for Japanese by American soldiers, and some were nearly shot. Each was given a bodyguard to keep him safe and to prevent the code, which was not written down on the battlefield, from falling into enemy hands. (This arrangement was the basis for the movie *Windtalkers*.) During the first two days of the battle for Iwo Jima, six code talkers worked around the clock to deliver over 800 messages without error.

The Japanese, experts at breaking codes, were mystified; they had never heard anything like the sounds that burbled from the radio. Even a Navajo soldier captured at Bataan was bewildered. The code that helped ensure victory in the Pacific was never broken, and the code talkers are finally beginning to get the recognition they deserve.

The Navajo Code

Officers
commanding general: *bih-keh-he* ("war chief")
major general: *so-na-kih* ("two star")
brigadier general: *so-a-la-ih* ("one star")
colonel: *atsah-besh-le-gai* ("silver eagle")

Places
Alaska: *beh-hga* ("with winter")
America: *ne-he-mah* ("our mother")
Australia: *cha-yes-desi* ("rolled hat")
Britain: *toh-ta* ("between waters")
Germany: *besh-be-cha-he* ("iron hat")
India: *ah-le-gai* ("white clothes")
Russia: *sila-gol-chi-ih* ("red army")
Spain: *deba-de-nih* ("sheep pain")

Airplanes
torpedo plane: *tas-chizzie* ("swallow")
fighter plane: *aa-he-tih-hi* ("hummingbird")
bomber plane: *jay-sho* ("buzzard")

Ships
battleship: *lo-tso* ("whale")
aircraft: *tsidi-moffa-ye-hi* ("bird carrier")
destroyer: *ca-lo* ("shark")
cruiser: *lo-tso-yazzie* ("small whale")

and communal dances with names such as When the Thunder Sleeps are also held. Often the setting is inside a traditional log hogan, which means "home" in Navajo. These eight-sided, one-room structures have a packed clay floor and a domed roof of mud or sod pierced by a smoke hole. The doorway faces east to greet the rising sun. Residences with tarpaper-and-shingle roofs and plywood walls are slowly replacing the hogan, but you'll still see the traditional log structures out in the countryside.

Navajo mythology includes a rich cast of characters including Turquoise Boy, Talking God, Spider Woman, and Water Monster. Their origin myth recounts a progression through three underworlds into this, the Fourth or Glittering World. Of the Navajo Holy People, one of the most important is Changing Woman (*Asdzaan Nadleehe*), considered the tribe's spiritual mother. Impregnated by the sun, she bore twin sons called Monster Slayer (*Naaee' Neezghani*) and Born for Water (*Tobdjishchini*). The Hero Twins went on to slay a series of monsters to make the earth safe for human beings. Several who pleaded for their lives—including Sleepiness, Hunger, Old Age, and Poverty—were spared as a lesson to humanity.

The Navajo live in a matrilineal clan system, in which kinship is extremely important. There are over 140 clans today, with names like Bitter Water Clan and the Corn People. Traditional greetings include a recitation of one's mother's ("born-to") and father's ("born-for") clans, and marriages must be to someone outside of one's clan. A complex chain of clan relationships can make avoiding this form of "incest" difficult.

In fact, family connections are of paramount importance to the Navajo, and nothing illustrates the intersection with tribal folklore better than the traditional *Chi Dlo Dil,* or Laughing Party. Newborn babies are considered to be in the "soft world," and are kept away from hard objects for fear they will adopt "hard" qualities. About six weeks after birth, relatives gather to eat and play with the baby. The first person to make the baby laugh, it is thought, will play an important role in the child's life.

HOPI

Demography

The westernmost group of Pueblo Indians, once called the Moqui, occupy 12 villages on three mesas in the middle of the Navajo Reservation. Most of the approximately 12,000 tribe members live on the 1.6 million-acre Hopi Reservation. It was created in 1882 with little thought given to the traditional boundaries of the Navajo and the Hopi, and subsequent legal rulings have only complicated things. The Hopi Reservation is as poor as its surrounding neighbor; the average annual income is $17,500, unemployment is around 25 percent, and over half of tribe members live below the poverty line. The Hopi live mostly on tourism, government aid, and farm products such as beans, corn, squash, melons, fruit, and wheat. They also herd cows and sheep. Despite the once-popular T-shirts saying "Don't Worry, Be Hopi," the tribe's traditional culture has faded. Many tribal members have moved away from the mesas and abandoned the complex instructions of *Sootukwnangwu,* the Supreme Creator. Yet the core values remain, and the improbable, lofty villages endure.

THE HAPPY HOPI

Louis Tewanima, one of the United States' greatest distance runners, grew up chasing jackrabbits on the Hopi Reservation. It's said that he would run 120 miles to Winslow and back just to see the trains pass. He met the legendary Native American athlete Jim Thorpe at an Indian school in Pennsylvania, where Tewanima once had to run 18 miles to a race after missing the train. He arrived in time and won the two-mile event. He went on to represent the United States at the 1908 and 1912 Olympic Games. At the second he won a silver medal and set an American record that stood for 52 years, until it was broken by another Native American. The "Happy Hopi from Shongopovi" died at age 92 when he tumbled from Second Mesa in the dark on his way home from a ceremony.

Organization

The 12 Hopi villages, largely autonomous, are loosely united under the Hopi Tribal Council. The majority rule incorporated by the 1936 Hopi constitution conflicts with the tribe's traditional way of making decisions, which relies more on building consensus. Like the Navajo Nation, the Hopi tribal government maintains relationships with the federal government, which acts as a trustee for the tribe, as well as with surrounding state and local agencies. Three villages have adopted Western-style governments. The others have held onto the traditional Hopi form of government to different degrees; Oraibi is the most traditional and independent. A chief or *kikmongwi* oversees each village's social and ceremonial life, while bowing to community consensus.

Traditional Culture

The Hopi speak a Uto-Aztecan language, part of a linguistic family that ranges from California into Mexico. The most famous Hopi crafts are the figurines that represent the spirits said to reside in the San Francisco Mountains near Flagstaff. Tribe members also make beautiful silver jewelry using an overlay technique, as well as pottery, baskets, and paintings.

The Hopi live according to the translation of their correct name, *Hopitu,* which means "peaceful people." Their worldview is based on humility, respect, cooperation, and caring for the earth. This last part is particularly important since, as farmers without a permanent water supply, they have had to learn dry-farming techniques that take extraordinary care and diligence. In this unforgiving land, it is crucial that the tribe follow the ceremonial Hopi Way, not only to ensure their own survival but also the well-being of everyone on earth.

The Hopi have a similar origin story to the Navajo: the Bear Clan, they say, led the Hopi from a *sipapu* (a small opening in the earth) into this, the Fourth World, where they wandered the globe before settling in the *Tuuwanasave,* or "earth center." Here the Hopi follow the laws of *Maa'sau,* the Guardian of the Fourth World, which tells them to live in harmony and balance with their surroundings. Only a careful balance protects the world from disaster. Help is available in the form of the kachinas (*katsinam*), benevolent spirit beings who live in the San Francisco Mountains and appear to the tribe between the winter solstice and mid-July. Hundreds of kachinas serve as messengers between the Hopi and the spiritual realm by controlling natural forces such as rain and meting out punishment for infringements of Hopi law. The spirits themselves can be represented in two ways: by men dressing up for ceremonies, and as dolls (*tihu* or *tithu*) that are used to teach children and are also sold. Some kachinas are frightening figures who stress discipline, while others serve as comic relief, such as the Navajo Clown (*Tasavu*) who mocks the neighboring tribe.

Hopi culture is divided into matrilineal clans, with villages providing an extra level of self-identification. A sophisticated religious calendar is closely followed; spiritual leaders calculate ceremonial dates by the position of the sun. Like other Pueblo tribes, the Hopi use ceremonial underground kivas, which a number of secret societies use for meditation and prayer. Important ceremonies include *Soyal,* the celebration of the winter solstice, and *Niman,* the Home Dance. All Hopi ceremonies used to be open to non-members, but so many broke the rules against recording that many dances have been closed to outsiders, including the famous Snake Dance held in late August, during which dancers performed with live snakes in their mouths.

UTE

The smallest tribal group in the Four Corners occupies two reservations, one in southwest Colorado and the other just over the border into New Mexico. (Members of the third modern Ute tribe, the Northern Utes, live on a reservation in northern Utah.) Colorado's oldest native residents began as a loose confederation of seven bands spread across Colorado, Arizona, New Mexico, Wyoming, and Utah, which was named after them. It is known that they originally came from the north and west, but when they arrived is still unclear. The Ute adopted horses from the Spanish and became respected hunters and feared raiders, going after buffalo on the eastern plains and settlers' livestock with equal ferocity. Utes speak a Shoshonean language similar to that of the Shoshones, Paiutes, and Comanches.

The **Ute Mountain Tribe** lives on a 600,000-acre reservation bordering Mesa Verde National Park, with the anthropomorphic mountain at its center. A population of nearly 1,400 lives mostly in Towaoc, the only real town on the reservation. The **Southern Ute Tribe** has a larger reservation (818,000 acres), but the homesteading system left it a checkerboard of Indian and non-Indian lands. The tribe owns just over 300,000 acres, and counts 1,250 members out of the reservation's population of 7,900. Tribal headquarters are in Ignacio. Both Colorado Ute tribes are run by elected tribal councils and depend on income from agriculture, livestock, construction, forestry, mining, and casinos.

On the Road

The Four Corners is a sprawling, roughly defined, rugged, all-around exotic place to visit, and there are as many ways to explore it as there are people who come here. Some want nothing more than to drive their RV to the edge of the Grand Canyon and gaze into the abyss. Others point their dusty van down the most remote dirt road and vanish for weeks on foot, bike, or raft. College students pile out of hostels and buses to explore national parks, families pore over jewelry at roadside stands on Indian reservations, and archaeology buffs poke around the crumbling ruins of long-gone cultures. You can approach this region any way you choose and rest assured it will satisfy just about anything you have on your to-do list—as long as you arm yourself with the right information and take a few simple precautions.

The ideal visit goes something like this: sometime in the spring or fall, you arrive somewhere in the Four Corners, probably Flagstaff or Moab, the two tourist centers closest to the interstates. You're driving your own vehicle or else a rental (preferably, but by no means necessarily, a four-wheel-drive). With three to four weeks free and a loose idea of what you'd like to see and do—say, Monument Valley, Chaco Canyon, an Indian festival, and some good mountain biking—you set out across the high desert with a full tank of gas, a good map, and a few gallons of water in the trunk, just in case.

Even if you're not in this ideal situation, don't despair. I've enjoyed the Four Corners in a weekend, in the middle of winter, and with a car so full of everything I own that my rear bumper scraped the pavement every time I took a corner too fast. Do, however, keep a few things in mind. This is a unique area and traveling here can be an unusual experience—climatically, geographically, and culturally.

White Rim, Canyonlands National Park

First, you're in the high desert, so exposure to the sun and your water supply take on added significance (the idea being to minimize the former and maximize the latter). Distances out here can be vast, often much longer than first-timers realize, and roads that may be winding, unpaved, or both can turn what looks like a simple jog on the map into a half-day odyssey. Finally, remember that the unfamiliar cultures you'll encounter, which give the Four Corners so much of its magic, require a measure of sensitivity and tact. Cultural interactions go both ways, and it's always nice to leave as many good feelings behind as you take home.

This chapter takes care of the rest: how to get around, where to go and stay, what to do, and how to stay safe, healthy, and happy. Arm yourself with the right information and pack a little patience, and you'll find first-hand that the Four Corners is truly like no other place on earth.

Getting There and Around

In a nutshell, the easiest way to explore the Four Corners is to fly to one of the nearest major airports, rent a car, and drive wherever you want to go. Local air, bus, and train service is limited to a few cities, and the distances involved and the remoteness of many of the attractions make a private vehicle the only practical way to get around. A network of highways connects the major cities and points of interest, but this still leaves much of the region inaccessible to drivers without a four-wheel-drive (4WD).

By Air

The nearest **international airports** are in Albuquerque (140 miles from Gallup), Phoenix (145 miles from Flagstaff), Denver (335 miles from Durango), Salt Lake City (235 miles from Moab), and Las Vegas (250 miles from Flagstaff, 270 miles from Page). Each of these cities is a major travel gateway served by most major airlines, and all offer a full range of hotels, restaurants, and tourist-related services. There are smaller **local airports** in Moab, Cortez, Grand Junction, Flagstaff, and Page, with limited service to each other and larger cities; information on these is included in the travel chapters.

By Car

The Four Corners is sandwiched between I-40 to the south, running between Albuquerque and California, and I-70 to the north, which runs from Denver to I-15 in the middle of Utah. I-15 runs from Salt Lake City southwest to St. George,

Las Vegas, and beyond. Major travel arteries within the area include **U.S. 89** and **U.S. 89A,** which connect Flagstaff to Kanab, close to I-15 at St. George. **U.S. 160** connects with U.S. 89 north of Flagstaff and runs east to the Four Corners Monument itself, Cortez, and Durango.

The unfortunately named **U.S. 666** leads north from Gallup across the Navajo Reservation, joining briefly with U.S. 160 and eventually meeting U.S. 191 at Monticello. **U.S. 191** joins I-70 near Green River and runs south through Moab and the other towns of southeast Utah before crossing the state line and the Navajo Reservation. It passes Canyon de Chelly and joins I-40 at Chambers. Other major routes (out here that means a two-lane paved road) include **U.S. 24** and **U.S. 95** across remote south-central Utah, and the spectacular **U.S. 12,** which winds across the northern border of the Grand Staircase–Escalante National Monument.

Car rental agencies can be found in the Four Corners' larger cities: Moab, Durango, Flagstaff, Gallup, and Farmington. When renting a car, consider how far out into the backcountry you want to go; 4WD vehicles are available but they cost more. A good option if you plan on staying on the pavement is to rent a recreational vehicle (RV), which is like piloting your own mobile mini-hotel. You can find developed campsites with water, electric, and sewer hookups for $20–30 per night, or just park on public land and rough it, relatively speaking. **Cruise America,** 480/464-7300, fax 480/464-7321, www .cruiseamerica.com, info@cruiseamerica.com,

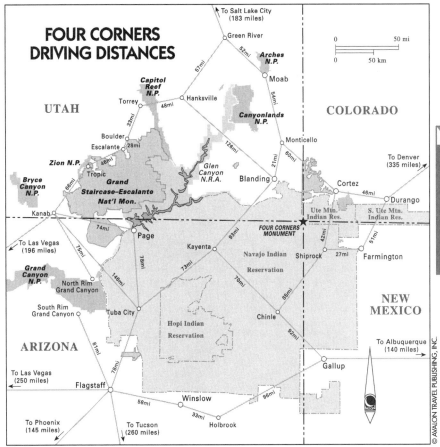

FOUR CORNERS
DRIVING DISTANCES

0   50 mi
0   50 km

To Salt Lake City
(183 miles)

Green River

Arches
N.P.

Moab

Capitol
Reef
N.P.

Torrey   Hanksville

UTAH

Canyonlands
N.P.

COLORADO

Boulder
Escalante

Monticello

Zion N.P.

Glen
Canyon
N.R.A.

Tropic

To Denver
(335 miles)

Bryce
Canyon
N.P.

Grand
Staircase-Escalante
Nat'l Mon.

Blanding

Cortez

Durango

Kanab

Ute Mtn.
Indian Res.

S. Ute Mtn.
Indian Res.

To Las Vegas
(196 miles)

Page

Kayenta

FOUR CORNERS
MONUMENT

Navajo Indian

Shiprock

Farmington

Grand
Canyon
N.P.

North Rim
Grand Canyon

Reservation

NEW
MEXICO

South Rim
Grand Canyon

Tuba City

Chinle

ARIZONA

Hopi Indian
Reservation

To Albuquerque
(140 miles)

To Las Vegas
(250 miles)

Flagstaff

Gallup

Winslow

To Phoenix
(145 miles)

To Tucson
(260 miles)

Holbrook

ON THE ROAD

has RV rental offices in Phoenix, Albuquerque, Salt Lake City, and Denver.

Many car rental agencies will give you a **map** with your car, or you can pick up an atlas that covers all four states. By far the best map of the region is the *Guide to Indian Country* map put out by the Automobile Club of Southern California. This is a true work of cartographic art, accurate to a tenth of a mile, and covers everything in this book, plus areas to the east (Albuquerque and Santa Fe) and west (to Kingman, Arizona, and St. George, Utah). It's the one Lt. Joe Leaphorn fills with pins in Tony Hillerman's Navajo mysteries, simply indispensable for any long-term exploration of the Four Corners area—John Wesley Powell would have killed for one. You can get it from AAA offices, and at bookstores and gas stations throughout the region.

By Bus

There's not as much bus service out here as you might expect (or hope). **Greyhound,** 800/231-2222, www.greyhound.com, has regular service to cities along the interstates: Green River, Durango, Gallup, Farmington, Holbrook, Winslow, and Flagstaff. Contact them for a schedule and information on special discounts and passes. **Golden State Bus Lines** stops at Ben's Cafe in Green

© JULIAN SMITH

The promise of Navajo crafts is one sign that you are entering Navajo country.

River on the way from Las Vegas to Denver. This line goes all over the Southwest and into northern Mexico; for information, contact them in Las Vegas (607 Maple St., 213/627-2940) or Denver (2301 Champa St., 303/675-0110. The Navajo Reservation is served by the **Navajo Transit System,** 928/729-4002/4111, www.navajotransit-system.com, with seven daily routes.

A few companies offer bus tours of the Southwest very different from the typical Greyhound experience. Both **AdventurePlanet,** 34560 Ave. B, Yucaipa, CA 92399, 208/726-8410 or 888/737-5263, www.adventureplanet.com, info@adventureplanet.com, and **Green Tortoise Adventure Travel,** 494 Broadway, San Francisco, CA 94133, 415/956-7500 or 800/867-8647, www.greentortoise.com, tortoise@greentortoise.com, have buses that double as rolling hotels, filled mostly with younger travelers. These trips, which usually include a food fund and communal cooking, focus on outdoor activities and national parks.

By Train

Amtrak, 800/872-7245, www.amtrak.com, runs the luxury *Southwest Chief* line along the path, more or less, of old Route 66. On its way from Chicago to Los Angeles, the *Chief* stops in Gallup, Winslow, and Flagstaff daily in both directions. This is a more comfortable but more expensive and much less flexible way to travel than by bus. Fares vary depending on time of year, and there are a number of discounts available; contact Amtrak for details.

Hitchhiking

This is still an accepted form of transport in the Southwest, particularly on the Indian reservations. It can be a good way to meet locals and get around for little or nothing, but it can also be an exercise in patience, not to mention downright dangerous. I do it from time to time—luckily, mostly on the driving end nowadays—and have never had a bad experience, but that's just one person's story. Trust your instincts when deciding whether or not to accept or offer a ride. It's polite to offer some money for gas if you do get picked up. Women traveling alone should not consider hitchhiking an option. **Ride boards** at universities such as Northern Arizona University in Flagstaff list people who are looking for riders to specific locations to help share the costs, as well as riders looking for drivers.

TOURIST INFORMATION

A number of state and regional tourism departments and governmental agencies exist to answer your travel-related questions. Additional resources, including various local Chambers of Commerce, Convention and Visitors Bureaus, and Travel Councils, are also listed in the text.

Arizona

Arizona Game & Fish Dept.
2221 W. Greenway Rd.
Phoenix, AZ 85023-4399
602/942-3000
www.gf.state.az.us

Arizona Office of Tourism
1110 W. Washington, Suite 155
Phoenix, AZ 85007
602/364-3700 or 888/520-3434
www.arizonaguide.com

Arizona State Parks
1300 W. Washington
Phoenix, AZ 85007
602/542-4174
www.pr.state.az.us

Colorado

Colorado Dept. of Wildlife
West Region Service Center
711 Independent
Grand Junction, CO 81505
970/255-6100
http://wildlife.state.co.us

Colorado State Parks
1313 Sherman St., Suite 618
Denver, CO 80203
303/866-3437
http://parks.state.co.us

San Juan National Forest (Southwest Colorado)
15 Burnett Ct.
Durango, CO 81301
970/247-4874
www.fs.fed.us/r2/sanjuan

Southwest Colorado Travel Region
295A Girard St.
Durango, CO 81301
800/933-4340
www.swcolotravel.org
swctr@frontier.net

New Mexico

New Mexico Dept. of Game & Fish
1 Wildlife Way
Santa Fe, NM 87507
505/476-8000
ispa@state.nm.us
www.gmfsh.state.nm.us

New Mexico Dept. of Tourism
491 Old Santa Fe Trail
Santa Fe, NM 87503
800/733-6396 ext. 0643
www.newmexico.org

New Mexico State Parks
P.O. Box 1147
Santa Fe, NM 87504
888/667-2757
www.emnrd.state.nm.us/nmparks
nmparks@state.nm.us

Utah

Dixie National Forest (South-central Utah)
1789 Wedgewood Ln.
Cedar City, UT 84720
435/865-3700
www.fs.fed.us/dxnf

(continued on next page)

TOURIST INFORMATION (cont'd)

Manti La Sal National Forest
(Southeast Utah)
599 West Price River Dr.
Price, Utah 84501
435/637-2817
www.fs.fed.us/r4/mantilasal

Utah Division of Wildlife Resources
Southeastern Region
475 West Price River Dr., Suite C
Price, UT 84501
435/636-0260

Southern Region
P.O. Box 606
Cedar City, UT 84721-0606
435/865-6100
www.wildlife.utah.gov

Utah State Parks & Recreation
2800 Rose Park Ln.
Salt Lake City, UT 84116
801/538-7220
http://parks.state.ut.us

Utah Travel Council
P.O. Box 147420
Salt Lake City, UT 84114-7420
801/538-1030 or 800/200-1160
www.utah.com
travel@utah.com

**Four Corners Region
Grand Circle Association**
6420 S. Quebec, Suite B
Englewood, CO 80111
303/850-9358 or 888/254-7263
www.grandcircle.org
info@grandcircle.org

National Park Service
Intermountain Region
12795 Alameda Pkwy.
Denver, CO 80225
303/969-2500
www.nps.gov

Navajo Parks & Recreation Dept.
P.O. Box 2520
Window Rock, AZ 86515
928/871-6647
www.navajonationparks.org
info@navajonationparks.org

Navajoland Tourism Dept.
P.O. Box 663
Window Rock, AZ 86515
520/871-6659 or 520/871-6436
www.discovernavajo.com
discovernavajo@lycos.com

U.S. Fish & Wildlife Service
Southwest Region
500 Gold Ave. SW
Albuquerque, NM 87102
505/248-6911
http://southwest.fws.gov

ON THE ROAD

Suggested Itineraries

With so many different destinations to choose from—not to mention a roadmap that looks like a spider web after a high wind—planning a trip around the Four Corners can be a tad overwhelming. A little guidance is therefore in order. The routes below are organized by type of activity, but they all follow roughly the same pattern. Starting at Flagstaff, the first three each describe a clockwise loop (following the layout of this book), touching New Mexico, Colorado, and stopping in Moab, Utah, before heading south to Arizona. This way you can start or stop in either Flagstaff, Durango, or Moab, the three main tourist cities in the Four Corners, and switch from one route to another along the way. Each will take two to four weeks, depending on how quick you are. The "Native Culture" route strays from the circular path somewhat and is shorter. It can be done in as little as a week. All these routes assume you have your own vehicle. They don't include everything in covered in this book, just the most outstanding sights in each category. Happy planning!

> *With so many different destinations to choose from—not to mention a roadmap that looks like a spider web after a high wind—planning a trip around the Four Corners can be a tad overwhelming. A little guidance is therefore in order.*

SCENERY AND PARKS

This route is for those who don't plan on venturing far from the pavement but nevertheless want to maximize their oohing and ahhing. Starting in **Flagstaff,** head east on I-40, stopping at the **Meteor Crater.** Take the scenic drive through **Petrified Forest National Park** and the Painted Desert, then head up U.S. 191 though Ganado to **Canyon de Chelly National Park.** You can tour this on your own or descend into the canyon itself on a guided tour.

No photo album of the Four Corners is complete without at least a roll shot of **Monument Valley,** so take U.S. 191 to U.S. 160 and 163 to get there, on the Arizona-Utah border. Keep going up into southeast Utah, stopping for a peek at the Goosenecks of the San Juan near **Mexican Hat,** and perhaps taking a detour up U.S. 261 onto Cedar Mesa (don't miss the views from **Muley Point** at the top); return to U.S. 191 via U.S. 95 through the giant gash in Comb Ridge. Colorado is a short distance east of Monticello on U.S. 666. It offers the cliff palaces of **Mesa Verde National Park** near Cortez and the day-long **San Juan Skyway** that loops in the mountains north of **Durango.**

Use **Moab** as a home base to visit **Arches National Park** and **Canyonlands National Park,** whose Island in the Sky District offers the quickest visual bang for the buck. Continue north on U.S. 191 to I-70 and head west through Green River to reach the turnoff for U.S. 24 south to Hanksville. Here the surroundings get downright weird, from the sawtooth bulwarks of the **San Rafael Swell** to the melting mudstone of **Goblin Valley State Park.** Continue on U.S. 24 to **Capitol Reef National Park,** where a short scenic drive gives access to a surprising chunk of the park's stupendous sights. At Torrey, turn south onto **U.S. 12,** one of the most spectacular drives in the country. It winds up onto Boulder Mountain for amazing views before descending into the slickrock wildness of the northern **Grand Staircase–Escalante National Monument.** Even better, **Bryce Canyon National Park** awaits at the western end.

Keep going on U.S. 12 to U.S. 89, which you'll take south to Kanab. From here you have a choice: if you haven't had enough Escalante yet, continue on U.S. 89 across the monument's southern reaches. Otherwise, hop south across the border to Fredonia (as have many fugitive polygamists over the years) and take U.S. 89A up onto the Kaibab Plateau, which gives the option of a detour south to the **North Rim of the Grand Canyon.** U.S. 89A continues east along the base of the Vermilion Cliffs to **Marble Canyon** and the impressive twin spans of Navajo Bridge (leave time to drive down to the river at Lees Ferry). U.S. 89A eventually rejoins U.S. 89 and continues south. At Cameron, you can hop onto U.S. 64 west to the **South Rim of the Grand Canyon,** or else continue south to Flagstaff to finish the loop, possibly taking in one more vista from the Arizona Snowbowl in the San Francisco Peaks high above the city.

OUTDOORS AND BACKCOUNTRY

If a beautiful view makes you want nothing more than to run out and disappear into it for as long as possible, this route is for you. From Flagstaff, drive east again on I-40 to the **Petrified Forest National Park,** where you can grab a free permit to camp in the **Painted Desert** portion north of the interstate. Head north on U.S. 191 to Chinle and **Canyon de Chelly National Park.** One trail here goes to the bottom without a permit required; otherwise, sign up for a guided hike among the Navajo farms and orchards at the bottom of this gorgeous canyon system. (The park campground is free.)

The detour east to Farmington is not as easy as it looks—U.S. 12, 134/32, 666, and 64 are probably the fastest way—but south of the city are two little-visited spots perfect for enjoying solitude. The **Bisti** and **De-Na-Zin Wilderness Areas** are full of otherworldly rock formations, and the badlands surrounding **Angel Peak** are amazing at sunset and sunrise. **Durango** is less than an hour north of Farmington, in the foothills of the trail-packed San Juan National Forest.

In any case, you'll eventually want to head north until you're on U.S. 191 in southeast Utah, which you've probably been waiting for since the beginning of the trip. If it's the right time of year and you have the time to spare, consider the quick, easy raft trip down the **San Juan River** from Bluff to Mexican Hat, or a hike down into **Grand Gulch** (or the less-traveled Owl and Fish Creek Canyons) up on Cedar Mesa. U.S. 191 continues north to Moab, the epicenter of the outdoor playground that is southern Utah. Take

one of the dozens of **mountain bike** trails that made the town famous, such as the famous Slickrock Trail, or backpack among the spires of the Needles district of **Canyonlands National Park.** The **White Rim** below the park's Island in the Sky district is an outstanding multi-day bike trip, and this area also has the highest concentration of **rock climbing** in the region.

Continue north to Green River on I-70 and back south down U.S. 24, where the slot canyons of the **San Rafael Swell** await, across the road from the excellent short hike to the stunning pictographs in **Horseshoe Canyon,** a detached part of the Maze district of Canyonlands National Park. U.S. 24 continues west to **Capitol Reef National Park,** with more slot canyons slicing through the Waterpocket Fold, accessed via the rough **Notom-Bullfrog Road.** U.S. 12 heads south from Torrey into the backcountry smorgasbord of the gigantic **Grand Staircase–Escalante National Monument.** Warm up on the short hike to Calf Creek Falls, or perhaps Box-Death Hollow or the Boulder Mail Trail near the town of Boulder, before taking the Hole in the Rock Road south from Escalante into the heart of the monument. The canyon trails off this route, from narrow slots to those along the wide, easy Escalante River itself, are worth years of exploring.

Make an end run around the western end of the monument along U.S. 12 and 89 through Kanab. East of the city is the **Paria Plateau,** bisected by an outstanding multi-day hike through the Paria River canyons. U.S. 89 gives access to the trailheads, as well as water sports on Lake Powell and the famous slot hike through Antelope Canyon near Page. You can also choose to take the U.S. 89A spur around the south side of the plateau, if you'd like to hit the (relatively) cool and less crowded **North Rim of the Grand Canyon.** The canyon's **South Rim** awaits on U.S. 64 west of Cameron. By now you're probably bushed, ready to straggle back south to Flagstaff.

HISTORY AND ARCHAEOLOGY

The past is everywhere you turn in the Four Corners, from ancient ruins to trading posts and museums. If history is your forte, try this itinerary. Start your journey before leaving Flagstaff at the excellent **Museum of Northern Arizona,** followed by the ruins at **Wupatki** and **Walnut Canyon National Monuments.** East on I-40 are two **classic hotels** of very different character: the Wigwam Motel in Winslow and La Posada in Holbrook. Up U.S. 191 onto the Navajo Reservation is the **Hubbell Trading Post National Historic Site** in Ganado. Take U.S. 3/264 east to Gallup, then U.S. 9 or I-40 to U.S. 371 and continue north toward Farmington. Your next destination is just a stone's throw away, but without 4WD, you'll have to go all the way up to Farmington, over to Bloomfield on U.S. 64, and down U.S. 550 to reach the turnoff to **Chaco Canyon National Historical Park,** the center of one of the Southwest's greatest prehistoric cultures. The ruins here are on a scale that's hard to believe, so you may understandably be a bit underwhelmed by those you'll hit next: **Aztec** and **Salmon Ruins** to the north, near the cities of Aztec and Bloomfield, respectively.

Take U.S. 550 north from Aztec to **Durango,** where you can return to the present, or at least the last century, for a breather. West of Durango on U.S. 160 is a place that will leave you awestruck all over again: **Mesa Verde National Park,** whose cliff dwellings have to be seen to be believed. The area around Cortez and the Four Corners itself is rich in archaeological sites such as the boulder-perched towers of **Hovenweep National Monument,** the sprawling **Canyons of the Ancients National Monument,** and the **Anasazi Heritage Center** near Dolores.

Continue west on U.S. 666 into southeast Utah at Monticello. On your way toward **Moab** to the north, you'll pass the turnoff for the **Needles district of Canyonlands National Park,** rich in rock art and ruins. More petroglyphs line roads near Moab, and if you have time, the full-day trip via Green River to the **Horseshoe Canyon** portion of Canyonlands' Maze district promises one of the most impressive walls of pictographs you'll ever see. Back down U.S. 191 is the **Edge of the Cedars State Park** in Blanding, full to the rafters with artifacts, and you can probably guess what the **Dinosaur Museum** exhibits. Experience more

prehistory in person during a canyon hike on **Cedar Mesa,** west on U.S. 95, or keep going south along U.S. 191, which becomes U.S. 163 as it enters Arizona at **Monument Valley.** Nearby are two **trading posts** not to be missed—Goulding's, a museum, and Oljato, and one of the most authentic posts left in the Southwest.

Near Kayenta, south on U.S. 163, is **Navajo National Monument,** where you can see more cliff palaces either from the road or after a long one-day or overnight hike. More trading posts await as you return to Flagstaff, including **Old Red Lake, Tuba City** and **Van's** in Tuba City, and **Cameron** on U.S. 89. Continue south on U.S. 89 to reach Flagstaff.

NATIVE CULTURE

The Four Corners' three largest Indian tribes—Navajo, Hopi, and Ute—each have their own reservation (the Ute actually have two), and you can visit each without going far out of Arizona. From Flagstaff, head north on U.S. 89 to **Tuba City,** where you can grab a Navajo taco at the Tuba City Truck Stop Cafe and peruse the wares at Van's and the Tuba City Trading Post. If you're here on a Friday, visit the flea market for an undiluted dose of life on the "Rez." Take U.S. 264 east from Tuba City across the **Hopi Reservation,** surrounded by the larger Navajo Reservation. If you time it right, you can watch a traditional Hopi festival in a timeless stone village perched on one of three long mesas. The road continues east to Ganado, where a detour north on U.S. 191 brings you to **Canyon de Chelly National Park,** a time-bubble of agrarian life little changed in centuries. Another side trip heads east to **Crownpoint,** where a rug auction is held on the third Friday of every month.

Back on U.S. 264/3 is **Window Rock,** the administrative center of the Navajo Nation, and **Gallup,** its commercial hub. The latter teems with trading posts and galleries with crafts made by tribes from across the Southwest. Head north on U.S. 666 to the town of **Shiprock,** stopping off at the Two Gray Hills Trading Post along the way, and consider a detour up into Colorado to visit the ruins in the **Ute Mountain Tribal Park,**

ON THE ROAD

similar to those at Mesa Verde but not reconstructed. Leave the soaring shape of Shiprock in your rearview as you drive west on U.S. 64 to Teec Nos Pos and the Carrizo Mountains, where it becomes U.S. 160 and passes Mexican Water before reaching **Kayenta.** To the north is **Mon-** **ument Valley,** whose looming mesas are sacred to the Navajo and famous around the world, thanks to Western movies and car commercials. Continue down U.S. 160 to Tuba City, catching anything here you missed the first time through, and take U.S. 89 south back to Flagstaff.

Accommodations and Food

ACCOMMODATIONS

Throughout the Four Corners, accommodations range from luxury guest ranches and spas to a sleeping bag under the stars. Unless you're camping the whole way through, you can count on accommodations eating up the largest part of your travel budget. Luckily, standards are high, and although it might be a long drive to the next town, you can rest assured that almost every place worth a dot on the map offers at least a few places to stay. The listings in this book are geared to travelers of all budgets. Prices quoted are for doubles rooms in peak season and do not include taxes, which can add another 10 percent. Reservations are always a good idea, particularly from spring to fall.

Hotels and Motels

Chain hotels and motels are well represented in the Four Corners. On top of that, several noteworthy historic hotels, such as the Weatherford and Monte Vista in Flagstaff and Durango's General Palmer and Strater Hotels, offer more character at the high end. Rates can vary drastically depending on the season, discounts you may qualify for (such as AARP, AAA, or business or corporate rates), and even when and how you book the room—in person or by phone, in the afternoon or evening. Holidays and local festivals can raise prices, while weekend or weeklong stays can lower them. Calling a hotel directly for a reservation, especially on a Sunday night, often earns you a lower rate than calling the chain's toll-free number or booking over the Internet. Ask to speak to the manager on duty or someone in the sales office. Also, it never hurts to ask the receptionist to put a note in your record requesting a room upgrade.

Bed-and-Breakfasts and Guest Ranches

Bed-and-breakfasts (B&Bs) and their more personal brethren—country inns, guest ranches, and the like—can turn an average trip into an outstanding one. The buildings are often historic homes, and owners are always full of information on the area. It's hard to beat the home-cooked gourmet breakfasts and the personal attention these places offer, even if you have to smoke outside or occasionally share a bathroom. Guests can often use the kitchen to prepare their own food, and some rooms come with a kitchenette. Since space is limited, advance reservations and a deposit are usually required, along with a minimum stay during the high season. Cancellation requires prior notice—at least 24 hours, sometimes as much as one week—to avoid paying a service charge. Deals on multi-night stays are sometimes available.

Each state has its own B&B association that can help you find information or book a reservation at member inns. Contact the **Arizona Association of Bed and Breakfast Inns,** P.O. Box 22086, Flagstaff, AZ 86002-2086, 800/284-2589, www.arizona-bed-breakfast.com, info@arizona-bed-breakfast.com; **Bed & Breakfast Innkeepers of Colorado,** P.O. Box 38416, Dept. W, Colorado Springs, CO 80937-8416, 800/265-7696, www.innsofcolorado.org, info@innsofcolorado.org; **Bed & Breakfast Inns of Utah,** www.bbiu.org, info@bbiu.org; and the **New Mexico Bed and Breakfast Association,** 505/766-5380 or 800/661-6649, www.nmbba.org, info@nmbba.org. Other helpful websites include **Bed and Breakfast Inns Online,** www.bbonline.com, info@bbonline.com, and **Bedand-Breakfast.com,** www.bedandbreakfast.com.

© JULIAN SMITH

Wigwam Motel, Holbrook, Arizona

Hostels

These budget lodgings are popular with students, foreign backpackers, and anyone else willing to share a room or accept a slightly scruffy private one in exchange for low rates and the chance to meet like-minded travelers. In the Four Corners, there are hostels in Moab, Durango, Flagstaff, and Page, and hostel-like accommodations in a few other towns such as Torrey and Tuba City. Breakfast is usually included in the price, and you can use the kitchen at other times to cook your own food, saving even more money. The lower rates ($12–15) are for bunk beds in shared rooms, but private rooms are also available for a little more. They often offer group meals, activities, and tours of the surrounding area.

A membership with **Hostelling International,** 733 15th St. NW, Suite 840, Washington, D.C. 20005, 202/783-6161, fax 202/783-6171, www.hiayh.org, hostels@hiayh.org, will save you a few dollars each time. Find more information and hostel listings at www.hostels.com, www.hostelworld.com, or www.find-hostels.com.

Camping

Among the best things about traveling in this country—which we Americans often take for granted—are the enormous swatches of public land that belong to all of us, at least in theory. In this respect the Colorado Plateau is a prime example. Most of the land you see out here is publicly owned—68 percent of Utah and 44 percent of Arizona, all told. There's nothing like the freedom of driving for hours, pulling your car onto a dirt road in a national forest or across a BLM-managed mesa, and finding your own private spot to set up camp just as the sun sets.

Any land managed by the U.S. Forest Service (USFS) and the Bureau of Land Management (BLM) is open to **dispersed (at-large) camping,** aside from areas specially designated as closed to camping or places already developed for camping (in these, stay in the campsites only). Dispersed camping ranges from hike-in backcountry sites to clearings alongside roads where you can park a car, camper, or trailer. Fires are often prohibited, and land ownership can be a confusing patchwork of public and private holdings, so check with the local office of the USFS or the BLM for details. There is often a maximum stay of two or three weeks, although this is seldom enforced. Developed campgrounds usually include bathrooms, picnic tables, and fire rings, and can sometimes be reserved ahead of time. State and national parks are subject to more regulations; here you often have to stay in developed campsites (often first-come, first-served), or at least secure a permit for backcountry camping, and you'll probably have to stay in designated zones or campsites once you're out there. Fees are around $10–15 per campsite.

On private land and the Indian reservations you are limited to **private campgrounds,** which are plentiful. These offer tent and RV spaces which include electricity, water, and sewer hookups, and many offer showers, laundry services, and other activities and services. More elaborate places, typified by **KOA Kampgrounds,** 406/248-7444, fax 406/248-7444, www.koa.com, come complete with pools, game rooms, hot tubs, saunas, and volleyball courts. Occasionally they'll have small **cabins** with a/c and heat for about the price of a budget motel room. Features such as bicycle rental, miniature golf, and summer children's programs cost extra. You can reserve their campsites online. Many campgrounds close for the winter, and reservations and/or deposits may be necessary in popular areas like the Grand Canyon or during peak seasons. Private campsites cost around $20–30.

Homestays

U.S. Servas, Inc., 11 John St., Room 505, New York, NY 10038, 212/267-0252, fax 212/267-0292, www.usservas.org, info@usservas.org, oversees a worldwide network designed to promote peace and foster intercultural understanding through person-to-person contact. After an initial interview, travelers 18 and over pay $65 per year to rent a list of hosts who offer room and board for two nights. Becoming a Servas traveler is an excellent way to meet interesting local people, and the modest fee is easily recouped.

FOOD AND DRINK

The larger towns in the Four Corners—primarily Moab, Durango, and Flagstaff—offer a wide variety of eateries, from fine Thai restaurants to vegetarian cafes serving organic coffee and fresh-baked bread. Outside of these, however, the cooking quickly becomes pedestrian, with a handful of notable exceptions such as Hell's Backbone Grill in Boulder and Cafe Diablo in Torrey. This isn't to say it's not good food—it often is, especially if you're a fan of hearty, spicy cuisine heavy on meats and carbohydrates. Expect to pay around $5–8 pp for an average breakfast or lunch and $10–20 for dinner.

Southwest cuisine takes its cue from the piquant fare of Mexico and reaches its apogee in the

Southwest cuisine takes its cue from the piquant fare of Mexico and reaches its apogee in the sublime cooking of New Mexico. Dishes like burritos and enchiladas are full of beans and cheese, and graced with the fiery kiss of locally grown chiles.

sublime cooking of New Mexico. Dishes like burritos and enchiladas are full of beans and cheese, and graced with the fiery kiss of locally grown chiles. Less lethal than, say, jalapenos, these come in two color varieties—order your dish with red, green, or both (code-named "Christmas"). Try a chile relleno (stuffed with cheese) and finish up with a sopaipilla, a puffy fried pastry served hot with honey. **Native American** specialties include the wafer-thin *piiki* bread of the Hopi and deep-fried Navajo fry bread. Topped with meat, beans, cheese, and lettuce, it becomes a Navajo taco; try an outstanding example at the Tuba City Truck Stop Cafe. **Cowboy cookouts** are a popular restaurant theme around here, offering steaks cooked on an open fire and, usually, an evening's entertainment. **Fast food** is everywhere, of course, as are Mom-and-Pop eateries and roadside diners with worn vinyl seats and a world-weary atmosphere—and, often, the smell of great homestyle cooking.

Getting a drink is complicated in two parts of the Four Corners. Utah's arcane liquor laws limit brewpubs and taverns to 3.2 percent beer and supermarkets to "near-beer." Wine and hard liquor are sold at state-run liquor stores and some restaurants, although you'll have to ask your server for a drink—he can't offer you one outright. What you probably call a bar back home, here they call a "private club." Locals pay an annual fee, but visitors can pay $5 or so to enter for an evening. (Technically, this is a "sponsorship" by a current member. If you find out who yours is, buy him a drink!) Alcohol is forbidden on both the Navajo and Hopi Reservations, but this doesn't stop—in fact, it causes—the proliferation of liquor stores at border towns.

Arts and Entertainment

ARTS AND CRAFTS

Navajo Crafts

The Diné tell how Spider Woman taught their ancestors to weave on looms built by her husband. The introduction of curly-horned Churro sheep by the Spanish in the 17th century, along with the embracing of pueblo-style looms and a more sedentary lifestyle, allowed the tribe to become expert weavers. Today their **rugs** can hold their own among the world's finest handmade textiles. Women traditionally own the sheep and weave the rugs, which can take months to make. (The Churro sheep, almost extinct by the 1970s, is being pulled back from the brink through careful breeding.)

Navajo rugs combine Mexican stylistic influences with geometric designs and representations of natural phenomena. On the advice of early Anglo traders, they expanded their repertoire to include brighter colors and more intricate patterns, as well as synthetic yarns. True Navajo rugs, however, are woven from sheep's wool, as a quick sniff will verify. Other things to look for in a quality rug include symmetry, straight edges, even coloration, and a tight, flat weave. You'll often find a "spirit line" running to the border in older rugs, included to keep the weaver's spirit from being trapped inside the pattern.

Patterns include the geometric Two Gray Hills, made of natural white, gray, and brown wool; the warm pastel of the Burnt Water style; the elaborately banded Wide Ruins; and the self-explanatory Eye Dazzlers and Pictorials. Sometimes rug patterns are dictated by the color of their background, from Dinnebito (black) to Ganado (red) and Klagetoh (gray). Yei rugs depict the Holy People, and Yeibichai illustrate ceremonies in which the Holy People are impersonated by human dancers. Prices range from the low hundreds to well into the thousands, with a quality 3-by-5-foot rug going for $500–600. This is an exacting art, and, sadly, a dying one, since fewer young girls are learning the old weaving techniques. For this reason, a quality rug will hold its price well and probably even climb in value. Good rugs will also last for years; some old ones have endured over a century of boot traffic.

The Navajo originally learned the technique of silversmithing from Mexicans in the 1850s, before taking it to new levels. They don't have to melt down silver coins any more, but today's **silver jewelry** is just as impressive: chunky bracelets, elaborately detailed concha belts, rings and watchbands inlaid with turquoise and coral, and gorgeous squash-blossom necklaces that make your neck ache just to look at them. Silver jewelry is usually sand-cast and then polished to a bright luster, and die-stamped with decorative details. You'll often see Navajo matriarchs decked out in their best necklaces and bracelets, dripping with enough turquoise to ransom a princess. Men wear the *ketoh*, or "bow guard," a wide forearm band that is now purely decorative. Turquoise is the most common inlay material, but new techniques have afforded the addition of gold and other precious minerals.

Navajo **sandpaintings** recreate the ceremonial designs drawn on hogan floors by medicine men. The paintings are drawn with glue on plywood or particle board, then sprinkled with minerals gathered and ground on the reservation. Look for precise workmanship, but know that you're not getting a true religious artifact: small details are changed in the paintings to avoid offending the Holy People. Other types of **paintings** in oils and acrylics depict life on the reservation, and are sometimes quite abstract.

One of the most widely recognized types of basket made in the Southwest is the Navajo **wedding basket,** a wide, shallow dish woven of sumac and mahogany fibers. Made using a concentric coil technique, these have geometric designs in muted colors. They are purely decorative, usually hung on the wall. Tribe members make many other types of crafts as well, including their own versions of Hopi **kachinas, woodcarvings,** ceramic and alabaster **sculpture,** and **"folk art,"** a generic term for figurines carved from wood or fashioned from clay.

Hopi Crafts

The "peaceful people" are best known for two types of crafts. Hopi **silver jewelry**, more delicate than the Navajo style, dates to the 1890s, when Sikyatala, the first Hopi silversmith, learned his craft from artisans at Zuñi Pueblo. Since World War II, it has been done in an overlay style, in which a design is cut from a flat sheet of silver and set in front of another sheet that has been textured and oxidized to black. Hopi jewelry is marked with the artist's name, clan, or village, and the design may be pictorial or abstract. Gold and inlaid precious stones are sometimes incorporated into pieces that range from rings, bracelets, and bolo tie clasps to necklaces, belt buckles, and button covers.

Kachina (katsina) dolls, used to teach children about the gods who live in the San Francisco Mountains, are called *tithu* by the Hopi. These brightly painted figures, carved from the root of the cottonwood, rest on an attached base and can be amazingly detailed. They come in all sizes,

and the quality of the carving and painting varies as widely as the price. Prime examples are true works of art, justifiably fetching thousands of dollars. There are dozens of kachinas depicted as dolls, including *Mongwa,* the Great Horned Owl; *Salako Mana* and *Salaka Taka,* the male and female kachina leaders; and the humorous Koyemsi and Koshare clowns. Kachinas are one of the most distinctive souvenirs of the Southwest. If they strike your fancy, it's well worth it to read up on the art and talk to the carvers.

Hopi artisans also make **baskets** and **paintings** not unlike those of the Navajo, as well as ground-fired **pottery.**

SHOPPING

One of the best things about traveling in the Four Corners is the incredible variety of high-quality arts and crafts items that are available. Navajo rugs and Hopi jewelry are sold around the world, but here you can chat with the artisan in person, and have a face and a story to attach to the beautiful piece you end up taking home. If there's something particular you'd like to buy—

© JULIAN SMITH

turquoise jewelry on display at the Hatch Trading Post in New Mexico

say, a Navajo rug—read up on the different styles and try to visit as many places as possible to get a feel for prices and availability. I usually take home one nice souvenir every time I travel in the Four Corners, and I've never gone wrong by waiting until I found just the right piece.

Crafts made by many different Indian tribes are available in the Four Corners, including jewelry from Zuñi Pueblo and wonderful pottery from Acoma and Santo Domingo Pueblos, but most of what you'll see will be made by the Navajo and Hopi tribes.

Where to Shop

There are two main options when it comes to buying indigenous crafts (well, three, if you count paying five times as much at a boutique back home): purchase direct from the artists themselves or from a trading post or gallery. Buying from the creator, either in their home or at a roadside or flea market stand, adds not only a personal touch but also the opportunity to get the best price. In this situation it helps to know what you're looking for and how to judge quality and price. To be honest, a lot of the merchandise for sale at tourist spots like Monument Valley is, for lack of a better word, cheap trinkets. Fortunately, this kind of stuff is relatively easy to spot.

Trading posts and galleries have higher prices, but at the better ones you can be assured you're getting a quality product, with the reputation of the store to back it up. Employees are happy to let you browse and to lend their expert advice if necessary, and can pack and ship your purchases back home. Many also have **pawn** departments where people leave goods as collateral for cash loans and often don't return for them. Pawn shops are also common. This is a great way to get a deal on crafts, especially jewelry. "Dead pawn" is sometimes auctioned off on a monthly basis.

You'll find the best selection and quality at places like the Tuba City Trading Post, Noteh Dineh in Cortez, Toh-Atin in Durango, Twin Rocks in Bluff, Fifth Generation in Farmington, and Blair's Dinnebito in Page. For atmosphere, don't miss Hatch Brothers near Farmington, Goulding's and Oljato in Monument Valley, Cow Canyon in Bluff, and the Hubbell Trading Post National Historic Site west of Window Rock. Richardson's Trading Company in Gallup can hold its own in both categories.

Wherever you buy a piece, try to find out where and when it was made, and ask for a **certificate of authenticity,** or at least a receipt with the name and contact information of the artist or gallery, the artist's name and tribal affiliation, and the price, including the original price if you received a discount.

Shopping Resources

Many trading posts and galleries have their own websites, continually updated as goods are bought and sold; these are listed in the travel chapters of this book. The **Southwest Indian Foundation,** 505/863-4037 or 877/788-9962, www.southwestindian.com, is a nonprofit organization with an extensive mail-order catalog of arts and crafts. Profits go to help native communities support schools, provide food during holidays, and establish homes for battered women.

Some of the many books on Southwest Indian crafts are listed in the "Resources" section. The Southwest Parks and Monuments Association puts out the pocket-sized *A Guide to Navajo Rugs,* available at most bookstores and gift shops in the Four Corners.

EVENTS

The list of annual events is long, from the delicate dawn launch of a hot-air balloon rally to the dirt and sweat of rodeos. County fairs, held in the larger towns, are a great way to see a slice of local life (or sometimes the whole pie). These include livestock and agriculture displays, music, arts and crafts, and sometimes a parade and the inauguration of the annual king and queen. Chili cookoffs, wine festivals, and other food-related events showcase local cuisine and vintages, and a wide spectrum of theater, film, art, and music festivals range from the Canyonlands Film and Video Festival in Moab to Flagstaff's Concerts in the Park.

The outdoors is well represented, of course, with mountain bike and foot races and 4WD gatherings. Farmington's Riverfest and the Annual Green River/Moab Friendship Cruise are two of the region's water-based events. Cultural festivals include celebrations of the area's Hispanic and native cultures, such as the annual dances on the Hopi and Navajo Reservations, the Shiprock Navajo Fair, and, the biggest of its kind, Gallup's Inter-Tribal Indian Ceremonial, held each August. Some events, like Durango's Railfest and Aztec's Fiesta Days, don't really fit into any one category. Finally, the holidays bring parades of lights and nativity scenes (both Anglo and indigenous versions) and strings of luminarias—lit candles in sand-filled paper bags, a legacy of Spanish New Mexico—to places like Mesa Verde and San Juan College in Farmington.

Recreation

You could easily spend a lifetime sampling the outdoor offerings of the Four Corners. A plethora of tour operators are on hand to lead the way, or you can head out on your own—just promise you'll go prepared.

HIKING AND CAMPING

Since most of the Four Corners is accessible only by foot, the possibilities for hiking and camping are almost endless. From paved paths in national parks to terrifying scrambles along canyon ledges, it's all here. Perhaps more than any other place in the Lower 48, the Four Corners offers something that's become increasingly rare: the opportunity to disappear, really and truly, into the backcountry. You can take a short ramble from a car to a canyon overlook, or descend into that canyon and its tributaries for weeks without seeing another person. Remote ruins, petroglyphs, slot canyons, and hidden springs are only a few of the goodies waiting in the backcountry. For those tired of the desert, there are mountain ranges with peerless views and snow cover from fall to spring. Many trails are developed and even accessible to disabled visitors, while countless more are rough, steep, and unmaintained. Many in this latter category are marked by small piles of rocks called **cairns.** Feel free to add your own pebble, but make sure you really are on the trail; false cairns can be dangerous.

Be aware of any and all land ownership regulations: state, national, and tribal parks have camping regulations, and the Indian reservations are considered private property and therefore off-limits to at-large (i.e., anywhere, anytime) camping. BLM lands and national forests are more liberal in their policies, although some restrictions still apply; see "Camping" under "Accommodations," above, as well as the special topic "Tourism Information" for details and contact information.

The canyon country is spectacular terrain, but not one to be taken lightly. Heed the advice on heat and water in the "Health and Safety" section below, and always carry an emergency survival pack. Be prepared for extreme weather conditions, especially at high altitudes. During the rainy or "monsoon" season (roughly July–Sept.), monumental cloudbursts are an almost daily occurrence. Summer temperatures often climb over 100°F, and sub-zero winter cold is common.

Since you'll be carry so much weight in water (one gallon weighs eight pounds), it's smart to minimize the weight of the rest of your gear. Many companies are starting to make **ultralight** camping gear, tested and perfected on long routes like the Appalachian Trail. One outfit specializes in it: **GoLite,** P.O Box 20190, Boulder, CO 80303, 303/546-6000 or 888/546-5483, www.golite.com, info@golite.com. Throw one of their Flash sleeping bags and a Lair tarp shelter inside a Breeze hiking pack, and you have a basic setup that weighs less than five pounds. Inspired and advised by ultralight hiking guru (and inventor of climbing cams) Ray Jardine, they also make clothing.

As you stay safe, protect the environment as well by following the guidelines of the **Leave No Trace** program, 284 Lincoln St., Lander, WY 82520, 307/335-2213, www.lnt.org. These include careful planning (let someone responsible know where you're going and when you plan to return); traveling and camping on durable surfaces (stay off the crypto!); disposing of waste properly (no burning toilet paper); leaving things as you find them (disturbing archaeological sites on federal land is a felony); minimizing the impact of campfires (better yet, use a stove); leaving wildlife alone; and being considerate of your fellow campers.

Maps are a critical part of any backcountry venture. National Geographic has acquired **Trails Illustrated**, www.trailsillustrated .com, whose water- and tearproof maps are the best going. For $10 each, you can find your way around Arches National Park, Bryce Canyon National Park, Canyonlands National Park (Maze district and northeast Glen Canyon National Recreation Area, or Needles and Island in the Sky), Glen Canyon & Capitol Reef Area, Grand Canyon National Park, the canyons of the Escalante, the San Rafael Swell, the Moab area, and the Grand Gulch Plateau. They also offer folding state map guides for $7 each.

The **U.S. Geological Survey** 1400 Independence Rd., Rolla, MO 65401, 573/308-3500, www.usgs.gov, has been creating topographical maps of the entire country since 1879. At last count they had over 80,000, including more than 57,000 of the 1:24,000-scale maps better known as 7.5-minute quadrangles, perfect for folding up and popping in a backpack or bike rack. You can buy these at many outdoor-gear stores and specialty map stores in the Four Corners, such as Times Independent Maps in Moab, or order them directly from the USGS for $6 each plus a $5 handling fee. Find ordering information online at http://mcmcweb.er.usgs .gov/topomaps and http://mapping.usgs.gov/ esic/prices/index.html.

Latitude 40 Maps, PO Box 189, Nederland, CO 80466, 303/258-7909, fax 303/258-0540, lat40@indra.com, www.angelfire.com/biz/lati-

Since most of the Four Corners is accessible only by foot, the possibilities for hiking and camping are almost endless. Perhaps more than any other place in the Lower 48, the Four Corners offers something that's become increasingly rare: the opportunity to disappear, really and truly, into the backcountry.

tude40, makes three excellent maps for mountain bikers and hikers: Moab East ($10), Moab West ($10), and the Slickrock Bike Trail ($7), as well as a recreation map of Southwest Colorado ($10).

Another good online source is **TopoZone**, www.topozone.com, which lets you create and download custom topographic maps based on the USGS line.

CANYONEERING

This relatively new pursuit involves descending or ascending narrow canyons that often require rock climbing skills to enter, negotiate, and exit. This is one of the more exciting ways to explore the canyon country, but it's also one of the most hazardous. In addition to the risk of falling and hurting yourself in some of the most remote country around, add the danger of flash floods in monsoon season as well as hypothermia, since you'll have to wade or even swim in icy water to get through some narrow canyons. Flash floods can arrive with little or no warning, even if the sky is blue overhead, and can fill a canyon with water, mud, trees, and boulders much more quickly than you can escape it. For a reminder of the forces involved, look for tree trunks lodged many yards overhead in narrow canyons by seasonal floods. Flash floods are often preceded by an earthy smell and a sound like a train rushing down the canyon. Smaller ones can be fun to watch from a safe vantage point, but big ones are deadly.

Take wading shoes, synthetic clothing (damp cotton is a killer), waterproof bags for your things, and a walking stick or pole for balance and to check for deep holes hidden under muddy water. Only tackle the really wet canyons in hot weather. If necessary, bring ropes and/or nylon webbing and climbing harnesses, and know how to use them or go with someone who does. Claustrophobes should find something else to do—some slot canyons are so narrow you'll have to remove your backpack and shimmy through sideways. Many excellent guidebooks list canyon hikes in detail; see the "Resources" section for a listing.

BICYCLING

As much as any other activity, **mountain biking** has put the Four Corners on the map. Hundreds or thousands of fat-tire fanatics descend in the spring and fall (summer is usually too hot) to try their hands—and legs, hips, and wisely helmeted heads—on the steep but sticky slickrock, meandering mountain singletrack, and old mining and logging roads. Moab's Slickrock Trail is world famous, and dozens of others nearby make this otherwise unassuming town a prime biking destination. There are just as many easy trails for the less adventurous. Durango is the Four Corners' other mountain biking hotspot, with precipitous tracks in just about every direction. Both towns have bike shops galore offering gear, rentals, and information. Guidebooks to mountain biking in these and other locations are listed in the "Resources" section.

Road biking is also an option out here, although long distances, high altitudes, steep climbs, and desert conditions make it more of an undertaking than rolling through an Iowa cornfield. You'll see many long-distance bikers enjoying the scenery from a bike covered with panniers or towing a full trailer. Camping is plentiful, but the quality of road shoulders varies. For tips on long-distance riding, contact the **Adventure Cycling Association,** 150 E. Pine St., P.O. Box 8308, Missoula, MT 59807, 406/721-1776 or 800/755-2453, info@adventurecycling.org, www.adventurecycling.org. They offer guided trips, maps, and plenty of other information.

CLIMBING

Rock climbing options are limited by the soft nature of the sedimentary stones, but certain layers—in particular, the cliff-forming Wingate sandstone—offer excellent protection. Once again Moab is the place to go: the cracks of Indian Creek to the south are world-famous for their sheer, merciless perfection, and classic desert towers fill Castle Valley to the north. There is more climbing along the Colorado River, up in the La Sal Mountains, as well as in Canyonlands

© JULIAN SMITH

Canyonlands' White Rim Trail is a popular site for mountain bikers.

THE FOUR CORNERS' MOST OFFBEAT SPOTS

"The Corner" (Winslow): Stand in the intersection The Eagles made famous (page 96)

Kokopelli's Cave (Farmington): A B&B with *serious* Anasazi influences (page 113)

Four Corners Monument: Play Twister in four states simultaneously (page 137)

Hole N' The Rock (Moab): An entire home carved out of a sandstone cliff (page 154)

Cisco (Green River): A modern ghost town just off the interstate (page 154)

Goblin Valley (southern Utah): Bizarre stone hoodoos ripe for the scrambling (page 178)

Fruita (Capitol Reef National Park): Pick your own fruit in the middle of the desert (page 185)

Pahreah (Grand Staircase–Escalante): Real ruins, a fake western town, and amazing scenery (page 203)

and Arches National Parks; see the guides listed in the "Resources" section for more details.

Mountaineering is limited to hike-up peaks, with more than a few towering over 13,000 feet above the high desert. The La Sals, Abajos, Henrys, San Juans, and San Francisco Mountains all offer great, steep trails and, of course, summit views to die for. Be careful of lightning up here, and make sure you're prepared for weather that can turn ugly in a hurry.

WATER SPORTS

The streams and rivers that carved the canyon country from the Colorado Plateau are open to floaters, boaters, and white-water aficionados. The rapids along the Colorado River through the Grand Canyon make for an unforgettable, once-in-a-lifetime trip, but more mellow options exist as well, including the stretch of the San Juan River from Bluff to Mexican Hat, and sections of the Colorado and Green Rivers near Moab. You can do these yourself, by renting a raft, canoe, or kayak locally and arranging for a vehicle shuttle, or let one of the dozens of rafting companies throughout

the region take care of the details. Some camping regulations apply along more popular routes.

Houseboating is one of the most common ways to experience Lake Powell; these floating apartments are available for rent from lakeside concessionaires. **Fishing** is also excellent in Lake Powell and many other lakes and waterways throughout the region. The trout streams that spill from the Rockies in southwest Colorado are among the best in the country. Check with the local Fish and Game Departments about licenses and restrictions.

WINTER SPORTS

The Four Corners sees a fair bit of snow in the winter, but it often doesn't last long except on mountain peaks. Beyond southwest Colorado, where Ski Purgatory sits north of Durango, **skiing** options are limited to cross-country and backcountry snowboarding or telemark skiing. On cross-country skis is a great way to experience national parks like Bryce, Mesa Verde, and the Grand Canyon in the winter, when the crowds vanish and many roads are closed.

TOUR COMPANIES

Whether you want to go hiking, biking, horseback riding, off-road driving, or river rafting, visit an Indian village, or try your hand at archaeology, you can depend on at least one tour company—and probably a few dozen—to lend a hand. Not surprisingly, local tour operators are concentrated in the major tourist hubs of Moab, Durango, Page, and Flagstaff; contact information is included under the various city listings throughout this book. Several national operators also offer tours of the area, including the **Sierra Club,** 415/977-5500, www.sierraclub.org, whose Outings program, www.sierraclub.org/outings, national.outings@sierraclub.org, offers many nature and cultural trips on the Colorado Plateau, from sightseeing to service programs. **Elderhostel** is similar for travelers over 55. Organizations like Monticello's Four Corners School of Outdoor Education are good for learning vacations, and in Moab the **Canyonlands Field Institute,** 1329 S. U.S. 191, 435/259-7750 or 800/860-5262, fax

ON THE ROAD

435/259-2335, www.canyonlandsfieldinst.org, cfiinfo@canyonlandsfieldinst.org, has been organizing tours of the Four Corners' ecology, geology, and native cultures since 1984.

Many local tour operators are ready to help you experience the Colorado Plateau like a cowboy, on **horseback.** Tours range from afternoon rides to overnight trips, and include the famous **mule trains** that still descend, tourist-laden, into the depths of the Grand Canyon. **Rockhounding** is popular with geology buffs and, at least briefly, just about anyone leaving the Petrified Forest National Park. A handful of geology tours are available, including Lin Ottinger's out of Moab. Several guidebooks to rock collecting on your own are listed in the "Resources" section.

Health and Safety

HEAT, WATER, AND THE SUN

In the high desert you have two things working against you whenever you step outside: the strong, nearly constant sunlight, and the thin, dry air. It's remarkably easy to get a **sunburn,** so use sunscreen (at least SPF 15) liberally, and always have a hat with you—the bigger the brim, the better. Consider wearing long sleeves and pants, preferably light colored; they can actually keep you cooler than shorts and T-shirts (just ask the Beduin). A handkerchief is handy to protect your neck if you burn easily. "Desert-rat" hats with built-in neck flaps are available at outdoor gear stores. Sunburn is the first step on the road to **hyperthermia** (overheating). This progresses through relatively common **heat exhaustion,** with its flu-like symptoms such as vomiting and dizziness, to **heat stroke,** a very serious condition in which the body's cooling mechanism breaks down. Heat stroke, marked by a significant change in behavior and brain activity, has an 80 percent mortality rate if untreated. If you suspect any of the above, get out of the sun, remove any restrictive clothing, and drink plenty of fluids, preferably with salts or electrolytes. If you can, splash cool water on the victim or use ice packs (over clothing) to cool him or her off.

Most visitors to the Four Corners will experience **dehydration** at some point; in this thin, dry, warm air, it's almost a way of life. Pay attention, though, and you'll soon be able to head it off before things get serious. The easiest way to judge how well you are hydrated, not to mince words, is to keep track of the color of your pee.

Clear or barely tinted urine is good; dark urine is bad. Get in the habit of paying attention to this and *drink constantly,* even if it's only a few sips of something non-caffeinated every so often. Carbohydrate drinks, like diluted Gatorade (the full-strength stuff is too much at once), help restore lost electrolytes. These are available in powered form, along with electrolyte tablets you can add to water in emergencies. Backpack hydration systems make constant sipping easier. Remember

DESERT SURVIVAL KIT

If you plan on doing any desert hiking or biking, throw these items into a small plastic bag and keep it in the bottom of your pack—it could make all the difference between safe or very sorry.

Lighter: Small, child-proof to prevent leaking

Pocketknife or **Swiss Army knife**

Light source: Mini-Mag flashlight or LED headlamp

Compass: To go with your map

Extra food: A few energy bars, gels, or some hard candy

Space blanket: Emergency versions roll up small.

First-aid kit: Just the essentials

Signal mirror: Plastic models available—practice first!

Signal whistle: Much better than screaming yourself hoarse

Water purification tablets: Iodine drops work as well.

Sunscreen: Slather it on—you'll sweat it off.

Electrolyte tablets: You'll sweat this off too.

© JULIAN SMITH

(or know) that *you become dehydrated before you get thirsty.* The thirst response only kicks in after a delay, so once you become thirsty, you've already been dehydrated for a while. Even if you aren't thirsty, drink! Just get in the habit. Besides, it's good for you.

Another thing to keep in mind is that often you won't have sweat to remind you you're losing water—the moisture evaporates straight into the air instead. During hard exercise in the hot sun—hiking or mountain biking, for instance—it's possible to lose up to two quarts of water per hour, and two gallons of water per day. That's why it's crucial to carry at *least* **one gallon of water per person per day** when doing these kind of activities. Always carry more water than you think you'll need to have some left over in case things go wrong. Stashing an extra gallon in the car or a quart in the backpack can make all the difference. Consider staying put, or in the shade, during the hottest part of the day, especially in summer. Night hiking by the light of the moon is cool and magical. *Always* take a full water bottle with you when you venture off the pavement, even if it's only a short hike to a ruin or overlook. Out here, water is life—don't get caught without it.

OTHER HEALTH ISSUES

Hypothermia

Too far at the other end of the thermometer is also reason to worry. Temperatures drop amazingly fast in the dry desert air: a plunge of 40°F from day to night is not unusual. Heat vanishes into the stratosphere as the sun falls, and if your body temperature drops below 95°F, you're in trouble. Shivering is a sign of mild hypothermia. If this happens, remove any wet clothes, find the warmest spot possible, and get the victim to eat and drink, preferably hot, sugary liquids like Jell-O mix. Then there's the hypothermic's favorite cure (which does actually work): huddling together in a sleeping bag. If weakness, slurred speech, apathy, and poor judgment appear, cover the victim gently with clothing or a sleeping bag and seek medical attention.

Impure Water

Thanks in part to grazing cattle, nearly all natural water sources in the country can be considered contaminated. Giardia is the most common bug, causing diarrhea and cramps that can become quite serious. Always filter or chemically treat all water with iodine before drinking it. Vitamin C (ascorbic acid) will remove the taste of iodine in water, but add this only after the required waiting period. Rivers like the Colorado, which like the Mississippi could be called "too thick to drink, too thin to plow," often carry runoff from fertilized fields and mine tailings rich in heavy metals. I try not drink out of big rivers in the Four Corners. If you must, let the sediment settle before filtering and consider double-treating the water.

In the Backcountry

Getting lost is a very real possibility in the trackless desert and canyon mazes that make up the Colorado Plateau. Always let someone responsible know where you're going and when you plan to return when you head off on a trip. Keep an eye out for unusual landmarks as you progress, and look back frequently so you can pick out the way home, if necessary. If you think you've lost the trail, backtrack to your last known point—a tree, a junction, or a trail marker. If this doesn't work, *stay put* and *signal* for help. Use your signal mirror, wave brightly colored clothing, and blow your whistle. Although it may be tough to just sit and wait, it's better than wandering farther off when a search party is trying to find you. *Always* check the weather forecast before venturing into narrow canyons to avoid **flash floods.**

Plants and Animals

At times it seems like every living thing in the desert either stings, bites, scratches, or impales. Life is a struggle, and living things have evolved many ways to secure and protect both scant resources and themselves. A fearsome appearance is often deceiving, however—tarantulas, for example, are no more dangerous than bees. **Rattlesnakes** are often found sunning themselves on rock ledges or sections of trail when the ground temperature is over 80°F. They're as afraid of you as you are of them, so if you don't torment them—or grab one unexpectedly—you should have nothing to worry about. The rattle is unmistakable; simply back off and go another way. **Scorpions, centipedes,** and poisonous **spiders** like the black widow are also present. The easiest way to avoid all of these creatures is to avoid putting your hands and feet where you can't see,

including ledges, overhangs, and behind logs. Avoid leaving clothing or sleeping bags lying around on the ground. If you have, shake them out before putting them on or crawling inside.

The most you'll probably ever see of a **mountain lion,** if you're lucky, is a flash of movement, but these large cats are present in the higher mountain ranges. **Coyotes** are ubiquitous, but they never attack people (nor do wolves, for that matter, despite what you may have heard). **Black bears** also live in the mountains; store your food in a bag hung from a branch, and don't leave any sitting around a campsite.

Poison ivy grows in wet areas; avoid its waxy leaves which grow in groups of three. **Nettles,** which grow in drier, rocky locations, can also cause severe itching. The sharp, stiff leaves of **agaves** and **yuccas** can be dangerous if you stumble into them (one species of yucca is aptly named the Spanish bayonet). **Cacti** are covered with spines, often including tiny ones you can't even see. Needless to say, avoid these, particularly the cholla, whose needles leave a nearly invisible sheath behind that itches madly. Keep an eye out for bits of cactus on the ground, too.

Hantavirus

This nasty virus appeared in the Four Corners in 1993, when a number of people suddenly developed acute breathing problems. About half died with alarming speed. Health authorities investigated and discovered that heavy snowmelt had caused a bumper crop of piñon nuts, which in turn had supported an unusually high mouse population. They figured out that the mice droppings carried the airborne virus that causes Hantavirus Pulmonary Syndrome (HPV). The symptoms, which appear one to five weeks after exposure, include fever, fatigue, aching muscles, nausea, and other flu-like symptoms. Left untreated, HPV is fatal. It is very rare, but to avoid it, minimize your contact with rodents and their droppings, particularly in enclosed spaces like old cabins. Clean up infested areas by wetting the droppings with a bleach solution (wear latex gloves) and mopping them up—don't sweep dry particles into the air. In the backcountry, avoid pack rat middens, and don't encourage the little critters into your campsite by leaving food within easy reach.

Interestingly, the Navajo were not surprised by the 1993 hantavirus outbreak. In their medical tradition, mice are consider the carriers of an ancient sickness that targets the healthiest and strongest, as does HPV, so they have always done their best to keep rodents out of residences and the food supply. The sickness had struck in 1918 and 1933-34, both years with high numbers of piñon nuts and mice. Some elders had even predicted the 1993 outbreak.

SAFETY

When driving, keep a special eye out for erratic drivers. Drunk driving is a serious problem out here; in 2002 alone, tribal police received over 8,500 DWI-related calls, and made over 5,000 DWI arrests.

The most common form of crime in the Four Corners is theft—don't leave anything valuable in view in your car or hotel room—but assaults and robberies do occur. Crime has increased on public lands in recent years, due to a rise in visitors and a decrease in funds for law enforcement, particularly in remote areas such as those patrolled by the BLM. I have traveled around this place alone for years without any trouble, sleeping in my car or camping on public land, but safety is something I always try to keep in mind. (I even unwittingly went backpacking in Grand Gulch during the largest manhunt in Southwest history in 1998, after three survivalist bank robbers killed a Cortez police office, wounded two others, and disappeared into the canyon country. One suspect eventually killed himself, another's body was found years later, and the third got away. The trip, thankfully, came off without incident, even if I did have to detour around Bluff, which had been completely evacuated.)

As a rule of thumb, don't sleep at highway rest areas, and keep one eye peeled and one ear open when alone in the backcountry, particularly if you are a woman alone—sorry to say. Lock your hotel door and your car as a matter of habit. Don't let fear ruin your trip; just be aware of your surroundings. Dial **911** from any pay phone, for free, in case of emergency. If necessary, contact local police, state police, or the various law enforcement agencies active on the reservations: the Hopi police (928/734-3700) and the Bureau of Indian Affairs (BIA) police (928/738-2233) on the Hopi Reservation, or the Navajo Tribal Police (928/871-6112 or 6113).

Tips for Travelers

CULTURAL ISSUES

You'll encounter conservative values in the Four Corners, particularly in southern Utah and on the Indian reservations. In this mostly rural region, tradition is highly valued and flashy displays of wealth and liberal (read: California or East-Coast) attitudes can be frowned upon. Gay travelers should avoid being overt in public. This slower pace of life may be difficult for some visitors to get used to, but do your best—people here are still overwhelmingly friendly and accepting. Polygamy still exists in some corners along the Utah-Arizona border, so some residents of towns such as Fredonia and Colorado City may view visitors with distrust.

A visit to an Indian reservation is really a visit to another country, with the expected concerns of cultural sensitivity and personal conduct. The poverty may shock you and the people fascinate, but try to avoid making a camera lens the first thing anyone sees of you. Photography (or any other kind of recording) is completely prohibited on the Hopi Reservation and allowed only in rare circumstances on the Navajo Nation. Indian culture is traditionally reserved and harmonious—the squeaky wheel gets ostracized, not greased—and older people are viewed with respect. Tribal members may seem aloof at first, but give them time to open up—and express a genuine interest in their culture and them as people, not objects—and you won't be disappointed.

TRAVELERS WITH DISABILITIES

The Four Corners is a rough neighborhood, in the sense that many roads are unpaved, trails are steep and crooked, and many buildings are not disabled-accessible. Most hotel chains require their facilities to be accessible, but B&Bs (often in old buildings) and restaurants are another story. If accessibility is an issue for you, always call ahead and check. The National Park Service is doing a good job of making its facilities accessible to travelers with disabilities, including most visitor centers and at least a paved trail or two at every location. For more information, check the individual park descriptions on the National Park Service website (www.nps.gov), which list degrees of accessibility. If you have more questions, contact the park directly and ask to speak to the accessibility coordinator. The NPS Golden Access Passport offers free lifetime entrance to visitors who are blind or permanently disabled, as well as a 50 percent discount on federal use fees.

For more information on disabled travel contact **Mobility International USA,** P.O. Box 10767, Eugene, OR 97440, 541/343-1284, fax 541/343-6812, www.miusa.org, info@miusa.org, or the **Society for Accessible Travel & Hospitality,** 347 5th Ave., Ste. 610, New York, NY 10016, 212/447-7284, fax 212/725-8253, www.sath.org, sath-travel@aol.com.

TRAVELING WITH CHILDREN

A trip to the Four Corners is one your kids will remember their entire lives—although it's up to you to make sure it's because of the sunrise over Monument Valley, not the hours driving across the desert looking for a bathroom. I can still vividly remember my own first-grade visit to the Grand Canyon (somersaulting across a bed and kicking out a cabin window—sorry Mom and Dad), so I can vouch that the area is as fun for the very young as it is for everyone else.

To start with, most of this place is one big rocky jungle gym. Nothing brings out the kids (or the kid in the rest of us) like scrambling over a pile of stones at the edge of a canyon or climbing a trail overlooking an ancient ruin. Many hikes, bike rides, raft trips, and backpack routes are family-friendly, even some slot canyons. Wild West history is always a surefire hit, from the old-time melodramas at the Strater Hotel in Durango to the trading posts and museums elsewhere. Native cultures are part of that appeal, and include festival dances in the Hopi villages (no running and screaming, please), Navajo tours into Canyon de Chelly, and even a night in an authentic hogan for those so inclined.

A few things are important to keep in mind, especially the harsh climate. Always make sure everyone has sunscreen, appropriate clothing, and enough water (get kids their own water bottles and make a game out of drinking, drinking, drinking) when you wander outside. Don't overestimate how far little legs can go on long, difficult trails, and be aware that the impressively vertical scenery often lacks safety features like guardrails and warning signs. Last but not least, know that it really *can* be an hour or more to the next pit stop when you pile in the car.

Local babysitting agencies can be found in the yellow pages or through hotel desks. The **Family Travel Times,** 40 5th Ave., New York, NY 10011, 212/477-5524 or 888/822-4388, www.familytraveltimes.com, info@familytraveltimes, publishes articles on vacationing with kids. The most recent one is always free; to access their back catalogue costs $49 for two years. Also try the "Travel With Kids" section of the **About.com** website, http://travelwith-kids.about.com.

> *A trip to the Four Corners is one your kids will remember their entire lives. Most of this place is one big rocky jungle gym. Nothing brings out the kids (or the kid in the rest of us) like scrambling over a pile of stones at the edge of a canyon or climbing a trail overlooking an ancient ruin.*

SENIOR TRAVELERS

Many hotels and attractions offer discounts for seniors; ask when making reservations or at the gate. The **American Association of Retired Persons,** 601 E St. NW, Washington, D.C. 20049, 800/424-3410, www.aarp.org, member@aarp.org, is the country's largest seniors' organization, with discounts for members ($12.50 pp per year) on hotels, car rentals, air travel, and tours worldwide. **Elderhostel,** 877/426-8056, www.elderhostel.org, organizes worldwide "extraordinary learning adventures" for people 55 and over (one half of a couple is sufficient). Some trips are pure fun, and others are more service oriented, including recording petroglyphs on the Hopi Reservation and cataloguing Anasazi artifacts in a Four Corners museum.

TRAVELING WITH PETS

Smaller pets are OK at some hotels and motels (often for a small surcharge), but most B&Bs will say no. Remember that pets must stay in vehicles or on pavement in all national parks.

VOLUNTEERING

Chronically underfunded as they are, most national parks and national forests gladly accept volunteers for varying positions and time commitments. Either contact the park's volunteer coordinator or take a look at the National Park Service's **Volunteers-in-Parks** program (www.nps.gov/volunteer). They can sometime provide housing and (very limited) living expenses. The **Student Conservation Association,** P.O. Box 550, Charlestown, NH 03603-0550, 603/543-1700, www.thesca.org, can also place volunteers (and not just students) in conservation-related positions. I've done two stints with the SCA; both were great experiences.

MONEY

Cash is always the easiest way to pay, but the fraud protection, insurance benefits, and other advantages of **credit cards** make them popular among travelers. Unfortunately, in some smaller towns in the Four Corners, and on large parts of the Indian reservations, many vendors can't accept credit cards. **Travelers checks** are another option, but these can also be somewhat of a problem outside larger towns. They offer the advantage of replacement if they're lost or stolen; American Express and Thomas Cook checks are widely accepted at banks, hotels, and restaurants. Forget about using **personal checks,** and foreign visitors should change to U.S. dollars at the earliest opportunity.

On the plus side, almost every town has a bank, service station, or bar with an **ATM** (Automated Teller Machine) where you can withdraw cash from your bank card or credit card, as long as you don't mind paying a small fee every time. The most popular ATM networks are Star, Cirrus, Plus, Visa, American Express, and MasterCard. **Western Union,** 800/225-5227, www.westernunion.com, lets you wire money (for a fee) to any of thousands of locations, as well as by phone and over the Internet. Each state charges a different amount of **sales tax:** Arizona (5.6 percent), Utah (4.75 percent), Colorado (2.9 percent), and New Mexico (5 percent). Not to be outdone, the Navajo Nation started charging a 3 percent sales tax in 2002.

Tipping is customary in restaurants, taxis, and wherever someone totes your bags (airports and hotels). As any former restaurant server will tell you (and there are plenty of us out there), a 15 percent tip on restaurant and bar bills is standard, since waiters make considerably less than minimum wage before tips. Leave 20 percent or more for outstanding service or if you're just feeling nice. Taxi drivers typically receive 15 percent, and airport porters and bellhops at least $1 per bag.

TRAVEL INSURANCE

A number of agencies offer specialized travelers' insurance in various combinations of health, accident, trip-cancellation and trip-interruption, and lost-luggage protection. Two dependable choices are **Travel Guard International,** 1145 Clark St., Stevens Point, WI 54481, 800/826-4919, www.travel-guard.com, and **Access America,** P.O. Box 90315, Richmond, VA

ON THE ROAD

23286-4991, 866/807-3982, fax 800/346-9265, www.accessamerica.com, service@accessamerica.com.

PARK PASSES

With admission fees climbing ever higher, it's usually a good idea to buy a **National Parks Pass** if you plan on visiting more than two or three parks. At $50, they quickly pay for themselves and are good for one year for the occupants of any private vehicle at any NPS facility in the country. Get one at any park or from the **National Parks Foundation,** 888/GO-PARKS, https://buy.nationalparks.org. You can also buy local **"passports"** for parks in certain areas, including the Southeast Utah Group (Arches, Canyonlands, Hovenweep, and Natural Bridges) and the national monuments near Flagstaff (Hovenweep, Wupatki, and Sunset Crater), both $25. **State park passes** are also available for each state.

WEIGHTS AND MEASURES

Time Zones

All four states are in the Mountain Time zone, which is two hours behind Eastern Time (New York), one hour ahead of Pacific Time (California), and seven hours behind Greenwich Mean Time (London). Sound simple? Not so fast. From April to October, Utah, Colorado, and New Mexico advance one hour according to daylight savings time ("spring forward, fall back"). Arizona apparently has enough sunshine, because that state stays on the same time year-round—except for the Navajo Reservation, which *does* participate in daylight savings time. To make things even more confusing, the Hopi Reservation *inside* the Navajo Reservation follows Arizona's lead and ignores daylight savings time. From April to October, then, set your watch forward one hour if you enter Utah, New Mexico, or the Navajo Reservation from Arizona, and when you enter the Hopi Reservation. Set it back an hour entering Arizona or leaving the Hopi Reservation. Got it?

Business Hours

Most businesses, aside from restaurants, are open Mon.–Sat. 9 A.M.–6 P.M., with varying hours on Sunday. In Utah, however, almost all businesses, including restaurants, are closed on Sunday. Banks and post offices are typically open for the first half of the day on Saturday. The highly seasonal tourism industry means many businesses close for the winter or at least significantly reduce their hours. This can also apply in the height of the summer in some locations, when visitation drops because of the heat. It's always a good idea to call ahead from October to April to make sure your favorite hotel, restaurant, or trading post hasn't closed up shop for the season.

Electricity

Homes and businesses in the United States operate on 110-220 volt electricity. Modern outlets have three plugs, including two flat prongs and one round (grounding) prong, but older buildings may only have two-prong plugs. If you're using an expensive piece of electronics such as a laptop computer, you should get a three-to-two-prong adapter that also protects against power surges.

COMMUNICATIONS

Every incorporated town, no matter how small, has a **U.S. post office,** 800/275-8777, www.usps.gov, usually open Mon.–Fri. 8:30 A.M.–5 P.M. and Saturday 8:30 A.M.–noon. The main telephone **area codes** in the Four Corners are 435 (southern Utah), 970 (southwest Colorado), 505 (most of New Mexico), and 928 (northern Arizona). (This last one was changed from 520 in 2001, so you may still see brochures and the like with the old area code.) **Toll-free numbers** start with 800, 888, 877, and 866. Reach **directory assistance** by calling 411 (local) or 1 + area code + 555-1212 (long-distance). Toll-free information is 800/555-1212. For **emergencies** dial 911. Ubiquitous **pay phones** cost 35 cents for a short local call. For longer and long-distance calls, it's cheaper to get a pre-paid **calling card,** available in many different amounts just about everywhere. Cell phone coverage in the Four Corners can be spotty at best outside of cities.

Most medium-to-large cities have their own **newspapers,** which are a good source of information on local events and attitudes. This includes the *Gallup Independent,* www.gallupindependent.com, Moab's *Times-Independent,* www.moabtimes.com, and the *Canyon Country Zephyr,* www.canyoncountryzephyr.com ("All the News That Causes Fits"), the Farmington *Daily Times,* www.daily-times.com, and the *Arizona Daily Sun,* www.azdailysun.com, available in Flagstaff. On the reservations look for the *Navajo Times,* www.thenavajotimes.com, and the *Navajo-Hopi Observer,* www.navajohopiobserver.com.

Radio is still an important medium in this wide-open countryside. As you roll across the Navajo reservation, tune in to KTNN (AM 660), "The Voice of the Navajo Nation," for a taste of daily life. Owned by the tribe, the station, www.ktnnonline.com, plays mostly Country and Western music, interspersed with chants and announcements in Navajo on pertinent topics like the news, weather, and livestock reports. The tribe also owns KWRK (96.1 FM), with a Top-40 format. KUYI (88.1 FM) serves a similar purpose for the Hopi tribe, and is online at www.kuyi.net ("kuyi" is the Hopi word for water). Arizona's only high-school radio station, KGHR (91.5 FM), is run by Navajo students at the Grey Hills Academy in Tuba City. They broadcast an interesting mix of country, classical, rock, and Native American music, plus NPR programs.

Internet cafes are starting to spread across the Four Corners, albeit slowly. Some coffeehouses and hostels offer web access for a fee, but the most dependable place to hop online (and for free at that) is still the public library. Ask nicely and they should put you on the waiting list even if you don't have a library card.

Navajo and Hopi Country

The high, wide tablelands of northeastern Arizona, northwestern New Mexico, and southernmost Utah encompass two of the country's largest Indian reservations, as well as one of the Four Corner's most vibrant cities (Flagstaff) near one of the country's most incredible sights (the Grand Canyon). These are some of the loneliest yet most extraordinary acres of the Colorado Plateau, averaging between 5,000 and 7,000 feet elevation. The wide-open country is a textbook of geology: buttes, washes, mesas, volcanic plugs, and dikes break the otherwise flat expanse, but all pale next to the biggest gorge of them all northwest of Flagstaff. Sagebrush, yucca, and desert grasses march to the rim of deep canyons, and the heights of Navajo Mountain, Black Mesa, and the Chuska Mountains on the Arizona-New Mexico border are dusted with snow in the winter. The largest ponderosa pine forest in the world spreads to both rims of the Grand Canyon, and virtually every hill in sight in the 1,800-square-mile San Francisco Volcanic Field is or was a volcano, some of which erupted as recently as nine centuries ago.

But it is the indigenous cultures that truly define this part of the Four Corners. Anasazi cliff

Cameron Trading Post, south of Tuba City, Arizona

© JULIAN SMITH

dwellings are scattered throughout the region, with those at Navajo National Monument rivaling anything in Colorado or Utah. The Navajo and Hopi have maintained their traditions into the 21st century in the face of almost overwhelming odds. Farming, ranching, herding, and tourism provide an income for many, while mining and logging enrich a few. With the exception of Flagstaff, the larger towns on or near the reservations, including Tuba City, Kayenta, Window Rock, and Gallup, are not very big, and the poverty on raw display can make them more depressing than inviting. But there is still much to do: shopping at the many native galleries in Flagstaff and Gallup, taking in breath-stopping views of Canyon de Chelly National Park or the Grand Canyon, walking the creaking floors of the Hubbell Trading Post in Ganado, and watching dances in the timeless villages of the Hopi Reservation. Flagstaff alone can keep visitors occupied for weeks, with three national monuments, some of the Southwest's best museums, a ski resort, and trails galore amid the 600-plus volcanic peaks that dot the skyline.

Outside of Gallup and Flagstaff, tourist services are few and far between. Most of the towns on the reservations have hotels, but food choices are often limited to fast food, and it may be an hour or more to the next gas station or water supply. Although the reservations are legally dry, alcoholism and drunk driving are serious problems. Keep in mind too that you need permission to hike or camp inside their borders, either from local landowners or the Navajo Nation Parks and Recreation Department. In your wanderings, you may find ceremonial offerings—you'll know them when you see them—and these should be left in peace.

Along I-40, which parallels the southern border of the Navajo Reservation, are the railroad towns of Flagstaff, Winslow, and Holbrook, as well as the gaudy palettes of the Painted Desert and Petrified Forest National Park. The interstate eventually heads east to New Mexico and west to California, and I-17 heads south from Flagstaff to Phoenix. U.S. 89 runs north from Flagstaff, splitting off U.S. 89A before reaching Page and the Utah border (covered in the "South-Central Utah" chapter).

The unfortunately named U.S. 666 cuts across the northern border of the Navajo Reservation from Tuba City to Shiprock via Kayenta (actually U.S. 64 from Tec Nos Pos), and U.S. 89 runs north from Flagstaff to Page along the western edge. Crossing the reservation, you have two main choices: U.S. 191 up the center, through Ganado and Chinle to Mexican Water, Utah (paralleled by U.S. 12 north of Window Rock), and the east-west U.S. 264/3, from Tuba City across the Hopi mesas to Ganado, Window Rock, and Gallup. Countless dirt roads reach much of the rest of the reservations, but a large portion remains inaccessible. These tracks can be very rough, particularly in bad weather, and they are seldom marked; the *Indian Country* map is your best weapon against getting lost.

If for some masochistic reason you're not driving your own vehicle, your only other transportation option (besides the Greyhound buses along I-40 and hitchhiking, which is common out here) is the **Navajo Transit System,** 928/729-4002/4111, www.navajotransitsystem.com. They send one bus daily along seven routes: Tuba City/Window Rock; Toyei/Window Rock; Kayenta/Fort Defiance; Crownpoint/Fort Defiance; Fort Defiance/Window Rock/Gallup; and Shiprock/Farmington/Window Rock. None are over $13 o/w.

For tours of the area, try **Largo Navajoland Tours,** 505/863-0050 or 888/726-9084, www .navajolandtours.com, jlargo@navajolandtours .com, run by tribe members John and Brenda Largo. They cover all the major sites on and near the reservation, from Monument Valley and Canyon de Chelly to the Grand Canyon and Chaco Canyon. They also run a traditional Navajo hogan B&B and offer horseback, hiking, and rafting trips.

Flagstaff and Vicinity

"Flag" (pop. 65,000) is still a railroad town—an average of 135 trains roar through every 24 hours, sounding their whistles (by law) and frustratingly dividing the city in two for up to half an hour. It's also a city very aware of its heritage, from the historical markers on downtown buildings to the great old neon motel signs on Route 66 out of town. With 20,000 students in residence at Northern Arizona University, there seems to be some sort of local ordinance that requires men under 25 to have beards, but the music and art scenes thrive and the outdoors beckon. Ski the Arizona Snowbowl, hike the Grand Canyon, visit Sedona or the nearby Indian reservations, and throw in the outstanding Museum of Northern Arizona and Lowell Observatory for good measure—in terms of tourist attractions, there is very little that Flagstaff lacks.

HISTORY

The Sinagua, less advanced cultural cousins of the Anasazi, were living in pithouses and canyon-edge dwellings in the foothills of the San Francisco Mountains when major eruptions in 1064 and 1065 covered 800 square miles of the surrounding countryside with lava and ash. They returned soon after to build Anasazi-style pueblos and farm the newly enriched soil, but moved on around the same time the Anasazi did, perhaps for similar reasons.

The area was explored by four separate military surveys before Flagstaff itself came into being. In 1876, a group of settlers arrived from Boston, and on July 4 they raised an American flag on a peeled pine tree in what is now Antelope Park. The early settlement didn't last, but the flagpole did, and travelers heading west were told to keep an eye out for the good campsite it marked. Some of these settlers eventually stayed, and the name stuck. The post office and the railroad both arrived in 1881, and by 1886 Flagstaff was the biggest city on the railroad line between Albuquerque and the Pacific Ocean. The Arizona Lumber and Timber Company

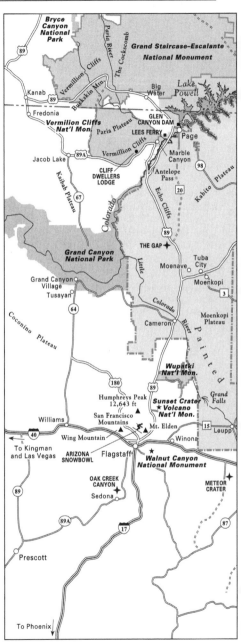

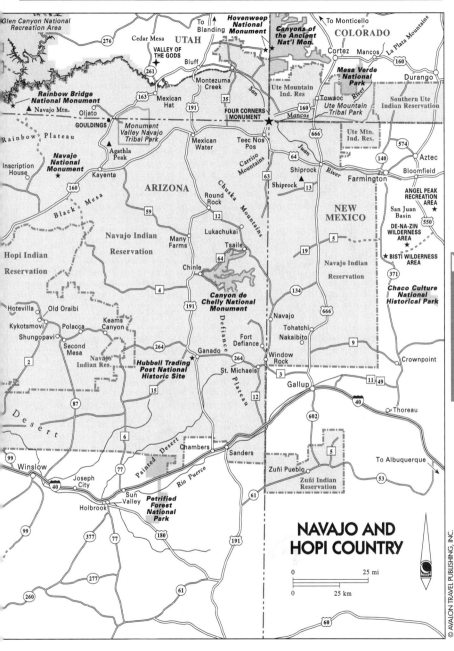

Glen Canyon National
Recreation Area

To ↑ **Hovenweep**
Blanding **National**
Monument

UTAH

To Monticello

COLORADO

Cedar Mesa

**VALLEY OF
THE GODS**

276

261

Bluff

Mexican
Hat

163

Montezuma
Creek

35

191

Cortez Mancos

La Plata Mountains

160

**Mesa Verde
National
Park**

Durango

Southern Ute
Indian Reservation

**Rainbow Bridge
National Monument**

▲ Navajo Mtn.   Oljato

GOULDINGS

Rainbow   Plateau

*Monument
Valley Navajo
Tribal Park*

**FOUR CORNERS
MONUMENT**

San

Ute Mountain
Ind. Res

160   Towaoc
Mancos

Ute Mountain
Tribal Park

**Navajo
National
Monument**

Inscription
House

160

▲ Agathla
Peak

Kayenta

Mexican
Water

Teec Nos
Pos

666

Ute Mtn.
Ind. Res.

574

Aztec

Bloomfield

ARIZONA

Black   Mesa

59

12

Round
Rock

Carrizo
Mountains

Chuska Mountains

63

64

Shiprock

Shiprock 13

Juan

River

Farmington

San Juan
Basin

550

**ANGEL PEAK
RECREATION
AREA** ★

**NEW
MEXICO**

**DE-NA-ZIN
WILDERNESS
AREA** ★

**Hopi Indian

Reservation**

Navajo Indian

Reservation

Many
Farms

Lukachukai

Tsaile

64

Chinle

4

19

5

Navajo Indian

Reservation

★ **BISTI WILDERNESS
AREA**

371

**Chaco Culture
National
Historical Park**

Hotevilla   Old Oraibi

Kykotsmovi   Polacca

Shungopavi

2

Keams
Canyon

Second
Mesa

Navajo
Indian Res.

264

**Canyon de
Chelly National
Monument**

191

Defiance

Ganado

264

St. Michaels

Navajo

Tohatchi

Nakaibito

Fort
Defiance

Window
Rock

3

134

666

9

Crownpoint

**Hubbell Trading
Post National
Historic Site** ★

15

87

6

Plateau

12

Gallup

11 49

40

Thoreau

Desert

Chambers

Sanders

602

5

99

Winslow

77

Joseph
City

40

Painted Desert

Rio Puerco

Sun
Valley

Holbrook

**Petrified
Forest
National
Park**

Zuñi Pueblo

**Zuñi Indian
Reservation**

61

To Albuquerque

53

99

377

77

180

191

60

61

260

277

**NAVAJO AND
HOPI COUNTRY**

0   25 mi

0   25 km

N

NAVAJO & HOPI COUNTRY

© AVALON TRAVEL PUBLISHING, INC.

NAVAJO AND HOPI HIGHLIGHTS

Museum of Northern Arizona: An extensive collection, clearly presented, makes this Flagstaff museum a must-see (page 62)

Monument Valley: World-famous rock monoliths make up one of the American West's best-known sights (page 82)

Canyon de Chelly National Monument: A gorgeous canyon system preserves a slice of Navajo life from centuries ago (page 84)

Petrified Forest National Park: Fossils, giant petrified trees, and the southern edge of the Painted Desert make this park a definite detour off I-40 (page 98)

Gallup: Outstanding shopping and cultural opportunities abound in the "Gateway to Indian Country" (page 100)

made a fortune from the abundant forests, shipping logs out cheaply by rail. Sheep and cattle ranches provided more jobs.

Coconino County, established in 1891, was soon the second largest in the country. Three years later the Lowell Observatory was built, and in 1930 Dr. Percival Lowell discovered the planet Pluto in Flagstaff's crystal skies. Route 66 and its attendant traffic arrived in the 1920s, allowing more and more visitors to discover the wonders of the Grand Canyon and the Indian reservations nearby.

SIGHTS

Museum of Northern Arizona

Founded in 1928, this outstanding museum, 3101 N. Fort Valley Rd., 928/774-5213, www.musnaz.org, has evolved into the best of its kind in the Four Corners. Displays on anthropology, biology, geology, and fine art are clearly laid out and comprehensive without being exhausting. The histories of the Colorado Plateau's tribes are clearly spelled out, and exquisite examples of crafts are on display, including weavings, kachinas, baskets, pottery, and jewelry. Changing exhibits examine topics such as the

role of Indians in Westerns. The museum's Kiva Gallery contains a mockup of a Hopi kiva with a beautiful mural by Michael Kabotie and Delbridge Honanie. Ideally you'd start your visit to the Colorado Plateau here, on North Fort Valley Road (U.S. 180) three miles northwest of downtown Flagstaff. Open daily 9 A.M.–5 P.M., $5 adults, $3 children.

Pioneer Museum

The 1908 Coconino County Hospital for the Indigent was converted to a boarding house and then a museum in 1963. Today, the northern division of the Arizona Historical Society, www.infomagic.net/~ahsnad, administers the building as a museum, 928/774-6272, on North Fort Valley Road on the way to the Museum of Northern Arizona. The collection includes over 10,000 bits of Flagstaff's past, from an old iron lung to farm gear and clothing. Nearby are a 1910 barn, a 1912 steam locomotive, and a historic cabin that was moved here from the east side of the San Francisco Mountains. In the blacksmith shop behind the museum, the sweaty craft is demonstrated Thursdays through Saturdays in summer. Open Mon.–Sat. 9 A.M.–5 P.M., free.

The Art Barn

Behind the Pioneer Museum is Flagstaff's Art Barn, 928/774-0822, a large gallery operated by local artists and their patrons. The work leans strongly in the Native American and Southwest directions, and prices, direct from the artists, are low. You'll find paintings, rugs, pottery, jewelry, and many other items for sale. They also organize workshops and offer a bronze foundry and matting services. Open Tues.–Sat. 10 A.M.–5 P.M. Music, theater, and dance performances are held in the 200-seat theater of the adjacent **Coconino Center for the Arts,** 928/779-2300.

Lowell Observatory

Boston aristocrat-turned-astronomer Percival Lowell founded this observatory, 1400 W. Mars Hill Rd., 928/774-3358, www.lowell.edu, in 1894. He spent 15 years gazing at Mars through the 24-inch refractor telescope, convinced that

Monument Valley is one of Arizona's most magnificent natural wonders.

he was looking at the remains of canals built by an intelligent race. On that matter he was way off, but his hunch about "Planet X" orbiting beyond Uranus proved correct. Fourteen years after his death in 1916, Pluto was discovered by Clyde Tombaugh, and Lowell is given most of the credit. Today the privately owned observatory, which sits at 7,260 feet in the clear mountain air above Flagstaff, is still used for serious research. The Steele Visitor Center offers tours of the original telescope inside historic Clark Dome, built of native ponderosa pine in the days before power tools, as well as the spectrograph used to prove the universe is expanding and plates with the first images of Pluto. Open daily 9 A.M.–5 P.M. (noon–5 P.M. Nov.–Mar.) for $4 adults, $2 children. Evening viewing programs are given at 7:30 or 8 P.M. some nights, weather depending, as are solar-viewing hours; call for a current schedule.

Riordan Mansion State Historic Park

Prominent local businessmen Timothy and Michael Riordan were responsible for the success of the Arizona Lumber and Timber Company near the turn of the century. They each married one of the Metz sisters, cousins of the famous traders the Babbitt brothers, and in 1904 commissioned the architect of the Grand Canyon's El Tovar Hotel to build them a monumental home of logs and volcanic stone. Actually two separate homes joined by a common area, it has 40 rooms totaling 13,000 square feet. Timothy's side of what the brothers dubbed *Kinlichi* ("Red House" in Navajo) is open for tours. Original fixtures and hand-carved American Craftsman-style furniture give a taste of life at the high end in early Flagstaff. The mansion, 409 Riordan Rd., 928/779-4395, www.pr.state.az.us/parkhtml/riordan.html, is open daily 8:30 A.M.–5 P.M. (from 10:30 A.M. Nov.–Apr.) for $5 adults, $2.50 children. Reservations are a good idea for the guided tours, offered every hour in the summer.

The Arboretum

More than 2,500 species of high-elevation plants thrive at the country's highest research botanical garden, 4001 S. Woody Mountain Rd., 928/774-1442, www.thearb.org. The garden is at 7,150 feet, which gives it an average growing season of just 75 days, but they still do an amazing job of raising plants from across the Colorado Plateau.

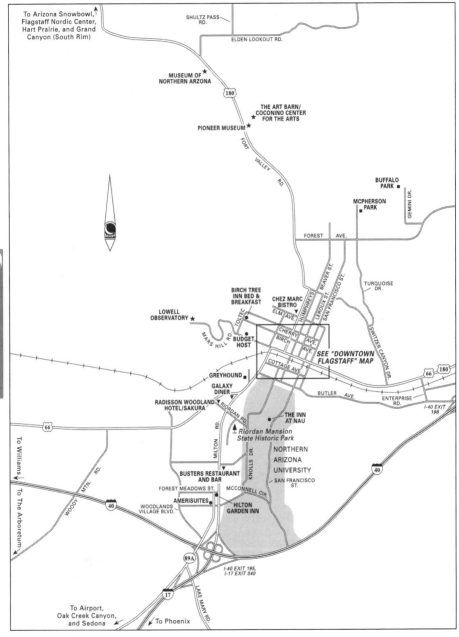

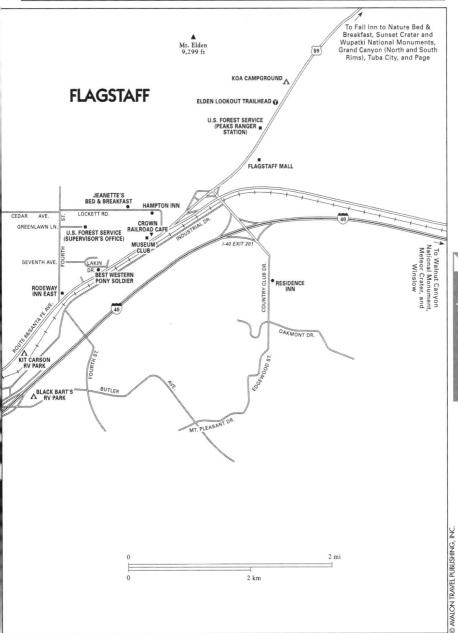

FLAGSTAFF

Mt. Elden
9,299 ft

To Fall Inn to Nature Bed &
Breakfast, Sunset Crater and
Wupatki National Monuments,
Grand Canyon (North and South
Rims), Tuba City, and Page

89

KOA CAMPGROUND

ELDEN LOOKOUT TRAILHEAD

U.S. FOREST SERVICE
(PEAKS RANGER
STATION)

FLAGSTAFF MALL

JEANETTE'S
BED & BREAKFAST

HAMPTON INN

CEDAR   AVE.

LOCKETT RD.

40

GREENLAWN LN.

CROWN
RAILROAD CAFE

U.S. FOREST SERVICE
(SUPERVISOR'S OFFICE)

MUSEUM
CLUB

INDUSTRIAL DR.

I-40 EXIT 201

SEVENTH AVE.

LAKIN
DR.

BEST WESTERN
PONY SOLDIER

COUNTRY CLUB DR.

RESIDENCE
INN

RODEWAY
INN EAST

40

OAKMONT DR.

ROUTE 66/SANTA FE AVE.

KIT CARSON
RV PARK

FOURTH

ST.

EDGEWOOD ST.

BLACK BART'S
RV PARK

BUTLER

AVE.

FOURTH ST.

MT. PLEASANT DR.

To Walnut Canyon
National Monument,
Meteor Crater, and
Winslow

NAVAJO & HOPI COUNTRY

0   2 mi

0   2 km

© AVALON TRAVEL PUBLISHING, INC.

FLAGSTAFF CLIMATE

Month	Average High	Average Low	Mean	Average Precipitation
January	43°F	16°F	30°F	2.18 inches
February	46°F	19°F	32°F	2.56 inches
March	50°F	23°F	37°F	2.62 inches
April	58°F	27°F	43°F	1.29 inches
May	68°F	34°F	51°F	0.80 inches
June	79°F	41°F	60°F	0.43 inches
July	82°F	50°F	66°F	2.40 inches
August	80°F	49°F	64°F	2.89 inches
September	74°F	42°F	58°F	2.12 inches
October	63°F	31°F	47°F	1.93 inches
November	51°F	22°F	37°F	1.86 inches
December	44°F	17°F	30°F	1.83 inches

Several miles of trails wind through the garden's 200 acres. Hour-long guided tours are given daily at 11 A.M. and 1 P.M. These are included in the admission ($4 adults, $1 children). Open daily 9 A.M.–5 P.M. Apr. to mid-Dec.

ACCOMMODATIONS

As northern Arizona's main tourist center, it's no surprise that Flagstaff has an abundance of lodging options. Rates fall by as much as half during off-season, and many inexpensive chain motels line the Route 66 "strip" on its way out of town. You can make hotel and tour reservations for free through **Flagstaff Central Reservations,** 928/527-8333 or 800/527-8388, fax 928/527-4272, www.flagstaffrooms.com, flagres@infomagic.com, which also covers Page and the Grand Canyon.

Under $50

The popular **Grand Canyon International Hostel,** 19 S. San Francisco St., 928/779-9421 or 888/442-2696, fax 928/774-6047, www.grandcanyonhostel.com, info@grandcanyonhostel.com, has dorm rooms ($14–16) and five private rooms ($29–36). They organize trips to Sedona and the Grand Canyon, and offer Internet access, a cable TV/VCR room, and laundry services. The same

couple owns and operates the nearby **Dubeau International Hostel,** 19 W. Phoenix Ave., 928/774-6731 or 800/398-7112, fax 928/774-6047, www.dubeauhostel.com, info@dubeauhostel.com, with dorm rooms for the same price and eight private rooms ($32–39). Breakfast is included at both places. It's a good idea to book private rooms a few weeks or even a month in advance, especially in the summer. The **Townhouse Motel,** 122 W. U.S. 66, 928/774-5081, is also centrally located.

$50–100

On January 1, 1900, John W. Weatherford opened a hotel in the dusty frontier town of Flagstaff that still bears his name today. The **Weatherford Hotel,** 23 N. Leroux St., 928/779-1919, fax 928/773-8951, www.weatherfordhotel.com, contact@weatherfordhotel.com, has gone through various incarnations since then—billiard hall, theater, and radio station, to name a few—but after two decades of work it has been restored to its pioneer peak, when Zane Gray wrote *Call of the Canyon* while staying here. Period touches include a 19-foot lobby ceiling, the wrap-around third-floor balcony, and a huge wooden bar in the ballroom, built for a Tombstone saloon over a century

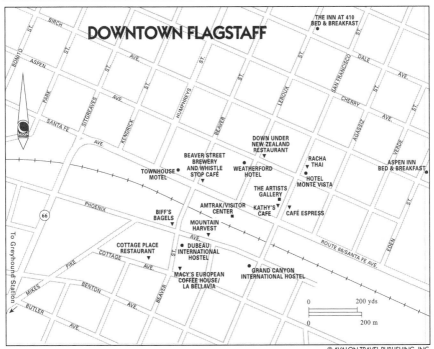

DOWNTOWN FLAGSTAFF

THE INN AT 410
BED & BREAKFAST

DOWN UNDER
NEW ZEALAND
RESTAURANT

BEAVER STREET
BREWERY
AND WHISTLE
STOP CAFÉ

TOWNHOUSE
MOTEL

WEATHERFORD
HOTEL

RACHA
THAI

HOTEL
MONTE VISTA

ASPEN INN
BED & BREAKFAST

THE ARTISTS
GALLERY

BIFF'S
BAGELS

AMTRAK/VISITOR
CENTER

KATHY'S
CAFE

CAFÉ ESPRESS

MOUNTAIN
HARVEST

COTTAGE PLACE
RESTAURANT

DUBEAU
INTERNATIONAL
HOSTEL

GRAND CANYON
INTERNATIONAL HOSTEL

MACY'S EUROPEAN
COFFEE HOUSE/
LA BELLAVIA

To Greyhound Station

0   200 yds

0   200 m

© AVALON TRAVEL PUBLISHING, INC.

ago. **Charly's** restaurant features live music on weekends. Rates are $50–60.

C. B. Wilson, cousin to Wyatt Earp, built the graceful 1912 home three blocks from downtown that has been turned into the **Aspen Inn Bed & Breakfast,** 218 N. Elden St., 928/773-0295 or 888/999-4110, www.flagstaffbedbreakfast.com, aspeninn77@aol.com. Just outside the city, the **Fall Inn to Nature,** 928/714-0237, www.bbonline.com/az/fallinn, fallinn@infomagic.com, is a cedar home on 2.5 acres, with a redwood deck and an outdoor hot tub with a view of Mt. Elden.

A number of chain hotels on Route 66 fall in this price category, including the **Budget Host,** 820 W. U.S. 66, 928/779-3631, 928/526-2200, and the **Best Western Pony Soldier,** 3030 E. U.S. 66, 928/526-2388, fax 928/527-8329. Students at NAU's School of Hotel and Restaurant Management run **The Inn at NAU,** 928/523-1616, www.hrm.nau.edu/inn, julene.boger@nau.edu,

on campus. Room rates ($80–100) include breakfast at the Garden Terrace Restaurant, also run by the program.

$100–150

The **Hotel Monte Vista,** 100 N. San Francisco St., 928/779-6971 or 800/545-3068, fax 928/779-2904, www.hotelmontevista.com, montev@infomagic.net, is downtown Flagstaff's other historic lodge. Since it was built in 1927, it has hosted presidents and such Hollywood stars as John Wayne, who reported a friendly ghost in his room. Most of the 50 rooms on four floors have good views; all are named after famous guests. With a day spa on site, the hotel also features the cool **Monte Vista Lounge** downstairs, with live bands Thurs.–Sat.

Once a fraternity house, the **Birch Tree Inn Bed & Breakfast,** 824 W. Birch Ave., 928/774-1042 or 888/774-1042, www.birchtreeinn.com, info@birchtreeinn.com, occupies a two-story

Country Victorian home with five rooms for $75–140. **Jeanette's Bed & Breakfast,** 3380 E. Lockett Rd., 928/527-1912 or 800/752-1912, www.bbonline.com/az/jbb, has been voted "most romantic" in town; maybe it's the clawfoot tubs, fresh flowers, and handmade soap that fill the Victorian building.

Both the **Hampton Inn,** 3501 E. Lockett Rd., 928/526-1885, fax 928/526-9885, and the **Hilton Garden Inn,** 350 W. Forest Meadows St., 928/226-8888, fax 928/556-9059, are also in this price range.

$150 and Up

Some of the nine rooms at **The Inn at 410 Bed & Breakfast,** 410 N. Leroux St., 928/774-0088 or 800/774-2008, fax 928/774-6354, www.inn410 .com, info@inn410.com, have fireplaces and/or Jacuzzis. The owners of the 1894 Craftsman home can arrange two-night packages including a tour of the Grand Canyon starting at $480. Rates include gourmet breakfast; $135–190. **Amerisuites,** 2455 S. Beulah Blvd., 928/774-8042, fax 928/774-5524, has efficiencies with high-speed Internet access for $90–160. The **Residence Inn,** 3440 N. Country Club Dr., 928/526-5555, fax 928/527-0328, has one-bedroom units with kitchens for $140–220.

Campgrounds

All of the following are open year-round. **Black Bart's RV Park,** 2760 E. Butler Ave., 928/774-1912, fax 928/774-1113, has 122 sites for $21–23 near I-40 exit 198. Featuring an on-site saloon and an antique store, they also host a musical revue in the steak house. The **Flagstaff KOA,** 5803 N. U.S. 89, 800/KOA-FLAG or 928/526-9926, fax 928/527-8356, www.koa .com/az/flagstaff, jsinaz@aol.com, offers both campsites ($22–28) and cabins ($37), five miles northeast of town near I-40 exit 201. Take exit 191 or 195 off of I-40 to reach the **Kit Carson RV Park,** 2101 W. U.S. 66, 928/774-6993, with campsites for $29 with all hookups.

In the Coconino National Forest, the **Bonito Campground** is on the loop road near Sunset Crater Volcano National Monument, with 44 sites open May to mid-October for $8–12. Turn left (west) at the Sunset Crater turnoff from U.S. 89 onto Forest Road 552 and follow the signs to the **Lockett Meadow Campground,** which has 15 sites for $6–12, open May–Sept. You can camp just about anywhere in the national forest that surrounds Flagstaff; just make sure you're not on private land (signs, fences, and houses are good clues), and be very careful with fires in this tinderbox woodland.

FOOD

Flagstaff has an amazing variety of places to eat, with plenty of inexpensive options priced for student budgets. Many restaurants are south of the train tracks, close to the university.

Startups

La Bellavia, 18 S. Beaver St., 928/774-8301, is a comfy spot that has earned Flagstaff's best breakfast title many times since they opened in 1976. Try their signature Swedish oat pancakes. (Open daily for breakfast and lunch.) Sixty-six omelets fill the menu at the **Crown Railroad Cafe,** 3300 E. U.S. 66, 928/522-9237, next to Museum Club. Lunch and breakfast specials are $4, and northern Arizona's largest electric train runs around the restaurant. It's one of two in town, open daily 6 A.M.–9 P.M. South of the train tracks, **Biff's Bagels,** 1 S. Beaver St., 928/226-0424, serves breakfast, coffees, and bagels, with sandwiches in the $4–5 range. Offering Internet access, they're open Mon.–Sat. 7 A.M.–3 P.M., Sun. 8 A.M.–2 P.M.

On the Healthy Side

Homemade vegetarian plates are a specialty of **Cafe Espress,** 16 N. San Francisco St., 928/774-0541, along with coffees and fresh-baked treats. It's also a gallery that exhibits local artists' works. Open daily for breakfast and lunch, and for dinner Wed.–Sat. The smell of fresh-roasted coffee permeates **Macy's European Coffee House, Bakery and Vegetarian Restaurant,** 14 S. Beaver St., 928/774-2243, thanks to the big red roaster by the tables. Their creative menu includes many vegetarian and vegan selections, with soups, salads, and sandwiches for $4–6. Open daily for all meals.

A few blocks away is **Mountain Harvest,** 6 W. Phoenix Ave., 928/779-9456, a natural market offering organic produce and a deli. Sandwiches and other wholesome bites are $5 and up. Open Mon.–Sat. 8 A.M.–8 P.M., Sun. 9 A.M.–6 P.M.

More Substantial

Meatloaf sandwiches, malts, movie posters, and waitresses in Hawaiian shirts sum up the **Galaxy Diner,** 931 W. U.S. 66, 928/774-2466, a neon-and-silver faux-Route 66 diner (it's only eight years old) that does American road staples for $5–9. The burgers are good, and they serve breakfast all day. Open daily for all meals. **Busters Restaurant and Bar,** 1800 S. Milton Rd., 928/774-5155, is an animated place open for lunch and dinner daily, with steaks, seafood, and chicken dishes. **Kathy's Cafe,** 7 N. San Francisco St., 928/774-1951, offers no pretense, just good smoothies and sandwiches ($4–6) served daily for lunch and dinner.

Stop by the **Beaver Street Brewery and Whistle Stop Café,** 11S. Beaver St., 928/779-0079, for catfish platters and wood-fired pizzas, or enjoy one of their home-brewed ales on the outdoor patio. There's a billiard room for after-dinner sport. Open daily for lunch and dinner. Occupying a restored 1909 bungalow, the **Cottage Place Restaurant,** 126 W. Cottage Ave., 928/774-8431, may just be Flagstaff's best restaurant. This intimate spot offers prix fixe dinners (a la carte entrees are $16–22), earning *Wine Spectator* magazine's "Award of Excellence" six times. Open daily for dinner; reservations are recommended.

International

Northern Arizona's finest sushi bar is probably **Sakura,** in the Radisson Woodland Hotel, 1175 W. U.S. 66, 928/773-9118. They also serve teppanyaki, and are open daily for all meals. Another excellent Asian option is **Racha Thai,** 104 N. San Francisco St., 928/774-3003, with candlelit tables and many vegetarian choices. Dinner entrees run $8–12, but they offer lunch specials for $6–7. (Open for lunch and dinner Tues.–Sat. and dinner on Sunday.) The patio is a good place to sample the kangaroo at **Down Under New Zealand Restaurant,** 928/774-6677, which is

in Heritage Square at 6 E. Aspen Ave. (#100). The menu includes lamb, venison, and rabbit as well. (Open daily for lunch and dinner.) Fine country French cooking is the signature of **Chez Marc Bistro,** 503 N. Humphreys St., 928/774-1343, set in a cozy historic house. Entrees range from beef and chicken to ostrich and bison, and cost up to $30 for dinner (although most are in the $12–18 range). (Open for dinner Thurs.–Sat.; reservations recommended.)

ARTS AND ENTERTAINMENT

Nightlife

Built in 1931, **The Museum Club,** 3404 E. U.S. 66, 928/526-9434, www.museumclub.com, has evolved into the best country-music roadhouse in Arizona and one of the most outstanding in the country, according to both *Country America Magazine* and *Car & Driver.* Enter through the ponderosa pine archway onto the state's largest wooden dance floor. Five more ponderosas support the A-frame roof, and the mahogany backbar dates to the 1880s. Live blues, country, rock, and reggae include national acts like Willie Nelson and John Lee Hooker.

For more live music, **The Alley,** 22 E. U.S. 66, 928/774-7929, is probably your best bet, with pool tables, a bar, and a stage in back. A block away is **Joe's Place,** 102 E. U.S. 66, 928/774-6281, another good bar with pool tables; if these don't fit the bill, try **Beaver Street Brews and Cues,** 3 S. Beaver St., 928/779-0079, open daily. The lounges at the Weatherford Hotel and the Hotel Monte Vista are also good spots for an after-hours drink. For more information on Flagstaff nightlife, try the Flagstaff Skinny website (www.flagstaffskinny.com).

The Arts

NAU's **Richard E. Beasley Gallery,** 928/523-3549, displays rotating exhibits of contemporary art by students and faculty on the second floor of the Fine and Performing Arts Building. (Open Mon.–Fri. 11 A.M.–3 P.M.) Eighteenth-century furniture, glassware, silver, and art fill the **Marguerite Hettel Weiss Collection,** on the third floor of the Old Main Building. These galleries are both under the auspices of the **Old Main Art Gallery,** 928/523-3471, www.nau.edu/artgallery, on the northern end of campus, whose varied collection is open Mon.–Fri. 8 A.M.–5 P.M., Sat. 10 A.M.–2 P.M.

The **Flagstaff Symphony Orchestra,** www.flagstaffsymphony.org, has been entertaining northern Arizona audiences since 1949. Performances are held in NAU's Ardrey Auditorium from Sept.–Apr., and tickets are available online.

Shopping

It makes sense that Flagstaff, surrounded by mountains, deserts, canyons, and rivers, has plenty of good sporting goods stores. Try **Aspen Sports,** 15 N. San Francisco, 928/779-1935, **Babbitt's Backcountry Outfitters,** 12 E. Aspen Ave., 928/774-4775, or **Mountain Sports,** 928/226-2885, 24 N. San Francisco St., www.mountainsport.com. **Peace Surplus,** 14 W. U.S. 66, 928/779-4521, stocks climbing, fishing, skiing, and backpacking gear.

The Artists Gallery, 17 N. San Francisco St., 928/773-0958, collects the works of over 40 local contemporary artists under one roof, ranging from blown glass and painting to sculpture and furniture. Herbs, jewelry, kachina dolls, and baskets are on sale at the **Winter Sun Trading Company,** 107 N. San Francisco St., 928/774-2884, www.wintersun.com. For more Indian crafts, try **Puchteca Indian Crafts,** 20 N. San Francisco St., 928/774-2414.

Events

Flagstaff's **Winterfest** in February rolls together over 100 snow-themed events, including skiing and sled-dog competitions. May brings the beginning of the Museum of Northern Arizona's **Heritage Program,** which highlights the food, music, dance, arts, and traditions of the Colorado Plateau's diverse cultures all summer long. This includes the **Festival of Hispanic Arts and Crafts** in late May, the **Hopi Marketplace** in early July, the **Navajo Marketplace** in early August, the **Zuni Mar-**

ketplace in late August, and the **Festival of Pai Arts** (including the Havasupai, Hualapai, Yavapai, and Paiute Nations) in late September.

June is full of events, from the **Gem and Mineral Show** to the **Great Fiesta del Barrio and Fajita Cook-off** and the **Pine Country Pro Rodeo and Parade.** The founding of the city and its county are celebrated during the **Fabulous Fourth Festivities,** which serve as a prelude to the **Flagstaff Summer Fest** the first weekend in August, featuring artists from across the Southwest. The **Coconino Country Fair** and an **Arts and Crafts Festival** both occur over Labor Day weekend, and the **Flagstaff Festival of Science,** www.scifest.org, comes in late September.

RECREATION
Hiking

Beyond the 22-mile **Flagstaff Urban Trails System,** hikers and bikers have to look no farther than the San Francisco Peaks to find some of the best trails this close to a city in Arizona. Many of them are in the **Mt. Elden/Dry Lake Hills Trail System** and start from the **Mt. Elden trailhead,** near the National Forest Service's **Peaks Ranger Station,** 5075 N. U.S. 89, 928/526-0866. (Take Route 66 east out of town until it becomes U.S. 89 and look across from the Flagstaff Mall.) The trails climb up through boulders and huge junipers and piñon pines. The two-mile **Fatman's Loop** overlooks the city, so named as a warning: you have to be at least somewhat fit to tackle this one. A steep, three-mile trail that climbs 2,400 feet leads to the **Elden Lookout Tower** at 9,300 feet, with views as good as you'd expect.

Buffalo Park on the north side of town serves as trailhead for the **Oldham Trail,** leading 5.5 miles through aspen, spruce, pines, and fir trees to views over Oak Creek Canyon, Sunset Crater, and the Painted Desert. To get there, take San Francisco Street north, take a right on Forest Av-

> *Hikers and bikers have to look no farther than the San Francisco Peaks to find some of the best trails this close to a city in Arizona, climbing up through boulders, huge junipers, and piñon pines.*

enue, which becomes Cedar, and then a left on Gemini; the park is at the end of the road. The Arizona Snowbowl offers access to a number of trails as well.

Mountain Biking

Cyclists can tackle the 19.6-mile **Mount Elden Loop,** which circles the mountains clockwise by connecting the Schultz Creek, Little Elden, Pipeline, Oldham, and Rocky Ridge Trails. This is a great all-day ride, and most of it is moderately difficult singletrack. The trailhead is 3.2 miles north of town on U.S. 180; turn right onto Schultz Pass Road (FR 557), then park at the intersection with Mount Elden Road (FR 420) and head north on the Schultz Creek Trail. The **Elden Lookout Road** is another good ride, one of many in the national forests near town—just make sure to stay out of the wilderness area. For more information on roads among the San Francisco Peaks, see "Near Flagstaff," below.

Absolute Bikes, 18 N. San Francisco St.,

THE PAINTED DESERT

The Navajo call it *halchíítah,* meaning "among the colors." The arid badlands of the late-Triassic Chinle Formation are famous for their psychedelic scenery, heavily eroded and dotted with buttes and mesas of nearly every color imaginable. Pastel pinks, reds, yellows, greens, and grays stain the barren hillsides, and crazy eroded shapes make up a surrealistic landscape that is almost unbelievable at sunrise and sunset.

The Painted Desert extends in a narrow arc for about 160 miles from Cameron to the Petrified Forest, between the Little Colorado River and the Hopi tablelands. Most of the soils were laid down as silt and volcanic ash, and are marked by clays that shrink and swell so much as they get wet and dry out that hardly anything can grow. A few different factors have dictated which colors ended up where. Reds, oranges, and pinks come from iron and aluminum oxides concentrated in slowly deposited sediments, while blues, grays, and purples are the results of rapid events, such as floods, that removed oxygen from the soils.

928/779-5969, rents full-suspension mountain bikes for $50 per day and cruisers for $15 per day. **Single Track Bikes,** 575 W. Riordan Rd., 928/773-1862, is another good source of local riding info, gear, and service.

Rafting and Kayaking

As the closest city to the Grand Canyon proper, Flagstaff is often the base of choice for river runners out to tackle the rapids of the Colorado River and other waterways nearby. **Canyoneers,** 7195 N. U.S. 89, 928/526-0924 or 800/525-0924, www.canyoneers.com, answers@canyoneers.com, traces its origins to 1936, when Norman Nevills first guided a trip down the San Juan River. Their Grand Canyon offerings range from week-long trips on powered boats ($1,725 pp) to 13-day excursions on oar boats for $2,895 pp.

In 1986 Tim and Pam Whitney, who have been running the Grand Canyon since 1973, founded **Rivers and Oceans,** 12620 N. Copeland Ln., 928/526-4575 or 800/473-4576, www.rivers-oceans.com, info@rivers-oceans.com. Their guided trips include the Grand Canyon and rivers in southern Utah and Idaho. **Arizona Raft Adventures,** 4050 E. Huntington Dr., 928/526-8200 or 800/786-7238, www.azraft-com, also offer Grand Canyon raft trips. **Canyon Rio Rafting,** 928/774-3377 or 800/272-3353, www.canyonrio.com, info@canyonrio.com, offers family raft trips on rivers in central Arizona, the San Juan, and the Chama River in northern New Mexico, ranging from two hours to all day ($100 adults, $80 children). They also offer gear rentals and kayak instruction.

Skiing

For information on downhill skiing at the Arizona Snowbowl in the San Francisco Mountains, see "Near Flagstaff," below. The **Flagstaff Nordic Center,** 928/779-1951, offers over 20 miles of groomed trails, rentals, refreshments, and instruction. It's 16 miles north of town on U.S. 180, open daily Dec.–Mar., depending on snow, from 9 A.M.–4 P.M. Other popular cross-country skiing trails are on Wing Mountain, northwest of Flagstaff via U.S. 180 and Forest Road 222B, and Hart Prairie, 9.5 northwest via U.S. 180

and Forest Road 151. Call 928/779-4755 for a current snow report, or try the Forest Service's Peaks Ranger Station.

Other Activities

Four Season Outfitters & Guides, 107 W. Phoenix Ave., 877/272-5032 or 928/226-8798, www.fsoutfitters.com, info@fsoutfitters.com, organize hiking, backpacking, climbing, and rafting tours throughout the Four Corners. Day hikes into the Grand Canyon are $140 pp, including transport, food, and park admission, and can be lengthened up to a week or more. Three days in the Escalante canyons costs $650 pp. They have a rental/retail shop on the premises, and rent gear too.

Maxis and Frank Davies have been guiding horseback trail rides into the San Francisco Peaks from their **Flying Heart Ranch,** 928/526-2788, for 50 years. Located next to the Horsemen Lodge about 20 minutes north of downtown on U.S. 89, their rides last from 90 minutes to all day.

GETTING THERE AND AROUND

Flagstaffs's local **Mountain Line** bus service, 928/779-6624, runs three routes through the city Mon.–Fri., and two on Saturday. **Greyhound,** 399 S. Malpais Ln., 928/774-4573, takes advantage of the city's location on I-40 with service to major cities to the east and west. **Amtrak,** 1 E. U.S. 66, 928/774-8679, sells tickets to Los Angeles and Albuquerque daily. **Northern Arizona Shuttle and Tours,** 928/773-4337 or 866/870-8687, www.nazshuttle.com, sends buses to the South Rim of the Grand Canyon on Monday, Wednesday, and Saturday mornings, returning in the afternoon, for $20 pp each way ($15 children). They also go to Phoenix for $30 pp ($20). **Open Road Tours & Transportation,** 928/226-8060 or 877/266-8060, www.openroadtours.com, offers similar routes. From Apr.–Oct., **Backpacker Bus,** www.backpackerbus.com, info@backpackerbus.com, stops by Flagstaff's hostels on its way from Las Vegas to Big Bear Lake, California. It leaves for Big Bear Lake on Wednesdays and Saturdays for $35 pp o/w. Their laid-back bus routes connect hostels throughout

the Southwest and California, and you can get on and off whenever and wherever you like.

From Pulliam Field, five miles south of town, **America West,** 800/235-9292, flies four or five times daily to Phoenix. (It's usually cheaper to fly to Phoenix and take a bus from there, or vice versa.)

INFORMATION

The **Flagstaff Convention and Visitor's Bureau,** 928/774-9541 or 800/842-7293, www .flagstaffarizona.org, www.flagstaff.az.us, cvb@ ci.flagstaff.az.us, visitor@flagstaff.az.us, runs a **visitor center** in the old train station at 1 E. U.S. 66, open daily 8 A.M.–5 P.M. Find information on the surrounding mountain country, including maps and brochures, at the **U.S Forest Service supervisor's office,** 2323 E. Greenlaw Ln., 928/527-3600, www.fs.fed.us/r3/coconino, behind the shopping center. (Open Mon.–Fri. 7:30 A.M.–4:30 P.M.) They also operate the **Peaks Ranger Station,** 5075 N. U.S. 89, 928/526-0866, open similar hours.

Internet access is available at Kinko's, Biff's Bagels (1 S. Beaver St.), Bookman's Used Books (1520 S. Riordan Rd.), and the Mad Cyberian Cafe & Pub (101 S. San Francisco St.), as well as Flagstaff's City Library (300 W. Aspen Ave.) and NAU's Cline Library.

NEAR FLAGSTAFF

The Grand Canyon is just the beginning: along with the Navajo and Hopi Reservations to the northeast, Sedona and Oak Creek Canyon to the south, and the San Francisco Mountains to the west, three national monuments are within half an hour of the city. A **local passport** to all three costs $25, good for one vehicle for a year.

Walnut Canyon National Monument

This steep, lush canyon south of Flagstaff was home to at least 100 members of the Sinagua ("without water") culture in the 12th and 13th centuries, who built homes in shallow alcoves on the steep walls. The sandstone gorge itself is a wonder, with abundant vegetation and wildlife nourished by Walnut Creek. Residents raised corn, beans, and squash in fields among the pine forests on the canyon rim, above limestone ledges in the upper canyon dotted with marine fossils. Eventually they moved on; today, some Hopi clans trace their ancestry to Walnut Canyon.

Six miles of the 20-mile canyon are protected today, including over 300 masonry ruins. The **visitor center,** 928/526-3367, www.nps.gov/waca, sits on the edge of the 400-foot-deep ravine, and holds exhibits on the Sinagua culture, a bookstore, and information on ranger-guided walks given in summer (backcountry hiking is not allowed). Open daily 8 A.M.–6 P.M. June–Aug. (from 9 A.M. Dec.–Feb., otherwise 8 A.M.–5 P.M.). The self-guided, mile-long **Island Trail** climbs down into the canyon past the ruins of 25 cliff dwellings. The trail's steepness and altitude (6,700 ft) make it harder than you'd think. Another short trail leads along the rim past viewpoints, a pithouse, and a small pueblo.

Keep your eyes peeled for the canyon's varied wildlife, who inhabit several overlapping ecological communities. About 70 species of mammals in the area include coyotes, mule deer, elk, mountain lions, black bears, pronghorn antelopes, and a host of smaller critters. Canyon wrens, Cooper's hawks, prairie falcons, and great gray owls are some of the 121 resident bird species.

To get there, take exit 204 from I-40 and drive south three miles to the visitor center. Admission is $3 pp, good for a week, and is free to children under 16.

Grand Falls of the Little Colorado

A tongue of lava from Merriam Crater created this 185-foot cascade about 100,000 years ago. It's only worth coming in the spring, when meltwater roars over the edge. At other times it can slow to a trickle or stop altogether. The falls are just over the border of the Navajo Reservation, about 30 miles northeast of Flagstaff. To get there, first get to Winona, via I-40 exit 207 or 211, or the Camp Townsend-Winona Road, which leaves U.S. 89 north of Flagstaff (just under two miles north of the Flagstaff Mall). Take U.S. 3 north from Winona toward Leupp for 13 miles, then

turn left (north) for another 10 miles on unpaved Indian U.S. 70. There are picnic tables, and the dirt roads can be muddy and impassible in bad weather. No admission fee.

Sunset Crater National Monument

In A.D. 1064, the youngest of over 600 volcanoes in the San Francisco Volcanic Field started to blow its top. Flowing lava and forest fires lit the night sky, and residents fled as firebombs rained down and earthquakes shook the ground. The eruptions subsided around 1180, but by then people had already begun moving back into the area north of the new black peak.

The dramatic cinder cone volcano is 1,000 feet high and nearly a mile wide at its base. Surrounded by deep cinders and lava flows, it is far from the most hospitable-looking landscape, but trees, shrubs, and flowers have recolonized the scorched habitat. The name comes from multicolored mineral deposits at the crater rim that seem to light up at sunset.

A 36-mile **loop road** off U.S. 89 connects Sunset Crater (8,029 ft), the Strawberry Crater Wilderness, and Wupatki National Monument in the Coconino National Forest north of Flagstaff. It's a lovely drive through a landscape of black and rust-colored volcanic debris, sagebrush, and juniper. The crater is on the southern end of the loop; turn right 12 miles north of Flagstaff and go two more to the **visitor center,** 928/526-0502, www.nps.gov/sucr, where you can find a bookstore, picnic tables, and information on daily guided walks and evening programs. Entrance is $3 pp for visitors over 17, good for a week both here and at Wupatki. (Open daily 8 A.M.–6 P.M. June–Aug., from 9 A.M. Dec.–Feb., otherwise 8 A.M.–5 P.M.) Across the road is the **Bonito Campground,** 928/526-1474 or 0866, open late May to mid-Oct. ($13). One of the monument's two trails begins a mile east of the visitor center: the steep **Lenox Crater Trail** goes a mile to the top of a cinder cone and will have the less fit gasping for air by the end. Another half mile down the loop road is the beginning of the **Lava Flow Trail,** a mile-long loop past sharp lava flows, spatter cones, lava tubes, and cinder drifts like black snow.

GRAND CANYON NATIONAL PARK

Northwest of Flagstaff stretches one of the world's natural wonders, a mile-deep chasm carved into the high desert by the relentless force of flowing water. Over tens of millions of years, the Colorado River has eaten away the surface of the Colorado Plateau, leaving the canyon to end all canyons: 277 miles long and up to 18 miles wide, with countless side gorges, each of which could be a national park in itself. It's one of the country's greatest tourist draws, and justifiably so: the view from the edge is something you'll never forget, and a trip to the bottom—particularly a raft voyage through the famous Colorado River rapids—is almost beyond words.

Entrance to the park is $20 per vehicle, good for a week. For more information, call the park's recorded **visitor information number,** 928/638-7888, stop by the **park website,** www.nps.gov/grca, or check out the **"Unofficial" Grand Canyon National Park Home-page,** www.kaibab.org. For complete coverage of the Grand Canyon, pick up *Moon Handbooks Grand Canyon* by Bill Weir.

South Rim

Most visitors approach the canyon from this side, which offers the quickest access from a major city (Flagstaff). As a result, the South Rim has more tourist amenities than the more re-mote North Rim. Highway 64 runs north from I-40 at Williams to **Grand Canyon Village,** the largest settlement in the park. Here you'll find **park headquarters,** a post office, a bank, med-ical services, many stores and gift shops, and the **Canyon View Information Plaza** at Mather Point. Six national park lodges offer accommodations, including the grand old **El Tovar,** open since 1905. Rates are $40–120 d, depending on season. For reservations, contact Xanterra Parks & Resorts, 303/297-2757 or 888/297-2757, fax 303/297-3175, www.xanterra.com. Most of the lodges have restaurants. You can camp at the **Mather Campground** or **Trailer Village.** (Reservations at the former are highly recommended; call 800/365-2267 or visit http://reser-vations.nps.gov). More tourist services are available at Tusayan, on U.S. 64 outside the park boundaries. A new light rail system carries visitors from here to Mather Point and Grand Canyon Village to ease congestion, and **Trans-Canyon Shuttle,** 928/638-2820, sends vans be-tween the North and South Rims daily May–October.

The **Rim Trail** offers access to many excellent viewpoints over the vastness of the canyon and its tributaries. For a closer look, the **Bright Angel Trail** heads 9.3 miles downhill to **Phantom Ranch** at the bottom. (Dorm beds here are $24, and cabins are $65 d.) Rangers have horror sto-ries about businessmen with briefcases and mothers with baby carriages heading down this dif-ficult trail—hopefully you'll leave better prepared. Keep in mind that it can hit well over 100°F in the inner gorge in the summer, even when it's balmy on the rims, and that it typically takes twice as much time, energy, and water to climb back out as it does to descend. Carry at least one gallon of water per person per day from spring to fall. Permits are necessary for overnight hikes ($10 plus $5 pp per night). Call the **Backcountry Information Line** (928/638-7875) for details, or stop by www.thecanyon.com/nps.

U.S. 64 runs east from Grand Canyon Village for 25 miles along the edge of the canyon, where it's called East Rim Drive inside the park. Along the way are ruins, viewpoints, and the **Desert View Watchtower,** a stone structure designed by Mary Coulter for the Fred Harvey Company in 1932 and lined with Hopi murals. Several other trails lead down into the gorge. One popular hike is the **Grandview Trail** from Grandview Point to Horseshoe Mesa, an old In-dian route improved by miners (six miles r/t). Another classic way to enter the canyon is via **mule ride,** a hoary tradition that's been lumbering along for over a century. Start at $108 pp for a day trip, these can be reserved through Xanterra. U.S. 64 continues east to Cameron.

North Rim

U.S. 89A climbs into the cool evergreen forests of the Kaibab Plateau and at almost 8,000 feet hits Jacob Lake, where it joins with U.S. 67 toward the northern edge of the abyss. The **Jacob Lake Inn,** 928/643-7232, www.jacoblake.com, offers a restaurant, year-round rooms and cabins ($70–90), and a campground ($10). Across the road, **Allen's Outfitters,** 435/644-8150, organizes horseback trips into the Kaibab National Forest, and the USFS Jacob Lake Campground has primitive sites for $10. From here, U.S. 67 reaches almost 9,000 feet as it winds through the parklike meadows and pine-clad hills of the Kaibab National Forest, one of the prettiest in the Lower 48. Buried by snow in winter, the road is open mid-May to mid-Oct., weather permitting (call 928/638-7888 or the Forest Service visitor center at Jacob Lake, 928/643-7298, for an update).

Though only about 10 miles as the raven flies from the South Rim, the less developed North Rim is over 200 miles away by road, so it sees fewer visitors. You can still depend on the same stupendous views and the same precipitous trails—you'll just share them with a few thousand less people. Plus, since it's over 1,000 feet higher, it's significantly cooler in the summer.

Built in 1928, the log-beam **Grand Canyon Lodge** boasts two porches and an octagonal Sun Room with huge windows to take advantage of the view from the edge. Rooms and cabins range from $60–95 per night, and it's a good idea to make reservations (through Xanterra, above) as far in advance as possible. The same goes for the restaurant, which serves all meals, as well as the **North Rim Campground,** 800/365-2267, http://reservations.nps.gov, with sites for $10–20, showers, laundry facilities, and a grocery and camping store.

From here you can take the **North Kaibab Trail** 15 miles from **Bright Angel Point** to Phantom Ranch. The steeper, unmaintained **North Bass** and **Thunder River** trails also go all the way to the river; the latter passes a river that gushes out of a sheer limestone cliff before flowing right into the Colorado, making it the shortest in the world. A 23-mile **scenic drive** leads to the overlook at **Point Royal,** passing half a dozen more viewpoints along the way, many with picnic areas and short trails.

Rafting the Canyon

Riding the rapids of the Colorado River ranks high up on the list of Things You Should Do Before You Die, Circumstances Permitting. Follow in the footsteps of daring explorers as you explore side canyons, float the placid stretches, shrink in significance next to billions of years of geology, and—OK, here the footsteps end—enjoy gourmet meals and the luxury of sleeping bags on a sandbar beneath the stars. Companies in Page, Flagstaff, and other cities in Utah and Arizona offer many different options for running the river, which is a good thing considering the waiting list for private permits is over a decade long. Choose from motor boats or the classic oar-powered dories, and either the full 226 miles from Lee's Ferry to Diamond Creek or a partial trip. The full journey takes 11–19 days by oar or 6–8 days with a motor, or you can join or leave a trip at Phantom Ranch, cutting your travel time considerably.

For more information, see the appropriate listings under Page and Flagstaff, write the park for the latest list (P.O. Box 129, Grand Canyon, AZ 86023), or contact the **Grand Canyon River Outfitters Association,** www.gcroa.org.

NAVAJO & HOPI COUNTRY

Other Crater Hiking

Just east of the Sunset Crater visitor center is the beginning of Forest Road 545A, leading north 5.5 miles to the fire tower on top of **O'Leary Peak** (8,965 ft). This lava-dome volcano offers excellent views of the Painted Desert and the San Francisco Volcanic Field, including Sunset Crater. You'll have to walk the last quarter mile of the road.

Farther north up the loop road is the 10,141-acre **Strawberry Crater Wilderness,** centered on yet another cinder cone and its accompanying lava flow. It's much older than Sunset Crater, formed between 50,000 and 100,000 years ago, and the wilderness area is full of prehistoric ruins. Indigenous residents used volcanic cinders as a sort of mulch to hold water, to make up for the area's dry location in the rain shadow of the San Francisco Peaks (only about seven inches of precipitation fall here every year).

The easiest access to the area is from U.S. 89. About 16 miles north of the Flagstaff Mall, take Forest Roads 546 and 779 east to the wilderness boundary, where an unmarked trail leads to the summit. You can also enter the wilderness area from the loop road to the east.

Wupatki National Monument

The only place in the Southwest where at least four separate cultures overlapped, Wupatki preserves four multi-storied pueblos, including the largest in the Flagstaff area. They rose during the 11th century A.D., when residents returning after the eruption of Sunset Crater Volcano found the soil much improved by the water-retaining ash and cinders. The Wupatki Basin bears the distinct signs of the Sinagua, Hohokam, Cohonina, and Kayenta Anasazi cultures, who arrived during a period of general population rise throughout the Southwest. By the 12th century, however, they had moved on to the north, east, and south, where they were assimilated into the cultures of those areas.

The Wupatki **visitor center,** 928/679-2365, www.nps.gov/wupa, is 14 miles from the northern end of the loop drive. You'll find a picnic area, vending machines, and a bookstore, along with exhibits inside on the various cultures that

Lomaki Pueblo, Wupatki National Monument

met and coexisted more or less peacefully here. A reconstructed pueblo room gives you an idea of life in the 12th century. Entrance is $3 pp for visitors over 17, good for a week both here and at Sunset Crater. (Open daily 8 A.M.–6 P.M. June–Aug., from 9 A.M. Dec.–Feb., otherwise 8 A.M.–5 P.M.) Ask about orientation programs and guided hikes, given daily in summer and less often in spring and fall.

A short self-guided trail leads to the multistory **Wupatki Pueblo** on a side branch of Deadman Wash. This 100-room structure is built from red stone that contrasts with the black lava and green vegetation. The trail circles the pueblo, passing rooms on the far side that were once used to house rangers. Nearby are a reconstructed ball court and a blowhole, a small opening to an underground chamber that expels or draws in air depending on barometric pressure.

A side branch from the loop road leads 2.5 miles to **Wukoki Pueblo,** which once housed two or three families and is the monument's best-preserved pueblo. Farther north on the loop road are three smaller pueblos. The 30-room **Citadel Pueblo** stands like a castle on a small butte, near

© JULIAN SMITH

Nalakihu Pueblo, about half as big. **Lomaki Pueblo** sits on the edge of a small box canyon and had nine rooms between two stories.

San Francisco Mountains

The most distinctive features of Flagstaff's skyline were named by Franciscan monks after St. Francis of Assisi, the founder of their order, as they went about their business converting Indians on the Hopi Reservation. The Hopi themselves call the mountain *Nubat-i-kyan-bi* ("place of the snow peaks") and believe their kachina spirits live among the summits for part of every year before flying to the Hopi mesas in the form of nourishing rain clouds. The play of light over the amazingly symmetrical peaks makes it easy to see why the Hopis revere them. The 1930s WPA guide to Arizona rhapsodized, "At sunrise they appear gold; at noon they are Carrara marble against a turquoise sky; at sunset they are polished copper, ruby, coral, and finally amethyst."

The range tops out at **Humphrey's Peak,** Arizona's highest point at 12,633 feet and home to a ski resort and miles upon miles of trails. Many of these lie inside the 18,960-acre **Kachina Peaks Wilderness,** which encloses most of the highest peaks north of Mt. Elden. A huge caldera created during the mountain's most recent eruption (about 2 million years ago) forms an inner basin filled with aspens, pines, and firs. As you can imagine, the views from up here are spectacular, from flower-covered meadows all the way down to the Painted Desert and, if it's a clear day, the Grand Canyon.

The easiest way to get into the heart of the hills is the road to the **Arizona Snowbowl,** 928/779-1951, www.arizonasnowbowl.com, which leaves U.S. 180 seven miles north of downtown and climbs another seven uphill. In the winter, 30 mostly intermediate runs are served by four lifts and a tow rope. Lift tickets are $40 adult and $22 junior; instruction and rentals are also available. Call for information or stop by their website. Call 928/779-4755 for a current snow report.

In summer, the chairlift continues to run to the 11,500-foot peak. It operates daily 10 A.M.–4 P.M. from late June to Labor Day, and Fri.–Sun. until mid-Oct. Two excellent trails leave from the lower parking lot; the five-mile **Kachina Trail** is a good, moderate hike south to Schultz Pass, and the six-mile **Humphrey's Peak Trail** leads above tree line to Humphrey's Peak. (Note that hiking is not allowed off trails above 11,400 feet to protect the fragile tundra vegetation.) The **Schultz Pass Road** is a gravel route connecting U.S. 180 and 89 between Mt. Elden and the wilderness area. This 26-mile drive traverses ponderosa forests, open glades, and streams perfect for an afternoon picnic. It's open Apr.–Nov., weather permitting, and offers access to the **Weatherford Trail,** built by hand in 1926 and popular with families for its gentle grade and views. This crosses the Fremont Saddle (11,354 ft) before connecting with the Humphrey's Peak Trail from the Arizona Snowbowl. The western end of the Schultz Pass Road joins U.S. 180 just north of the Museum of Northern Arizona. It begins as Forest Road 420 and heads left (north) where the Elden Lookout Road heads right (east).

Another good drive through the mountains is the **Around the Peaks Loop,** a 44-mile gravel route around Humphrey's Peak that's also open Apr.–Nov, weather permitting. Like the Schultz Pass Road, it is particularly gorgeous in autumn when the aspens are turning gold. To do the loop counterclockwise, drive 14 miles north of Flagstaff on U.S. 89 to Forest Road 418, go west 12 miles to Forest Road 151, and then south eight miles to U.S. 180, 9.5 miles north of Flagstaff.

Sedona

South of Flagstaff on U.S. 89A is one of Arizona's more famous destinations, part art center, part resort retreat, and part New Age nexus. Blessed with spectacular red-rock scenery, a moderate climate, and (according to many residents) seven spiritual energy "vortexes," Sedona draws an interesting crowd and makes for a fascinating and wonderfully scenic day trip from Flagstaff. Getting there is half the fun; **Oak Creek Canyon** (U.S. 89A north of Sedona) is an amazing drive past rock monoliths, swimming holes, viewpoints, and secluded resort lodges. It gets very crowded on summer weekends, so consider coming at some other time if you can (the same applies to Sedona itself).

In Sedona, you can choose from dozens of B&Bs. Try the **Stoneflower Bed & Breakfast,** 90 Chavez Ranch Rd., 928/282-2977 or 800/338-2334, www.stoneflower.com ($100). If your budget permits, you can opt for the **Enchantment Resort,** 928/282-2900 or 800/826-4180, www.enchantmentresort.com, with a spa, athletic facilities, and restaurants at the mouth of Boynton Canyon ($200 and up). If it doesn't, there's always the **Hostel Sedona,** 928/282-2772, on Soldiers Wash Drive ($15–35).

Food choices are just as broad, ranging from the elegant French fare at **L'Auberge de Sedona,** 301 L'Auberge Ln., 928/282-1667, to the innovative American cuisine of the **Heartline Cafe,** 1610 W. U.S. 89A, 928/282-0785. The home-baked goodies at the **Desert Flour Bakery & Bistro** are particularly yummy; there's one in the Pink Jeep Plaza.

For more information on Sedona and the surrounding area, contact the **Sedona-Oak Creek Canyon Chamber of Commerce,** N. U.S. 89A and Forest Road, 928/282-7722 or 800/288-7336, www.visitsedona.com.

Navajo Reservation

TUBA CITY AND VICINITY

One of the Navajo Reservation's most diverse communities, Tuba City sits just off U.S. 89 between Flagstaff and Page. It was named by early Mormon settlers after a Hopi called Tuuvi, chief of the Water and Corn Clans at Oraibi. Tuuvi was the first Hopi to meet Brigham Young, and after converting to the Mormon faith in Salt Lake City, he donated a plot of land to the church on the condition that Mormon settlers would protect the Hopi from Navajo and Paiute raiders. Jacob Hamblin, the "Buckskin Missionary," helped establish a settlement at a well-watered area called Moenave at the foot of a cliff to the north. Mormons heading south along a trail blazed by Hamblin to the Little Colorado River Valley often stopped here to rest and resupply. (The trail became known as the Honeymoon Trail, since young Mormon couples had to travel all the way back to St. George, Utah, to have their wedding vows officially solemnized by the church.) The last Latter-Day Saint left Moenave near the turn of the century, when the area was added to the Navajo Reservation.

Although predominantly Navajo, Tuba City has many residents who belong to the Hopi and other tribes, as well as Anglos. The Basha's grocery store serves as the unofficial community gathering place. Although most travelers zip past on their way to the North Rim of the Grand Canyon without a second glance, Tuba City is worth a detour for the shopping and the Navajo tacos.

Sights

Tuba City sits on a mesa north of U.S. 160 in one of the most striking expanses of the **Painted Desert.** About two miles east on U.S. 160 from U.S. 89, a dirt turnoff leads to the top of a small hill, a great place to take photos and enjoy the view.

Three more miles bring you to another turnoff marked by a hand-lettered sign for **Moenave,** the site of the original Mormon settlement. Near the turnoff are a set of **dinosaur tracks** laid down by the nine-foot *Dilophosaurus* in the late Triassic mud. Navajo children are usually on hand to give you a short tour (a small tip is expected) and will point out the three-toed footprints, petrified eggs, and even an embedded claw. The settlement of Moenave itself, at the base of Hamblin Ridge, is a green oasis fed by springs. John D. Lee, of Lees Ferry, hid out here for a while before being tracked down and executed for his role in the Mountain Meadows Massacre.

Accommodations and Food

The **Quality Inn,** 928/283-4545, fax 928/283-4144, has rooms for $90–135, a restaurant serving all meals, and an RV park with six tent sites. Students at the Greyhills Academy High School run the 32-room **Greyhills Inn,** 928/283-6271 ext. 141, as part of a training program in hotel management. Hostel beds are $20, and rooms with shared baths start at $50 pp. Back at the intersection of U.S. 160 and 264, the **Tuba City Truck Stop Cafe,** 928/283-4975, is a must-eat for road-food gourmands. They boast the "best Navajo taco in the Southwest," and the messy, heaping concoction of beans, lettuce, tomatoes, and cheese on top of fry bread is hard to beat. Navajo matriarchs decked out in their best jewelry munch quietly beneath signed photos of various celebrities who have stopped in for a bite.

Shopping and Events

A huge red building on U.S. 160 as the base of the mesa houses **Van's Trading Company,** 928/283-5343, which is half supermarket and half general-goods store. The pawn department, open daily 9 A.M.–6 P.M., has lots of jewelry and rugs. Dead pawn is auctioned off on the 15th of every month. In Tuba City proper is the **Tuba Trading Post,** 928/283-5441, built in 1870 out of local blue limestone and logs from the San Francisco Peaks. Teddy Roosevelt stayed here in 1913 on his way back from hunting mountain lions on the North Rim of the Grand Canyon, and Zane Gray also stopped by. Today the two-story octagonal showroom holds a wealth of quality crafts, particularly jewelry. Open Mon.–Fri. 8 A.M.–6 P.M., Sat. 8 A.M.–5 P.M., Sun 9 A.M.–5 P.M.

Every Friday the **Tuba City Flea Market** coalesces behind the Community Center. A little bit of everything is for sale—car parts, used clothing, medicinal herbs, turquoise jewelry—and you can listen to the lilting sounds of the Navajo language over a bowl of mutton stew and fry bread when you need a breather. The **Western Navajo Fair** is held in the Rodeo and Fair Grounds every October, the first weekend after Columbus Day.

East of Tuba City

Twenty miles east of Tuba City on U.S. 160 is the **Red Lake Trading Post,** 928/283-5194, at the foot of the squat, 200-foot rock formations called the Elephant Feet. Started in 1891 by the Babbitt Brothers Trading Company, the post was acquired as a debt payment for an early settler who was shot in a card game. They don't have much for sale any more, but notice the upper story

made of Arbuckle Brothers coffee boxes. Open daily 7 A.M.–9 P.M.

North of Tuba City

U.S. 89 follows Hamblin Wash and a ridge of the same name to the east, as it rolls toward Marble Canyon and Lees Ferry. Where Hamblin Ridge meets the Echo Cliffs, 17 miles north of the U.S. 160 intersection, is a break in the cliffs called The Gap, home of **The Gap Trading Post,** 928/283-5635. Originally built around 1880 by Joe Lee, great-grandson of John D. Lee, The Gap has been rebuilt twice—this last time in solid stone—after repeated fires. It's now a Thriftway gas station and convenience store with a small selection of jewelry, rugs, and other crafts.

South of Tuba City

In 1911, a suspension bridge was built over the Little Colorado River about 50 miles north of Flagstaff. Five years later, Hubert and C. D. Richardson established a trading post where the Navajo and Hopi exchanged wool, blankets, and livestock for dry goods. Today the **Cameron Trading Post and Gallery,** 928/679-2231 or 800/338-7385, fax 928/679-2350, www.camerontradingpost.com, is owned by Joe Atkinson, grandnephew of the Richardsons, who has remodeled the old place into a beautiful enclave that's the perfect home base for a Grand Canyon visit.

About a mile north of the intersection of U.S. 89 and 64, the Cameron Trading Post has a lodge with 66 rooms ($90–120) featuring hand-carved furniture and balcony views of the Little Colorado Gorge. Many are arranged around the hotel's exquisite gardens, where Chinese elms, fruit trees, and rose bushes were originally planted by Hubert's wife, Mabel. A large stone fireplace, pressed-tin ceiling, and native crafts from throughout the Southwest decorate the dining room, serving all meals daily.

There's a food market, gas station, RV park ($15), and post office elsewhere in the complex, and an active trading post where locals buy craft supplies and sundries, and sell wool and piñon nuts. Make sure you visit the gallery, which has an outstanding collection of antique and contemporary native art. Rugs, concha belts, pottery,

NAVAJO & HOPI COUNTRY

kachinas, baskets, and Old West memorabilia fill the place from wooden floor to wide-beamed ceiling. The best (and most expensive) pieces are on display upstairs, in a series of rooms restored to look like living quarters.

KAYENTA AND VICINITY

The largest city in the northern part of the Navajo Reservation (pop. 4,500) takes its name, loosely, from the Navajo word *teehindeeh*, meaning "bog hole" or "natural game pit," after the glue-like soil around a nearby spring that mired livestock. (The Navajo call it *Tódínéeshzheé*, meaning "water spreading out like fingers" and referring to nearby springs.) In truth, it's not the most inviting place, with little of interest besides a few motels, inexpensive restaurants, and a shopping center at the intersection of U.S. 160 and 163. It's a dusty town of pickup trucks and cowboy hats, home to miners and farmers.

Accommodations and Food

Kayenta has only a few chain hotels, all near the main intersection. In the $100–150 range are a **Best Western Wetherill Inn,** 928/697-3231, fax 928/697-3233l; the **Hampton Inn,** 928/ 697-3170, fax 928/697-3189; and the **Holiday Inn,** 928/697-3221, fax 928/697-3349. More representative lodgings can be found 10 miles southwest on U.S. 163 at the **Country of Many Hogans Bed & Breakfast,** 888/291-4397, pin 4617, zenbah@hotmail.com. At the foot of Boot Mesa, 2.5 miles west of U.S. 163 on Route 6450, the Bedonie family offers private accommodations in a traditional Navajo hogan. It's part of a reservation-wide economic development program to encourage local businesses, and the price ($125) includes a hearty breakfast (other meals can be arranged on request). Built of cedar logs hauled from hundreds of miles away, the hogan doesn't have electricity or running water, but the friendly family can organize activities like a sweat lodge, horseback rides, and guided hikes.

Back at the main intersection, the **Blue Coffee Pot,** 928/697-3396, is a local favorite. Named after a type of container commonly seen on the reservation, it serves good steaks and Mexican and Navajo dishes for $4–8. Open Mon.–Fri. for all meals. The Basha's supermarket complex contains a hardware store, a movie theater, a Wendy's, a Blimpie, and a Burger King, with an interesting exhibit on the Navajo code talkers.

THE OWL, THE SNAKE, AND THE PILE OF WOOL

Monument Valley is just the beginning of the fascinating geology near Kayenta. Just north of Kayenta on U.S. 163, **Agathla Peak** (6,096 ft.) is a jagged volcanic neck with the same blackened, ominous look of Shiprock. This is believed to be the center of the Navajo world, set in place by the Holy People to prop up the sky. In Navajo *'aghaalá* means "much wool." The peak's name recalls the legend of a huge snake that made his home at the base of the rock. His wife, an owl, lived nearby—look for distinctive **Owl Rock** (6,547 ft.) across the road, formed of Wingate sandstone. The snake grew fat on the plentiful local antelope, and tossed so much leftover hair outside his home that the name stuck. Kit Carson later renamed the peak El Capitan, and the classic Western *Stagecoach* was filmed here in 1938.

Half Dome stands closer to Kayenta near **Church Rock** (5,580 ft.), looming west of the town on U.S. 160. Heading south along U.S. 160 toward Tuba City, you'll pass along the south side of the **Organ Rock Monocline,** also called Skeleton Mesa. Huge sandstone teeth point northwest in the remains of this geologic uplift, raised 75–80 million years ago. **Marsh Pass** (6,750 ft.) brings you to **Tsegi Canyon,** home to the Anasazi Inn. This beautiful canyon, coming in from the north, was carved by Laguna Creek and is relatively lush, boasting many Anasazi sites and fields of Navajo corn in the summer. U.S. 160 continues southwest through **Long House Canyon** to the turnoff for Navajo National Monument. An electric coal train passes over the road here, leading south to **Black Mesa** and the Peabody coal mines.

(Owner Richard Mike's father, King, was a code talker.) You can buy more food at the Kayenta Trading Post, a supermarket down the hill behind the Best Western.

Activities and Information

Crafts, Western wear, and craft supplies are sold at the **Navajo Arts and Crafts Enterprises** outlet, 928/697-8611, near the main intersection (open Mon.–Fri. 9 A.M.–6 P.M.). Independence Day brings the **Todineeshzhee Fourth of July Rodeo and Fair** to Kayenta. Find more information on the area at the **Visitors Center,** 928/697-3572, in a round building next to the Burger King. Local dancers perform in the courtyard on summer evenings. It's open daily 10 A.M.–7 P.M. in summer, and Mon.–Sat. until 6 P.M. otherwise.

Navajo National Monument

Twenty miles south of Kayenta, U.S. 564 leads north to this small monument that protects three of the most impressive and intact Anasazi ruins in the Four Corners. Start at the **visitor center,** 928/672-2700, www.nps.gov/nava, on the Shonto Plateau nine miles north of U.S. 160. It's open year-round 8 A.M.–5 P.M. (entrance is free) and contains a craft shop and museum. Next door is a **campground** with 31 sites, also free. Two short, easy trails lead to overlooks above the **Betatakin** cliff dwellings, but to really experience the monument you should take a ranger-led tour, offered Memorial Day to Labor Day. Betatakin sits in a 435-foot-high alcove, which has dropped so much sandstone lately that tours now stop outside instead of entering. This is a little more of an undertaking—the five-mile trail is steep and sandy, and you'll need a free permit—but it's well worth it.

Keet Seel is 17 miles from the visitor center, meaning you can stay the night or do the whole thing in an epic, one-day push. Either way, you can follow a ranger through this entire town of over 100 rooms, tucked under a cliff overhang. The inhabitants kept their stored food safe from rodents in ingeniously sealed storage chambers. Stone slabs fit perfectly into small doorways, and were held in place by poles slid through wooden loops set into the masonry on either side.

RAINBOW BRIDGE, THE OLD-FASHIONED WAY

If you're up for a bit of a trek, you can reach Rainbow Bridge in the only way it was possible before the filling of Lake Powell—by land. The **Rainbow Trail** circles Navajo Mountain, and begins off Hwy. 98 between Page and Kayenta. Between mileposts 349 and 350, turn north onto the partly paved Navajo Mountain Rd. Drive 32 miles and turn left at the fork to reach the ruins of the old Rainbow Lodge. (If you arrive at the Navajo Mountain Mission, you turned right.)

From here the South Rainbow Trail (marked by red mileposts) leads west across First and Horse Canyons, then down into Cliff Canyon, where you'll find first water at a campsite after eight miles. Take a side canyon to the right another mile down, then climb out and over Redbud Pass (blasted out by John Wetherell's party in 1922) to Redbud Creek, which you'll follow down to the bridge at the water's edge, about 13 miles from the trailhead. The remains of an old tourist camp are under an overhang nearby. Remember, don't camp under the bridge or approach it too closely, as it is still holy to the Navajo.

You can return the same way, or take the North Rainbow Trail back to complete the circle. This leaves the bridge to the east up Bridge Canyon, and crosses Oak, Masja, Blad Rock, and Cha Canyons and the tablelands between them. From Cha Canyon a dirt road takes you back around to the Navajo Mountain Mission. A vehicle or mountain bike shuttle will save you another ten miles of walking back to the Rainbow Lodge. The whole loop should take 3–5 days, and there is little water away from the lake (which you should take care to purify carefully).

You can also climb Navajo Mountain from the mission; take a rough road west that eventually turns into a track as it reaches the summit at 10,388 ft. Since the route crosses the Navajo Reservation, you'll have to get a permit in advance from tribal offices in Window Rock (928/871-6647) or Cameron (928/679-2303).

The closest lodgings to the monument are in Tsegi Canyon, about five miles northeast on U.S. 160. Here the **Anasazi Inn,** 928/697-3793, fax 928/697-8249, www.anasaziinn.com, has 56 rooms ($40) and a small cafe serving all meals daily. It's nothing special room-wise, but you can't beat the setting in the pink sandstone gorge.

MONUMENT VALLEY

Driving north of Kayenta on U.S. 163 toward the Utah border, it's easy to feel like you've entered a Western movie sunset just as the credits start to roll. Rising from the flat plain like the gods' own rock garden, the stone monoliths of Monument Valley are the unmistakable symbol of the American West, embedded in the imagination of the world by countless movies, photos, and car commercials.

The Navajo consider all of *Tsébii' nidzisgai* (the "Valley Within the Rocks") to be one huge hogan, with the traditional east-facing door situated near the visitor center. Tribe members sought refuge here during Kit Carson's campaign in the 1860s, and many still live and farm here. Despite the valley's near-mythic status, visitation is limited to a single loop road and permitted tours. (Rock climbing is forbidden, despite what you saw in *The Eiger Sanction* or *Vertical Limit.*) More prosaically, the buttes of Monument Valley are formed of Cedar Mesa sandstone on top of sloping bases of Halgaito shale. Over the millennia, the softer shale has eroded more quickly, causing the sandstone to fracture vertically into the towering formations. Many are capped by ledges of red Organ Rock shale.

At an intersection on the state line, a short road leads east to the Monument Valley Navajo Tribal Park **visitor center,** 435/727-3218, www.navajonationparks.org, open daily 7 A.M.– 7 P.M. (entrance is $3). Here you'll find a snack shop, gift shop, and a restaurant upstairs. There's

Driving north of Kayenta on U.S. 163, it's easy to feel like you've entered a Western movie sunset just as the credits start to roll. Rising from the flat plain like the gods' own rock garden, the stone monoliths of Monument Valley are the unmistakable symbol of the American West.

a desk where you can sign up for a tour, and dozens of local operators have set up booths in the parking lot, offering trail rides, hikes, and vehicle tours through the monument. One of them, **Sacred Monument Tours,** 435/727-3218 or 928/380-4527, www.monumentvalley.net, has daily offerings starting at $20 for a one-hour Jeep tour, with an all-day horse tour for $140. Longer tours leave the loop road for obscure petroglyphs and ruins. Other operators include **Roland's Navajoland Tours,** 928/697-3524, fax 928/697-3374, out of Kayenta, and **Fred's Adventure Tours,** 435/739-4294, based in Mexican Hat.

The visitor center is perched on the edge of the sandy valley filled with massive square buttes, including the Totem Pole, Castle Rock, the Stage Coach, and the famous Mittens. Some of the 100 sites in the **Mitten View Campground** share the great views, well worth getting up for sunrise. Group, tent, and RV sites are available ($10), along with coin-operated showers. From here the 17-mile **loop road** descends into the valley, past many Navajo homes and a viewpoint named for director John Ford, who made this place world-famous through his films. Allow at least two hours to traverse the dirt road, which is good enough for most 2WD vehicles and closes shortly before sundown (it's also a great mountain bike ride).

For the classic road-trip shot of Monument Valley, approach from the north on U.S. 191 (which changes to U.S. 163 in Arizona). A little over 13 miles north of the Utah border there's a small hill, with the highway heading straight as an arrow toward the valley below. Trust me—you'll recognize the view.

Goulding's Lodge and Trading Post

Opposite the valley at the state-line intersection is a complex centered around a trading post opened in a 10-man tent in the 1920s by Harry Goulding and his wife, "Mike." Harry,

© JULIAN SMITH

view of Monument Valley from Goulding's Lodge and Trading Post

called *Dibé Nééz* ("Tall Sheep") by the Navajo, purchased 640 acres at the base of Black Door Mesa for $320 in 1937. Goulding bought local crafts, settled disputes, and acted as a liaison between the Navajo and the government. He also convinced director John Ford that the local scenery would make an ideal movie backdrop, hoping to bring jobs to the area during the Great Depression. The rest is celluloid history. The valley has been used as backdrop for countless movies including such classic Westerns as *Stagecoach, My Darling Clementine,* and *Fort Apache.* As Hollywood glitterati started to arrive, the Gouldings opened a lodge that became a second home to stars like John Wayne. Movie memorabilia and trading-post artifacts fill the original trading post, which has been turned into a museum (open daily year-round). A suggested donation of $2 is put toward scholarships for local children.

The immaculate modern **lodge,** 435/727-3231, www.gouldings.com, gouldings@gouldings.com, boasts 62 rooms ($70–160 depending on season) and the Stagecoach Dining Room, built for the filming of *She Wore a Yellow Ribbon.* Each room features a VCR so you can watch the many Westerns available for rent—or just look out from your balcony at the real thing. A modern **campground** has views of the valley as well, along with a heated indoor pool, Laundromat, hot showers, and a grocery store. It's also open year-round, with sites for $16 (tents) and $26 (full RV hookups). Sign up at the lodge for Navajo-guided **tours** to nearby ruins, petroglyphs, crafts demonstrations, and movie locations ($33 pp half day, $63 full day).

Oljato

Eight miles past Goulding's is one of the most authentic trading posts left on the reservation, and one of my personal favorites. The **Oljato Trading Post & Museum,** 435/727-3210, http://a-aa.com/monumentvalley, oljatotp@hotmail.com, was built in 1921, making it one of the oldest still in operation. Step past the rusting gas pumps into the U-shaped "bullpen" for everything from hose clamps to ice cream sandwiches. A few things are still for sale in the back, alongside museum pieces and old photo albums. They don't sell gas anymore and the airstrip is growing weeds, but this gem hasn't closed yet. The owners also offer trail rides in the area.

THE NUMBER OF THE BEAST

Let him who has understanding calculate the number of the beast, for it is the number of a man: His number is 666.

Revelation 13:18

They say U.S. Highway 666 is cursed. It's been nicknamed the "Devil's Highway," and national newspapers quote locals saying they "blame Satan" for numerous unexplained accidents. There's even a *New Yorker* cartoon showing two devils driving past the ominous highway sign that featured prominently in Oliver Stone's 1994 paean to car-borne slaughter, *Natural Born Killers.*

But is this dark cousin of Route 66, America's "Mother Road," really evil? Ironically, the number itself was a mere coincidence. The original route was called the Navajo Trail, listed as 141 miles long in the official log of numbered U.S. highways in the 1920s. As the sixth branch off U.S. 66 between Chicago and Los Angeles, this stretch—linking Cortez, Colorado, with Gallup, New Mexico—was dubbed Highway

666 in 1926, following the standard system for interstate highways.

Apparently no one was bothered by the Biblical allusion. According to the numerological system called gematria, which assigns a value to each letter of the alphabet, 666 is the sum of the letters that make up the name of the "beast" (perhaps Roman Emperor Nero, originally, but today usually referring to the Antichrist).

In any case, the road was eventually extended to Monticello, Utah, and Douglas, Arizona. When Route 66 was officially replaced by I-40 in 1985, its branches weren't immediately renumbered. Although parts of it eventually were given new numbers (south of Gallup it has become U.S. 191), U.S. 666 from Gallup to Monticello kept its old blasphemous digits. Short of the Rapture, the only thing that will change it is if the states themselves request a number change—and they haven't yet.

Regardless of what you believe, late at night, on the long dark, lonely stretches, skeptics and the credulous should both be wary of drunk drivers.

Canyon de Chelly National Monument

Joseph Campbell, international guru of mythology, once called this canyon system in northeast Arizona "the most sacred place on Earth." There is definitely something about this place, which has been inhabited for thousands of years, that makes it stand out even among the Four Corners' scenic and historical marvels. Covering 130 square miles of precipitous gorges and fertile canyon bottoms, Canyon de Chelly (de-SHAY) has an ageless quality, as Navajo families farm and tend orchards and herds of animals beneath soaring stone monoliths. It's almost as if a pane of glass had been laid across the cliff tops, preserving a way of life that once came dangerously close to extinction. The Navajo still own the land that comprises the monument, which is administered by the National Park Service. Roads run along the canyon's north and south rims, with sweeping overlooks that take in rock spires, Anasazi ruins, and farmland. Aside from one

trail to the bottom, the only other way to break the glass floor is to join a Navajo-led tour.

The Setting

The monument comprises three ravines—Monument Canyon, Canyon del Muerto, and Canyon de Chelly—whose rims range 5,000–7,000 feet in elevation. Down the center runs the Rio de Chelly, from its beginnings in the Chuska Mountains in the east to the mouth of Canyon de Chelly near the town of Chinle, "the place where the water flows out." The amazingly red sandstone walls are over 1,000 feet high in places, and as sheer as the side of a skyscraper. Temperatures range from well below 0°F in winter to over 100°F in summer, but the river-deposited sediments and reliable water supply make the canyon bottom excellent for farming. Side streams dry up in the summer and rage with flash floods during the summer rainy seasons and spring snowmelt. Quicksand is often a danger in wet, sandy spots.

History

People have lived in this sheltered canyon system for millennia, starting with the Basketmaker-phase Anasazi, who left some 700 ruins here between about A.D. 350 and 1300. They pecked hand and foot trails in the stone faces and progressed from pithouses to apartment-style stone dwellings in alcoves, similar to those at Navajo National Monument but on a smaller scale. Plentiful rainfall from 1050–1150 allowed the population to grow significantly, with as many as 800 people living in the main canyon. This bounty was short-lived, however: a regional drought during the 1200s lowered the water table and dried up the canyon's streams, forcing the Puebloans to move on.

The Hopi tribe occupied Canyon de Chelly sporadically thereafter, but by 1700 the Navajo had taken over. They named the place *Tséyi'*, meaning "rock canyon," but it was the Spanish spelling of the word that stuck. From the Hopi, the Navajo acquired dry-farming techniques (peacefully) and women and food (by force), and from the Spanish they stole livestock and horses. Members of many tribes fled here after the Pueblo uprising of 1680, but it was the Navajo who suffered most during Kit Carson's merciless campaign against them in 1863. Carson's men swept the length of the canyon, laying waste to the orchards and slaughtering livestock. After a brave but futile resistance, the survivors were forced on the "Long Walk" to eastern New Mexico. Carson signed a peace treaty with the tribe in 1864 on the present site of the national monument headquarters.

The canyons were declared a national monument in 1931 under a rare arrangement in which management is shared by the tribe and the National Park Service. The Navajo still grow melons, corn, beans, and squash on the fertile canyon bottom, where sheep and goats wander among cottonwoods and peach orchards.

Visiting Canyon de Chelly

Just east of the town of Chinle, a seasonal wash of the same name marks the beginning of the canyon system. You can only descend the rough road leading down into the canyons if you're a resident or on a guided tour. At the **visitor center,** 928/674-5500, www.nps.gov/cach, three miles west of Chinle, are exhibits on the area's history and geology, along with restrooms, pay phones, and drinking water. (Open daily 8 A.M.–6 P.M., 5 P.M. Oct.–Apr.) Entrance to the monument is free, as is a spot at the pleasant **Cottonwood Campground,** open year-round. (There is also a privately owned campground on the South Rim Drive; see below.) Nearby is the beautiful **Thunderbird Lodge,** 928/674-5841, fax 674-8264, which began as a trading post built by Sam Day in 1902. The original post building is now the cafeteria, decorated with Navajo rugs. The lodge is open year-round, with rooms for $100–120, and a gift shop with a selection that would make Day proud. They also offer tours of the canyon.

Canyon de Chelly consists of four main gorges and many side canyons, slicing generally eastward into Defiance Plateau. From a car you can access only the northern and southern edges, but the fantastic views almost make up for the limitation. Short trails lead to the cliff edges. Beware at the overlooks, not only of sharp drop-offs but also of highly skilled and incredibly fast car thieves. Break-ins have been a serious problem in the past; ask at the visitor center for an update. You definitely don't want to leave anything of value in plain view. The two rim drives would make an excellent bicycle ride except for the complete lack of anything close to a bike lane.

North Rim Drive

Also called U.S. 64, this road runs along the Canyon del Muerto, connecting Chinle to Diné College and Tsaile on U.S. 12. The canyon was named the "Canyon of the Dead" in Spanish by a Smithsonian anthropologist who excavated many buried bodies among its ruins. Just over five miles from the visitor center is the **Ledge Ruin Overlook,** looking down on a ruin dated to the 11th and 12th centuries. Two more miles brings you to the **Antelope House Overlook,** above a ruin named for pictographs of running antelopes painted by a Navajo artist around 1830. The ruins themselves, and artwork left by the Anasazi, are more than a thousand years older. Directly

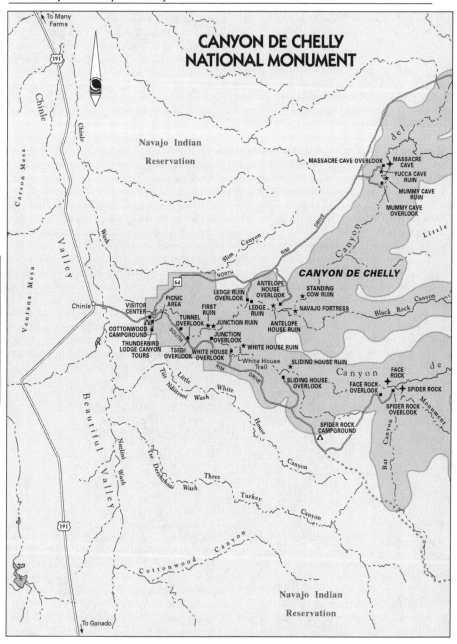

NAVAJO & HOPI COUNTRY

across the canyon, above the junction of the Canyon del Muerto and Black Rock Canyon to the south, is the **Navajo Fortress,** an aerie where Navajo warriors hid from Kit Carson, sneaking down at night for water and food. Carson waited below, enduring showers of stones, until the starving Navajo surrendered. Just upcanyon is **Standing Cow Ruin,** where Navajo pictographs show a blue and white cow and a priest accompanying a Spanish cavalry unit.

The next turnoff is 18 miles from the visitor center. Take a right at the fork for **Mummy Cave Overlook,** named for two mummies found in the ruins that fill two caves, thought to be occupied between 300 and 1300. A right at the fork will bring you to **Massacre Cave Overlook.** When the Spanish sent Lt. Antonio de Narbona into the canyon in 1805 to quell Navajo raids, he found a group of women, children, and elders hiding here while the men were off hunting deer in the Lukachukai Mountains. In two days, Spanish riflemen killed 115 of the Navajo by bouncing bullets off the canyon ceiling from the rim above, and took 33 prisoners. The bones of the victims remain in the cave untouched, per Navajo custom.

South Rim Drive

Although not a through road, the South Rim Drive offers even more impressive views than the northern route. You'll pass the **Tunnel Overlook** and the **Tsegi Overlook** over the upper canyon before reaching the **Junction Overlook,** where Canyon del Muerto joins Canyon de Chelly. **First Ruin** and **Junction Ruin** are both visible from here. Six miles from the visitor center is the turnoff for the **White House Overlook,** which offers not only a great view but also the only way to reach the canyon bottom without a guide. The trail down to **White House Ruin,** dated to about A.D. 1200, is just over one mile from the canyon edge 500 feet down to the canyon floor and across it. The steep, rocky trail passes through a few short tunnels, a farm, and an orchard before crossing the stream in front of the well-preserved ruins (bring water). Tribal members sell jewelry near the well-preserved ruins (restrooms nearby). Don't wander off the trail without a guide.

Farther down the rim drive is the turnoff for the overlook above **Sliding House Ruin** and the **Spider Rock Campground,** 928/674-8261 or 877/910-CAMP, spiderrock@earthlink.net, home.earthlink.net/~spiderrock. Owned by tribal member Howard Smith (no relation), this place has tent sites for $10 and RV sites for $15, as well as solar-heated showers ($2) and two authentic hogans starting at $25. The South Rim Drive continues southeast as Route 7 (unpaved), but follow the pavement northeast back into the monument to the **Spider Rock Overlook,** the park's most outstanding viewpoint. An 800-foot rock tower thrusts from the canyon bottom where three canyons come together. The monolith is understandably special to the Navajo, who call it *Tse' Na' ashjé'ii* and tell of the supernatural being who lives on top. Spider Woman teaches weaving on a loom whose warp is the rays of the sun. Navajo mothers once warned their children to behave or else Spider Woman would carry them to her perch, which is white with tiny bones.

Tours

Canyon de Chelly Unimog Tours, 928/674-5433 or 309-9988, www.canyondechellytours.com, leonskyhorse@yahoo.com, offers tours of the canyon bottom in a Jeep, the military-esque, natural-gas-powered Unimog, or your own 4WD vehicle, starting at $50 for half a day. Three-hour tours leave the Holiday Inn parking lot at 9 A.M. and 1 P.M. for $12 pp. The **Tseyi Guide Association** also offers vehicle tours for $15 per hour, and hiking tours (15 people max) for the same price. Ask at the visitor center for details. Vehicle tours booked at the Thunderbird lodge run $40 pp for a half day and $65 for a full day, all the way to Spider Rock and back. Lupita and Jon McClanahan live in the canyon and operate **Foot Path Journeys,** 928/724-3366, www.footpathjourneys.com, tours@footpathjourneys.com, offering hiking, backpacking, and camping trips.

Chinle

There isn't much in the town of Chinle itself aside from a **Best Western,** 928/674-5875, fax 674-3715, with 100 rooms for $100–140, and the **Holiday Inn,** 928/674-5000, fax 674-8264 ($100–120). Both have heated pools and restaurants open daily for all meals. The Chinle Comprehensive Health Care Facility is one of the best hospitals on the reservation, combining traditional Navajo healing practices with modern medicine; it even includes a hogan for ceremonies. Look for labels in Navajo on products in Basha's Grocery Store, and for souvenirs try **Navajo Arts & Crafts Enterprises,** 928/674-5338, at the main intersection.

Many Farms

North of Chinle at the intersection of U.S. 59 and 191 is a settlement called *Dá'ák'ehaláni* by the Navajo. Several hundred small farms are cultivated in the area. The **Many Farms Inn,** 928/781-6362, mfhsinn@manyfarms.bia.edu, behind the Many Farms High School, is run by Navajo students studying hotel management and tourism. Rooms in a school dormitory with shared bathrooms are $30 per night, and there's a TV lounge, a gym, and basketball courts.

HUBBELL TRADING POST NATIONAL HISTORIC SITE

The oldest continuously operating trading post on the Navajo Reservation was built on the bank of Ganado Wash in 1871. Clerk and interpreter John Lorenzo Hubbell bought the place seven years later, and it stayed in his family until the National Park Service took over in 1967. Hubbell quickly turned the post into one of the most successful in the Southwest, buying out and opening other posts throughout the Four Corners and earning the nickname "Don" Lorenzo, a Spanish term of respect, for his fair trading and hospitality.

A true friend of the Navajo, Hubbell spoke their language fluently (along with three others) and advised weavers on which designs would fetch the best prices. (The handsome Ganado pattern, with its deep red wool and cross motif, is still woven.) He brought a silversmith from Mexico to teach his art and treated Navajo struck down by smallpox. The Hubbells—Lorenzo, his

© ED CHAMBERLIN

The old Hubbell Trading Post, opened on the Navajo Reservation in 1871, is still open for business.

wife Una Rubi, and their four children—amassed one of the largest art collections in the Southwest in their home next to the post.

Today the original 160-acre homestead is administered by the National Park Service, 928/755-3475, www.nps.gov/hutr, and the old trading post is run by the Western National Parks Association (www.spma.org). They still buy and sell crafts, food, and supplies, though most sales now are to tourists, and they stock a king's ransom in Navajo rugs in the rug room. Demonstrations and auctions of Indian crafts are held throughout the year, and daily tours take visitors into the Hubbell home ($2 pp), which retains all its original furnishings (except for the rugs). The ceiling in the main hallway is covered with dozens of woven baskets, and works by artists who visited the family adorn the walls, including many of E. A. Burbank's "red

heads"—portraits, mostly of Indians, done with red conté crayon.

The post, one mile west of Ganado on U.S. 264, is open daily 8 A.M.–6 P.M. (5 P.M. in winter), and admission is free. More information on the post, including its craft auctions, can be obtained from the nonprofit organization **Friends of Hubbell Trading Post National Historic Site,** www.friendsofhubbell.org, hogan@friendsofhubbell.org.

Lorenzo Hubbell also helped start the **Ganado Mission,** the largest Presbyterian mission to the Navajo, in 1903. The mission concentrated on education and health care early on, and was transferred to the Navajo Nation Health Foundation in 1974. On its grounds, across U.S. 264 from the trading post, you'll find the **Cafe Sage,** 928/755-3411 ext. 292, serving inexpensive cafeteria fare Mon.–Fri. 7 A.M.–7 P.M., Sat. 9 A.M.–2 P.M.

Hopi Reservation

A cultural island within the larger Navajo Reservation, the Hopi Reservation centers around 12 ancient villages on three fingerlike mesas that rise to 7,200 feet. First, Second, and Third Mesas were named from east to west, since early explorers arrived from the east, and are strung together by U.S. 264 between Tuba City and Ganado. A few of the Hopi villages have been inhabited for over eight centuries. This is a quiet, isolated place, whose main draw is the almost tangible sense of tradition that hangs in the clear air.

The boundaries of the Hopis' ancestral lands, or *Tutsqua,* extended from Canyon de Chelly and the Four Corners to the San Francisco Peaks, and from Navajo Mountain to the Zuñi Pueblo near Gallup. The 600-foot-high Hopi mesas are dotted with homes made from adobe, cinderblock, and stone, standing alongside trailers, pickup trucks, and the shells of unfinished or abandoned buildings. Ladders poke out of kivas, both above and below ground level, and scattered outhouses indicate which of the traditional villages do not have plumbing. Most of the Hopi are peaceful farmers or artisans and highly respectful of tradition, although more and more live in modern towns in between the older villages perched atop the steep-walled mesas.

A few of the Hopi villages have been inhabited for over eight centuries. This is a quiet, isolated place, whose main draw is the almost tangible sense of tradition that hangs in the clear air.

The Hopi welcome visitors; they just expect you to behave yourself. The tribe guards its privacy and traditions even more than the Navajo, so photography, videotaping, sketching, and any other methods of recording are *strictly* prohibited—no exceptions. Accept the fact that this is one part of your vacation you'll have to recall from memory, because if you're caught breaking this rule, you will be asked to leave.

Most social dances are open to non-Hopi, but many kachina dances and all snake dances and flute ceremonies are closed to visitors. If you want to watch a ceremony, be aware that you will be considered a part of the collective spiritual effort, so you should act and dress respectfully. This means no shorts, short skirts, or T-shirts, no loud talking, and no striding across the plaza to get a closer look at someone's headdress. Many residents sell crafts and food from their homes, advertising with signs out front—try some traditional, wafer-thin *piiki* bread, made with blue corn flour. Don't wander far down back alleys, though, particularly during ceremonies, and get permission from a village leader if you plan on spending more than a few hours in any village.

Visitors are barred from certain culturally sensitive areas on the reservation; check with the Hopi Cultural Center on Second Mesa for a list of these sites and a schedule of religious ceremonies open to the public. A number of tribal members offer guided cultural and archaeological tours of the area; try **Gary Tso,** P.O. Box 434, Second Mesa, AZ 86043, 928/734-2567, lhhunter58@hotmail.com, or **Bertram "Tsaava" Tsavadawa,** P.O. Box 412, Second Mesa, AZ 86043, 928/306-7849 or 928/306-7849. Professional anthropologist **Micah Loma'omvaya** offers archaeological tours to ruins and other sites on the reservation, starting at $65 pp for a half day. Contact him at P.O. Box 627, Kykotsmovi, AZ 86039, 928/734-9549, hopianthro@yahoo.com, www.hopitours.com.

The information in the section below is listed from east to west, following U.S. 264 from Ganado to Tuba City.

EAST OF FIRST MESA

The natural oasis of **Keams Canyon,** called *Pongsikya* by the Hopi, was originally known to Anglo settlers as Peach Orchard Springs. Englishman Thomas Keam, once a trooper under Col. Kit Carson (whose 1863 signature is inscribed in the canyon wall), opened a trading post here in 1869. He married a Hopi woman

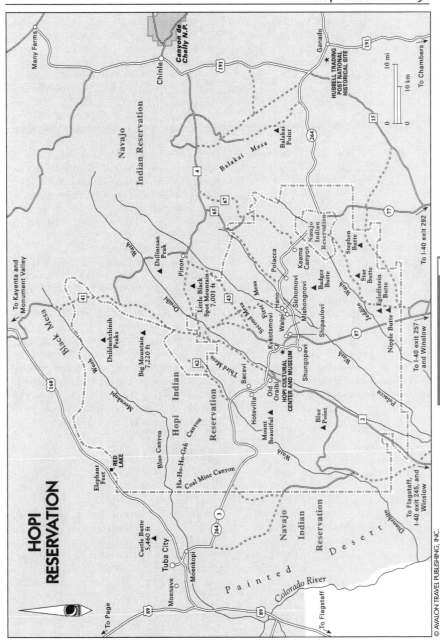

HOPI RESERVATION

© AVALON TRAVEL PUBLISHING, INC.

NAVAJO & HOPI COUNTRY

and quarreled strongly with the BIA superintendent, who demanded that the Hopi stop their ceremonial dances and send their children to the nearby BIA boarding school under threat of force. The superintendent was eventually dismissed.

Today, Keams Canyon is a U.S. government town with a hospital, post office, and **Keam's Canyon Shopping Center.** McGee's Indian Art Gallery, 928/738-2295, www.hopiart.com, inside, centers around Keam's original trading post and sells an excellent selection of local crafts, particularly kachinas. They've added a grocery store, a Laundromat, and a small cafe (928/738-2296), open Mon.–Fri. for all meals and Sat. for breakfast and lunch. They also offer lodgings; call for details. Follow the road up Keams Wash 1.5 miles to a shelter on the west (left), marking an inscription left by Kit Carson.

At the southern tip of Antelope Mesa are the ruins of **Awatovi** (ah-WAHT-oh-vee), which has a bloody history. A Franciscan church built in this Hopi village in 1629 was destroyed by the tribe and residents of other pueblos who feared the friars' influence. When Awatovi's residents allowed the missionaries back in two decades later, however, the other Hopi villages took drastic steps. Almost all of the men in Awatovi were killed, and its women and children scattered among other villages. The area is closed to the public.

FIRST MESA

At the base of First Mesa is **Polacca** (po-LAH-kah), founded in 1890 by a resident of Hano. The BIA tried to convince Hopi in the older villages up above to move here, but to this day most of Polacca's residents still consider themselves to be from Walpi or Sichomovi. In Polacca is the turnoff for the road to the top of First Mesa, a steep and narrow paved road just over a mile long. (Larger vehicles must park at the bottom.)

The first traditional village on the mesa is **Hano,** which was founded by Tewa Indians from the Rio Grande near Albuquerque. Fleeing the Spanish after the Pueblo Revolt of 1680, the Tewa were allowed to settle here by the Hopi if they agreed to guard access to the mesa. This was the home of the famous Hopi potter Nam-

peyo, born in 1860, who based her work on the ancient techniques used in pottery shards dug up by anthropologists. Her legacy continues in various homes selling pottery; look for signs.

Sichomovi (see-CHO-mo-vi), just beyond Hano, was founded in 1750 by residents of Walpi. Here in Ponsi Hall, 928/737-2262, you can arrange tours of Walpi, offered Mon.–Fri. from 9 A.M. to 4 or 5 P.M. ($10 pp). **Walpi** (WAHL-pee) itself perches on the narrow southernmost tip of the mesa, and is one of the most evocative spots in the Four Corners. The name, meaning "the gap," refers to the narrow neck of stone that isolates it almost completely from the rest of the mesa—and, it seems, the modern age. With nothing but sky and stone in every direction, Walpi anchors a striking panorama that has hardly changed in centuries.

The tiny, exceedingly traditional village sits above the original settlement of Old Walpi, which was inhabited since the 13th century but abandoned for this more secure location after the Pueblo Revolt. The ruins of an old Spanish mission are also visible (although closed to visitors), as are prehistoric foot trails up the mesa and stone depressions used to catch rainwater. Walpi lacks running water and electricity, and can be visited only on an authorized tour arranged in Sichomovi. Along with its setting, the village is known for its crafts and its ceremonies, which are unfortunately closed to the public.

SECOND MESA

U.S. 264 is joined by U.S. 87 at the foot of Second Mesa. Near the intersection are a **post office,** the **Sekakuku supermarket,** 928/737-2632, which offers takeout deli food, and **LKD's Diner,** 928/737-2717, serving a small menu for breakfast and lunch Mon.–Sat. in season (Mon.–Fri. otherwise). Al Sakakuku's **Hopi Fine Arts** has a good selection of crafts.

Villages

Two routes take U.S. 264 to the top of Second Mesa. They split half a mile west of the U.S. 87 intersection, where you'll find a **gas station** and the **Honani Crafts Galery,** 602/737-2238, which has an excellent array of jewelry behind four stained glass windows depicting kachinas. From here a steep, twisting track—more of a loading ramp than a road—leads up to two traditional villages. **Shipaulovi** (shih-PAW-lohvee) has little more than an old abandoned trading post and a few homes. The name means "place of the mosquitoes." **Mishongnovi** (miSHONG-no-vee) sits at the very top of the mesa, with not a yard to spare between the building walls and the cliff edges.

The other route takes you past the turnoff for **Shungopavi** (shon-GO-pah-vee), meaning "sand grass spring place." Its story is similar to Walpi's— an older village at the base of the mesa was abandoned for a more secure spot after the Pueblo Revolt. A number of galleries sell jewelry and other crafts, including Dawa's and Qöötsa-Omaw Arts & Crafts. You can grab a bite here at Hilda-Burger, 928/734-9278.

Hopi Cultural Center

Where the two routes rejoin on top of Second Mesa, this small complex, 928/734-2401, fax 928/734-6651, hopi@psv.com, serves as unofficial nexus of the reservation. It has a museum of Hopi crafts and cultural items (open Mon.–Fri. 8 A.M.–5 P.M., $4 pp), as well as a motel with modest but clean rooms for $95 ($65–70 Oct.–Mar.) and a campground. A restaurant, serving dishes ($5–7) such as burgers, blue corn pancakes, and *nöqkwivi,* a traditional hominy and mutton stew. Across the way another small gallery, 928/734-2412, sells paintings and beautiful kachinas for $300 and up; it's open Tues. noon–5:30 P.M., Wed. 9:30 A.M.–4:30 P.M., Thurs.–Sat. 9:30 A.M.–5:30 P.M., Sun 10 A.M.– 3 P.M., and Monday and Tuesday morning by appointment only (call 928/737-2756). **Hopi Arts and Crafts,** 928/734-2463, is nearby in a two-story pink building (open Mon.–Sat.). Artisans are trained in this cooperative silvercafting guild, established in 1949, and they sell a variety of crafts. Many trainees have gone on to start their own successful businesses.

A mostly dirt road (U.S. 43) leaves from here north up Second Mesa, joining U.S. 41 at Pinon, offering a scenic alternate way to reach Chinle

and Canyon de Chelly. Other galleries are scattered along the roads on Second Mesa. A short drive east of the Cultural Center is Janice and Joseph Day's **Tsakurshovi,** 928/734-2478, a store with a great selection of Hopi and Navajo work, including jewelry, kachinas, baskets, and exquisite jewelry by Emerson Smith, a Navajo who works while he's out herding sheep. The Days supply the Hopi with materials for their ceremonies, which explains all the turtle shells, furs, and herbs around, and are a font of information on the area.

THIRD MESA

Kykotsmovi (kee-KOOTS-moh-vee) was founded by residents of Old Oraibi near a spring at the base of Third Mesa. Today it's surrounded by fruit trees and is the home of the modern Hopi government. The **Hopi Tribe Cultural Preservation Office,** 928/734-2244, provides visitor information out of the Tribal Headquarters building, and the **Kykotsmovi Village Store,** 928/734-2456, offers sandwiches, pizzas, and other deli items. U.S. 2 heads south from here for I-15 at the town of Leupp ("loop"). This is the quickest way back to Flagstaff, and is a lovely, empty drive that's paved the entire way. At the turnoff is **Gentle Rain Designs,** 928/734-9535, a friendly place that sells clothing made from cotton, denim, and recycled-plastic fleece, all decorated with Hopi motifs. (Open Tues.–Sun. 9 A.M.–5 P.M.)

On the way up onto Third Mesa to Old Oraibi you'll pass **Pumpkin Seed Point,** a picnic area with a great view of the Hopi Buttes to the south. Soon comes the turnoff for Old Oraibi, two miles west of Kykotsmovi, where you'll find the pink **Monongya Gallery,** 928/734-2344, with a large selection of paintings, jewelry, pottery, and baskets made by various tribes. Their selection of kachinas is one of the largest around. Open Mon.–Sat. 9 A.M.–5 P.M., Sun 10 A.M.–4 P.M.

Inhabited since the mid-12th century, **Old Oraibi** (oh-RYE-bee) is arguably the oldest continuousy occupied community in the country. In 1906, this windswept collection of stone and cinderblock buildings was split by internal strife. The Bear clan, led by Tawaquaptewa, wanted to cooperate with the U.S. government's Indian Service, while the Skeleton clan, led by Youkeoma, refused. They settled the dispute with a pushing contest: a line was etched in the mesa, and the groups lined up on either side, with their respective leaders in front. At a signal each started shoving, and when the dust cleared Tawaquaptewa's clan had won. Youkeoma led his people off to found Hotevilla, where they were labeled "hostiles" by the U.S. government. The event is commemorated by an inscription in the mesa, near the line itself, which reads:

> *Well it have to be this way not*
> *pass me over this LINE*
> *it will be DONE.*
> *Spt. 8, 1906.*

Wandering the streets of Old Oraibi is an experience in time travel. Notice the ruins of the old Mennonite church at the south end of the mesa, built in 1901 and destroyed by lightning (a second strike) in 1942, to the quiet delight of many of the town's traditional residents. A few homes sell crafts, including the **Monongya Gallery,** 928/734-2344. Resident Bertram Tsavadawa offers guided walking tours; contact him at 928/734-9544 or 928/306-7849.

A few miles west on U.S. 264 are the villages of **Hotevilla** (HOAT-vih-lah), founded by Youkeoma's people, and **Bacavi** (BAH-kah-vee), founded three years later by another Oraibi splinter group. These are residential villages without much to see.

WEST OF THIRD MESA

Just over 30 miles west of Bacavi and Hotevilla is **Coal Mine Canyon,** a marvelous ravine that leads north to join Blue Canyon and, eventually, Moenkopi Wash toward Tuba City. Look for a dirt road between mile markers 336 and 337 leading to a windmill, beside the rodeo grounds. The Navajo call this serrated landscape *hááhonoojí,* or "jagged," and the Hopi tell of *Quayowuuti,* the Eagle Woman from Old Oraibi, who stepped from the edge of the canyon to her death. Her ghost is said to appear under the full moon.

Just east of Tuba City on U.S. 264 is the town of **Moenkopi,** a small cultural island separated from the greater Hopi Reservation. "The place of running water" was founded in the 1870s by farmers from Oraibi, who would run to their fields and back—a distance of over 30 miles— several times a week. Like many Hopi villages, it is split into upper and lower sections.

East of Flagstaff

I-40 leaves the San Francisco Mountains for the high desert plains as it rolls east toward New Mexico. It follows the Little Colorado River upstream from Winslow to Holbrook, where it is joined by the Rio Puerco. Rugged hills dotted with buttes and junipers continue past the Petrified Forest and Painted Desert to the southern end of Defiance Plateau at the state line.

METEOR CRATER

About 50,000 years ago, a meteorite 150 feet across slammed into the Arizona plain at upwards of 30,000 mph, igniting an explosion greater than 20 million tons of TNT. The impact threw 175 million tons of stone into the atmos-

phere, uplifted the bedrock by 150 feet, and turned graphite into diamond at pressures of over 20 million pounds per square inch—and it left a really, *really* big hole in the ground.

You can fit 20 football fields into the crater, which is 2.5 miles in circumference and deeper than the Washington Monument is tall. It was originally thought to be volcanic in origin, but the tireless research of Philadelphia mining engineer Daniel Barringer convinced the world otherwise, even though his efforts to find the meteorite itself didn't pan out.

The "first proved and best preserved meteorite crater in the world" is privately owned, with a well-done museum on its edge with exhibits on astrogeology and space travel. (A computer simulation of a meteor impact offers the perverse pleasure of seeing how big and fast you can make your imaginary comet before it vaporizes the earth.) There's a gift shop and snack bar, and guided walks around the rim trail included in admission ($12 adults, $5 children 6–17). On the crater floor, a dummy figure in a space suit provides a sense of scale; Apollo astronauts trained here before going to the moon. The crater, 928/289-2362/5898, www.meteorcrater.com, info@meteorcrater.com, is open daily 8 A.M.–5 P.M., located five miles south of I-40 exit 233. On the way here you'll pass the **Meteor Crater RV Park**, 928/289-4002, with 71 sites ($18–20), a gas station, showers, and laundry.

WINSLOW

This city was founded in 1882 as a railroad stop near Sunset Crossing, one of the few places to ford the sandy-bottomed Little Colorado River. Winslow hit its stride in the early 1900s, when cross-country traffic poured in off the new Route 66 and local ranchers shipped their stock out through the rail terminal. Fred Harvey opened La Posada, perhaps the prettiest of his Spanish-style hotels, and in 1930, Charles Lindberg flew to Winslow Airport, which he had designed as a stop between Chicago and Los Angeles.

The town slid toward the end of the 20th century, when traffic began to pass by on both the interstate and the railroad. Still, you've probably heard of Winslow if you've ever listened to pop radio: the Eagles sang about "Standing on a corner in Winslow, Arizona" in their hit "Take it Easy." Today, Winslow (pop. 11,000) has a rundown, south-of-the-border ambiance, with lots of crumbling and boarded-up adobe buildings. It's hoped that the restoration of La Posada will inject some much-needed vitality into the town, which has a number of interesting sights within day-trip distance.

The Winslow corner made famous in the Eagles song "Take it Easy" is commemorated by Ron Adamson's bronze statue and John Pugh's mural.

© JULIAN SMITH

NAVAJO & HOPI COUNTRY

Sights

The actual corner that Jackson Browne and Glen Frey sang about is commemorated at the **Standin' on a Corner Park** at Second Street (Route 66) and Kinsley Avenue. You can have your photo taken next to the statue of one of the Eagles holding a guitar, or the "girl, my Lord, in a flatbed Ford" painted in a two-story mural on the facing wall. This part of downtown is starting to cash in on its Route 66 heritage, with shops offering souvenirs and memorabilia.

The quirky **Old Trails Museum,** 212 Kinsley St., 928/289-5861, is housed in a 1921 bank building, nicknamed "Winslow's attic." An interesting collection includes dinosaur bones, Route 66 memorabilia, and the still of a local moonshiner, who lived to the age of 97 on a daily breakfast of black coffee, raw eggs, and a shot of his own firewater. Open Tues.–Sat. 1–5 P.M. (closed Wed. Nov.–Mar.), free.

North of Winslow on the banks of the Little Colorado River is **Homolovi Ruins State Park,** 928/289-4106, www.pr.state.az.us/parkhtml/homolovi.html, opened in 1993. The site's four main pueblo ruins were inhabited in the 13th and 14th centuries by the ancestors of the Hopi, who eventually migrated north to the three Hopi mesas. Their name for the group archaeologists call the Anasazi (or the Ancestral Puebloans) is the *Hisat'sinom,* and the Hopi still consider this part of the ancestral homeland and make periodic pilgrimages. Over 300 archaeological sites have been uncovered here, and three of the four pueblos are open to the public. There is also a visitor center and a 53-site campground ($12–22); admission is $5. To get there, take I-40 exit 257 to U.S. 87, go north 1.3 miles to the entrance on the left, then proceed another 2 miles to the visitor center. Open daily 7 A.M.–7:30 P.M. (visitor center 8 A.M.–5 P.M.).

Accommodations and Food

Architect Mary Coulter designed **La Posada,** 303 E. Second St., 928/289-4366, www.laposada.org, for hotelier Fred Harvey in 1930, calling it her masterpiece. Built in the style of an old Spanish hacienda, the "Last Great Railroad Hotel" counted among its guests luminaries such as Albert Einstein, Howard Hughes, Dorothy Lamour, and the Crown Prince of Japan. All trains between Los Angeles stopped here, as did planes before better designs let them make the trip without refueling. It was closed for 40 years and nearly razed before it was rescued from the wrecking ball in the late 1990s and put on the historical preservation list.

Restorations were still ongoing as of 2002, but the hotel was already well on its way to its former glory. Suits of armor, paintings, and religious icons make up the eclectic art collection, and trains still rumble past the cottonwoods and gardens out back. The **Turquoise Room Restaurant,** 928/289-2888, serves contemporary Southwest cuisine including recipes from the Harvey heyday of the 1930s (open for all meals). On either side of the restaurant are the Martini Lounge and the excellent gift shop. This is truly a special place, well worth a stop if only for lunch. Rooms are $80–100.

Winslow has many inexpensive hotels, including a **Days Inn,** 2035 W. U.S. 66, 928/289-1010, fax 928/289-5778, **Motel 6,** 520 W. Desmond St., 928/289-9581, fax 928/289-5642, and an **Econo Lodge,** 1706 N. Park Dr., 928/289-4687, fax 928/289-9377, with rooms from $50–100. The **Best Western Adobe Inn,** 1701 N. Park Dr., 928/289-4638, fax 928/289-5514, has a restaurant and a heated outdoor pool ($120). **Freddie's RV Park,** 928/289-3201, is north of I-40 exit 255 east of Winslow, and has sites for $15 with all hookups.

Bonnie and Rob Garrett run the **Santa Fe Whistle Stop,** 114 E. Third St., 928/289-5277, serving up "burgers that stop trains" in a 1940s-era diner. **The Seattle Grind,** 106 E. Second St., 928/289-2859, is near the Corner Park, and has local art on display and live music to complement the java. Family owned for half a century, the **Casa Blanca Cafe,** 1201 E. Second St., 928/289-4191, serves up genuine Mexican food every day of the week for lunch and dinner.

Shopping

The photogenically weathered Lorenzo Hubbell Co. Trading Post, 523 W. Second St., now also houses the **Arizona Indian Artists Coopera-**

tive, 928/289-3986. A good variety of crafts are offered at competitive prices, direct from the artisans. Open Mon.–Fri. 9 A.M.–5 P.M. **Roadworks Gifts & Souvenirs,** 101 W. Second St., 928/289-5423, is on the second floor overlooking the Corner Park. They stock every kind of Route 66 souvenir you can think of, plus a few hundred more: T-shirts, bumper stickers, books, magnets, postcards, mugs. Don't miss R. Waldemire's postcards and map-guide to Route 66; he used to run the Route 66 visitor center in Seligman, west of Flagstaff, before moving south to the mountains. His detailed drawings are works of art.

Getting There

Amtrak serves Winslow, but the station (next to La Posada on East Second Street) is unstaffed; call 800/872-7245 for information. The **Greyhound** station, 928/289-2171, is at 2201 N. Park Dr.

Information

The **Winslow Chamber of Commerce,** 300 W. North Rd., 928/289-2434, www.winslowarizona.org, winslowchamber@cybertrails.com, operates a visitor center north of I-40 exit 253, open Mon.–Fri. 8 A.M.–5 P.M.

HOLBROOK

This ranching center was founded, as so many other Southwestern cities were, with the arrival of the railroad in 1881. The second-largest ranch in the county, the Hashknife, was based nearby, with cowboys herding up to 60,000 cows and 2,000 horses across two million acres. This attracted rustlers, naturally, and for a time Holbrook was known as the town "too tough for women and children." Patrons at the Bucket of Blood Saloon tried to outdo each other in downing shots of whiskey "before they touched the bottom of the glass," and cowboys would gallop through town on payday with guns blazing, crying "Hide out, kids, the cowboys are in town!" In 1887, Sheriff Perry Owens (scoffed at on his arrival as a bit of a dandy) single-handedly killed three members of the Cooper-Blevins gang in a

gunfight, and wounded a fourth. Until 1914, Holbrook was known as the only county seat in the country without a church.

Today Holbrook (pop. 4,700) provides a rest stop along I-40 and the easiest access to Petrified Forest National Park.

Sights and Information

Holbrook's 1898 county courthouse has been turned into the **Navajo County Museum,** 100 E. Arizona St., full to the rafters with local history. The collection focuses on Holbrook's colorful Wild West past, and the claustrophobic jail downstairs is decorated with prisoners' graffiti. (Open daily 8 A.M.–5 P.M., free.) The offices of the **Holbrook Chamber of Commerce,** 928/524-6558 or 800/524-2459, www.ci.holbrook.az.us, holbrookchamb@cybertrails.com, are here as well. (The museum shares the same telephone numbers.)

Accommodations and Food

Fittingly, Hopi Drive and Navajo Boulevard are Holbrook's main commercial arteries. Here you'll find most of the city's hotels and restaurants. Leading the least-expensive category by a wide margin is the **Wigwam Motel,** 811 W. Hopi Dr., 928/524-3048, pages.zdnet.com/john3248. It looks like a classic car collection parked among big fake teepees, and that's just what it is. Built in the 1940s, the wigwams still contain their original furniture and all their Route 66 charm. Other options under $50 include the **Budget Host,** 235 W. Hopi Dr., 928/524-3809, and the **Relax Inn,** 2418 E. Navajo Blvd., 928/524-6815, fax 928/524-2328.

In the $50–100 category are a **Days Inn,** 2601 Navajo Blvd., 928/524-6949, fax 928/524-6665, and a **Comfort Inn,** 2602 E. Navajo Blvd., 928/524-6131, fax 928/524-2281. The **OK RV Park,** 1576 Roadrunner Rd., 928/524-3226, has 120 sites for $14–22. There's also a **KOA Kampground,** 928/524-6689 at 102 Hermosa Dr., with 208 sites plus all the usual KOA amenities for $29 (full hookups) or $20 (tents).

Authentic diner fare befitting Holbrook's location on Old Route 66 is what makes **Joe & Aggie's Cafe,** 120 W. Hopi Dr., 928/524-6540, such a gem. From the honey bottles for the sopaipillas to the chicken-fried steak platters, Holbrook's oldest restaurant (1946) does Mexican and American road food right. **El Rancho Restaurant,** 867 Navajo Blvd., 928/524-3332, also serves good and inexpensive Mexican meals for breakfast, lunch, and dinner Tues.–Sun. For tasty Italian food try the **Mesa Italiana,** 2318 E. Navajo Blvd., 928/524-6696, open daily for lunch and dinner.

Shopping

With all the petrified wood for sale in town, it's hard to believe there's any left in the park—but luckily the law dictates that anything offered for sale must be taken from private land. Polished specimens, geodes, turquoise, and other geological curiosities are offered at places like the **Rainbow Rock Shop,** 101 Navajo Blvd., 928/524-2384, with huge green dinosaurs guarding its entrance near the train tracks. **McGee's Beyond Native Tradition Gallery,** 2114 E. Navajo Blvd., 928/524-1977, is the best of Holbrook's many native crafts stores, stocking an excellent collection of rugs, kachinas, baskets, jewelry, and pottery.

Entertainment and Events

If you happen to arrive in Holbrook in late January and have someone in Scottsdale you want to write to, you're in luck: re-enactors with the **Hashknife Pony Express** carry mail on horseback along the old express route. (Send your mail, marked "Via Pony Express" in the lower left-hand corner, enclosed in another envelope addressed to "Postmaster, Holbrook, AZ 86025.") Holbrook's **Old West Days** in mid-June bring more re-enactors, music, crafts, dancing, and bike and foot races. In September the **Navajo County Fair** arrives, and the **Christmas Parade of Lights** illuminates downtown Holbrook the first Saturday in December.

Native American dances are held weekend evenings in summer on the lawn next to the courthouse; ask for a schedule inside.

Getting There

The town **Greyhound** stop, 928/524-3832, is at the Circle K at 101 Mission Lane and Navajo Blvd.

PETRIFIED FOREST NATIONAL PARK

In the late Triassic Period, 225 million years ago, this part of Arizona crawled with giant reptiles and fish-eating amphibians. Some of the first dinosaurs plodded among cycads, ferns, and early conifers. Huge *Araucarioxylon arizonicum* trees, some up to 200 feet high, were uprooted by wind or old age and swept down into a vast floodplain to be buried in silt and mud. Over the eons, silica-bearing groundwater seeped through the wood and replaced it, cell by cell, with silica. Iron-rich minerals tinted the silica a rainbow of brilliant colors: hematite made red and pink; goethite caused yellow, orange, and brown; and manganese dioxide created purples and blues. Erosion eventually exposed the fossilized logs in the hillsides of the Painted Desert. (The native legend regarding the logs' origins is even more colorful: a weary goddess had killed a rabbit and tried to make a fire, but the logs were too wet, so in anger she cursed them to remain forever fireproof—as stone.)

Today this 93,500-acre park protects one of the world's largest and best-preserved concentrations of petrified wood. The petrifaction process was so slow and exact that in some trees the original cell structure is still clearly visible. A wealth of late-Triassic fossils and ruins and petroglyphs from 10,000 years of human habitation complete the picture. It's hard to believe that this area wasn't always valued for its historic significance, but the logs were once pulverized to make industrial grinding powder. The area was declared a national monument by President Theodore Roosevelt in 1906, and in 1962 it was made a park.

Visiting the Park

A 28-mile drive is the park's backbone, arcing from I-40 exit 311 to U.S. 180 east of Holbrook. Everything is on or near this road, which connects to seven short trails. Very few people venture off it, but backcountry camping is permitted (with a free permit) in the psychedelic Painted Desert section north of the interstate. Entrance is

$10 per vehicle, and the park, 928/524-6228, www.nps.gov/pefo, is open daily 8 A.M.–5 P.M. (7 A.M.–6 P.M. in summer).

Warnings against stealing petrified wood are everywhere, but some people still do it even though there is plenty for sale in Holbrook legally gathered from private lands. "Conscience wood" displays showcase pieces that guilt-ridden visitors have returned after taking them home, often after a rash of mysteriously bad luck. It doesn't need repeating, but I will anyway: Don't remove *anything* from the park, lest you become like the visitors then-ranger Edward Abbey would ask about smuggled wood at the park gate: "The driver would look me back straight in the eye, sincere and honest as only an American can be, and reply, 'No sir, we don't.' One of the kids in the back seat would say, 'But Daddy, what about that big log we put in the trunk?' "

Starting at the northern end, the **Painted Desert Visitor Center,** offers an introductory video, a bookstore, restrooms, and general information on the park. (Open daily 8 A.M.–5 P.M.) A short distance farther, past viewpoints over the Painted Desert, is the **Painted Desert Inn,** a historic Fred Harvey lodge decorated inside with murals by Hopi artist Fred Kabotie. Native American artists demonstrate crafts here, and rangers lead tours. (Open daily 8 A.M.–4 P.M.)

Keep going past more viewpoints and cross the interstate (no access) and the train tracks to reach the central portion of the park, where most of the prehistoric ruins and petroglyphs are found. The **Puerco Indian Ruins** and **Newspaper Rock** are two of these, but **The Tepees** and **The Haystacks** are actually rock formations. (The ruins are believed to have been occupied twice, between A.D. 1100–1200 and 1300–1400.) A short side road leads to **Blue Mesa,** with panoramic viewpoints and a mile-long interpretive loop trail. Farther down the main road, **Agate Bridge** is a gully under a large petrified log.

The southern part of the park is where you'll find the best petrified wood. A turnoff to the south, 2.6 miles from the southern end of the road, leads to the popular **Long Logs Trail** and **Agate House,** a seven-room structure built by ancient inhabitants entirely out of petrified wood, which has been partially restored. The **Rainbow Forest Museum** displays astounding fossils near a bookstore and information desk (open daily 8 A.M.–5 P.M.) Out back is the short **Giant Logs Trail,** true to its name: one stone stump stands taller than a man. Across the road, **Fred Harvey's Rainbow Gift Shop and Fountain** sells souvenirs and snacks.

Just inside the scenic drive's southern entrance are two places not affiliated with the park: the **Petrified Forest Museum Gift Shop,** 928/524-3470, and the **Crystal Forest Museum and Gift Shop,** 928/524-3500. Both let you satisfy your acquisitive cravings with beautiful petrified wood for sale. They also allow camping on their properties.

Gallup and Vicinity

Although it's outside reservation boundaries, Gallup (pop. 20,000) is the Navajo Nation's most important commercial center. A plethora of arts and crafts shops and galleries, along with a good slice of turn-of-the-century history and the country's premiere Indian gathering, await those who look past the city's weather-beaten facade. Surrounded by the Navajo Reservation and Zuñi Pueblo (and within an hour of Acoma and Laguna Pueblos and Jicarilla Apache Reservation), unpretentious Gallup easily earns the title "Gateway to Indian Country."

A classic, neon-signed stretch of Old Route 66 serves as Gallup's Main Street, parallel to the train tracks. The 12-block downtown area, bounded by Main Street, Hill Avenue, First Street, and Fourth Street, contains most of Gallup's galleries and trading posts, along with a reassuring amount of public artwork. On Second Street near Main Street, there's a mural depicting the Navajo code talkers. Motels and restaurants (mostly serving Mexican food) line Route 66/Main Street toward either end of town. Gritty pawn shops sidle up next to high-end craft boutiques, and Navajo cowboys share the sidewalks with tourists hopping off the interstate for a quiet browse.

Note: The scourge of drunk driving reaches a pinnacle in Gallup. Keep a sharp eye out behind the wheel, especially on weekend nights.

HISTORY

Coal was discovered in the area near the middle of the 19th century, helping to ensure that the Atlantic & Pacific Railroad chose a route that passed near this tiny stagecoach stop. The town itself, named after a railroad paymaster, was founded in 1881 and quickly became a timber and coal mining hub. Between 1880 and 1948, over 50 mines were in operation near Gallup, which stayed relatively quiet as Western cities went. In 1929 alone, 25,177 railroad cars full of coal left the city's freight station, averaging one 70-car train every day of the year. The coal boom drew people

from around the world to Gallup's already diverse ethnic mix, which included members of the Navajo and Hopi tribes and the Acoma and Zuñi Pueblos. Workers from Germany, Italy, Spain, Greece, China, Japan, Austria, Wales, Scotland, and Yugoslavia, among other countries, left descendants who still call the city home.

A 30-car coal train still rumbles out of Gallup seven days a week, and the Santa Fe Railroad passes through town every 15 minutes, but the city has shifted its focus to tourism, particularly the rich arts and crafts traditions of the nearby Indian tribes. Making Gallup "Indian Capital of the World" has been a successful marketing strategy; the city now boasts over 100 trading posts, shops, and galleries, along with a few good museums and some 2,000 hotel and motel rooms for the traffic from I-40.

SIGHTS

The 1916 Santa Fe Train Depot in the center of town was renovated in 1995 and turned into the **Gallup Cultural Center,** 201 E. U.S. 66, 505/863-4131. A sculpture of Manuelito, the famous 19th-century Navajo chief, stands in front of the large blue and gray building. On the second floor is the Storyteller Museum, with dioramas and displays on trading posts and native crafts, illustrated with great old black-and-white photos, and the Ceremonial Gallery, filled with modern Indian art. Films are shows in the Navajo Cinema, and you can grab a bite at El Navajo Cafe, serving an inexpensive breakfast and lunch, including organic espresso drinks, on wood tables and chairs carved by the owner (they're also for sale). Open Mon.–Fri. The gift shop, run by the Southwest Indian Foundation, stocks a good variety of crafts. The whole complex is open daily 8 A.M.–5 P.M.

The Gallup Historical Society runs the **Rex Museum,** 300 W. U.S. 66, 505/863-1363, in what was once the Rex Hotel (c. 1900). Vestiges of Gallup's mining heyday are on display inside. Open Tues.–Sat., 8 A.M.–3:30 P.M. for $2 pp. The **Red Mesa Art Center,** 105 W. Hill,

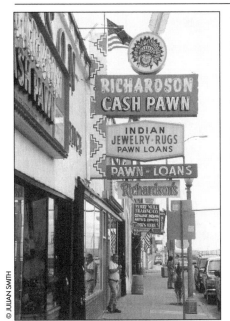

© JULIAN SMITH

Gallup sidewalks evoke a bygone era.

505/722-4209, is a nonprofit run by the Gallup Area Arts Council dedicated to encouraging local artists. They hold a monthly artist lecture series; call for details.

The local Chamber of Commerce has brochures detailing a **walking tour** of historical Gallup. Some two dozen buildings downtown date to the turn of the 20th century or before, including the 1925 Grand Hotel (306 W. Coal Ave.), Kitchen's Opera House (218 W. U.S. 66, built around 1890), and the ornate El Morro Theater, 207 W. Coal Ave., built in 1928 in the Spanish Colonial Revival style and still in operation.

ACCOMMODATIONS

Gallup has no shortage of hotel rooms, although some of the cheaper ones along Route 66—advertising rates as low as $15—are best avoided. For under $50, you can find a dependably clean and secure place at the **Economy Inn,** 1709 W. U.S. 66, 505/863-9301, fax 505/722-9112,

the **Howard Johnson Inn,** 3404 W. U.S. 66, 505/863-6801, fax 505/722-5102, and the **Red Roof Inn,** 3304 W. U.S. 66, 505/863-3804, fax 505/863-8089.

There is one place in Gallup you should stay if at all possible, or at least peek inside: the **El Rancho Hotel,** 1000 E. U.S. 66, 505/863-9311 or 800/543-6351, fax 505/722-5917, www.elranchohotel.com. Opened in 1937 by D. W. Griffith's brother, it became a second home to movie stars filming nearby during the 1940s, '50s, and '60s. Ronald Reagan, Spencer Tracy, Kirk Douglas, and Katherine Hepburn all stayed here, and their signed photos grace the hallways today. It's a proud shrine to Hollywood's golden age of Westerns, with a flamboyant balconied lobby full of Indian art, big fireplaces, animal heads, and dark wood furniture. Armand Ortega's Indian Store sells quality crafts, and live music floats from the 49er Lounge. Plates named after Carmen Miranda and Anthony Quinn are served at the restaurant, open daily for all meals. Rates start at $57, with suites up to $85, but rooms at the attached motel start at only $33.

In the $50–100 price range you'll also find a **Best Western,** 3009 W. U.S. 66, 505/722-2221, fax 505/722-7442, a **Days Inn,** 3201 W. U.S. 66, 505/863-6889, and a **Travelodge,** 3275 W. U.S. 66, 505/722-2100. The only campground in town, aside from the one at Red Rock State Park, is the **USA RV Park,** 2925 W. U.S. 66, 505/863-5021, where tent sites are $20 and RV sites are $24–26. Take exit 6 off of I-40, then go a mile east on Route 66. It's next to the Holiday Inn.

FOOD

The parking lot is always packed at lunch at **Don Diego's Restaurant and Lounge,** 801 W. U.S. 66, 505/722-5517, which is a good sign that the Baca family is still cooking up the same great Mexican food they have been for decades. Dishes are $4–6 for breakfast, $6–8 for lunch, and $8–12 for dinner, including baby back ribs and carne adovada. There's a lounge serving the "best margaritas in town," too. Open Mon.–Sat. for all meals. **Earl's Family Restaurant,** 1400 E. U.S. 66, 505/863-4201, is another local landmark, open since 1947. They serve inexpensive Mexican and American family fare daily for all meals.

For fine dining, the only game in town is **Chelles,** 2201 W. U.S. 66, 505/722-7698, open for dinner Mon.–Sat. This place specializes in seafood, but they will also accommodate fans of Mexican cooking—a given this close to the border. **The Coffee Shop,** 203 W. Coal Ave., 505/726-0291, is next to El Morro Theater, open from 7 or 8 A.M. to 10 or 11 P.M. (Sun. 10 A.M.– 4 P.M.). Live music, poetry readings, and local art on the walls make it a cozy neighborhood spot, serving snacks and the usual caffeinated beverages. Western BBQ and Navajo tacos have been on the menu of **The Ranch Kitchen,** 3001 W. U.S. 66, 505/722-2537, for four decades (open daily for all meals), and **PeeWee's Kitchen,** 1644 Cedar Hills Dr., 505/863-9039, serves "family fare, cooked with care," particularly the breakfasts. Open for breakfast and lunch Mon.–Sat.

SHOPPING

The real reason most people spend time in Gallup is to browse the wares in the city's seemingly endless array of trading posts, art galleries, pawn shops, and gift stores. This is one of the Four Corners' top shopping destinations, and a stroll down Old Route 66 near the Santa Fe Train Depot is enough to burn a hole in the wallet of any devotee of Southwestern arts and crafts. Of them all, **Richardson's Trading Company,** 222 W. U.S. 66, 505/722-4762, www.richardson-trading.com, is the most steeped in history—and around here, that's saying a lot. Opened in 1913, it stocks an overwhelming selection of crafts and goods from the wooden floor to the roof. At last count there were 2,000 rugs in the rug room, which is just behind the stuffed white buffalo (this one was bleached).

Tobe Turpen's Trading Post, 1710 S. Second St., 505/722-3806 or 800/554-7958, www.tobeturpens.com, was started in 1939 by Tobe Sr., and is run today by Tobe Jr. with the help of Tobe III. They have tons of jewelry in the pawn vault, along with hundreds of pawned saddles. The Tanner family traces its trading history back to the arrival of Seth Tanner in the company of

THE CROWNPOINT RUG AUCTION

On the third Friday of every month, the gymnasium of the Crownpoint Elementary School fills to brimming with Navajo artisans, browsers, and visitors at one of the best shopping—and cultural—opportunities on the Res. This isn't oriented to tourists, but is rather a major local social event that draws friends and families for a fun night out. Previewing starts at 3 P.M., and students set up table with snacks and drinks around 5 P.M. Artisans display jewelry, pottery, and other crafts in the halls, but inside the gym the focus is on rugs. You can pick up and examine any one that strikes your fancy and talk directly to its creator. Not only are prices lower here than just about anywhere else, but the event also provides a major source of income for the weavers, who get the money directly. Rugs sell for under $100 and up into the thousands. The auction starts at 7 P.M. and lasts until around midnight.

The school is off U.S. 371 in Crownpoint east of Gallup. If you're heading north from Thoreau (pronounced "through," no kidding), turn left (west) at the Crownpoint sign, then take a right at the second four-way stop. The school is on the right (look for all the cars). Admission is free, and they don't take credit cards. For more information contact the **Crownpoint Rug Weavers Association,** 505/786-7386, www.crownpoint-rugauction.com.

Brigham Young in the 19th century. Today, his fourth-generation descendants run some of Gallup's better stores. The **Ellis Tanner Trading Co.,** 1980 U.S. 602, 505/863-4434 or 800/ 469-4434, www.etanner.com, stocks (among many other things) lots of pawned goods and paintings. The **Shush Yaz Trading Co.,** 1304 W. Lincoln, 505/722-0130, www.cia-g.com/ ~shushyaz, is named after Seth's son Don, nicknamed "Little Bear" by the Navajo. The **Kiva Gallery,** 202 W. U.S. 66, 505/722-5577 or 800/338-2140, www.kiva-gallery.com, specializes in original paintings, while **Yazzie's Indian Art,** 236 W. U.S. 66, 505/726-8272, has a good selection of outstanding jewelry.

ACTIVITIES AND EVENTS

Behind the Gallup Community Service Center, 410 Bataan Veterans St., is the trailhead of the **Northside bike trail,** an 18-mile technical singletrack ride through the piñon-juniper desert. The **Scoreboard bike shop,** 107 W. Coal Ave., 505/722-6077, has maps and info. **Indian Country Expeditions,** 505/722-9755, jbrown@indiancountryexp.com, www.indiancountryexp.com, offers guided 4WD tours around Gallup and throughout the Four Corners. Guests can meet craftspeople, sleep in hogans, and herd sheep on horseback, among other activities. These start at $125 pp per day. The Red Rock Hikers Group meets at the Outlaw Trading Post at Red Rock State Park every Saturday and Sunday at 8:30 A.M.

All of Gallup's annual events are held at **Red Rock State Park,** 505/722-3829, which is almost five miles east of town off I-40 exit 33 (follow the signs from Frontage Road). Among the 640 acres of scarlet scenery are a 103-site campground ($14 with hookups, $10 without), a small historical museum (505/863-1337), and the 1888 Outlaw Trading Post. The **Lion's Club Rodeo** arrives at the Red Rock arena in June, but the biggest event of the year comes in August.

The **Gallup Inter-Tribal Indian Ceremonial,** 505/863-3896 or 800/233-4528, www.ceremonial.org, brings together members of over 30 tribes from as far away as Canada for four days of rodeos, dances, parades, and art displays. This event, called "The Greatest American Show" by none other than Will Rogers, has been held since 1922 and is one of the biggest of its kind. It's a good idea to get tickets ahead of time; dances are $12–25, rodeos are $10, and to get on the grounds alone will run you $3. The same goes for hotel reservations, which are booked solid months in advance.

Close to 200 hot-air balloons float skyward during the **Red Rock Balloon Rally,** the first weekend in December, and the **Gallup Community Concerts Association,** 505/863-3075, hosts an ongoing series of concerts and plays, and free **Indian dances** are held for the public every night from May–Aug. at the Cultural Center. For a listing of other cultural events in town, check out the website www.cia-g.com/~whatson.

Information and Transportation

For more information on Gallup and the surrounding area, stop by the Gallup Chamber of Commerce's **visitor center,** 103 W. U.S. 66, 505/722-2228 or 800/380-4989, www.gallupchamber.com, which includes a small display on the Navajo code talkers. Open Mon.–Fri. 8:30 A.M.–5 P.M. The **Gallup Convention & Visitors Bureau,** 800/242-4282, www.Gallup-NM.org, is another good source. Gallup's **Greyhound** station is at 255 E. U.S. 66, 505/863-3761, and **Amtrak** is located at 201 E. U.S. 66, 505/863-3244.

WINDOW ROCK

The administrative center of the Navajo Nation straddles the New Mexico-Arizona border 24 miles west of Gallup on U.S. 264/3. It owes its importance to John Collier, commissioner of Indian Affairs in the 1930s, who brought the reservation's various offices together here as the Navajo Central Agency. He is remembered for his sympathetic ear in matters such as the tribe's education and health care, including the replacing of boarding schools with day schools for children.

Sights

The **Navajo Museum, Library, and Visitor Center,** 928/871-6673, is in the Navajo Arts and Crafts Enterprises building near the intersection of U.S. 264/3 and 12. This large building houses a museum with spare but well-done displays on tribal history, geology, and archaeology. Open Mon. 8 A.M.–5 P.M., Tues.–Fri. 8 A.M.–8 P.M., Sat. 9 A.M.–5 P.M., free. Sharing the same parking lot are the **Navajo Parks & Recreation Department,** 928/871-6636 or 871-6647, where you can pick up permits for camping on the reservation, and the **Navajo Zoological & Botanical Park,** 928/871-6574, a sad but hopeful little place (as most small zoos are) that houses animals injured or otherwise unfit for the wild. The collection ranges from ducks and sheep to a cougar, black bears, bobcats, and one endlessly pacing wolf. Open daily 8 A.M.–5 P.M. for free (pets are not allowed "for many reasons").

The headquarters of the Navajo Tribal Government sit in front of **Window Rock Tribal Park,** centered around *Tségháhoodzání,* the "Perforated Rock," a natural window which figures in the Water Way ceremony. The tribe's executive offices, council chamber, and police headquarters (for readers of Tony Hillerman's novels) are all here. To find it, take a right half a mile north of the intersection of U.S. 264/3 and 12.

Accommodations and Food

Most tourist activity in Window Rock centers around the **Navajo Nation Inn,** 48 W. U.S. 264, 928/871-4108, fax 871-5466, a modest place with 56 rooms ($60–75) near the main intersection. The restaurant is also the local favorite, serving good food (plates $5–7) including a breakfast buffet, burgers, Navajo tacos (of course), and a spicy roasted corn-chile soup. Open daily for all meals. Other than that, your only choices are the Days Inn in St. Michaels and the bevy of fast-food outlets in Window Rock.

Shopping

A big selection including concha belts, books, jewelry, and craft supplies awaits at the **Navajo Arts & Crafts Enterprises** outlet, 928/871-4090, near the Navajo Nation Inn. One of four on the reservation, it shares an entrance with the **Horned Moon Apparel Company,** which stocks Western wear. (Open Mon.–Fri. 9 A.M.–6 P.M., Sat. 9 A.M.–5 P.M.) **Griswold's Inc,** 1591A U.S. 264, 928/371-5393, is between the KFC and the Napa Auto Parts Store a few hundred yards east of the Arizona-New Mexico border. Although it's been in business only since 1988, the front room is laid out in the classic bullpen design, and is full of locals cashing paychecks on Friday afternoons. They have a little of everything in stock, from cradleboards to saddles and pottery, as well as a few hundred rugs in the rug room.

Information

The main office of the **Navajo Tourism** department, 928/871-6436, www.discovernavajo.com, discovernavajo@lycos.com, is in the governmental complex at Window Rock, although it's not a visitor-center setup.

St. Michaels

Heiress to an investment banker's fortune, Katharine Drexel followed a higher calling and founded the Sisters of the Blessed Sacrament for Indians and Colored People, a Franciscan mission just west of Window Rock, in 1896. With the help of two priests from Ohio, the Rev. Mother turned the 440-acre spread (obtained by purchasing squatter's rights to the property) into a successful mission, and named it after her childhood home in Pennsylvania. One of the Ohio priests was said to have written over 3,000 letters to help the tribe increase the size of the reservation. Among their guests was Father Bernard Haile, who helped develop the written form of the Navajo language and published the first Navajo dictionary.

Turn south at the mustard-colored trailer housing the St. Michaels post office to reach the mission, shaded by large old cottonwoods. Across from the church, a small stone building houses the **St. Michaels Historical Museum and Bookstore,** 928/871-4171, which still sells some of Father Haile's publications (open Memorial Day–Labor Day 9 A.M.–5 P.M.).

St. Michaels is also home to a **Days Inn,** 392 W. U.S. 264, 928/871-5690, fax 871-5699, with a heated indoor pool, a fitness center, and rooms in the $50–100 range. As an alternative, you can stay in a traditional **Navajo hogan,** which is five miles up a dirt road from town and has no running water or electricity. A traditional home-cooked breakfast is included in the price ($105–145), and the owners can organize sweat lodges, weaving and pottery demonstrations, and walking tours. Contact Christine Wallace, P.O. Box 1187, St. Michaels, AZ 86511, 928/871-4360, for information and reservations.

NORTH OF GALLUP
Highway 666

The northeastern corner of the Navajo Reservation is a stark lesson in geology. Heading north from Gallup, U.S. 666 parallels the Chuska Mountains on the Arizona border, rising darkly to almost 10,000 feet. About 40 miles north of Gallup, U.S. 134 heads west from Sheep Springs. On its way to Window Rock it crosses Washington Pass, named (to the chagrin of locals) after a U.S. Army soldier. Ten miles farther north on U.S. 666 is a side road at Newcomb that quickly turns to dirt and leads 6.5 miles to the **Two Gray Hills Trading Post,** 505/789-3270. Les Wilson runs this timeless place, which was built in 1897 and gave its name to the distinctive white, black, and gray geometric rug pattern. Ask to see the small rug room in back, where he stocks a good selection made by local weavers. Open Mon.–Sat. 8:30 A.M.–5:30 P.M.

U.S. 666 continues through a bizarre landscape of mesa, monoclines, and volcanic detritus. **Bennett Peak** and **Ford Butte,** on opposite sides of the highway near milepost 64, are both volcanic necks, left behind when softer outer layers eroded away. Dikes of hardened lava radiate from the necks like crazed bicycle spokes across the flat terrain.

To the north are **Rol-Hay Rock** to the west, sharp little **Barber Peak** and the **Hogback** monocline to the east, and the main attraction, **Shiprock.** The perfect impression of the inside of a volcano, Shiprock towers 1,700 feet above the desert, with a shape that seems to explain why the Navajo call it *Tsé Bit' A'i,* the "Rock with Wings." The name, however, actually comes from a legend that tells how the Navajos' ancestors, praying for deliverance from their enemies far to the north, felt the ground rise up beneath their feet and carry them here. Other stories tell how the Hero Twins, Monster Slayer and Child Born For Water, scaled Shiprock to kill a nestful of monstrous birds that were preying on their people. Shiprock was first climbed by Anglos in 1939, but is now off-limits as a sacred site. (The English name comes from early Anglo settlers who were reminded of a 19th-century clipper ship.)

Town of Shiprock

There's not much to the town at the crossroads of U.S. 64 and 666 of interest to tourists, aside from a handful of fast-food restaurants and a few good places to shop. The **Shiprock Trading Company,** 505/368-4585 or 800/210-7847, www.shiprocktrading.com, has been operating at the same location since 1894. It is now run by Jed Foutz, the fifth-generation Foutz to own the business. Ask to see the back rooms full of dead pawn, crafts, and antiques, which were once the original post's rug rooms. The Foutz family, one of the oldest trading families on the reservation, also runs the **Foutz Trading Co.,** 505/368-5790 or 800/383-0615, www.foutzrug.com, with a good selection of Navajo folk art, knives with embroidered sheaths, and Navajo kachinas. The store is also full of craft supplies, including a colorful wall of yarn, and has separate rooms for rugs and sandpaintings. (There's another Foutz Trading Co. on U.S. 64 toward Farmington, across from a huge pile of scrap metal, but that one stocks mostly pawned goods.)

Shiprock is also the home of the **Northern Navajo Fair** in early October, which brings a rodeo, a powwow, a parade, traditional song and dance, and arts and crafts to the town fairgrounds. This colorful event has been going for almost a century, making it one of the oldest on the reservation.

NAVAJO & HOPI COUNTRY

New Mexico and Colorado

Slashed by arroyos and backed by pine-covered peaks, the rolling plains of northwest New Mexico and southwest Colorado aren't as dazzling as, say, southern Utah, but the lively mountain city of Durango and the states' archaeological wealth more than make up for it. Most of this region is part of the San Juan Basin, a shallow bowl that encompasses 7,800 square miles of desert scrub and low, dun-colored hills. The region is rich in oil and gas, and is also heavily grazed. More than 10,000 head of cattle graze among 20,000 wells, which pump 10 percent of the country's domestic supply of natural gas.

This area's true riches, however, are rooted deep in the past. Southwest Colorado and northwest New Mexico boast the highest concentration of developed archaeological sites in the Four Corners, starting with the world-famous cliff dwellings of Mesa Verde National Park on the piney tablelands south of Cortez. Chaco Canyon in New Mexico is equally impressive, albeit in a more subtle way, as the center of a culture that once traded as far away as Central America. Smaller sites like Hovenweep, Salmon and Aztec Ruins, the Canyons of the Ancients, and the Anasazi Heritage Center near Dolores, Colorado, can each be easily explored in a day.

the badlands of the Angel Peak National Recreation Area, New Mexico

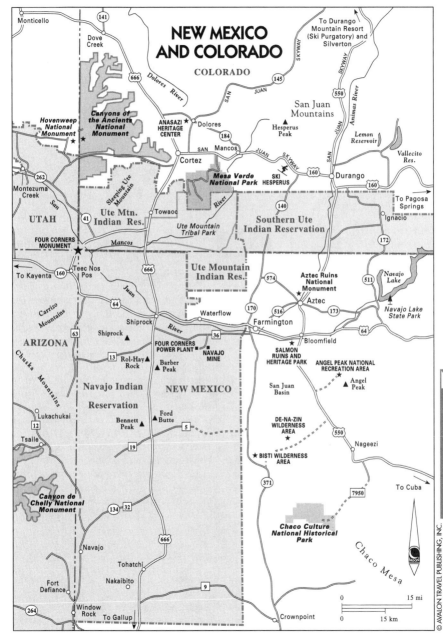

NEW MEXICO AND COLORADO

COLORADO

To Durango Mountain Resort (Ski Purgatory) and Silverton

Monticello

Dove Creek

Dolores River

San Juan Mountains

Hovenweep National Monument

Canyons of the Ancients National Monument

ANASAZI HERITAGE CENTER

Dolores

Hesperus Peak

Lemon Reservoir

Vallecito Res.

Mancos

Cortez

Mesa Verde National Park

SKI HESPERUS

Durango

Montezuma Creek

Sleeping Ute Mountain

UTAH

Ute Mtn. Indian Res.

Towaoc

Ute Mountain Tribal Park

Southern Ute Indian Reservation

To Pagosa Springs

Ignacio

FOUR CORNERS MONUMENT

Mancos

To Kayenta

Teec Nos Pos

Ute Mountain Indian Res.

Aztec Ruins National Monument

Navajo Lake

Carrizo Mountains

Juan

Aztec

Navajo Lake State Park

ARIZONA

Shiprock

Waterflow

Farmington

Chuska Mountains

Shiprock

Bloomfield

FOUR CORNERS POWER PLANT

NAVAJO MINE

SALMON RUINS AND HERITAGE PARK

ANGEL PEAK NATIONAL RECREATION AREA

Rol-Hay Rock

Barber Peak

NEW MEXICO

San Juan Basin

Angel Peak

Navajo Indian Reservation

Ford Butte

DE-NA-ZIN WILDERNESS AREA

Lukachukai

Bennett Peak

Nageezi

Tsaile

BISTI WILDERNESS AREA

Canyon de Chelly National Monument

To Cuba

Navajo

Chaco Culture National Historical Park

Chaco Mesa

Tohatchi

Nakaibito

Fort Defiance

Window Rock

To Gallup

Crownpoint

0   15 mi

0   15 km

NEW MEXICO & COLORADO

NEW MEXICO AND COLORADO HIGHLIGHTS

Chaco Culture National Historical Park: The remote and enigmatic remains of the Four Corners' ancient cultural hub (page 108)

Aztec and Salmon Ruins: Influenced by the Chacoan culture, each of these smaller sites is impressive on its own (page 117, 118)

Durango: A lively mountain town with a historic railroad and plenty of options for outdoor fun (page 119)

Mesa Verde National Park: Apartment-sized cliff dwellings in one of the Southwest's archaeological jewels (page 128)

Durango, the largest city in southwest Colorado, is an energetic college town enviably close to great skiing, hiking, and biking in the San Juan Mountains, and home to one end of a famous scenic railroad, to boot. For fans of places to visit just to say you did, the Four Corners Monument commemorates the only place in the country where four states meet at one remote, arbitrary point.

Durango and Cortez are linked by U.S. 160, which joins U.S. 666 in the latter as it heads north to Monticello, Utah, and south to Shiprock, New Mexico. U.S. 550 connects Durango to Aztec, Bloomfield, and points southeast, while U.S. 64 runs from west to east near the state line, stringing together Shiprock, Farmington, and Bloomfield.

Chaco Culture National Historical Park

The road to Chaco Canyon is long, rough, and nearly impossible in bad weather—putting you in the perfect frame of mind to experience one of the country's premiere archaeological sites. The cultural hub of the Ancestral Puebloans once teemed with as many as 5,000 inhabitants, who lived in a society unequaled north of Mexico. Today, this dry valley in the remote high desert of northern New Mexico isn't the easiest place to reach, but Chaco rewards anyone interested in the monumental remains of a vanished civilization.

About 1,200 ruins have been found in the park, which has been declared a UNESCO World Heritage Site. Some of these are the "great houses," huge stone complexes that were linked to each other; many others are "outliers" beyond the park boundaries, once connected by an astounding system of roads. Chaco flourished for almost 400 years, peaking in the 11th century, and its cultural repercussions lasted much longer. An abundance of enigmatic petroglyphs and trade items from far-off lands add to the aura of mystery that surrounds these isolated ruins. Overlooking Pueblo Bonito as the sun rises or sets, it's easy to imagine this windswept canyon full of the bustle of life or haunted by the ghosts of the past.

THE SETTING

Chaco Wash is a wide, shallow canyon near the center of the San Juan Basin. It drains to the northwest, eventually crossing the Arizona state line and becoming the Chaco River, an intermittent tributary of the San Juan River. The landscape is dry and uninviting, with escarpments, mesas, and buttes breaking the drab monotony. If you're wondering the obvious—why here?—keep in mind the changing climate and the skill of Chaco's builders in growing crops with hardly any rain. One theory holds that Chaco actually served as a buffer against the harsh, unpredictable environment. The unpredictable climate may have made it necessary to organize the agriculture of the entire San Juan Basin, and the cultural leaders at Chaco may have stored and redistributed food during bad harvest years.

HISTORY

Chaco was inhabited from the beginning of the Christian era; people began settling here more or less permanently during the Modified Basketmaker Period (A.D. 450–750). Underground pithouses became multi-room, multi-story surface dwellings, stick-and-mud walls became stone fortifications, and by A.D. 900 Chaco's heyday had begun.

This is when the characteristic **great houses** were first constructed. These massive, multi-story structures were built using unique masonry techniques that, to a great extent, stand unaltered to this day. Containing hundreds of rooms and dozens of ceremonial kivas, the great houses were unlike anything that had been built before in the Southwest. They were planned in detail, oriented to the sun, moon, and stars and linked by line of sight to each other to ensure direct communications. It's not clear what their exact purpose was; in this marginal land, they were too big to be simple farming villages. Their size might have served some greater ceremonial or symbolic purpose—perhaps, as much as anything, to demonstrate the power of their builders. If so, they might have been occupied only part of the time.

The great houses of Pueblo Bonito, Peñasco Blanco, Una Vida, Hungo Pavi, Pueblo Alto, and Chetro Ketl were erected in the 9th and 10th centuries. New masonry techniques (surrounding thick rubble cores with thin, intricate facing layers) allowed the builders to raise taller structures than any that had yet been constructed. By the 11th century, Chaco was connected to over 150 other great houses throughout the San Juan Basin. Population estimates range from 2,000 to 5,000 people, who lived in some 400 settlements in and near Chaco Canyon.

By now Chaco's importance as a cultural center matched its architecture, and most important social, religious, and commercial activity in the San Juan Basin passed through the valley at some point. A trading network that extended into northern Mexico brought tropical birds, copper, and seashells that were exchanged for distinctive black-on-white pottery and turquoise mined nearby and processed into jewelry at Chaco. Pottery was painted with detailed geometric designs using mineral or carbon paints.

Containing hundreds of rooms and dozens of ceremonial kivas, Chaco's great houses were unlike anything that had been built before in the Southwest. They were planned in detail, oriented to the sun, moon, and stars and linked to each other by line of sight to ensure direct communications.

The cultural zenith began to pass in the 12th century, when new construction stopped. By 1200 the place was almost completely deserted. The jury is still out on the reason for this massive, sudden emigration. Pressure from Athapascan tribes arriving from the north may have been a factor, although lacking the horses the Spanish would later bring, these tribes couldn't have done much damage. Some archaeologists think Chaco was an northern outpost of the Toltec Empire of Mexico, which fell around the same time and took Chaco with it. The most compelling evidence, however, points to a combination of poor planning and environmental catastrophe. A prolonged drought that hit the San Juan Basin between 1130 and 1180 may have overcome the inhabitants' ingenious irrigation methods and diminished the food supply. By then the valley was also likely overfarmed, having supported thousands of people for centuries. Social upheaval may have followed, and those that didn't kill each other simply moved on to places with a more dependable water supply and smaller crowds.

Chaco's influence was still felt into the 13th century to the north, west, and south, in places such as Aztec and Salmon Ruins, but its peak had passed. As the Mesa Verdean culture grew, Chaco faded, and its residents moved the south and east, eventually metamorphosing into the Hopi and Rio Grande Pueblo cultures. These groups still trace a spiritual lineage to Chaco and return from time to time to honor their spiritual and biological ancestors. They remember the connection in songs and prayers and also participate in management decisions with the park. The Navajo lived in the canyon until 1948, and still trace the origins of certain clans to Chaco, which they call *Tse' biyahnii'a'ah,* "the home of the great gambler." The word "Chaco" itself may be a Spanish corruption of the Navajo word *Ts'koh,* meaning "canyon," or **Tzak aik,** meaning "white string of rocks" (referring to the light-colored sandstone atop Chacra Mesa).

Anglos first discovered the ruins in 1949, when the expedition under Lt. James Simpson surveyed the area. Further photographic expeditions led to excavations near the turn of the century, including some by cowboy/amateur archaeologist Richard Wetherill. The Hyde Expedition (1896–1900) from the American Museum of Natural History excavated Pueblo Bonito, and tree-ring dating by a National Geographic party during the late 1920s pinpointed the ages of the sites. The area became a National Monument in 1949, a National Historical Park in 1980, and a UNESCO World Heritage Site in 1987.

ACCESS

The most direct and easy way to drive to Chaco, relatively speaking, is via the road from U.S. 550. This route, which involves 16 miles of dirt road, can become impassable after bad weather, so call ahead to check on conditions if it has been raining. Turn off U.S. 550 onto Country Road 7900 at the sign at mile 112.5, three miles southeast of Nageezi, and follow it 21 miles to the park boundary.

Two other routes access Chaco to the southeast, from U.S. 9 between Crownpoint and Cuba, but they are longer, rougher, and not recommended for casual visitors (definitely not for RVs).

VISITOR CENTER AND VICINITY

The **Gallo Campground,** about 20 miles from U.S. 550, is open year-round with 47 sites available on a first-come, first-served basis for $10 per night. A trail from the campground (also a good mountain bike ride) leads 1.5 miles to the pueblo of **Wijiji,** built in the early 1100s. This ruin is unusual in its symmetry and the fact that it seems to have been built in one go, rather than added to over the years. A Navajo legend tells that a Pueblo woman living near here taught the tribe how to weave.

A mile farther lies the park **visitor center,** 505/786-7014, www.nps.gov/chcu. This houses a museum and bookstore as well as telephones,

restrooms, and drinking water, which is it as far as amenities go. Pay the entrance fee ($4 pp, $8 per vehicle, good for one week), and check here for information on campfire talks, ranger-guided hikes, and free permits for longer trails. A short trail from the parking lot leads to the partially excavated **Una Vida** ruin, with five kivas and about 150 rooms.

LOOP ROAD AND RUINS

The visitor center is at the beginning of a nine-mile paved **loop drive** that passes the park's major archaeological sites or trailheads leading to them. Heading counterclockwise around the one-way loop, you'll first pass **Hungo Pavi,** a minor ruin, before reaching **Chetro Ketl,** built in the 11th century and enlarged in the early 12th. It has about 500 rooms, 16 kivas, and a huge, elevated plaza. At the far end of the loop, **Pueblo Bonito** is the largest and best known of Chaco's great houses. This four-story, D-shaped complex was occupied from the 10th through the 13th centuries and built in stages, ending up with about 600 rooms and 40 kivas. If you can, take the steep trail up the cliff to overlook the massive structure. Pueblo Bonito, a sacred place to native tribes, is one of the most studied ruins in North America. A leaning sandstone tower known as Threatening Rock once loomed over the rear of the pueblo. The Chacoans braced it with earth and masonry, and the Park Service monitored its tilt carefully, but in January 1941 it finally made good on its promise and fell, crushing about 30 excavated rooms. A short trail leads along the road to Chetro Ketl.

From the far end of the loop a short spur heads to **Pueblo del Arroyo,** a 280-room complex with some two dozen kivas, built in a short period about 1100. From here the **South Mesa Trail** leads south to **Tsin Kletzin,** dating to the early 12th century. The 4.1-mile loop trail leads to several good viewpoints and reconnects with the loop road at Casa Rinconada. Another trail leaves the Pueblo del Arroyo parking lot for **Kin Kletso,** down Chaco Wash, which was built in two stages around 1130 and may have had three stories on one side. The trail continues past numerous

ALL ROADS LEAD TO CHACO

Archaeologists always knew it must have taken a sophisticated transportation system to link the scattered settlements of the Chacoan society, but it took the advent of aerial photography to reveal the amazing extent of the Chaco road system. More than 400 miles of ancient roadway (much easier to pick out from the air) have been identified, linking Chaco Canyon to some 75 surrounding communities. The longest of these reached all the way to Salmon and Aztec ruins, over 40 miles north, while others seemed to begin and end in the empty desert.

These were not just foot trails, either. Averaging 30 feet across, the roads were built on leveled beds that were raised above sloping terrain, with rock borders or masonry walls to keep the dirt fill in place. They were laid out in amazingly straight lines, and double and quadruple road segments were sometime built near the great houses. Settlements were spaced about a day's travel apart on the longer north-south routes.

The network must have taken an amazing amount of planning and effort to build and maintain, and it is thought that the roads were more than just ways to move goods and people. Most dating to the 11th and 12th centuries, when Chaco's population was expanding, the roads may have helped bind the burgeoning culture into a cohesive whole. By facilitating communications and bringing spiritual pilgrims to Chaco, the roads may have helped spread the Chacoan religion across the inhospitable landscape and provide yet another way to reflect their worldview in earth and stone.

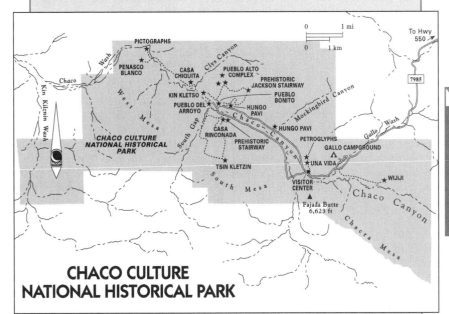

**CHACO CULTURE
NATIONAL HISTORICAL PARK**

NEW MEXICO & COLORADO

petroglyphs (including one that may depict a supernova in A.D. 1054) and the **Casa Chiquita** ruins near the mouth of Clys Canyon to **Peñasco Blanco,** 3.2 miles from the trailhead. This is one of Chaco's oldest pueblos, begun along with Pueblo Bonito and Una Vida in the 10th century. The Pueblo Alto Trail heads east from Kin Keltso to **Pueblo Alto,** at the intersection of several ancient roads on top of a mesa. Great views and farming terraces and a prehistoric staircase are visible from the 5.4-mile loop.

As the loop road heads back to the visitor center, it passes **Casa Rinconada** on the south side of the canyon, containing the largest known "great kiva" in the park.

NEAR CHACO

South of Farmington, a dreamlike terrain of multicolored stone hoodoos spreads between U.S. Highways 371 and 550. The best of these are preserved within the 45,00 acres of the **Bisti and De-Na-Zin Wilderness Areas.** Both are equally acid-etched, like bad science-fiction movie sets, with strange tabletop formations set off against bands of earth the color of charcoal and burgundy. Barely 10,000 people visit per year, so chances are you'll have it mostly to yourself. Bisti means "large area of shale hills" in Navajo, and De-Na-Zin comes from the Navajo word for "cranes," since petroglyphs of cranes have been found just to the south. Many fossils from the late Cretaceous, the end of the dinosaur age, have also been found here. To get there, turn east (right) off of U.S. 371, 36.5 miles south of the San Juan River (46 miles north of Crownpoint) onto State Road 7297. Follow the gravel road

two miles to a T intersection, then head left and continue just over a mile to a parking area on the right surrounded by boulders. For more information, contact the BLM's Farmington office at 505/599-8900.

Twenty miles south of Bloomfield on U.S. 550 is another small but striking area of badlands. The **Angel Peak National Recreation Area** is presided over by a rock spire know to the Navajo as *Tsethi Gizhi,* the "Rock with Two Prongs on Top." It's easy to zip by the turnoff, but fans of striking scenery won't be disappointed by stopping. About eight miles down the dirt road are several overlooks taking in the colorful, eroded landscape along with a few dozen primate campsites. Most of the time you'll have this place all to yourself as well. For more information contact the BLM's Farmington office.

Ten miles farther south is the **Blanco Trading Post,** 505/632-1597, with a large selection of rugs as well as groceries, crafts, fresh mutton, gas, and sheep for sale. The owners do most of their business with local residents and operate the area's post office. Slightly farther, at milepost 117, is the Nageezi Trading Post, home of **The Inn at the Post B&B,** 505/632-3646 or 800/96CHACO, chaco@fisi.net. Opened as a trading post in 1939, this place added accommodations in 1990 under the guidance of postmaster Don Batchelor. It's open Mar.–Oct., with three rooms for $70–80, depending on whether you want a shared or private bathroom. A continental breakfast is included, and they offer a kitchen guests can use, which is a good thing as there aren't any restaurants around. The Inn is the closet lodging to Chaco Canyon that involves a bed, and they also sell groceries and gas.

Farmington and Vicinity

At the northeastern corner of the Navajo Reservation, the La Plata and Animas Rivers join the San Juan in a dusty landscape of bluffs and mesas the Navajo call *Totah* ("the place where rivers meet"). Farmington (pop. 34,000), the urban hub of northwest New Mexico, is joined by smaller Bloomfield and Aztec. West of the reservation boundary lie Morgan Lake and its two industrial neighbors: the Navajo Mine, one of the largest open-pit coal mines in the world, and the Four Corners Power Plant that feeds on it. (The power plant keeps the waters of the lake at 75°F year-round, to the delight of local windsurfers.)

Farmington was founded in the late 19th century by Anglo settlers drawn to the fertile riverside soils. Initially called Farmingtown, eventually the "w" was dropped, and the small farming and ranching town took off in the 1950s when oil and gas deposits were discovered nearby. Uranium was eventually added to the list. Farmington is now home to San Juan College, with over 6,000 students, as well as some of the best mountain biking in this part of the Four Corners.

SIGHTS

Main and Broadway run parallel through Farmington's historic downtown area, where you'll find a few classic old theaters. The Totah Theater has a great neon sign but wasn't in operation in 2002, but the Allen Theater at 208 W. Main, 505/325-9313, still shows second-run movies. Located 2.5 miles to the east, the **Gateway Park Museum and Visitors Center,** 3041 E. Main St., 505/599-1174, features exhibits on local history as well as lectures and art shows year-round. (Open Mon.–Sat. 9 A.M.–5 P.M., Sun. noon–5 P.M., $2 pp.) The Farmington Convention & Visitors Bureau's visitor center, 505/326-7602 or 800/448-1240, www.farmingtonnm.org, is open similar hours.

Also in Animas Park are the **Riverside Nature Center,** with interpretive exhibits on riverine ecology (open Sat. 9 A.M.–4 P.M., Sun. 1–4 P.M. in summer) and the **Harvest Grove Farm & Orchards Exhibit Barn,** which is open

Saturday mornings during the summer, when a farmer's market is held. Kids might also like the **E3 Children's Museum & Science Center** at 302 N. Orchard, open Wed.–Fri. noon–5 P.M., Sat. 10 A.M.–5 P.M., free admission.

ACCOMMODATIONS

For under $50 you can find at room at the **Knight's Inn,** 701 Airport Dr., 505/325-5061, or the **Travelodge,** 510 Scott Ave., 505/327-0242, fax 327-5617. A **Super 8,** 1601 E. Broadway, fax 505/325-1813, and a **Comfort Inn,** 555 Scott Ave., 505/325-2626, fax 325-7675, both have rooms for under $100.

Much more distinctive are the Juniper and Cottonwood Rooms at the **Silver River Adobe Inn,** 3151 W. Main St., 505/325-8219 or 800/382-9251, www.cyberport.com/silveradobe, sribb@cyberport.com, a B&B on a cliff overlooking the San Juan and La Plata Rivers. It's an adobe-and-wood place with a cozy library, a mini-spa, and organic breakfasts included with the rooms ($105–115) and the four-person suite ($175). The turnoff for the Inn is at the La Plata bridge. Built by Indian traders in the 1940s, the **Casa Blanca Bed & Breakfast,** 505 E. LaPlata St., 505/327-6503 or 800/550-653, fax 505/327-5680, www.farmingtonnm.lodging.com, casablancanm@hotmail.com, is a Mission-style home on a bluff overlooking the town. Rooms are $80–135, and a private cottage is $175.

Even *more* distinctive is **Kokopelli's Cave Bed & Breakfast,** 206 W. 38th Ave., 505/325-7855, fax 505/325-9671, www.bbonline.com/nm/kokopelli, kokoscave@hotmail.com, a 1,650-square-foot cave for rent that's been featured on *Oprah* and CNN. It was dug out in the 1980s, originally intended to be the office of a consulting geologist. A waterfall shower, a replica kiva in the den, and the steep descent to reach the front door complete the experience. Rates are $220 per night for two people, and $260 for up to four.

Campsites are available at **Dad's RV Park,** 202 E. Piñon, 505/564-2222 or 888/326-DADS

($13.50) and **Mom & Pops RV Park,** 901 Illinois, 505/327-3200 ($14, or $5 pp for tents), as well as at Navajo Lake State Park.

FOOD

If Farmington is your first foray into New Mexico and its cuisine, be prepared for some belt-tightening meals. **Los Hermanitos,** 3501 E. Main St., 505/326-5664, does New Mexico fare right, including green chile and carne adovada. It's run by native New Mexicans Sam and Cathy Gonzales in the Middle Fork Square, open daily for lunch and dinner. The **Chipotle Grill,** 1000 N. Butler, 505/324-1595, is another good, unpretentious place, serving Mexican dishes ($6–7) for all meals Mon.–Sat.

At **Jean's Cafe,** 321 W. Main St., 505/324-5556, they make everything fresh ("Not Fast Food," says the sign), from the mutton stew to the best fry bread in town. It's a local favorite with rugs on the wall and a red police light rotating in the window. Nothing costs over $7; breakfast and lunch are served Mon.–Sat.

The **Three Rivers Eatery and Brewhouse,**101 E. Main St., 505/324-2187, occupies the 1912 Andrew Building downtown. It's decorated with artifacts from the building's former tenants: a drug store and the *Farmington Times-Hustler* newspaper (now the *Daily Times*). It has an outdoor patio and the biggest collection of beer labels and coasters in the state. Burgers, steaks, pasta, and burritos are $6–15. You can find a good cup of tea at the **Something Special Bakery and Tearoom,** 116 N. Auburn, 505/325-8183. Head to **K.B. Dillons,** 101 E. Broadway, 505/325-0222, for cocktails at the dark bar, or steak, lobster, and other entrees starting at $14. (Open for lunch and dinner Mon.–Sat.)

RECREATION
Mountain Biking
San Juan County, a high-desert landscape of rolling hills, river alleys, and piñon-juniper forests, is filled

> *San Juan County, a high-desert landscape of rolling hills, river alleys, and piñon-juniper forests, is filled with great mountain biking trails.*

with great mountain biking trails. Many of these, including a network of dirt roads built to access petroleum deposits, are on public lands and within easy range of Farmington. North of San Juan College bike trails crisscross the mesa, which offers everything from hilly jumps to sandy arroyos. The **Glade Run Trail** is an easy 3.4-mile loop. The 29-mile **Road Apple Rally** loop is a New Mexico classic, offering views of the San Juan Mountains and Shiprock. Both start from Lions Wilderness Park at the north end of College Avenue; to get there, take Piñon Hill Boulevard north from Main Street, then turn onto College Boulevard.

Other popular trails include two loops on **Piñon Mesa,** three miles north of Main Street on U.S. 170 (to spot the trailhead, look for a large cottonwood on the east side of the road), and **Kinsey's Ridge,** an eight-mile trail (o/w) through scrubby forests that starts at the end of Foothills Drive. A 5.6-mile loop circles **Lake Farmington** northeast of the city. The trail to Hart's Canyon near Aztec, supposed crash site of a UFO, is another good local ride.

For more riding information contact one of the local bike shops: **Cottonwood Cycles,** 4370 E. Main St., 505/326-0429, or **Havens Bikes and Boards,** 500 E. Main St., 505/327-1727.

There's a public pool and water slide at the **Farmington Aquatic Center,** 1151 N. Sullivan, 505/599-1167, open daily (hours vary) for $5 adults, $3.25 children.

ARTS AND ENTERTAINMENT
The Arts
Theater performances are given at the James C. Henderson Fine Arts Center of **San Juan College,** 505/326-3311, www.sanjuancollege.edu, on the north side of town. The college also has a planetarium, 505/566-3389, which gives free shows for the public on Friday evenings. Ballet, musicals, and theater productions are held at the **Farmington Civic Center,** 200 W. Arrington Ave., 505/599/1148 or 877/599-3331, including

performances by the San Juan Symphony, www
.sanjuansymphony.com.

From late June to August, the **Black River
Traders** historical drama is held in the natural amphitheater at Lions Wilderness Park north of San
Juan College. This outdoor drama depicting life at
a turn-of-the-century trading post plays Wed.–Sat.
evenings. Call 800/448-1240 for information.

Nightlife

Aside from occasional live music as K.B. Dil-
lons, local say the only other thing that quali-
fies as nightlife in Farmington is the live comedy
at **Señor Peppers** restaurant, 1300 W. Navajo,
505/327-0436, by the airport. For gamblers the
SunRay Park and Casino, 505/566-1200, is
one of the largest in the area, with slot machines
and live horse racing. It's between Farmington
and Bloomfield on U.S. 64.

Shopping

With the Navajo Reservation just on the edge of
town, Farmington boasts a number of excellent
places to shop for Indian crafts. Most are concentrated in the downtown area. The **Fifth Generation Trading Company,** 232 W. Broadway,
505/326-3211, in operation since 1875, stocks
rugs, kachinas, jewelry, alabaster sculptures, and
one of the largest collections of sandpaintings in
the Southwest. **Emerson's Gallery,** 121 W. Main
St., 505/599.8597, www.emersongallery.com, displays the vivid paintings of Anthony Chee Emerson, as well as folk art by his mother and brother.

Original crafts by local artisans, including some
you can wear, are for sale at **The Dusty Attic,**
111 W. Main St., 505/327-7696 or 800/253-
6966. Other good places to shop in Farmington
include the **Foutz Indian Room,** 301 W. Main
St., 505/325-9413, **Beasley Pawn & Trading,**
117 W. Main St., 505/599-0881, and **Jack's Boots
& Saddles,** 312 W. Broadway, 505/325-2652.

Events

In late April the **Badlands Battle Mountain
Bike Race** takes place on Piñon Mesa, and in
late May the **Farmington Invitational Balloon
Festival** sees hot-air balloons launch from the
shore of Farmington Lake at dawn on Saturday

and Sunday. Also in late May, Farmington's
Riverfest brings music, food, art, raft rides, and
live entertainment to Animas Park.

The **San Juan County Sheriff's Posse Rodeo,**
the largest open rodeo in northern New Mexico,
rides into the San Juan Rodeo Grounds on U.S.
516 east of Farmington in June. Early August
brings some of the county's best amateur baseball to
Farmington during the **Connie Mack World Series,** 505/327-9673, in Rickett's Park. Later that
month is the **San Juan Country Fair,** the largest in
the state, with livestock, live music, fiddlers, a parade, and more. It happens in McGee Park on
U.S. 64 between Farmington and Bloomfield.

The **Totah Festival** celebrates native cultures in
the Farmington Civic Center near the end of the
month, with a powwow, rug auction, and juried art
show only a few of the activities. In October the
Road Apple Rally, www.roadapplerally.com,
brings riders from all over the country to test their
skill on the loop courses north of the city. This is
the oldest continuously held mountain bike race in
the world, open to beginners and veterans alike.

INFORMATION AND
TRANSPORTATION

The **Farmington Convention & Visitors Bureau,** 505/326-7602 or 800/448-1240, fmncvb@
cyberport.com, www.farmingtonnm.org, operates out of the Gateway Park complex at 3041 E.
Main St. **Mesa Air,** 800/637-22478, www.mesa-
air.com, flies daily to Durango at 1 P.M. and to
Albuquerque at 7 P.M. The **Greyhound** bus station, 505/325-1009, is at 101 E. Animas St.

WEST OF FARMINGTON

Cottonwoods rustle over fields, orchards, and herds
of sheep along the banks of the San Juan River as it
flows west of town. In **Waterflow,** 15 miles west, is
the **Hogback Trading Company,** 3221 U.S. 64,
505/598-5154 or 598-9243. Established in 1871
by owner Tom Wheeler's great-grandfather, Joseph,
the two-story octagonal building has served as a
bank, mercantile store, and livestock brokerage
over the years. Rugs are the focus of the first floor,
while upstairs looks like a metropolitan art gallery,

with alabaster sculptures by Navajo artist Greg Johnson. Nearby is **Bob French Navajo Rugs,** 3459 U.S. 64, 505/598-5621, where you should head for the back room piled high with rugs of all sizes, styles, and quality. If money is tight, ask to see the sale pile of rugs that haven't sold in a while.

South of Waterflow is **Fruitland,** an anomalous Mormon community founded in 1877. Here you'll find the **Hatch Brothers Trading Post,** 36 Riverside Dr., 505/598-6226, a gem of a place in business since 1949, with an old-style bullpen layout and just about everything from food to pawned items and rugs for sale. Venerable owner R. S. Hatch says he'll be here for another half century. To get there, take the turnoff from U.S. 64 to Fruitland and pass the FINA gas station on your left. Go straight through the light (if the gas station comes up on your right, turn left instead) and bear right immediately onto a dirt road. Pass the boarded-up Fruitland Trading Co. and go another quarter of a mile to the riverbank.

AZTEC

Hilly streets lined with trees and historic homes make Aztec (pop. 6,000) stand out from its neighbors, as do the signs at the edge of town:

Welcome to Aztec
Pop. 6,000
and Six Old Soreheads

The town began as a trading post on the bank of the Rio de las Animas, and was most likely named Aztec after the distant Mexican civilization that early inhabitants thought had built the ruins nearby. (The river itself may have been dubbed the "River of Spirits" in Spanish for the same reason.) A farming and ranching center, it shared in the 1950s oil and gas boom as well as the Cold War–era UFO fever. Today Aztec is a quiet and friendly community, misanthropes notwithstanding. (The Soreheads belong to a tongue-in-cheek tradition whose honorees help raise funds for community projects.)

Sights and Activities

Many buildings in Aztec's downtown area date to the 19th century, celebrated at the **Aztec Museum, Pioneer Village and Oil Field Exhibit,** 125 N. Main, 505/334-9829. Old buildings, including a sheriff's office and the city's first jail, stand next to a 1920s oil rig, a narrow-gauge railroad caboose, and collections of historic artifacts, fossils, and minerals. Open

ALIENS IN AZTEC

On March 18, 1950, the headline of the *Farmington Daily Times* blared "HUGE 'SAUCER' ARMADA JOLTS FARMINGTON. Crafts Seen by Hundreds, Speed Estimated at 1000 MPH, Altitude 20,000 feet." The Cold War was just gearing up, and the state that gave birth to the Nuclear Age was gripped by UFO fever. Whatever streaked through the New Mexican skies on those spring nights—residents reported up to 500 saucer-shaped objects visible for a number of nights—the story that sticks is that one of them crashed near Aztec on the night of March 25. The silver craft was 100 feet in diameter and undamaged by its detour, but its inhabitants weren't so lucky. Sixteen humanoid bodies between three and four feet tall were removed and spirited away to government labs.

Whether you buy it or not, Aztec's **UFO Crash Site** makes for a scenic side trip from town. To get there, drive four miles north on U.S. 550 and turn right (east) at mile marker 164 onto Hart Canyon Road (County Road 2770). Follow this six more miles and take a left to a parking area, following the "Crash Site" signs. Mountain bikers can ride the popular **Alien Run** trail through Hart Canyon, which makes a seven-mile singletrack loop and starts about four miles earlier on Hart Canyon Road, before the large pump station (a race is held here every April). Find more information at the **Aztec UFO Information Center**, 106 N. Main, 505/334-9890, www.aztecufo.com, which has a gift shop and reference library. They sponsor monthly talks on all things alien, as well as the annual **Aztec UFO Symposium** in late March.

© JULIAN SMITH

kivas, Aztec Ruins National Monument

Mon.–Sat. 9 A.M.–5 P.M. in summer (10 A.M.–4 P.M. winter).

Step even farther back in time at **Aztec Ruins National Monument,** 505/334-6174, www.nps.gov/azru, northwest of the center of town at the intersection of U.S. 550 and 44. This set of ruins is unusual both in its size and the fact that it was inhabited for some two centuries, a relatively long time in the scheme of the prehistoric Southwest. The first inhabitants, who arrived around A.D. 1100, were either from Chaco or at least strongly influenced by that culture. They built what is known today as the West Ruin, a three-story, 400-room structure that included more than two dozen kivas, including the Great Kiva in the central plaza. The site was abandoned in the late 12th century and recolonized by Mesa Verdeans in the early 13th century, who built more structures to the east (not open to visitors). By 1300 it had been abandoned again.

Today you can take a short, self-guided walk through the ruins, marveling at the intricate construction of the well-preserved walls—at least those that weren't dismantled by early Anglo settlers to build their own homes. Much of the masonry and wooden beams are original. The Great Kiva, built by the Chacoans and remodeled by the Mesa Verdeans, was excavated and rebuilt by archaeologist Earl Morris in the 1920s and 1930s. It is the only reconstructed great kiva in the Southwest. The site is open daily 8 A.M.–5 P.M. (extended hours in summer). The fee for access is $4 pp, good for a week. A museum in the visitor center presents some of the many artifacts recovered at the site.

Accommodations and Food

All of Aztec's hotels are in the $50–100 range. **Miss Gail's Inn,** 300 S. Main St., 505/334-3452, or 888/534-3452, fax 505/334-9664, has four rooms in a 1907 building near the center of town. Downstairs is **Giovanni's Restaurant,** serving fresh Italian fare for lunch Mon.–Fri. and dinner by advance reservation. **The Step Back Inn,** 103 W. Aztec Blvd., 505/334-1200, fax 9858, 800/334-1255, is furnished with turn-of-the-century antiques. There's also the **Enchantment Lodge,** 1800 W. Aztec Blvd., 505/334-6143, with 20 more rooms, and campsites ($18) at the **Ruins Road RV Park,** 312 Ruins Rd., 505/334-3160.

The **Aztec Restaurant,** 107. E. Aztec Blvd., 505/334-9586, has a varied menu of healthy

NEW MEXICO & COLORADO

breakfasts, steaks, and other fare for $6–8. An old car impaled on a post marks the **HiWay Grill,** 410 N. Aztec Blvd., 505/334-6533, with more Mexican, sandwiches, and blue plate specials for $6–13. Famous for its breakfast burrito, **Oliver's,** 1901 W. Aztec Blvd., 505/334-7480, serves Mexican dishes, pasta, steaks, and seafood for breakfast and lunch Mon.–Sat. and dinner Wed.–Sat. Grab a cup of coffee and a tasty sandwich at the **Atomic Espresso Bistro,** 112 N. Main St., 505/334-0109, or a book with your latté at **Hardbacks Books & Espresso,** 200 S. Main St., 505/334-5545.

Information and Events

The folks at the **Aztec Chamber of Commerce and Visitor Center,** 110 N. Ash, 505/334-9551, www.aztecnm.com, aztec@cyberport.com, can tell you about **Aztec Fiesta Days** in June, featuring a parade, food, crafts, the election of new Soreheads, and the burning of an effigy of Old Man Gloom. The **Festival of Lights** in December illuminates Aztec's downtown with traditional New Mexican *farolitos* (lit candles in sand-filled bags, also known as luminarias). The visitor center is open Mon.–Sat. 8 A.M.–5 P.M., with extended hours in the summer.

Navajo Lake State Park

Created by the construction of Navajo Dam in 1962, **Navajo Lake** is now a state park, 505/632-2278, www.navajolake.com. The 35-mile-long lake straddles the Colorado border and is very popular, particularly on warm weekends. Visitors come to boat, fish, swim, water ski, even scuba dive, and usually start at the visitor center near the dam on U.S. 511. The San Juan River, flowing west toward Aztec and Farmington, is famous for its record trout fishing (get information on permits and choice spots from **Arcom,** 505/327-0642 in Farmington, or **Sandstone Anglers,** 505/334-9789, in Aztec). A total of 145 campsites can be found at three campsites: Sima Mesa and Pine among the piñons and junipers on the lake itself, and Cottonwood, downstream along the San Juan River (about half have RV hookups). Primitive camping is permitted along the lakeshore. Keep an eye out for bald eagles November through March.

BLOOMFIELD

Founded in 1877, Bloomfield's story is similar to Farmington's: a farming and agricultural economy supplanted by coal, natural gas, and petroleum discovered in the 1940s and 1950s. To historians, though, Bloomington is best known as the home of the Stockton Gang, a notorious gang of rustlers who terrorized the town during the late 19th century. The gang was led by Port Stockton, who arrived in Bloomfield fresh off the Lincoln County War down south (where Billy the Kid cut his outlaw teeth), supposedly with 15 notches already on his gun barrel. Stockton served briefly as Bloomfield's sheriff before hopping the fence and leading a gang in robbing stagecoaches, seizing widows' ranches, and stealing enough cattle to open their own butcher shop in Durango. All the gang members were eventually killed by locals in a brief flurry of violence called the Stockton War.

Sights

Just west of Bloomfield is the **Salmon Ruins and Heritage Park,** 6131 U.S. 64, 505/632-2103, a Chacoan outlier built in the shape of a C. This choice spot, overlooking the fertile banks of the San Juan River, was originally inhabited by the Chacoans, who stayed for less than half a century. It stood empty for 50 more years before new settlers arrived from Mesa Verde in the late 1100s and added to the construction. By the late 1200s the buildings stood empty again. One reason for the second abandonment may have been a fire that broke out around 1263. From the evidence, it's thought that a handful of adults and 35 children were standing on the roof of a kiva, perhaps to escape the flames, when it collapsed, killing them all and sealing up a time capsule that has been a boon to archaeologists. The blaze burned hot enough to fuse the kiva sand into glass.

Some 250 rooms made up the two-story complex, which measures 430 by 150 feet. The four-meter-high tower kiva is unusual, with two-meter-thick walls and six log-and-masonry buttresses similar to those found in European cathedrals. You can walk around the ruins themselves or take a trail to the Heritage Park, where eight reconstructed dwellings represent the valley's wide variety of inhabitants over the last 10,000 years. There's a Navajo hogan, Jicarilla Apache teepees, a Ute lodge, Basketmaker pithouses, a replica trading post, and even an original homestead built by farmer George Salmon around the turn of the century. The site is open daily 8 A.M.–5 P.M. (Sun. noon–5 P.M. Nov.–Mar.), for $3 pp.

Practicalities

Inexpensive rooms are available at the **Super 8,** 525 W. Broadway, 505/623-8886, and the **Bloomfield Motel,** 801 W. Broadway, 505/632-3383. There's a **KOA Kampground** at 1900 E. Blanco Blvd., 505/632-8339. Bloomfield doesn't have much in the way of food besides the fast-food joints along U.S. 64; try the **Five Seasons Restaurant,** 1100 W. Broadway, 505/632-1196, or the **Roadside Restaurant,** 319 S. Bloomfield Blvd., 505/632-9940, both local favorites for regional cooking.

The **Bloomfield Chamber of Commerce,** 224 W. Broadway, 505/632-0880, www.cyberport.com/citybloomfield, maintains a small hogan-shaped visitor center at the intersection of U.S. 64 and 550.

Durango and Vicinity

Rivaling Moab and Flagstaff in setting, history, and outdoor offerings, the city of Durango (pop. 14,000) is, in the words of Will Rogers, "out of the way, and glad of it." Enviably situated in the Animas River Valley between the mountains and the desert, Durango clings to its heritage as it welcomes visitors on their way to Mesa Verde or the skiing, biking, and hiking in the San Juan Mountains to the north. The 4,400 students attending Fort Lewis College help keep it a young, active place—a kind of Moab in the Mountains, if you will (though here they'd probably call Moab a "Durango of the Desert"). There are plenty of brewpubs, gear stores, and coffee shops, with the scent of pine and patchouli wafting through the air. A plethora of old stone buildings in the historic districts of Third and Main Avenues, and the historic rail line to Silverton, hearken back to Durango's raw early days.

HISTORY

Durango was founded in 1881 by the Denver & Rio Grande Railroad. In its early years it was a rough-knuckled frontier town catering to the cattle and mining industries. The grid of the streets, with residential areas uphill from the business district, was the only orderly thing about it. Prospectors, claim-jumpers, gamblers, cowhands, railroad workers, and the occasional desperado crowded the young town's barrooms and dancehalls, and brawls and gunfights were common. This account from the WPA Guide to Colorado captures Durango's rough-and-tumble early years:

Court was held in a large room over a general store, and on one occasion when the jury in a murder trial was out, the spectators cleared the floor and had a dance. When the jurors returned, the judge ordered silence while the verdict of guilty was pronounced, after which the dance was resumed, with the judge, lawyers, and jurors, but presumably nor the prisoner, participating in great glee.

An early streetcar line didn't last even a year because, according to the WPA guide, "the crews were abusive and insulting to patrons, and the cars invariably pulled away from the railroad station before all incoming passengers could get aboard."

In decline after the 1893 Silver Crash, Durango found new life in the tourist traffic to Mesa Verde National Park, the Silverton railroad, and the lucrative industries spawned by thrill-seeking recreationists, namely skiing, mountain biking, and river running—not to mention hiking, camping, and fishing.

NEW MEXICO & COLORADO

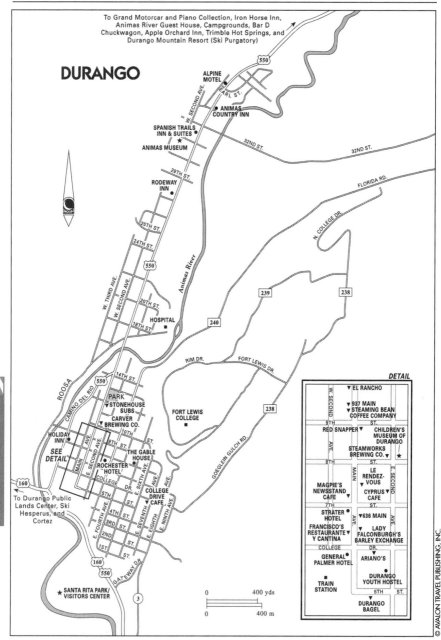

To Grand Motorcar and Piano Collection, Iron Horse Inn,
Animas River Guest House, Campgrounds, Bar D
Chuckwagon, Apple Orchard Inn, Trimble Hot Springs, and
Durango Mountain Resort (Ski Purgatory)

DURANGO

ALPINE MOTEL

550

CARL ST.

W. SECOND AVE.

ANIMAS COUNTRY INN

SPANISH TRAILS INN & SUITES

ANIMAS MUSEUM

32ND ST.

32ND ST.

29TH ST.

RODEWAY INN

FLORIDA RD.

25TH ST.

24TH ST.

550

N. COLLEGE DR.

W. THIRD AVE.

W. SECOND AVE.

20TH ST.

Animas River

18TH ST.

HOSPITAL

239

238

240

ROOSA

CAMINO DEL RIO

RIM DR.

FORT LEWIS DR.

14TH ST.

550

PARK

STONEHOUSE SUBS

CARVER BREWING CO.

FORT LEWIS COLLEGE

238

GOEGLEIN GULCH RD.

HOLIDAY INN

SEE DETAIL

MAIN AVE.

E. SECOND AVE.

10TH ST.

THE GABLE HOUSE

ROCHESTER HOTEL

COLLEGE DR.

E. SIXTH AVE.

E. EIGHTH AVE.

E. NINTH AVE.

160

To Durango Public
Lands Center, Ski
Hesperus, and
Cortez

COLLEGE DRIVE CAFE

5TH ST.

E. FOURTH AVE.

4TH ST.

3RD ST.

E. SEVENTH AVE.

2ND ST.

1ST ST.

COLLEGE DR.

160

550

GATEWAY DR.

SANTA RITA PARK / VISITORS CENTER

3

0   400 yds

0   400 m

DETAIL

W. SECOND AVE.

9TH ST.

EL RANCHO

937 MAIN

STEAMING BEAN COFFEE COMPANY

RED SNAPPER

CHILDREN'S MUSEUM OF DURANGO

MAIN AVE.

E. SECOND AVE.

STEAMWORKS BREWING CO.

8TH ST.

LE RENDEZ-VOUS

MAGPIE'S NEWSSTAND CAFE

CYPRUS CAFE

7TH ST.

STRATER HOTEL

636 MAIN

FRANCISCO'S RESTAURANTE Y CANTINA

LADY FALCONBURGH'S BARLEY EXCHANGE

COLLEGE DR.

GENERAL PALMER HOTEL

ARIANO'S

DURANGO YOUTH HOSTEL

TRAIN STATION

5TH ST.

DURANGO BAGEL

DURANGO CLIMATE

Month	Average High	Average Low	Mean	Average Precipitation
January	39°F	9°F	24°F	1.29 inches
February	45°F	15°F	30°F	1.11 inches
March	53°F	23°F	38°F	1.37 inches
April	62°F	28°F	45°F	0.84 inches
May	72°F	35°F	53°F	0.94 inches
June	83°F	42°F	63°F	0.40 inches
July	87°F	49°F	68°F	1.19 inches
August	85°F	48°F	67°F	1.71 inches
September	77°F	41°F	59°F	1.51 inches
October	65°F	31°F	48°F	1.43 inches
November	50°F	21°F	36°F	1.27 inches
December	41°F	12°F	27°F	1.02 inches

SIGHTS

One of the city's biggest tourist draws, **Durango & Silverton Narrow Gauge Railroad,** 479 Main Ave., 970/247-2733 or 888/872-4607, www.durangotrain.com, has been chugging through the spectacular mountain scenery for over a century. The experience is authentic down to the 36-inch tracks, restored Victorian coaches, and the loud, smoke-spewing engine. The train runs daily from May–Oct., leaving at 7–9 A.M. (check for a current schedule) for $60 adults, $30 children. The trip takes three hours each way, with a two-hour stopover in Silverton. Winter service to Cascade Canyon, 26 miles up the line, leaves daily at noon Dec.–May ($45/$22), and full-moon rides leave at 7:30 P.M. in July and Aug. Hundreds of thousands of people hop on board every year, so advance reservations are a good idea.

Durango's past, from prehistoric times through the Victorian era and beyond, is preserved in the **Animas Museum,** 31st Street and W. Second Avenue, 970/259-2402, www.frontier.net/~animas-museum. Located in the 1904 Animas City School building, it displays everything from Pueblo pottery to a reconstructed 1900 classroom. Open Mon.–Sat. 10 A.M.–6 P.M. (Wed.–Sat. 10 A.M.–4 P.M. in winter), admission $2.50 pp. The **Chil-**dren's **Museum of Durango,** 802 E. Second Ave., 970/259-9234, www.childsmuseum.org, has exhibits on everything from robots to the Anasazi. Open Wed.–Sat. 9 A.M.–4 P.M., Sun. 10 A.M.–2 P.M., admission $4 adults, $3 children. Over $1 million worth of grand pianos and classic cars, including Packards, DeSotos, and Hudsons, are housed in the **Grand Motorcar and Piano Collection,** 586 Animas View Dr., 970/247-1250. (Open daily 9 A.M.–7 P.M., with shorter hours in winter, for $6 adults, $4 children.) The **Center for Southwest Studies** at Fort Lewis College has a museum, 970/247-7456, with exhibits on subjects like ranching and Navajo textiles. It's open Mon.–Fri. 1–4 P.M., free admission.

National Historic Site **Trimble Hot Springs,** 6475 County Rd. 203, 970/247-0111, www.trimblehotsprings.com, is seven miles north of Durango on U.S. 550. Offering spa services in addition to hot and cold pools, they are open year-round from 8 or 9 A.M. to 10 or 11 P.M. daily, for $8.50 adults, $6 children.

ACCOMMODATIONS

Under $50

The **Durango Youth Hostel,** 543 E. Second Ave., 970/247-9905, fax 970/382-9150, has dorm and private rooms starting at $18. The **Country View Lodge** is a bit out of town (six miles, to be exact, at 28295 U.S. 160 East), 970/247-5701, but it boasts a rural setting and hostel and private rooms starting at $35, as well as tent sites and a deck overlooking a beaver-dammed stream.

$50–100

Durango has many inexpensive motels, particularly on U.S. 160 toward the outskirts of town. Places in this price range include the **Alpine Motel,** 3515 N. Main Ave., 970/247-4042, fax 970/385-4489, the **Animas Country Inn,** 3310 N. Main Ave., 970/247-4895, fax 970/382-8099, and the **Spanish Trails Inn & Suites,** 3141 Main Ave., 970/247-4173, www.spanishtrails.com.

$100–150

This price range is mostly the domain of chain hotels, including the **Holiday Inn,** 800 Camino del Rio, 970/247-5393, the **Rodeway Inn,** 2701 Main Ave., 970/259-2540, and the **Best Western Durango Inn & Suites,** 21382 U.S. 160 West, 970/247-3251, fax 970/385-4835. The **Iron Horse Inn,** 5800 N. Main, 970/259-1010 or 800/748-2990, fax 970/385-4791,www.iron-horseinndurango.com, has a fireplace in every room and an indoor pool and spa.

$150–250

Built in 1892, the **Rochester Hotel,** 726 E. Second Ave., 970/385-1920 or 800/664-1920, fax 970/385-1967, www.rochesterhotel.com, stay@rochesterhotel.com, has 15 rooms with high ceilings and "cowboy funky decor," according to *Condé Nast Traveler.* A full breakfast is included with night's stay. Built the same year, the **Gable House B&B,** 805 E. Fifth Ave., 970/247-4982, www.creativelinks.com/Gablehouse, ghbb@frontier.net, is a Queen Anne Victorian filled with antique furniture on a quiet street in the heart of town. Breakfast is served on fine china and silver.

Four miles north of town between red cliffs and the Animas River is the **Animas River Guest House,** 2725 County Rd. 250, 970/385-7829, www.durangoguesthouse.com. The fully furnished two-bedroom place is available nightly ($150–200) or weekly ($1,000–1,400). A bit

Durango's landscape

© JULIAN SMITH

further out is the **Apple Orchard Inn,** 7758 County Rd. 203, 970/247-0751 or 800/426-0751, fax 970/385-69776, www.appleorchard-inn.com, info@appleorchardinn.com. Voted best B&B in the state in 1999 by the *Denver Post,* it's near Trimble Hot Springs in Hermosa and has rooms in the main house ($85–150) and separate cottages with covered porches ($100–195). Some rooms feature river-stone fireplaces and views over the old apple orchard.

$250 and Up

Main Avenue is home to two outstanding hotels that date back to Durango's 19th-century roots. Located next to the train depot, the **General Palmer Hotel,** 567 Main Ave., 970/247-4747 or 800/523-3358, fax 970/247-1332, www.generalpalmerhotel.com, gphdurango@yahoo.com, is the only AAA four-star place in town, built in 1898. Brass lamps and hand-crocheted canopies over wooden four-poster beds give you an idea of the Victorian opulence on display here. Grab a bite at the Palace Grill or a tipple at the Quiet Lady Tavern.

A short walk away is the ornate red and white facade of the **Strater Hotel,** 699 Main Ave., 970/247-4431 or 800/247-4431, fax 970/259-2208, www.strater.com, built in 1887 and run by the third generation of the Barker family. Antiques grace the rooms and historical artifacts fill display cases in the lobby. In the Diamond Belle Saloon, waitstaff dress in Victorian finery and a piano player tinkles ragtime beneath an $11,000 chandelier (Louis L'Amour wrote a few of his Western page-turners here, soaking in the atmosphere). Italian combines with Southwest fare on the menu at Henry's Chop House & Bistro, and the Diamond Circle Melodrama performs nightly.

Campgrounds

No shortage here: there are over 900 public and private campsites within 40 miles of Durango. The San Juan National Forest's Columbine Ranger District, 970/247-4874, has 18 campsites, ranging from free to $10 per night. Many are northeast of town by the Lemon and Vallecito Reservoirs, 20 miles from Durango (head east on Florida Road/County Road 240). The Junction Creek campground is also popular and closer to town; turn right (west) on 25th Street and go eight miles to the campground ($8). Private campgrounds include the **Alpen Rose RV Park,** 27847 U.S. 550 North, 970/247-5540, www.alpenroservpark.com, camp@alpenroservpark.com ($30); **United Campground,** 1322 Animas View Dr., 970/247-3853, www.unitedcampground.com; and the **Durango RV Park,** 970/247-5199, www.durangorvpark.com, 10.5 miles south of where U.S. 160 leaves U.S. 550 ($16).

FOOD
Snacks and Starters

Near the train station **Durango Bagel,** 106 E. Fifth St., 970/385-7297, open daily from 6:30 A.M., advertises that "Bikers love bagels because they fit easily on your handlebars." The **College Drive Cafe,** 666 E. College Dr., 970/247-5322, offers breakfast all day, including half

© JULIAN SMITH

the Strater Hotel, Durango

a dozen tasty versions of eggs Benedict all for around $6 (open for all meals Wed.–Sun.). More inexpensive fare can be found at **Stonehouse Subs,** 140 E. 12th St., 970/247-4882, with sandwiches for ($4–8) on bread made from scratch.

Coffee Shops and Brewpubs

The **Steaming Bean Coffee Company,** 915 Main Ave., 970/385-7901, is a cozy place with Internet computers and local art on the walls (open daily until 8 or 9 P.M.). Another good place for a caffeinated pick-me-up and a newspaper in the morning is **Magpie's Newstand Cafe,** 707 Main Ave., 970/259-1159, with outdoor seating when the weather is nice. For local brews of a different sort try the **Carver Brewing Co.,** 1022 Main Ave., 970/259-2545, with live music and an outdoor beer garden. **Lady Falconburgh's Barley Exchange,** 640 N. Main Ave., 970/382-9664, stocks over 150 microbrews and imported beers downstairs in the Century Mall. Open for lunch and dinner until late.

Oven-fired pizza is a specialty (along with the homebrewed beers, of course) of the **Steamworks Brewing Co.,** 801 E. Second Ave., 970/259-9200. They brew their own sodas too and serve food ($7–11) on an outdoor patio. Open daily for lunch and dinner. **El Rancho,** 975 Main Ave., 970/259-8111, has been around since 1915, when a 20-year-old Jack Dempsey scored his first knockout on the premises before going on to become World Heavyweight Champion. Some historians now say it happened across the street, but in either case a mural on the wall of the old Central Hotel commemorates the event, which earned the future "Manasa Mauler" $50.

Regional Fare

A local favorite for their northern Italian cuisine is **Ariano's,** 150 E. College Dr., 970/247-8146, with early-bird specials from 5–6 P.M. Entrees, served daily for dinner, are around $16. The **Cyprus Cafe,** 725 E. Second

Ave., 970/385-6884, specializes in Mediterranean dishes like lamb souvlakia and cherry tomato linguine, served daily for lunch ($7–9) and dinner ($13–17). Opened in 1968, **Francisco's Restaurante y Cantina,** 619 Main Ave., 970/247-4098, is the oldest restaurant in Durango, serving the "best margaritas in town." Their Mexican fare is available daily for lunch and dinner ($8–11). Pastries, breads, sandwiches, and salads are all on the menu at **Le Rendez-Vous,** 750 Main Ave., 970/385-5685, a Swiss bakery and restaurant that offers breakfast and lunch daily.

Other Durango Restaurants

Opened by Ken and Sue Fusco in 1998, **937 Main,** 937 Main Ave., 970/259-2616, has become a local favorite for its reasonably priced Asian-inspired food, including shiitake and goat cheese omelets and udon noodle bowls. Entrees at "Ken & Sue's place" are $15–20; dining is available on the patio near the fountain. They've done so well that they opened a second place called **636 Main,** 636 Main Ave., 970/385-1810, just a few blocks away. Both are open daily for lunch and dinner. **Red Snapper,** 144 E. Ninth St., 970/259-3417, is a sure bet for good seafood, served daily for dinner in an aquarium-filled dining room, as well as for steak and other hearty dishes.

RECREATION
Mountain Biking

Durango is one of the most fat-tire-happy cities in the country, an infatuation that dates to the 19th-century Durango Wheel Club. In 1990 it was home to the first ever Mountain Bike Championships, and in 2001 it hosted one of the World Cup Mountain Biking competitions. Many world-champion riders have or still do live in town. Good rides include the short and long loops at **Log Chutes** (moderately difficult); the tough, steep climb over 11,750-foot **Kennebec Pass** northwest of town (28 mi o/w); and the **Dry Fork Loop** on the edge

> *Durango is one of the most fat-tire-happy cities in the country, an infatuation that dates to the 19th-century Durango Wheel Club. In 1990 it was home to the first ever Mountain Bike Championships, and in 2001 it hosted one of the World Cup Mountain Biking competitions.*

of town, with six miles of singletrack in an 18-mile ride. This is a segment of the 460-mile **Colorado Trail,** which crosses eight mountain ranges, seven national forests, six wilderness areas, and five rivers on its way from Durango to Denver. For more information on biking in the area, stop by **Durango Cyclery,** 143 E. 13th St., 970/247-0747, or **Mountain Bike Specialists,** 949 Main Ave., 970/247-4066, which rent bikes starting at $25 per day.

Hiking

Durango's choices for hiking are even more extensive, with the steep forested slopes of the La Plata Mountains and the San Juan National Forest practically surrounding the city. Be warned that most trails involve at least some steep slopes. For starters, try a popular trail like the **Animas River Trail,** which runs along the river from Santa Rita Park to 32nd Street, or the easy one-mile climb to **Raider Ridge** overlooking the Fort Lewis College campus and the city. The trail along **Junction Creek** in the San Juan National Forest links to the Colorado Trail, and the steep, two-mile **Hogsback Trail** starts near the Durango Mountain Park east of town.

You can climb 3,000 feet up **Haflin Canyon** through different ecological zones to reach **Missionary Ridge,** and more good views await from **Animas Mountain** northwest of Durango, which has educational signposts along the way (both are around 6 miles r/t). West of town, **Barnroof Point** is another stout climb, and you'll probably spot some critters in **Dry Creek,** which traverses a wildlife feeding area (5 mi o/w). Look for Peregrine falcons from **Perins Peak,** a difficult five-mile hike that passes the remains of the Boston Coal Mine and the site of Perins City, an old mining town.

Rafting and Kayaking

The Animas River frothing through downtown Durango is only the beginning; Durango's river offerings extend to the nearby Dolores and Piedras Rivers as well. You can get inspired watching kayakers tackle the course set up in the Animas River just off the Santa Rita Park, and then sign up with one of the city's many white-water guide services in kiosks along Main Avenue. These include **Flexible Flyers Rafting,** 2344 County Rd. 225, 970/247-4628 or 800/346-7741, www.flexibleflyersrafting.com; **Mountain Waters Rafting,** 643 Camino del Rio, 970/259-4191 or 800/748-2507, www.durangorafting.com; and **Mild to Wild Rafting,** 53 Rio Vista Circle, 800/567-6745, www.mild2wildrafting.com. The **Four Corners Riversports Paddle School,** 360 S. Camino del Rio, 970/259-3893, www.paddleschool.com, offers rentals, sales, and lessons in kayaks and canoes.

Skiing

The **Purgatory** ski resort, 970/247-9000 or 800/982-6103, www.ski-purg.com, is 25 miles north of Durango on U.S. 250. This top-flight resort offer 40 miles of trails spread over 1,200 acres and 2,000 vertical feet, with 11 lifts, including a six-person high-speed quad, to get you to the top. Backcountry Snowcat skiing trips take advantage of an average annual snowfall of 260 inches. Lift tickets are $55 per day for adults, and a full range of dining, accommodations, and shopping choices is available at Purgatory village. In summer the slopes are taken over by hikers, mountain bikers, and guests enjoying the alpine slide. Mountain Transport, 970/247-9000 ext. 3, runs buses to the resort from Durango Nov.–Apr. for $5 pp r/t.

At the other end of the spectrum is the family-run hill called **Ski Hesperus,** 9848 U.S. 160, 970/259-3711, www.skihesperus.com, 11 miles west of Durango, with only one lift and a handful of runs. On the bright side, it's cheap (adult passes are $25 per day) and usually much less crowded.

For ski supplies and information in Durango, stop by **The Ski Barn,** 3533 Main Ave., 970/247-1923. **Hassle Free Sports,** 2615 Main Ave., 970/259-3874 or 800/835-3800, www.hasslefreesports.com, has information on **cross-country skiing** near Durango, including popular trails at Haviland Lake, Molas Pass, and the Purgatory Ski Touring Center.

Fishing

Southwest Colorado has some of the best fishing in the country, from free-flowing rivers to high mountain lakes. Anglers can start with the

Animas River in town and fan out to nearby lakes like Molas, Little Molas, Andrews, Haviland, and Henderson, or to rivers like the San Juan, Dolores, and Piedras. The Vallecito, McPhee, and Navajo reservoirs are also good spots for going after trout, salmon, pike, bass, crappie, and bluegill. Try **Duranglers, 923 Main Ave.,** 970/385-4081 or 888-FISHDGO, www.duranglers.com, for guided fly-fishing trips and gear.

Other Activities

The closest **rock climbing** to town is at "Golf Wall," at the edge of the national forest, 17 miles north on U.S. 550. Look for a parking area on the right, just beyond a golf course. You'll find about 40 bolted routes up the limestone cliffs near the road, ranging from 5.8 to 5.13 in difficulty.

For **horseback rides** into the mountains, contact the **Rapp Corral,** 47 Elektra Lake Rd., 970/247-8454, www.rappguides.com, rapp@frontier.net. **D Bar G Outfitters,** 971 D Bar K Dr., 970/385-6888, does overnight horse-packing trips for around $100/day pp. The **Durango Soaring Club,** 27290 U.S. 550 North, 970/247-9037, offers glider rides over the Animas Valley mid-May–Sept., weather permitting, starting at $85 pp for half an hour.

Many stores in Durango, such as **Backcountry Experience,** 12th and Camino del Rio, 970/247-5830 or 800/648-8519, stock a wide variety of outdoor gear. **Gardenswartz** has two locations: 863 Main Ave., 970/247-2660, and 780 Main Ave., 970/259-6696. The latter has a machine that prints out customized, water- and tearproof topographic maps for $8. **Southwest Adventures,**1205 Camino del Río, 970/259-0370 or 800/642-5389, www.mtnguide.net, has rock climbing, hiking, and biking gear, and organizes classes, tours, and shuttles.

ARTS AND ENTERTAINMENT

Nightlife

The Strater Hotel's **Diamond Circle Melodrama,** 970/247-3400, www.diamoncirclemelodrama.com, has been hailed as one of the best of its kind in the country. Boo the villain and cheer the hero nightly starting at 7:45 P.M. ($17 adults,

$12 children). Advance reservations are a good idea. The musical stage show at the **Bar D Chuckwagon,** 970/247-5753 or 888/800-5753, www.bardchuckwagon.com, is accompanied by country music and hearty frontier recipes. Located nine miles north of Durango at 8080 County Rd. 250, the show plays nightly at 7:30 P.M. Memorial Day–Labor Day.

In town, the **Scoot'n Blues Café and Lounge,** 900 Main Ave., 970/259-1400, www.scootnblues.com, is a good bet for live music. It claims Durango's "best happy hour" from 4–6 P.M. Mon.–Fri. For a schedule of performances at the **Fort Lewis College Community Concert Hall,** contact the box office at 970/247-7657, www.durangoconcerts.com. Just south of Durango is the **Rocket Drive-In Theater,** 26126 U.S. 160, 970/247-0833, with shows at dusk for $5 pp.

Shopping

Many of Durango's art galleries are open during the Gallery Walk in late September, part of the Colorfest celebration. Two of the best are the **Gallery Ultima,** 1018 Main Ave., 970/247-1812, www.galleryultima.com, and **New West Galleries,** 747 Main Ave., 970/259-5777, both specializing in Southwest art, crafts, and jewelry. The **Toh-Atin Gallery,** 145 W. Ninth St., 970/247-8277 or 800/525-0384, www.toh-atin.com, in business since 1957, stocks gorgeous and expensive native and Southwest art and crafts, including piles of Navajo rugs. Pick up a handmade chapeau at **O'Farrell Hatmakers,** 563 Main Ave., 970/259-5900 or 800/895-7098, with a choice of Panama, palm leaf, beaver-fur felt, and cowboy models.

Events

Durango's Wild West roots live on in its many annual **rodeos,** including the Durango Pro Rodeo Series every Tuesday and Wednesday evening June–August, the Durango Cowgirl Classic over the Fourth of July, and the Family Ranch Rodeo the first week of October.

Snowdown, www.snowdown.org, includes a plethora of winter-themed fun in late January and early February. In March the **Durango Film Festival,** 970/259-2291, www.durangofilmfestival.com, brings American and world premieres and juried events. That same month, **Hozhoni Dayz,** http://hozhoni.fortlewis.edu, attracts over 5,000 people to Native American events on the Fort Lewis College campus.

April brings bluegrass picking and plucking to downtown during the **Durango Meltdown,** www.durangomeltdown.com. Over Labor Day weekend the **Iron Horse Bicycle Classic,** www.ironhorsebicycleclassic.com, one of the 10 largest bicycle events in the country, sees cyclists racing the train to Silverton, among other events. Two days of kayak races in June make up the **Animas River Days,** an event attended by many professional paddlers. Contact Four Corner River Sports, 970/259-3893, www.riversport.com, for information. **Music in the Mountains,** www .musicinthemountains.com, in July consists of three weeks of classic music performances at the Fort Lewis College campus and the Durango Mountain Resort.

Tractor pulls, auctions, and a livestock show happen in August during the **La Plata County Fair,** 970/247-4355, the same month the **Main Avenue Juried Arts Festival,** 970/259-2606, comes to the Durango Arts Center. August is also the month of the four-day **Narrow Gauge Railfest,** www.durangotrain.com, with visiting locomotives and rail-themed events.

September hears the roar of Harley-Davidson motorcycles as the **Four Corners Iron Horse Motorcycle Rally,** 970/375-0777 or 888/284-9212, www.fourcornersrally.com, combusts in nearby Ignacio. Events include scenic tours, bands, and arm-wrestling competitions. During October the **Durango Cowboy Gathering** consists of rodeos, cowboy poetry readings, and exhibits of mountain skills, and the**Durango Songwriters Expo,** www.durangosong.com, gives visitors and locals the chance to enjoy over 100 unsigned performers and songwriters.

The **San Juan Symphony** performs at Fort Lewis College's Community Concert Hall, 970/247-7657.

GETTING AROUND

For destinations out of walking distance, hop aboard the **trolley** that runs up and down Main Avenue (50 cents pp), or take one of the **Durango Lift** buses, 970/247-5438, www.durangogov.org, that go to Fort Lewis College and elsewhere ($1 pp). The **Durango-La Plata County Airport,** 970/247-8143, www.durangoairport.com, located 14 miles southeast of the city on U.S. 172, is served by United Express, America West Express, Mesa Air, and Rio Grande Air as well as by Avis, Hertz, Dollar, Budget, and National car rental agencies. Durango's **Greyhound** station, 970/247-2756, is at 275 E. Eighth Ave.

INFORMATION

Durango's main **visitor center** is run by the Durango Area Chamber Resort Association, 970/247-0312 or 800/525-8855, fax 970/385-7884, www.durango.org, info@durango.org, in the Santa Rita Park at the south end of town. You can make reservations for hotels, events, skiing, and the train through **Durango Central Reservations,** 945 Main Ave., 970/247-8900. For more information on public lands near town, contact the local offices of the **San Juan National Forest,** 970/247-4874, www.fs.fed.us/r2/sanjuan, or the **Bureau of Land Management,** 970/247-4874, www .co.blm.gov/sjra/index.html. Both are in the Durango Public Lands Center at 15 Burnett Court.

Mesa Verde and Vicinity

MESA VERDE NATIONAL PARK

Between Cortez and the Mancos River looms a series of forested mesas that harbor such a wealth of prehistoric architecture they have been declared both a national park and a UNESCO World Heritage Site. Amid the steep canyons that slice across this "green table" (from the Spanish) lie more than 4,000 known archaeological sites and probably thousands more yet undiscovered. About 600 of these are the famous **cliff dwellings** built when Mesa Verde reached its height A.D. 1100–1300.

Resembling apartment blocks in a city made of stone, these extraordinary structures are built from the same rock as the huge ledges that soar above them. Natural forces and looters have taken their toll—only a few cliff dwellings have been excavated and reinforced enough to admit visitors—but a stroll down these dusty lanes is enough to make 700 years seem like a moment, and the echo of residents' voices and the smoke of their campfires more than a distant memory.

The Setting

The park covers a series of mesas and canyons that form the northern drainage of the Mancos River, which flows through the Ute Reservation to the south. The fingerlike mesas are formed by three sandstone formations, or layers, that together make up the Mesa Verde Group. Most of the large alcoves are found in Ute, Navajo, Soda, and Morfield Canyons, hollowed out of Cliffhouse Sandstone, the uppermost formation. This sedimentary layer was formed beneath an inland sea 70–100 million years ago. Fine-grained sands deposited in shallow water formed layers of sandstone and shale. When the softer Mancos shale beneath it crumbles, the harder sandstone splits away in blocks or, occasionally, huge arches, some of which eventually weather into caves reaching back deep into the mesa. This often happens near springs, which—like any flowing water—help hasten the weathering of the soft sandstone.

Percolating rainwater gets redirected horizontally above the less permeable layer of shale, creating larger caves and convenient springs for their inhabitants.

This area is a better place to live than you might think. Sure, the water supply is limited, and no streams run year-round. Most canyons see flowing water only during summer monsoons or spring runoff. The growing season is long, however: up to 171 frost-free days per year, and up this high (7,000 feet) the summer heat isn't so bad, which makes it easier to grow crops. In summer, only the front buildings in the caves are hit by the sun's vertical rays, leaving the rest back in the cool shadows. In the winter, however, the low sun reaches far back into the caves, warming the stone walls and even the cave walls themselves. It's not unusual for it to be 10 to 20 degrees warmer up here than in Montezuma Valley to the north, even though Mesa Verde is 600 feet higher. Over the millennia, dust deposited by winds from the southwest covered the mesa tops with a layer of deep red soil. Combine that with the dependable summer rains from July to August, and Mesa Verde becomes a relatively comfortable, fertile place.

The highest portions of Mesa Verde are covered with large Douglas firs, ponderosa pines, and aspen. Utah juniper and piñon pine, the most common tree species, provided wood for building, tools, and fires, as well as tasty, nutritious nuts. Brush species such as mountain mahogany, Gambrel oak, and serviceberry are concentrated toward the northern end of the park. Big sagebrush, cacti, and flowers grow in the sandy canyon bottoms. Over 200 species of birds live here, from sociable groups of wild turkeys to hummingbirds. Mule deer and coyotes are common, but bears and mountain lions are rarely seen.

History

Mesa Verde was occupied for about 1,300 years. Nomadic tribes first arrived here at the fringe of the Rocky Mountains thousands of years ago, but semi-permanent dwellings weren't built until

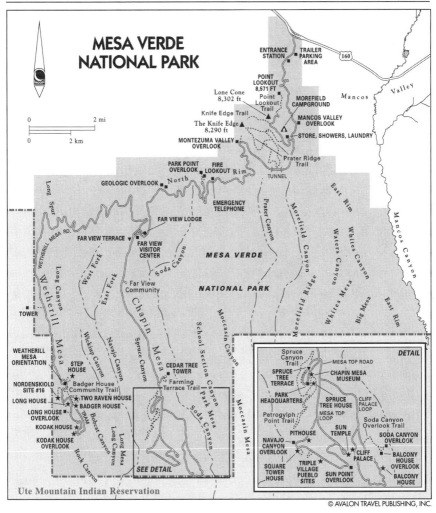

MESA VERDE
NATIONAL PARK

0   2 mi

0   2 km

ENTRANCE
STATION
TRAILER
PARKING
AREA
160
POINT
LOOKOUT
8,571 FT
Lone Cone
8,302 ft
Point
Lookout
Trail
MOREFIELD
CAMPGROUND
Mancos   Valley
Knife Edge Trail
The Knife Edge
8,290 ft
MANCOS VALLEY
OVERLOOK
MONTEZUMA VALLEY
OVERLOOK
STORE, SHOWERS, LAUNDRY
Prater Ridge
Trail
PARK POINT
OVERLOOK
FIRE
LOOKOUT
Rim
North
TUNNEL
GEOLOGIC OVERLOOK
East Rim
EMERGENCY
TELEPHONE
FAR VIEW LODGE
FAR VIEW TERRACE
FAR VIEW
VISITOR
CENTER
MESA VERDE
Mancos Canyon
WETHERILL MESA RD.
Long Spur
West Fork
East Fork
Soda Canyon
Far View
Community
NATIONAL PARK
Prater Canyon
Morefield Canyon
Morefield Ridge
Waters Canyon
Whites Canyon
Whitsis Mesa
Big Mesa
East Rim
TOWER
Long Canyon
Wetherill Mesa
Wickiup Canyon
Navajo Canyon
Spruce Canyon
Chapin Mesa
School Section Canyon
Moccasin Canyon
Park Mesa
Soda Canyon
Moccasin Mesa
WEATHERILL
MESA
ORIENTATION
STEP
HOUSE
CEDAR TREE
TOWER
Farming
Terrace Trail
NORDENSKIOLD
SITE #16
Badger House
Community Trail
TWO RAVEN HOUSE
LONG HOUSE
BADGER HOUSE
LONG HOUSE
OVERLOOK
KODAK HOUSE
Bobcat Canyon
Long Mesa
Long Canyon
KODAK HOUSE
OVERLOOK
Rock Canyon
SEE DETAIL
Ute Mountain Indian Reservation

DETAIL
Spruce
Canyon
Trail
MESA TOP ROAD
SPRUCE
TREE
TERRACE
CHAPIN MESA
MUSEUM
PARK
HEADQUARTERS
SPRUCE
TREE HOUSE
CLIFF
PALACE
LOOP
Petroglyph
Point Trail
MESA TOP
LOOP
Soda Canyon
Overlook Trail
NAVAJO
CANYON
OVERLOOK
PITHOUSE
SUN
TEMPLE
SODA CANYON
OVERLOOK
TRIPLE
VILLAGE
CLIFF
PALACE
BALCONY
HOUSE
OVERLOOK
SQUARE
TOWER
HOUSE
PUEBLO
SITES
SUN POINT
OVERLOOK
BALCONY
HOUSE

© AVALON TRAVEL PUBLISHING, INC.

NEW MEXICO & COLORADO

around A.D. 500. People dug pithouses in canyon alcoves and on top of the mesas, covering them with flat or raised roofs of logs and soil. They wove outstanding baskets from plant fibers, and started to make pottery and use the bow and arrow. By A.D. 1000, these houses were being built primarily aboveground on the mesa tops. Roofed dwellings gradually became grouped together to form small villages, called "pueblos" (Spanish for "village") by archaeologists. Con-

struction methods changed from mud-covered poles to layer masonry, and the builders left open courts amid the rooms. Pithouses deepened until they became the mostly underground ceremonial chambers called kivas.

Mesa Verde culture reached its climax during the Classic Pueblo Period (1100–1300), when inhabitants moved down into the canyons and built most of the grand constructions visible today. It's not sure how many they raised, but

FIRE ON THE MOUNTAIN

Wildfires are a natural part of Southwestern ecosystems, so when fighting fires becomes part of the management strategy for places like Mesa Verde, it's no surprise that things can quickly get out of balance. Four-fifths of the park has been burned since a policy of total fire suppression was adopted in 1908, with an average of eight fires racing across the high mesas every year since 1920. Since 1975, the numbers have climbed to 20–25 burns every year, including four major fires between 1996 and 2002 that burned over half the park.

In July 2000, an unusually hot, dry month, a lightning strike outside the park sparked a blaze that eventually scorched 23,607 acres on the eastern side of Mesa Verde. Flames reaching 300 feet were too hot for flame retardants to quell, and the path of destruction eventually covered an area eight miles long and four miles wide. It took 1,106 firefighters nine days to put out the Bircher Fire, and much of this area is still scarred from that blaze.

Unnaturally large wildfires, caused by a combination of hot, dry weather and the buildup of fuels, are expensive by any calculation. The Bircher Fire cost $5.5 million to fight and closed the park for two weeks, spelling lost revenue to the park and local businesses. Big fires can also alter the local ecology: while oak and berry shrublands can regenerate quickly, non-native grasses can outcompete burned-over piñon and juniper forests, and evergreen woodlands can take centuries to fully regrow. On the bright side, the fire burned only a few park buildings, and scorched areas can reveal previously hidden archaeological treasures. After a 1996 fire, one quarter the size of the Bircher Fire, 372 new sites were discovered.

over 600 cliff dwellings have been recorded within the park. Large alcoves facing south or southwest were preferred for the sunlight they captured in the winter. If the floor of an alcove was uneven, builders brought in dirt to even out the surface. Kivas were dug for religious rituals and possibly social events, held most likely by the men, and rocks too big to move were incorporated into the construction. It obviously took a large population working in harmony to erect buildings like this; Cliff Palace alone had over 200 rooms and was home to some 250 people. Exquisite pottery was a hallmark of this period, with black geometric designs on a gray or white background. Shell jewelry, bone scrapers, and stone tools have all been unearthed in garbage piles or burial sites.

Farming still provided most of the food. The classic trio of corn, beans, and squash was grown, including the violet-striped bean and a variety of corn resistant to drought (which eventually proved too little, too late). The lack of constantly flowing streams means the Mesa Verdeans had to depend on what little rain fell, but this was enough. Archaeologists experimented with growing corn in the park 1918–1973 using dryland farming techniques like those of the Hopi, and the crop failed in only three of those years. Storage rooms were incorporated into the buildings to hold excess crops over the winter.

Drought arrived around A.D. 1276 and lasted for over a decade. By this point the masonry had begun to get sloppy, suggesting some sort of cultural failure was already underway. The soil may have become less fertile, overtaxed by the demands of a rising population. Residents began to leave as the local springs dried up, moving south into northern Arizona and New Mexico. It's thought that their descendants make up parts of the Hopi and Rio Grande Valley Pueblo tribes. Shortly after A.D. 1300 Mesa Verde was mostly deserted.

The ruins stood empty for centuries. Anglo settlers explored them in the 19th century, interest sparked by an 1859 geological report on the enigmatic ruins by one Professor J. S. Newberry. In 1874, surveyor W. H. Jackson became the first Anglo to enter a cliff dwelling when he crawled inside Two-Story Cliff House in Ute Mountain Tribal Park. Prospector S. E. Osborn scratched his name and the date on the wall of Balcony House on March 20, 1884.

In December 1888, local rancher Richard Wetherill and his brother-in-law Charles Mason rode out onto Sun Point to look for lost cattle.

Through the blowing snow they spotted Cliff Palace. They tied together trees to scramble down into the ruin, and within a day they had discovered Spruce Tree House and Square Tower House as well. Richard returned with three of his brothers to explore the canyons and dig for artifacts in a fit of amateur archaeology. In less than a year and a half they discovered over 180 cliff dwellings. In 1906 Mesa Verde was declared the first (and is still the only) cultural national park in the country. It became a World Cultural Heritage Site in 1978.

Recreation

Hiking trails at Mesa Verde take you from mesatop ruins down into the canyons to see the remarkable cliff dwellings up close. Because the ruins and other cultural resources are so fragile, hiking is limited to designated trails only. A park ranger must be present whenever you enter a cliff dwelling, and no backcountry camping is permitted. A number of trails are short and near the loop roads. Keep in mind that most of the park is over 7,000 feet high, and trails can be steep and the weather hot and dry.

One way to have the place almost to yourself (aside from touring Wetherill Mesa on a weekday) is to explore the park in winter on **cross-country skis**. This offers a taste of what it was like when the Wetherills discovered it over a century ago, with walls looming in dark alcoves amid the whiteness. Mesa Verde gets 80 to 100 inches of snow in an average winter, and all roads beyond the Far View Visitor Center are unplowed and open to skiers. (Stay on roads only, though.)

Even if you don't go farther than a few steps from your car, the six-mile **Mesa Top Loop Road** passes a dozen spots of interest with easy access, including pithouses and overlooks.

Entering Mesa Verde

The entrance to the park is off of U.S. 160, an hour from Cortez and 90 minutes from Durango. After passing through the entrance station ($10 per vehicle), the park road winds its slow, painful way up the face of the mesa before reaching the **Moorefield Ranger Station**, 970/529-6005, and the adjacent **Moorefield**

Campground after four miles. The ranger station is open late May–Aug. 5 A.M.–8 P.M., and the campground (open mid-Apr.–mid-Oct.) is one of the nicest in the national park system. Four hundred sites ($19–25) are first-come, first-served. Talks are given in the campground amphitheater nightly, and there's a grocery store, gas station, showers, and laundry facilities nearby.

Three **trails** leave from the campground, and none require permits. The 2.3-mile Point Lookout Trail climbs switchbacks up the highest point in the park, with excellent views, and the Knife Edge Trail (1.5 mi) heads to an overlook over Montezuma Valley, which is especially pretty at sunset. In 2002, the 7.8-mile Prater Ridge Trail was still scorched from the Bircher Fire, but it may have been reopened by the time you read this.

From the campground the road continues to wind and climb, passing a viewpoint at Park Point before reaching the **Far View Visitor Center,** 970/529-5036, 15 miles from the entrance. The center, open 8 A.M.–5 P.M. early Apr.–mid-Oct., has exhibits on Native American crafts and sits next to the **Far View Lodge,** 970/529-4421, fax 970/529-4411, where rooms with great views and private porches are $90–110. The lodge itself, open Apr.–Oct., features the Metate Room restaurant open daily for all meals, the Far View Terrace cafeteria, and a gift shop. Get tickets at the visitor center for tours of Cliff Palace, Balcony House, and Long House ($2.25 pp).

Here the road splits: head left (south) to reach the Far View Sites complex and Chapin Mesa. Go right (west) to reach Wetherill Mesa, which is open only Memorial Day–Labor Day.

Chapin Mesa

The road onto Chapin Mesa leads south from the Far View Visitor Center. After passing turnoffs to small sites at the **Far View Sites Complex** and **Cedar Tree Tower,** you'll reach a turnoff 20 miles from the park entrance to **Park Headquarters,** 970/529-4465, www.nps.gov/meve, and the **Chapin Mesa Museum,** 970/529-4631, open daily year-round 8 A.M.–5 P.M. (until 6:30 P.M. mid-Apr.–mid-Oct.). The entire history of Mesa Verde is on display here, with an orientation video shown every half hour. There's also a snack bar and gift shop, and you can buy tickets for ranger-led tours ($2.25 pp).

From here an easy three-mile loop trail to **Petroglyph Point** leads to a petroglyph panel and views over Navajo and Spruce Canyons. It starts out low, climbs to the rim, and returns up high. A more popular two-mile trail that descends into Spruce Tree Canyon to **Spruce Tree House**. The third-largest and the best-preserved cliff dwelling in the park, Spruce Tree House had eight kivas and 114 rooms, and was thought to house 125–150 residents. This is the easiest cliff dwelling to enter, and in relatively good shape compared to the other ruins. You can tour it yourself for free from spring to fall (rangers are on duty), and take a ranger-guided tour three times a day in the winter. Both trails are gated—open only during visitor hours—and rangers ask that you register before starting out.

The road splits into two loops beyond the park headquarters and museum, leading to three other large cliff dwellings. The Cliff Palace Loop Road, the eastern loop, leads to two cliff dwellings you'll need a ticket to tour. To reach **Balcony House** visitors have to climb ladders and stone steps and crawl through a tunnel, so it's not for the faint of heart or the easily winded. The other is the huge **Cliff Palace,** the jewel of Mesa Verde, with 217 rooms and 23 kivas sheltered in an exceptionally large alcove. It's estimated that up to 250 people lived here at its peak. (This tour involves climbing four smaller ladders.)

Square Tower House is visible from the Chapin Mesa's western loop, and it's easy to see where it gets it name. The 1.5-mile **Soda Canyon Overlook Trail** starts at a parking area on the loop road past the Balcony House parking area, and goes to the canyon edge for views of Balcony House and other ruins.

Wetherill Mesa

You'll find less traffic on this side of the park, which is good for at least half a day of exploring. (Maximum vehicle length on this road is 25 feet.) You can reach all the sites here by foot trails or (I kid you not) a tram. Twelve miles from the Far View Visitor Center is a parking area where you can hike to **Step House,** open for self-guided

tours via a steep trail. Rangers on duty will explain the evidence of two separate occupations at the site around A.D. 600 and 1200. Otherwise, stop by the snack bar or just load onto the tram, which takes you to the head of the trail to **Long House** as well as to **Bader House, Kodak House,** and the poetically named **Nordenskiold Site #16.** The moderately strenuous tour of **Long House,** the second-largest cliff dwelling at Mesa Verde, includes a steep staircase and covers almost a mile. This one can be visited only on a ranger-led tour.

Other Practicalities

Mesa Verde is open daily, year-round, with limited services in the winter. You can book hotel and campground reservations, as well as guided tours of the ruins ($35–55), through **ARAMARK,** 970/533-1944 or 800/449-2288, fax 970/533-7831, www.visitmesaverde.com.

UTE MOUNTAIN RESERVATION

Colorado's southwest corner cradles this 595,787-acre reservation, 303/565-3751, leading up to the Utah and New Mexico lines (and a bit over each). The main town is Towaoc (toe-WAY-ock), Ute for "all right," located 11 miles south of Cortez on U.S. 160/666. This is where most of the reservation's 1,300 residents live and where you'll find the **Ute Mountain Casino and RV Park,** 970/565-8800 or 800/258-8007, www.utemountaincasino.com. Take your pick from bingo, keno, poker, and blackjack tables and a variety of slot and video poker machines. Kuchu's Restaurant serves Southwest-style food (open daily for all meals). The RV Park, 970/565-6544 or 800/889-5072, charges $17 per night for full hookups. As of 2002, plans were underway to add a 90-room hotel to the tune of $7–8 million. The casino is open from 8 A.M.–3 A.M. daily, with free shuttles to and from Cortez (call 970/565-8800 ext. 133). Dances are held in the Indian Village outside, including the Ute Mountain Bear Dance and Tribal Activities Pow Wow in June.

The area south of Mesa Verde was set aside in 1971 as the **Ute Mountain Tribal Park,** 970/565-9653 or 800/847-5485, www.utemountainute.com/tribalpark.htm, utepark@ fone.net, centered around **Sleeping Ute Mountain** (9,977 ft), a laccolithic peak that really does look like a slumbering giant with his head pointing north, complete with headdress, folded arms, and volcanic plugs for toes. According to legend, the mountain was once a great warrior god, whose violent battle against evil threw up the mountains and valleys all around. Wounded, he lay down to rest, and his blood formed the Mancos River and its tributaries. When his blanket of trees is light green it means spring has arrived; it turns darker in summer, red and yellow in fall, and white in the winter.

The visitor center, 970/564-5317, is 22 miles south of Cortez. With a landscape similar to the national park, the tribal park is also full of Ancestral Puebloan sites, but they have been left in their natural, unreconstructed state. The only way to see them is on a native-guided tour, which leaves from the visitor center daily at 8:30 A.M. The half-day tour to Mancos Canyon ($18 pp) is easier, while the full-day tour to Lion Canyon ($30 pp) involves less time spent driving, proportionally. On this one you'll climb five ladders to visit four cliff dwellings, including the "Eagle's Nest," which has been described as "worth every penny." Bring lunch and water and your own vehicle; if you don't have your own transportation it costs another $6 pp. Make reservations ahead of time by calling 800/847-5485. The park also offers overnight camping at primitive sites along the Mancos River ($11).

SOUTHERN UTE RESERVATION

South of Durango is the smaller (307,000 acres) Ute reservation, 303/563-4525. Most of the 7,880 residents live in the town of Ignacio on U.S. 172. Tribal crafts and historic artifacts, including powwow outfits and amazing beadwork, are on display at the **Southern Ute Indian Cultural Center,**

> *Sleeping Ute Mountain really does look like a slumbering giant with his head pointing north, complete with headdress, folded arms, and volcanic plugs for toes. According to legend, the mountain was once a great warrior god, whose violent battle against evil threw up the mountains and valleys all around.*

970/563-9583 or 563-4649, www.southernute-museum.org, open Mon.–Fri. 10 A.M.–6 P.M., Sat. and Sun. 10 A.M.–3 P.M. (Tues.–Fri. 10 A.M.–5:30 P.M. in winter). Nearby, the **Sky Ute Lodge & Casino,** 970/563-3000 or 888/842-4180, www .skyutecasino.com, is the state's only 24-hour house of gambling, with a lineup similar to its cousin in Towaoc. Hotel rooms are $60–80, the Pino Nuche Restaurant is open daily for all meals, and free shuttle service to Durango, Farmington, and Pagosa Springs is provided.

CORTEZ AND VICINITY

The closest city to Mesa Verde National Park and the Four Corners Monument is surrounded by mountains and sage flats, with huge mesas rising to the south. Sleepy Cortez (pop. 7,300), founded in 1886, occupies land rich in native history, ranging from the Anasazi to the Navajo, who called this spot *Tsaya-toh* ("rock water") for a nearby spring used to water sheep. Irrigation workers trying to bring water from the Dolores River Valley to the north were some of Cortez's first Anglo inhabitants. Sheep and cattle pastured west of town were traded here at the turn of the century, when many of the stone buildings that still line Main Street were built. The 1930s WPA guide to Colorado described the town's importance as an Indian trading center, painting a more lively picture than you'll probably find today: "Cortez is interesting on Saturday nights, when its main street is filled with ranchers, farmers, and Indians; the latter are usually dressed in brilliant velveteens and calicoes, and aglitter with silver and turquoise jewelry."

Sights

Occupying the ornate 1909 E. R. Lamb & Co. Mercantile Building, the **Cortez Cultural Center,** 25 N. Market St., 970/565-1151, www.cortez-culturalcenter.org, lives up to its name with a

NEW MEXICO & COLORADO

© JULIAN SMITH

junkyard near Cortez

museum on the area's rich indigenous heritage, as well as a gift shop and a gallery featuring work by local artists. Native dances are held here at 7:30 P.M. (or thereabouts) Mon.–Sat. Memorial Day–Labor Day, and there's a local farmers market Saturday mornings June–Oct. Other native cultural programs at the center include demonstrations of Navajo sandpainting, flute playing, storytelling, and talks on the famous WWII code talkers. The center is open Mon.–Sat. 10 A.M.– 5 P.M. (to 10 P.M. June–Aug.)

A bit out of town is the **Crow Canyon Archeological Center,** 23390 Road K, 970/565-8975 or 800/422-8975, www.crowcanyon.org, a nonprofit organization focusing on the long-term archaeological investigation of the earliest inhabitants of this corner of the state. The dusty buses parked at the entrance tell you this place isn't really for casual visitors; most people come to participate in the center's long list of research and educational programs or to use the extensive research library. If you've ever wanted to try your hand at the boring half of Indiana Jones's job, this is the place. They organize trips across the Southwest and as far away as Greece, but also offer day programs during the summer for a taste of Mesa Verde archaeology

(Wed. and Thurs. June–Aug., $50 adults, $25 children). The center is open Mon.–Fri. 9 A.M.– 4:30 P.M. To get there, go half a mile north of town on U.S. 666, then take a left on Road L and two more lefts, following the signs for the center. Along the way you'll pass Indian Camp Ranch, "America's first archaeological subdivision," with over 200 Anasazi sites in situ (not including the fake ruins at the gate).

Accommodations

The **Capri Motel,** 2100 S. Broadway, 970/565-3764 or 877/511-9859, offers very tidy lodgings for under $50. In the $50–100 category, choose from the **Tomahawk Lodge,** 728 S. Broadway, 970/565-8521, fax 970/564-9793; the **Anasazi Motor Inn,** 640 S. Broadway, 970/565-3773, fax 970/565-1027; or the **Budget Host Inn,** 2040 E. Main St., 970/565-3738, fax 970/565-7623.

Ten miles west of town, in McElmo Canyon at the foot of Sleeping Ute Mountain, is a singular B&B called **Kelly Place,** 970/565-3125 or 800/745-4885, www.kellyplace.com, kellypl@fone.net. This endearingly schizophrenic spot is half B&B and half educational center,

THE SAN JUAN SKYWAY

A spectacularly scenic loop winds for 236 miles through the San Juan and Uncompahgre National Forests north of Durango. This 236-mile National Scenic Byway passes historic mining towns, prehistoric ruins, and hot springs as it crosses four mountain passes over 10,000 feet. Depending on the season, you can take your pick from waterfalls, wildflowers, Victorian mansions, alpine forests, icy peaks, or starry skies. Although you can drive the Skyway in a day, the spectacular view and recreational opportunities galore demand at least two or three. It's paved the whole way, but countless dirt roads head off into the hills for bicycling, hiking, backpacking, fishing, rafting, and off-roading.

Starting in Durango, the Skyway heads north on U.S. 550, parallel to the Animas River and the train line past Trimble and Hermosa before heading on its own toward Purgatory ski resort. As you climb over Coal Bank Pass (10,640 ft) and Molas Pass (10,910 ft), you'll appreciate how difficult and expensive the "Million Dollar Highway" was to build. (The moniker is also thought to come from the value of the ore-bearing fill used to build the road.) The town of **Silverton** is a National Historic Landmark at the other end of the train line from Durango.

Keep going up U.S. 550 to Red Mountain Pass (11,008 ft), the highest paved pass in the San Juans, which is surrounded by mining ghost towns and alpine scenery. Following the route of an historic toll road, you'll pass through the rust-colored Red Mountain, a collapsed volcanic cone that gave up $750 million worth of gold, silver, and other minerals to early miners. Keep going through the tunnels and waterfalls of the precipitous Uncompahgre Gorge to reach **Ouray,** another Victorian-era mining town turned tourist magnet. Box Canyon Falls and the Ouray Hot Springs are two of the more popular attractions in the area, and Mt. Sneffels (14,150 ft) rises to the west in the center of its own wilderness area. U.S. 550 continues north to **Ridgway,** home to another great public hot spring (this one is outdoors) and authentic enough to be chosen as the film location for classic Westerns like *How the West Was Won* and *True Grit.*

Turn left (west) onto U.S. 62 and cross the Dallas Divide (8,970 ft) to reach **Placerville** on the San Miguel River, where you should take U.S. 145 southeast. Soon a short side road leads east to the box canyon sheltering the painfully picturesque mining town of **Telluride,** where locals and celebrities rub elbows at music festivals and a world-famous ski resort.

U.S. 145 continues south over Lizard Head Pass (10,222 ft), with trails leading into the Lizard Head Wilderness near Mt. Wilson (14,246 ft). Picnic pullouts and historic markers dot the roadway, as does the Ames Power Plant, producer of the world's first commercial supply of alternating current. The road passes more cliffs and waterfalls to tiny **Rico.** Follow the Dolores River, named one of the top 50 trout streams in the United States by Trout Magazine, southwest to **Dolores,** home to the Anasazi Heritage Center and only a short hop from **Cortez.** U.S. 160 from Cortez to Mesa Verde National Park and Durango makes up the southern leg of the Skyway.

offering horse rides, guided botany hikes, and archaeological excursions to the two-dozen-plus sites on the 100-acre property. The lodge itself is an adobe building graced with roses, an orchard, and a courtyard, with seven guest rooms and three private cabins, some of which have kitchenettes, fireplaces, and hot tubs. Owners Rodney and Kristie Carriker have been in business for over two decades and love what they do. Rates are $60–100.

The **Grizzly Roadhouse B&B,** 3450 U.S. 160 South, 970/565-7738 or 800/330-7286, www.grizzlyroadhouse.com, grizbb@fone.net, is more refined than its name might suggest. With two rooms in the main house or a two-bedroom private guest cottage decorated in Victorian style, this getaway is set on 30 acres about 10 miles south of Cortez. The emphasis is on restful: they even offer a "hibernation" spiritual retreat. Rates are $80–100.

On the eastern edge of town is the **Cortez-Mesa Verde KOA Kampground,** 27432 East U.S. 160, 970/565-9301, fax 970/565-2107, www.koa.com/where. Tent sites start at $21 and full hookup sites at $26, with teepees going for $30 and cabins for $40. A heated pool and whirlpool are just a few of the amenities. The **Mesa Oasis Campground,** 5608 U.S. 160, 970/565-8716, four miles south of Cortez, has 72 sites for $16–21.

Food

Quotations about drinking and fools line the walls at the **Main Street Brewery,** 21 E. Main St., 970/564-9112, including my favorite: "Avoid heart attacks—drink beer." They brew their own tasty Mesa Cerveza beers and serve steaks, pizzas, pasta, and burgers for $6–12. Open daily for dinner. An Old West theme pervades the **Homesteaders Restaurant,** 45 E. Main St., 970/565-6253, with old-fashioned favorites like liver and onions and chicken-fried steaks for $9–20, served Mon.–Sat. for lunch and dinner. **Nero's Italian Restaurant,** 303 W. Main St., 970/565-7366, puts a Southwest twist on Italian standbys, with dinner daily for $10–20.

At the intersection of U.S. 160 and 666, the **M & M Family Restaurant,** 970/565-6511, is a 24-hour truck stop featuring roadhouse atmosphere and utilitarian fare for less than you'd expect.

The old wooden post office building is home to the **Quality Book Store & Earth Song Haven Tea Room,** 34 W. Main St., 970/565-9125, which isn't that impressive on the bookstore side but does serve homey fare opposite for breakfast and lunch daily. Next to the cultural center, the **Magpie Coffee House,** 15 N. Market St., 970/564-8595 is a no-frills caffeine filling station open from 7 A.M. Mon.–Sat. For a few more frills, stop by the **Silver Bean,** 410 1/2 W. Main St., 970/946-4404, which occupies a gleaming 1969 Airstream International trailer near the U.S. 666 intersection. This drive-through coffee shop recalls the era of beehive hairdos and pink lawn flamingos (a few even stand out front). There are also a few seats inside, where they serve coffee drinks, Italian sodas, smoothies, and a few sandwiches and burritos. Open Mon.–Fri. 6:30 A.M.–3 P.M., Sat. 7:30 A.M.–1 P.M.

Shopping

A large selection of high-quality native crafts fills the **Notah Dineh Trading Company and Museum,** 345 W. Main St., 970/565-9607 or 800/444-2024, www.notahdineh.com, including pawned items and weaving supplies. Don't miss the

© JULIAN SMITH

Silver Bean café, Cortez

museum downstairs, with its displays cases full of old guns, scalps (really!), and beautiful weavings. The centerpiece is the largest Two Gray Hills rug known (12 by 18 feet), woven by Rachel Curly from 1957 to 1960, a year before the original Notah Dineh opened in the center of town. **Mesa Verde Pottery Gallery Southwest,** 27601 U.S. 160 East, 970/565-4492 or 800/441-9908, also has a large selection, and the **Clay Mesa Art Gallery and Studio,** 29 E. Main St., 970/565-1902, displays colorful pottery wall plates by local artists Rick St. John and Lesli Diane.

Events
Late May brings the **Mesa Verde Country Indian Arts and Culture Festival,** which spreads to Dolores, Mancos, Towaoc, and Mesa Verde National Park with close to a week of music, arts, crafts, and dancing. Highlights include the traditional Ute Mountain Ute Bear Dance and an Old Time Fiddlers' Contest in Mancos. The **Montezuma County Fair** arrives at Cortez in late July or early August.

Information
Stop by the **Colorado Welcome Center,** 928 E. Main St. at Mildred, 970/565-3414, by City Park, for information on local activities and events. Open daily 8 A.M.–5 P.M. You can also call the Cortez **Visitor Information Bureau** at 800/253-1616, or try these websites: www.cortezchamber.org, www.cortez-colorado.com, or www.mesaverdecountry.com.

NEAR CORTEZ
Anasazi Heritage Center
Up in the foothills of the San Juan Mountains near Dolores, this excellent museum, 970/992-4811, www.co.blm.gov/ahc/hmepge.htm, covers all the native cultures of the region, particularly the Anasazi. From the parking lot, a half-mile paved interpretive trail leads uphill to the Escalante Ruins, the size of a modest modern house, with 360-degree views of the surrounding countryside. The smaller Dominguez Pueblo ruins are outside the museum itself: imagine four or five families crammed in these three rooms. Over

three million artifacts and records are housed in the museum's research collection, along with hands-on exhibits, computer programs, and a replica of an ancient pithouse. To get there, turn off U.S. 666 onto U.S. 184 eight miles north of Cortez, or else take U.S. 145 north from the east end of town. Open daily 9 A.M.–5 P.M. Mar.–Oct. (to 4 P.M. otherwise), $3 pp.

Canyons of the Ancients National Monument
The Heritage Center is also the starting point for trips to this new monument, covering a ragged 164,000-acre chunk of BLM-managed land west of Cortez to the Utah border. Set aside in 2000, the monument protects one the of highest known densities of archaeological sites in the United States—more than 20,000 all told—belonging to the Ansazi, Ute, and Navajo cultures. That works out to more than 100 per square mile in some cases. The two largest sites are the Lowry Pueblo National Historic Landmark, with 40 rooms, eight kivas and a great kiva, which is along County Road CC nine miles west of Pleasant View, itself on U.S. 666 about 20 miles north of Cortez. The huge Sand Canyon Pueblo, with 420 rooms, 90 kivas, and 14 towers, was estimated to hold over 700 people at its peak.

There's little to see here—most of it is being reburied to protect it after cataloguing—but the road here is a nice mountain bike ride. Take U.S. 666 south of Cortez a few miles to County Road G (McElmo Canyon Road), then go west 12 miles to the trailhead. From here, four miles of slickrock and dirt track lead past several cliff dwellings (the last mile is too rough to ride). Find more information at their website, www.co.blm.gov/canm/index.html.

Four Corners Monument
The only point in the country where four states meet is a strange little place in a blasted landscape, 30 miles from anywhere. The small park surrounding the monument, run by the Navajo Nation, is open 7 A.M.–7 P.M. Memorial Day–Labor Day and 8 A.M.–5 P.M. the rest of the year ($2 pp). All there is, really, is a granite and brass monument with a small platform to take picture

from—a hand and foot in each state is a popular pose—surrounded by a ring of vendor stands selling T-shirts, crafts, and food. Picnic tables and restrooms are also available. Cortez, Farmington, and Bluff are all about the same distance away.

Hovenweep National Monument

This remote, little-visited monument straddling the Utah-Colorado border preserves five Ancestral Puebloan villages spread across 20 miles. Astonishingly well constructed towers balance on the rims of canyons and even on boulders, centuries after their original inhabitants mysteriously vanished.

Most of the structures here were built A.D. 1200–1300 by groups closely associated with those at Mesa Verde (perhaps jealous country cousins) and abandoned soon after. In addition to the square and circular towers, the D-shaped homes and kivas exhibit such careful masonry that many of these structures have survived more or less intact for over 700 years. The classic Hovenweep ruin is a multi-story pueblo at the head of a canyon with a perennial spring. These often include water-control features such as dams to trap and redirect the precious summer rains into gardens. It's unknown what purpose the towers served; they may have been defensive fortifications, homes, storage structures, celestial observatories, or some combination of the above. "Hovenweep" is a Paiute/Ute term that means "deserted valley," fittingly adopted by photographer William Henry Jackson in the last 19th century.

Start your tour at the **visitor center,** 970/562-4282, www.nps.gov/hove, where there is a campground for tents and small RVs ($10 per night). It's open daily from 8 A.M.–4 P.M. year-round, with longer hours in the summer. The nearby **Square Tower Group,** the only set of structures accessible by paved road, is the largest collection of ruins in the monument. Close to 30 kivas and the striking three-story Square Tower itself are at the head of Little Ruin Canyon. As many as 500 people may have lived here. A moderately rough trail leads along the canyon rim.

Hovenweep's four outlying groups are accessed by dirt roads that aren't regularly maintained and may be impassable to low-clearance vehicles (and to anything in bad weather). The **Holly Group** includes the multi-storied Tilted

© TIM VON PEIN

The Four Corners Monument is the only place in the United States where you can stand in four states at once.

inside the Hatch Trading Post

Tower and Boulder House, another tower perched on a large boulder at the head of Keeley Canyon. The top floor of the latter fell when the boulder shifted centuries ago. Access the **Horseshoe Group** via the Canyon Rim Trail (one mile r/t) to the Tower Point Ruin and the four-unit Horseshoe House. Thanks to a constant spring in Hackberry Canyon, as many as 350 inhabitants may have lived in the **Hackberry Group** a short hike east. Many kivas characterize the **Cutthroat Castle Group,** and a circular tower built on three boulders highlights the **Cajon Group** (ca-HONE).

Hovenweep is open year-round for $3 pp ($7 per vehicle), and passes are good for a week. You can get there by taking County Road G (McElmo Canyon Road) west from U.S. 666 at Pleasant View, north of Cortez, or via U.S. 262, which leaves U.S. 191 between Blanding and Bluff. (County Road G is dirt and may be impassible when wet.)

Hatch Trading Post

This venerable place is a short drive east of Hovenweep. Built in 1903 by Joseph Hatch on the banks of Montezuma Creek, the post is still owned by his descendants. Peacocks bark in the shade of apricot and apple trees out back. The post carries primarily canned food and other staples.

Ismay Trading Post

Somehow feeling even more isolated than Hatch, this adobe structure built in 1921 near the state line has kept its original bullpen configuration. Surrounded by junked cars and a big pile of broken glass, it looks like it could use some historical preservation funds. They sell mostly car parts, groceries, and a few rugs.

NEW MEXICO & COLORADO

© JULIAN SMITH

Southeast Utah

Mention southeast Utah to folks who have heard of the place and the words will typically conjure images of RVs trundling through Arches National Park, mountain bikes careening down Slickrock Trail, and rafters braving raging white water in the canyons of the Colorado and Green Rivers. True, this is the outdoor-recreation epicenter of southern Utah's canyon country, bursting with more opportunities to hike, bike, raft, and gawk at amazing scenery than a vacation of a week or two can contain.

But there's much more to southeast Utah than what's pictured on glossy tour brochures and slick websites. Snowcapped mountains tumbling into thousand-foot river canyons, hot-air balloons soaring over desert towers, and viewpoints that make

you weak in the knees are just a few of the other options in this land of extremes. The 12,000-foot peaks of the La Sal and Abajo Mountains tower over two national parks, a national monument, and plenty of other countryside that could qualify as either. Backcountry trails lead to Anasazi ruins, natural bridges, and quiet towns (yes, including Moab, the epicenter's center) perfectly spaced for the occasional cooked meal and hot shower.

About 34,000 people live in Grand County, San Juan County, and the southern half of Emery County, which combined spread over 13,500 square miles. Residents are independent, conservative, and hardy, many of them descendants of the settlers, homesteaders, and ranchers who arrived when this area was almost completely isolated

Land of Standing Rocks, Canyonlands National Park

© JUAN SMITH

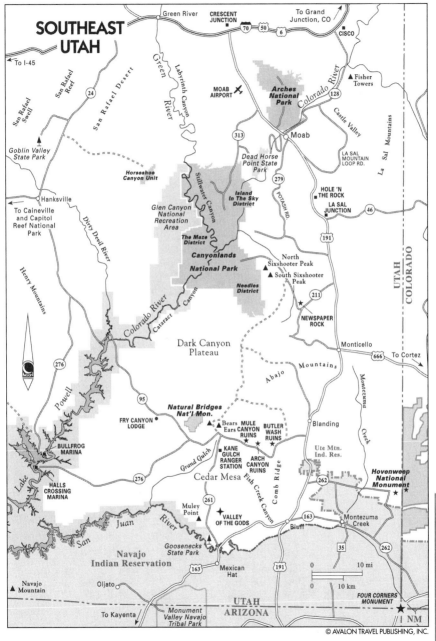

SOUTHEAST UTAH

To I-45

San Rafael Swell
San Rafael Reef
San Rafael Desert
San Rafael Reef

Green River
Labyrinth Canyon
Green River

Green River

CRESCENT JUNCTION
70 50
6 To Grand Junction, CO
CISCO

Colorado River
Fisher Towers
128

24

Goblin Valley State Park

Hanksville

To Caineville and Capitol Reef National Park

Horseshoe Canyon Unit

MOAB AIRPORT

Arches National Park

313

Moab

Castle Valley

La Sal Mountains

LA SAL MOUNTAIN LOOP RD.

Dead Horse Point State Park

279
POTASH RD.

HOLE 'N THE ROCK

LA SAL JUNCTION
46

Glen Canyon National Recreation Area

Stillwater Canyon

Island In The Sky District

The Maze District

Canyonlands National Park

Needles District

191

North Sixshooter Peak
South Sixshooter Peak

211

NEWSPAPER ROCK

UTAH
COLORADO

Dirty Devil River

Henry Mountains

Colorado River
Cataract Canyon

Dark Canyon Plateau

Abajo Mountains

Monticello
666 To Cortez

Montezuma Creek

276

Powell

95

FRY CANYON LODGE

Natural Bridges Nat'l Mon.

Bears Ears
MULE CANYON RUINS
BUTLER WASH RUINS

Blanding

BULLFROG MARINA

HALLS CROSSING MARINA

Lake

276

Grand Gulch

KANE GULCH RANGER STATION

ARCH CANYON RUINS

Cedar Mesa

Fish Creek Canyon

Comb Ridge

Ute Mtn. Ind. Res.

262

Hovenweep National Monument

Juan River

San

Navajo Indian Reservation

Muley Point

261

VALLEY OF THE GODS

Goosenecks State Park

163

Mexican Hat

Bluff

163

Montezuma Creek

35 262

191

0   10 mi
0   10 km

Navajo Mountain

Oljato

To Kayenta

Monument Valley Navajo Tribal Park

UTAH
ARIZONA

FOUR CORNERS MONUMENT

NM

SOUTHEAST UTAH

SOUTHEAST UTAH HIGHLIGHTS

San Juan River: A relaxing raft ride from Bluff to Mexican Hat, easy enough for first-timers (page 143)

Edge of the Cedars State Park, Blanding: One of the Four Corners' most extensive archaeological collections, with a reconstructed Anasazi village in back (page 146)

Moab Mountain Bike Trails: Too many outstanding rides to mention, including the grand-daddy of them all, the Slickrock Trail (page 157)

Arches National Park: A world-famous wonderland of arches, fins, domes, and towers only a short drive from Moab (page 162)

Canyonlands National Park: Choose from the amazing views from the Island in the Sky, hiking and backcountry driving in the Needles District, or the spectacular petroglyphs of Horseshoe Canyon in the Maze District (page 166)

from the rest of the country (we're talking well into the 20th century). Even though southeast Utah is the poster child of Four Corners recreation, the region's remoteness and unforgiving landscape still keep much of it off the tourist radar.

U.S. 191 is the transportation backbone of the region, with side braches at Monticello (U.S. 666 east to Cortez, Colorado) and Blanding (U.S. 95 northwest to Hanksville). At Mexican Hat, most travelers continue southwest on U.S. 163 to Monument Valley on the Arizona border, but U.S. 191 continues south across the Navajo Reservation.

Mexican Hat to Moab

MEXICAN HAT

This tiny town on the San Juan River consists of little more than a few gas stations and hotels, even though it swelled to as many as 1,000 people during various 20th-century mineral-mining booms. As usual, however, the surrounding geology takes up any slack in significance, from the rock formation that gives the town its name to the vibrant patterns in the hillsides above and the black cockscomb of Alhambra Rock across the river.

Accommodations and Food

Nestled in the gorge of the San Juan River by the U.S. 191 bridge, the **San Juan Inn,** 435/683-2210, fax 435/683-2210, has 37 rooms, including two with kitchens, as well as a small but respectable trading post and the **Olde Bridge Bar & Grill,** decorated with Western antiques and open daily for all meals. Rooms are $75. At **Burch's Motel and Trading Company,** 435/683-2221, fax 435/683-2246, http://go-utah.com/burchmotel, rooms are $55, and the trading post has been mostly converted to a convenience store and gas station, although it still dis-

plays a case of dusty jewelry. The **Hat Rock Cafe** next door serves all meals daily, from a $1.50 grilled cheese to $8 chicken-friend steak.

Across the street from the Texaco Station, the **Mexican Hat Lodge,** 435/683-2222, offers 10 rooms for $60 in summer and an outdoor restaurant where you can enjoy a steak cooked by a cowboy on a swinging grill over a cedar-wood fire (platters are $9–25). Once the Top O Hat Bar, this place was bought in 1979 by Bobby and Vonnie Mueller, part of a traveling band who fell in love with the area and decided to stay. **Valle's RV Park,** 435/683-2226, has a dozen sites for $15 including all hookups. They also operate a vehicle shuttle service and storage for river trips, and serve pizzas in their convenience store starting at $8.

Goosenecks State Park

Just north of Mexican Hat is the turnoff to the west for U.S. 261, which climbs the Moki Dugway up onto Cedar Mesa. A short side road leads to a small park, 435/678-2238, overlooking a tortuous series of curves carved by the San Juan River a thousand feet into the desert. The Goosenecks are a textbook example of "entrenched meanders," which begin when a waterway winds across a relatively flat surface. As the landscape is lifted upwards the river cuts deeper and deeper, eventually becoming trapped in the meandering curves it cut long ago. Here the San Juan winds so tightly that it crams five river miles of curves into one mile of landscape. Facilities include four free primitive campsites, rest rooms, and a picnic area.

Valley of the Gods

At the foot of the precipitous climb up Cedar Mesa, another side road heads east into this Monument Valley in miniature. Hundreds of rock formations jut skyward in the mesa's shadow. (Come in late January for the Bluff Balloon Festival, which fills the valley with hot air and color.) The 17-mile dirt road is good enough for cars,

---

RAFTING THE SAN JUAN RIVER

The popular, modestly challenging raft trip down the San Juan River starts three miles west of town on U.S. 191 at the Sand Island Recreation Area. Primitive camping is available for $6, and there's an impressive panel of pictographs on a rock wall, including geometric shapes, humanoid figures with three-tiered headdresses, and one half-ram, half-Kokopelli figure brandishing a flute.

The three-day raft trip to Mexican Hat passes through Class III rapids and the famous Goosenecks of the San Juan, with lots of rock art and ruins en route. Another five or so days will bring you to Clay Hills Crossing just above Lake Powell, the only viable takeout below Mexican Hat (there's a 30-foot waterfall just downstream). You'll need a BLM permit to launch, and mandatory campsites are assigned downstream of Mexican Hat. Contact the Monticello BLM office, 435/587-1544, www.blm.gov/utah/monticello/river.htm, for more information. Call 801/539-1311 for riverflow information, and pick up a copy of the booklet "Running the San Juan River from San Island to Clay Hills Crossing" from the Canyonlands Natural History Association.

---

but impassable when wet, and eventually reconnects to U.S. 191 north of Mexican Hat. Along the way you'll pass the **Valley of the Gods Bed & Breakfast,** 970/749-1164, www.zippitydodah .com/vog, with rooms in a snug stone ranch house and the best porch for hundreds of miles.

BLUFF

Founded in 1880 on the banks of the San Juan River by the exhausted Hole-in-the-Rock expedition, this anomalously liberal enclave is on its way to becoming a sleepier alternative to Moab. Bluff's tiny size (pop. 400) gives it one of the highest per-capita populations of archaeologists, naturalists, and artists in the United States. Restored pioneer homes made from buff-colored sandstone stand along dusty streets lined with huge cottonwoods, and crazy formations with names like Locomotive Rock loom above. The **pioneer cemetery** on a hill overlooking the town pays tribute to Bluff's determined settlers. It's next to an ongoing archaeological excavation thought to be a great house outlier of Chaco Canyon, built by the Anasazi.

Accommodations

For a motel room under $50, try the **Mokee Motel,** 435/672-2242, mokeemotel@sanjuan .net, or the **Kokopelli Inn,** 435/672-2322 or 800/541-8854, fax 435/672-2385, www.kokoinn .com, office@kokoinn.com, both on Main Street (U.S. 191) as it passes through town. All the rest of Bluff's lodgings are in the $50–100 price range. This includes the **Recapture Lodge,** 250 Main St., 435/672-2281, fax 435/672-2284, recapturelodge@hubwest.com, a comfy place with a pool, hot tub, and nightly slide shows on the area.

Navajo rugs and art decorate the **Calf Canyon B&B,** 7th East at Black Locust, 435/672-2470 or 888/922-2470, www.calfcanyon.com, hosts@calfcanyon.com, which has three rooms and a shady patio. Breakfast is also included with a room at the **Pioneer House Inn,** 189 3rd East, 435/672-2446 or 888/637-2582, www.pioneerhouse-inn.com, rmcbluff@sanjuan.net. An 1898 pioneer home in Bluff's historic district, the Pioneer House has five suites with one to three bedrooms

© JULIAN SMITH

Cow Canyon Trading Post, Bluff

each, kitchenettes, and plenty of space to relax outside. Local artwork adorns the inside.

You can't miss the relatively new **Desert Rose Inn & Cabins,** 701 W. Main St., 435/672-2303 or 888/475-7673, fax 435/672-2217, www.desertroseinn.com, information@desertroseinn.com, a three-story log building on the western edge of town. The 30-room place also has six detached cabins for rent. In addition to the Sand Island Recreation Area along the river, you can also camp at the **Cadillac Ranch RV Park,** 435/672-2262 or 800/538-6195, ranch@sanjuan.net, or the **Cottonwood RV Park,** 435/672-2287, both on U.S. 191.

Food

Great homemade pies are the forte of the diner-style **Turquoise Restaurant,** 435/672-2433, on U.S. 191 across from the Recapture Lodge. Offerings start at $5 for sandwiches, and include Navajo fry bread, fried chicken, and steaks up to $11. (Open daily for all meals.) Cowboy-style grilled steaks and catfish ($16–20) are served outdoors at the **Cottonwood Steakhouse,** Main Street and 4th West, 435/672-2282, open daily from 6 P.M. Apr.–Nov. You can eat out on the porch of the **Twin Rocks Cafe,** 913 E. Navajo Twins Dr., 435/672-2252, next to the trading post of the same name. On the menu are pit BBQ and mesquite-smoked chicken ($7–8), as well as vegetarian fare like garden burgers. (Open daily for all meals.)

At one end of Bluff's historic loop on the east end of town, the **Cow Canyon Trading Post and Restaurant,** 435/672-2208, serves up gourmet Southwest fare with fresh local produce so popular that reservations are often necessary. The dining room is in a glassed-in porch out back of the trading post, looking over green fields on the banks of the San Juan River. You can browse the wares while waiting for your entree ($8–12); serves dinner Apr.–Nov.

Shopping

At the foot of the Navajo Twins, a distinctive pair of stone formations on the edge of town, sits the **Twin Rocks Trading Post,** 913 E. Navajo Dr., 435/672-2341, www.twinrocks.com, with one of the best selections of native arts in southeast Utah. The wide stone building with two cigar-store Indians out front holds plenty of high-quality merchandise such as baskets, knives with inlaid handles, rugs, jewelry, and carvings. A short hop away on U.S. 191 is the timeworn **Cow Canyon Trading Post,** 435/672-2208, www.zunifetishes.com, cowcanyn@sanjuan.net, fairly reeking of history from the antique cars out front to the low ceilings and exposed brickwork inside. Built with stones from an old Mormon house in the 1880s, it operated as a trading post in the mid-20th century. Their eclectic collection of souvenirs, art, and books includes lots of pottery and Thomas Begay's "wooden sandpaintings," brightly painted wooden representations of Navajo sandpaintings. They try to be open daily 9 A.M.–5 P.M.

Among the many artists who have set up shop in Bluff is Margaret Labounty, whose **Rock Speaks Studio,** 6th West and Rabbitbrush Avenue, 435/672-2337, www.rockspeaks.com, margaret@labounty.com, displays her nature-inspired ceramics, rock sculptures, and sconces.

Tours and Activities

The highly recommended **Far Out Expeditions,** 7th and Mulberry, 435/672-2294, www.faroutexpeditions.com, farout@sanjuan.net, offer hikes, backpack trips, and vehicle-supported trips to view rock art and ruins throughout the area, including Monument Valley. Half-day tours start at $80 pp, and customized day tours go for $150 pp (two-person minimum). They also offer vehicle shuttles, cookouts, and a guesthouse in a historic home with a kitchen, living room, and two porches for $65 d.

Wild River Expeditions, 101 Main St., 435/672-2244 or 800/422-7654, fax 435/672-2365, www.riversandruins.com, wildriv@sanjuan.net, have been running the San Juan and other nearby rivers since 1957. Their trips run from one to eight days for $120 to $1,500 pp. **Bluff Expeditions,** 435/672-2446 or 888/637-2582, operates out of the Pioneer House, with trips from $50 pp for half-day excursions to $82 for full-day jaunts. River trips start at $120. (To do it yourself, see the special topic "Rafting the San Juan River.")

Buckhorn Llama, 435/672-2466, www.llamapack.com, buckhorn@llamapack.com, organizes llama pack trips (they carry your pack, not you) into the backcountry of southeast Utah and Colorado's San Juan Mountains. Guided trips are $200–300 pp per day, but if you'd rather do it on your own, they also rent the temperamental camelids, with a mandatory getting-to-know-your-llama session included. Explore the area on a more familiar animal with **Cottonwood Creek Cowboy Tours,** 435/672-2321, fax 435/672-2320, www.luckyw.com, el-whip@lasal.net, which hosts horsepack trips ranging from two-hour rides ($50 pp) to overnight trips to Mexican Hat and the Valley of the Gods ($250 pp per day).

Events

The **Bluff Balloon Festival** held the third weekend in January has grown from one balloon to three dozen in 2002. They lift off from the Valley of the Gods near Mexican Hat, adding splashes of color to an already vivid palette. In May the **Herbert Maryboy Memorial Rodeo** brings an authentic Navajo rodeo to town, and the **Utah Navajo Fair** in late August or early September offers traditional song and dance, crafts, food, and more rodeo action. Writers and storytellers gather to exchange words in six languages during the early October **Fandango** at St. Christopher's Mission.

BLANDING

The largest town in Utah's largest county (San Juan) counts just 3,200 residents or so. Set on White Mesa at the southern edge of rolling plains of sagebrush, Blanding hosts three museums and one end of U.S. 95, the "Trail of the Ancients," appropriate given its location in the middle of the ancient territory of the Anasazi. It's a deeply conservative town where alcohol is forbidden.

Archaeological excavations show that the Anasazi occupied this area A.D. 600–1200. Later, the Navajo named the location after the abundant sagebrush that rolls into piñon and juniper at the base of Blue Mountain.

First known as Grayson, the settlement was renamed under somewhat unusual circumstances. In 1914, a wealthy Easterner named Thomas Bicknell offered a thousand-book library to any town in Utah that would take his name. In the ensuing scramble, Grayson came in neck and neck with Thurber, near what is now Capitol Reef National Park. Thurber became Bicknell, Grayson adopted his wife's maiden name of Blanding, and the towns split the books.

In 1923, an abortive uprising by a forlorn group of Utes on the edge of town brought Blanding briefly into the national spotlight as the site of the "Posey War," billed—debatably—as the last Indian uprising in the United States.

Sights

Displays on the Anasazi, Navajo, and Utes fill the **Edge of the Cedars State Park Museum,** 660 W. 400 North, 435/678-2238, http://parks .state.ut.us/parks/www1/edge.htm, which serves as the regional archaeological repository for all of southeast Utah. The extensive collection includes hundreds of everyday objects from sandals to pottery. Many of the artifacts, including much of the extensive pottery collection, were found by locals in pot-hunting excursions in nearby canyons. Don't miss the vibrant parrot-feather decoration on the second floor. A partly excavated Anasazi pueblo stands out back. Native American arts festivals are held here in September; call for information. Open daily 8 A.M.–7 P.M., $1 pp.

Delve even farther into the past at the **Dinosaur Museum,** 754 S. 200 West, 435/678-3454, www.dinosaur-museum.org, a cavernous building filled with the bones, eggs, tracks and even fossilized skin of creatures like the *Allosaurus,* Utah's official state fossil. The museum also houses dinosaur sculptures, exhibits on the latest research, and a great collection of posters from old Hollywood dinosaur movies like *The Beast of Hollow Mountain* and *The Valley of Gwangi.* Open Mon.–Sat. 9 A.M.–5 P.M. Apr.–Oct. (8 A.M.–8 P.M. June–Aug.), $2 pp.

At the edge of town the **Nations of the Four Corners Cultural Center,** 500 S. 700 West, 435/678-3980, offers a series of self-guided trails past dwellings typical of Blanding's earliest residents, from a reconstructed Mormon pioneer cabins to a Navajo hogan. The free educational center is administered by Utah State University.

© JULIAN SMITH

reconstructed kiva at the Edge of Cedars State Park

Accommodations

All of the lodgings listed below have rooms in the $50–75 range. The **Grayson Country Inn,** 118 E. 300 South, 435/678-2388, fax 435/678-2220, occupies a 1908 family home, with nine rooms and a lauded country breakfast every morning. The Grayson was once the only hotel in town, but a few more have opened since then. The **Rogers House Bed & Breakfast Inn,** 412 S. Main St., 435/678-3932 or 800/355-3932, fax 435/678-3276, www.rogershouse.com, hosts@rogershouse.com, dates to 1915, with a large front porch and antique furniture.

Chain motels include the **Best Western Gateway Inn,** 88 E. Center St., 435/678-2278, fax 435/678-2240, and the **Comfort Inn,** 711 S. Main St., 435/678-3271 or 800/622-3250, fax 435/678-3219. Slightly less expensive (under $60) are the **Four Corners Inn,** 131 E. Center St., 435/678-3257, fax 435/678-3186, and the **Prospector Motor Lodge,** 591 S. Main St., 435/678-3231.

Food

Choices reflect the town's name—this isn't a stop for gourmands. "Home style family dining" is the name of the game at the **Old Tymer Restaurant,** 733 S. Main St., 435/678-2122, open daily for all meals (mostly Mexican and steaks) next to the Comfort Inn. The Four Corners Inn also serves lunch and dinner Mon.–Sat. starting at $6, including pizzas for $10–18. There's also the **Homestead Steak House,** 121 E. Center St., 435/678-3456, serving up Navajo tacos, pizza, BBQ ribs, fried ice cream, and homemade pies.

Shopping

Deceptively uninviting, **Huck's Museum and Trading Post,** 435/678-2329, just south of town on U.S. 191, is a log building filled with sundry knickknacks up front and one of the largest private collections of Anasazi artifacts anywhere in the back room. Ask for a tour for a small fee—it's worth it. Across the road, the **Purple Sage Trading Post,** 790 S. Main St., 435/678-3620 or 877/853-6149, www.purplesagetradingpost.com, stocks a wide range of native crafts including Navajo sandpaintings, rugs, pottery, jewelry, and kachinas. You can browse the collection at their website.

Tours

Short day trips to little-known scenic and archaeological spots near town are the specialty of **Back Country Expeditions,** 435/678-3662/3290, lpat@sanjuan.net. Jeff Black's **Black Tracks Jeep Tours,** 435/678-3123, www.blacktrackstours.com, jeff@blacktrackstours.com, offers one- to three-day tours of the surrounding areas for $75, which just might include a campfire performance by Stan Bronson, "The Storysinger."

Information

The **Blanding Chamber of Commerce,** 435/678-2791, www.blandingutah.org, info@BlandingUtah.org, runs a visitor center, 435/678-3662, on U.S. 191 at the north end of town, open daily 8 A.M.–8 P.M. in season.

HIGHWAY 95

Heading west from U.S. 191 just south of Blanding, the "Bicentennial Highway" crosses some of the most scenic backcountry in southern Utah. Built in 1946 but unpaved until 1976, U.S. 95 came with its share of controversy over opening up beautiful but remote Cedar Mesa to the general, non-4WD public. (This road was one target of the environmental saboteurs in Edward Abbey's *The Monkey Wrench Gang.*) The area is particularly rich in archaeology, giving U.S. 95 another nickname aimed squarely at tourists: The Trail of the Ancients. It's one of the easiest ways to access dozens of canyons filled with remnants of prehistoric civilizations, in particular the Anasazi's. (Mileposts are measured west to east from I-15.)

Speaking of the Anasazi, between mileposts 111 and 112 lies a trailhead for a short hike to **Butler Wash,** where a well-preserved pueblo is visible from an overlook. Look for a hand-and-foot trail chipped into the rock to the left of the alcove. West of that is the unmistakable barrier of **Comb Ridge,** a monocline that slashes 80 miles from north to south in an 800-foot jagged wall like the ramparts of an enormous castle. The road crosses the ridge via a gash dynamited from the sheer stone face, to the horror of environmentalists. There's an overlook between mileposts 108 and 109.

A few miles farther, between mileposts 107 and 108, is the turnoff for **Arch Canyon,** where day hikers can find an Anasazi ruin just past the canyon mouth. The entire canyon is good for two or three days' worth of exploration, with plenty of ruins, arches, and side canyons. Another six miles west on U.S. 95 brings you to **Mule Canyon,** where a 12-room dwelling, a kiva, and a two-story circular tower have been excavated and stabilized by the BLM. These structures, all linked by tunnels, were occupied during the Pueblo I to Pueblo III periods. Two miles southeast down the canyon are the **Cave Towers** with half a dozen towers and several cliff dwellings.

Detour: Highway 261

Connecting U.S. 95 with 191, this road heads out across Cedar Mesa proper, providing access to one of the region's most popular overnight hiking loops before literally dropping off the edge. Five miles south of U.S. 95 is the **Kane Gulch Ranger Station,** starting point for the 23-mile loop hike into **Grand Gulch.** Anasazi aficionados know this loop as one of the easiest (and prettiest) ways to access a treasure trove of ruins and rock art. The usual two- to three-day hike connects Kane Gulch with Bullet Canyon and has become so popular that the BLM has instituted a mandatory permit system ($2 pp for day hikers, $8 overnight) for trips during March, April, June, September, and October. The same permit regulations apply to all overnight canyon hikes on Cedar Mesa off U.S. 261. Contact the Monticello Field Office at 435/587-1532 for details.

> *Five miles south of U.S. 95 is the starting point for the 23-mile loop hike into Grand Gulch. Anasazi aficionados know this loop as one of the easiest (and prettiest) ways to access a treasure trove of ruins and rock art.*

Another loop, which sees less traffic than Grand Gulch, connects **Owl** and **Fish Creek Canyons** to the east of U.S. 261. Most often done clockwise, starting down Owl Creek Canyon first, the 15-mile hike takes two to three days. **Slickhorn Canyon,** farther down U.S. 261 to the west, is another popular hike, descending 500 feet in 12 miles to the San Juan River.

About 23 miles south of U.S. 95, U.S. 261 gives up the ghost and plunges off the sheer edge of Cedar Mesa in an astounding display of road-building determination known as the **Moki Dugway.** A series of white-knuckled, guardrail-deficient gravel curves descends 1,100 feet in three miles to the Valley of the Gods and the town of Mexican Hat. At the top of the dugway, take a detour down a dirt road to the west a few miles to **Muley Point Overlook,** a stunning view off the edge of the plateau as far as Monument Valley. Camping up here for sunset and sunrise is an unforgettable experience; you might even see hot-air balloons rising from the Valley of the Gods at dawn.

Natural Bridges National Monument

Back on U.S. 95, near the distinctive double peaks known as the **Bears Ears,** are three huge sandstone bridges spanning White Canyon. The monument, 435/692-1234, www.nps.gov/nabr, also protects many prehistoric cliff dwellings and storage rooms built by the Anasazi. Sipapu, Kachina, and Owachomo bridges were formed when the river changed course and cut across tight bends, eventually tunneling through the fins of rock.

Originally called "President," "Senator," and "Congressman" by prospector Cass Hite in the 1880s, the bridges were briefly renamed "Augusta," "Caroline," and "Edwin" before being *re*-renamed with native terms. The area was set aside by President Theodore Roosevelt in 1908, four years after *National Geographic* magazine sponsored an expedition here, making it the oldest National Park Service area in the state. The solar array that powers the Park Service facilities today— the largest in the world when it was built in 1980—includes a quarter of a million solar cells that produce up to 100 kilowatts.

You can see each bridge from the overlook drive, and short, steep trails (connected by an 8.5-mile loop) lead to the base of each bridge. Admission is $3 pp or $6 for a vehicle, good for a year, and the 13-site campground is $10 per night. The $25 passport to the Southeast Utah Group gives access to Natural Bridges, Arches National Park, Canyonlands National Park, and Hovenweep National Monument for a year.

Dark Canyon Primitive Area

This large, rugged canyon system is one of the wildest and least-explored in the state, even though it's just south of Canyonlands National Park. It takes a multi-day trip to do it justice, but if you have the time and determination, you'll be rewarded with thousand-foot-deep gorges spilling from the western slope of the Abajo Mountains all the way to the Colorado River. The lower canyon is hikeable year-round, and water is available throughout (though only intermittently in the upper reaches).

The most direct access is via an unpaved road that heads north from the entrance road to Natural Bridges National Monument to an 8,500-foot pass between the Bears Ears. Head right at the next intersection and park at the corral. From here you can descend either Woodenshoe or Peavine Canyons, which spill west from Elk Ridge at 8,200 feet in the Manti–La Sal National Forest. Ponderosa pine and Douglas fir grace the wide canyons, both contained within a 46,000-acre wilderness area. As you descend you enter BLM land and the canyons become progressively narrower and deeper. The entire canyon, about 30 miles long, takes three to four days to descend to the furthest reaches of Lake Powell upstream from Hite.

West of Natural Bridges

From Natural Bridges National Monument, U.S. 95 follows White Canyon west to Lake Powell. The dark red Organ Rock shale layer on top of the lighter Cedar Mesa sandstone contrasts wonderfully with the vibrant green of pine trees. At milepost 75 is **Cheese Box Butte,** which looks like, well, a cheese box. A cairned trail at the end of a short dirt track leads down into White Canyon, which you can cross to ascend **Cheese Box Canyon** and its narrows just a few miles up.

Just west of Cheese Box Butte is the **Fry Canyon Lodge,** 435/259-5334, lodge@frycanyon.com, www.frycanyon.com, which bills itself as "Utah's Most Remote Desert Lodge" (a bit like claiming to be "New York's Toughest Cab Driver"). Yet it's hard to imagine a more isolated hotel than this place, established in 1955 as a mining supply center. A post office then a school before it was transformed into a cozy getaway, it is still the only building on U.S. 95 between Blanding and Hanksville. For a base from which to explore one of Utah's more remote corners, it's hard to beat. A gas station and cafe serving all meals are adjacent. Rates: $65–90.

The next major stop along U.S. 95 is **Hite Marina,** 435/684-2457, on the upper reaches of Lake Powell near two bridges over what were once the Colorado and Dirty Devil Rivers. Before Glen Canyon Dam was built, this was the best natural crossing upriver from Lees Ferry. Prospector Cass Hite dubbed it "Dandy Crossing" in the 1880s about the time he discovered gold nearby

and opened the only post office in Glen Canyon. Here in the northernmost Glen Canyon National Recreation Area the scenery becomes an eye-popping spectacle of red, orange, and white mesas, buttes, and spires, sandwiched between the waters of the lake and the gray ramparts of the Henry Mountains. A ranger station, a grocery store, boat rentals, a launching ramp, and a primitive campground ($6 per vehicle per night) are available. West of the rivers is **Hite Overlook,** a grand view over the biblical landscape. (Notice how both interpretive plaques talk about things that have been flooded over.)

About 15 miles west of Hite is the **Hog Springs picnic area** amid red-walled canyons you can hike into after lunch and a nap. Keep an eye out for petroglyphs and pictographs. It's only a few more miles to the junction of U.S. 276 at the base of the Henry Mountains, which leads south to Bullfrog Marina and Halls Crossing on Lake Powell. U.S. 95 heads north across the Burr Desert to join U.S. 24 at Hanksville.

Henry Mountains

The last mountain range to be named in the Lower 48, the Henrys thrust 2,000 feet above the canyon country. Mt. Ellen (11,615 ft) is the highest of three peaks over 10,000 feet, and the northernmost summit in the relatively small range. John Wesley Powell named the range in 1871 after Joseph Henry, his friend at the helm of the Smithsonian Institution, and assigned geologist Grove Karl Gilbert to study their geology. Out of this came Gilbert's classic *Report on the Geology of the Henry Mountains* (1877), which identified the range as laccolithic and made the peaks familiar to geologists worldwide. Near the turn of the century outlaws hid in the mountains among ranches grazing cows, sheep, and goats. Overgrazing still scars the hillsides, which are now home to a herd of about 200 buffalo. One of the few free-roaming herds in the country, these beasts are descended from 18 released in 1941. The Utah Department of Wildlife Resources manages the herd and organizes a yearly hunt. Rusting equipment and abandoned mineshafts are all that remain of the uranium boom of the 1950s.

The views from the mountains, needless to say, are impressive, from the tilted layers of the Waterpocket Fold and the Pink Cliffs to the canyons surrounding Lake Powell and the La Sal Mountains. The Bull Creek Pass Backcountry Byway is one way to access viewpoints like Burr Point and Angel's Point over the Dirty Devil River. A four-mile trail leads from Bull Creek Pass to the summit of Mt. Ellen. The BLM maintains three campgrounds: Starr Springs, McMillan Springs, and Lonesome Beaver, which is near the Dandelion Flat picnic area. For more information, contact the BLM's Henry Mountains Field Station in Hanksville, 435/542-3461.

MONTICELLO

Moab's quiet cousin sits at the foot of the Abajo Mountains, also called the Blue Mountains. Monticello, the San Juan County seat, was founded in 1888 near springs known to travelers for centuries. It took the name of Thomas Jefferson's Virginia country retreat, although in these parts the "c" is soft, not "ch."

Accommodations

The nicest place to stay in town is the **Grist Mill Inn,** 64 S. 300 East, 435/587-2597 or 800/645-3762, www.thegristmillinn.com, reservations@thegristmillinn.com. The B&B occupies the 1933 Monticello Flour Mill, which was used until the mid-1960s. Rooms ($55–85) are full of antiques, and there's a library and a fireplace in the sitting room. A full country breakfast is included in the price. Chain motels include the **Best Western Wayside Inn,** 197 E. Central St., 435/587-2261, fax 435/-587-2920 ($60–75), and a **Days Inn,** 529 N. Main St., 435/687-2458, fax 435/587-2191 ($70–90), both of which have heated pools. Both the **Super 8,** 649 N. Main St., 435/587-2489, fax 435/587-2070, and the **Triangle H Motel,** 164 E. U.S. 666, 435/587-2274, fax 435/587-2175, have rooms for under $50.

Campsites at the **Bar-TN RV Park,** 348 S. Main St. 866/587-1005 or 435/587-1005/2332, www.bar-tn.com, barthhall@sanjuan.net, run $18 for full hookups and $12 for tents, and they also

have cabins for $30 and cable TV. If they're full try the **Mountain View RV Park,** 632 N. Main St., 435/587-2974, or the **Westerner RV Park,** 516 S. Main St., 435/587-2762. Four **Forest Service campgrounds** can be found in the Abajo Mountains: Dalton Springs and Buckboard are both west of town, and Devils Canyon and Nizhoni are south off of U.S. 191. These sites are open from spring to fall for $6–10 per site per night; call 435/587-2041 for more information.

Food

The "cowboy gourmet" cooking at the **MD Ranch Cookhouse,** 380 S. Main St., 435/587-3299, starts with a Buffalo Breakfast of chicken-fried buffalo steak and eggs, and goes from there. Lunch sandwiches are around $5 and dinner entrees are $8 and up. The Western theme continues into the gift stop, art gallery, antique museum, and live music on weekend evenings. Open daily in season for lunch and dinner. Inexpensive subs and salads can be found at **Wagon Wheel Pizza,** 154 S. Main St., 435/587-2766, and **Mesa Java,** 516 N. Main St., 435/587-2601, is the only espresso bar for an hour in any direction. It shares a roof with the Weeds Gallery, plying Southwest art, jewelry, and rugs and pottery from Mexico. Open Thurs.–Tues. in season from 7 A.M. (8 A.M. on Sunday) to 5 P.M.

Activities and Events

Monticello's **Four Corners School of Outdoor Education,** 435/587-2156 or 800/525-4456, fax 435/587-2193, www.fourcornersschool.org, fcs@sanjuan.net, has been running "ed-ventures" throughout the Southwest since 1984. Rafting, hiking, and backpacking trips to Lake Powell, Chaco Canyon, the Grand Canyon, and Yellowstone all have a strong conservation bent. The list also includes family tours, llama treks, women-only trips, and explorations of native culture, rock art, and geology.

March brings the **Blue Mountain-to-Canyonlands Triathlon,** and **Pioneer Days** in July includes parades, games, and food. In August the **San Juan County Fair & Rodeo** arrives in a cloud of dust with various livestock-centered events, dances, and agricultural exhibits.

Information

The **San Juan County Multi-Agency Visitor Center,** 117 S. Main St., 435/587-3235 or 800/574-4386, www.southeastutah.com, is in the San Juan County Administrative Building. It's open Mon.–Fri. 8 A.M.–5 P.M. and 10 A.M.–5 P.M. on weekends Apr.–Oct., then just Mon.–Fri. 9 A.M.–5 P.M. the rest of the year.

Getting There

Bighorn Express, 801/328-9920 or 888/655-7433, www.bighornexpress.com, runs a daily shuttle to and from Salt Lake City via Price, Green River, and Moab. The trip takes 5.5 hours and costs $55 pp o/w (Fri. and Sat. only in Jan. and Feb.).

Abajo Mountains

The Abajo Mountains were named with the Spanish word for "below" when early Spanish explorers gazed down on them from the higher La Sals to the north. Cresting at 11,362-foot Abajo Peak, this small laccolithic range was formed by an underground magma bulge like the ones that formed the La Sals and Navajo Mountain. Aspens, firs, pines trees, and alpine lakes are the perfect respite from the desert's summer heat. (Look for the shape of a horse's head formed by the trees towards the north end of the range when seen from Monticello.) A 22-mile paved road connects Monticello with U.S. 211 to the Needles, crossing the northeast flank of the range.

Moab and Arches National Park

After wandering for 40 years in the wilderness, the Israelites rested in the biblical kingdom of Moab before finally entering the Promised Land. The similarities to the modern seat of Grand County are uncanny: set in a narrow, verdant valley where the Colorado River slices between thousand-foot walls of rock, Moab is surrounded by enough stunning scenery that the Mormons' choice of a name ("beautiful land" in Hebrew) makes perfect sense. Moab has gone through more transformations than many cities 10 times its size, and exerts a force on southern Utah and the consciousness of the country—at least the outdoor-loving part—far out of proportion to its population.

HISTORY

Spanish Valley, also called Moab Valley, was formed when a thick layer of underground salt dissolved, causing the valley floor to sink. Native groups from the Anasazi and Fremont to the Sabuagana Utes lived here for the relatively mild climate, riverside soils, and shallow ford of the Colorado River. A Spanish expedition led by Juan Maria Antonio de Rivera arrived in 1765 from New Mexico, and things picked up in 1830 when the blazers of the Spanish Trail between

Santa Fe and Los Angeles first took advantage of the easy river crossing.

Mormon settlers came to stay in 1878 after a previous group of missionaries was run off by native tribes. The biblical name of Moab was adopted two years later. The townsite, on the south bank of the river near the foot of the La Sal Mountains, saw its first ferry begin operating in 1885. A modest economy at the turn of the century was based on ranching, farming, and the growing of fruit such as grapes, apples, and peaches. The first bridge spanned the river in 1912, but traffic was sparse.

The Cold War ushered in the town's first economic boom. The sudden demand for uranium brought hundreds of prospectors to comb the hills with Jeeps and Geiger counters. Charlie Steen's 1952 discovery of the La Vida mine, in the Lisbon Valley southeast of town, proved that there actually were fortunes to be made. Moab's population more than tripled during the 1950s; almost overnight the sleepy farming community became known as "The Uranium Capital of the World."

A smaller oil boom lasted into the 1960s, but Moab would have to wait another few decades for its next revolution. It was already obvious that Moab was rich in the natural beauty department: Arches National Monument had been set aside in 1929 (and made a park in 1971),

SLICKROCK CAMPGROUND

PORTAL RV PARK

To Butch Cassidy's King World Water Park, Colorado River bridge, Hwy. 128, Hwy. 279 (Potash Rd.), Arches National Park, Hwy. 313 (Canyonlands National Park, Dead Horse Point State Park), and I-70

MOAB

191

Swiss Cheese Ridge

Slickrock Bike Trail

Slickrock Bike Trail

SUNSET GRILL

MCGILL

500

Practice Loop

0   0.25 mi

0   0.25 km

MOAB ROCK SHOP

400 N. ST.

POISON SPIDER BICYCLES

TAG-A-LONG EXPEDITIONS

CITY PARK

PARK DR.

EKLECTICAFE

KNAVE OF HEARTS BAKERY

200 N. ST.

SUNFLOWER HILL B&B INN

TRAILHEAD FOR SLICKROCK BIKE TRAIL

OUTLAW SALOON

JAILHOUSE CAFE

100 N. ST.

RIM CYCLERY

ARROYO RD.

CENTER ST.

Swiss Cheese Ridge

CLUB RIO

CALI COCHITTA HOUSE OF DREAMS B&B

City Dump

Mill Creek

BLUE HERON B&B

FAT CITY SMOKEHOUSE

SEE DETAIL

100 S. ST.

KANE

ADOBE ADOBE

GONZO INN

MOAB DINER

APACHE MOTEL

200 S. ST.

To Moab Skyway, Scott M. Matheson Wetlands Preserve, and Colorado River

VIRGINIAN MOTEL

DREAM KEEPER INN

Moab Rim

CREEK BLVD

WOODY'S TAVERN

300 S. ST.

LOCUST LN.

MOAB CYCLERY

DAVE'S CORNER MARKET & CAFE

GEARHEADS

Mill Creek Dr.

SAND FLATS RD.

BIG HORN LODGE

CANYONLANDS CAMPGROUND AND RV PARK

Mill Creek

CHILE PEPPER BIKE SHOP

MOAB BREWERY

191

Pack Creek

LAZY LIZARD INTERNATIONAL HOSTEL HOLYOAK LN.

To Hole 'N the Rock and Monticello

DETAIL

POPLAR PLACE PUB & EATERY

BACK OF BEYOND BOOKS

100 N. ST.

TOM TILL GALLERY

DAN O'LAURIE CANYON COUNTY MUSEUM

MOAB INFORMATION CENTER

TIMES INDEPENDENT MAPS

CENTER ST.

HOGAN TRADING CO.

CENTER CAFE

LIBRARY

EDDIE MCSTIFF'S/ MONDO CAFE/ GEARHEADS

PAGAN MOUNTAINEERING

KOKOPELLI LODGE

© AVALON TRAVEL PUBLISHING, INC.

M

SOUTHEAST UTAH

Canyonlands National Park had been declared in 1964, and river running was a tourism staple by the early 1970s.

In the 1980s, though, word started to get out that the slickrock landscape, so beloved by local motorcyclists and Jeep drivers, was perfectly suited to a brand-new sport called mountain biking. Knobby tires stuck to the smooth sandstone like glue, and the endless hills, dips, bowls, and mountain trails were soon recognized as some of the best and most challenging mountain bike terrain in the world.

Thus Moab was reborn once again as one of the prime tourist destinations in the Southwest, set smack in the middle of an outdoor adventurer's nirvana. Today, thousands of visitors throng the streets on weekends in the spring and fall, particularly during festivals celebrating mountain biking or 4WD vehicles. Drawn by famous parks and adrenaline sports, visitors arrive from around the world and just next door; they say you can tell spring has arrived when all the license plates in town turn Colorado green. Like them or not, arrive they do, and they are an increasingly crucial (in an economic sense) and worrisome (from the environmental angle) fact of life to the undisputed tourist epicenter of canyon country. T-shirt and trinket shops along the town's short Main Street are packed in spring and fall, but in the heat of summer and chill of winter the place can be almost eerily quiet.

Moab is a diverse community for southern Utah, with Spandex-clad mountain bikers and overall-ed cowboys rubbing elbows with Italian tourists and Jeep-driving frat boys from Boulder. Although still mostly Mormon, Moab (pop. 4,000) has a steadily growing liberal spirit that keeps alive the spirit of Edward Abbey, who penned the classic *Desert Solitaire* after a few seasons as a ranger in Arches in the 1960s. Hollywood finally caught on to Moab's natural beauty in the 1960s, and dozens of films have been shot in the immediate environs from the classic (*Wagon Master* and *Cheyenne Autumn*) to the not-so-classic (*Indiana Jones and the Last Crusade* and *Warlock*).

SIGHTS

For a break from the desert, visit the **Scott M. Matheson Wetlands Preserve,** 435/259-4629, which protects 875 acres of marsh between Moab and the Colorado River. Birding is especially good here from spring to fall; over 180 species have been seen. Administered by the local office of The Nature Conservancy, it's open daily from sunrise to sunset (free admission). Guided nature walks leave from the main entrance at 8 A.M. on Saturday mornings Mar.–Oct. The preserve is three-quarters of a mile down Kane Creek Boulevard from the McDonald's on Main Street.

Offering another way to escape the heat is **Butch Cassidy's King World Water Park,** 435/259-2837, whose entrance is north on U.S. 191 almost to the Colorado River bridge (look for the sign). It fills a secluded box canyon, supposedly used by Butch Cassidy's Wild Bunch to hide rustled cattle, with five water slides, three pools, and a host of other facilities. Also on the premises is a 40-ton boulder carved with strange pictures by an eccentric European immigrant in the early 1930s. Open May–Aug. Tues.–Sat. 11:30 A.M.–7 P.M., admission $11.50 adults, $9.50 children 12 and under (Sun. and Mon. hours are 1–6 P.M., admission $10 adults, $8 children 12 and under).

Moab's history gets a good workout at the **Dan O'Laurie Canyon County Museum,** 118 E.

© JULIAN SMITH

Balanced Rock, Arches National Park

ODDNESS NEAR MOAB

One of the better offbeat destinations in the Southwest is the **Hole N' The Rock,** 11037 S. U.S. 191, 435/686-2250, a 14-room home that was chipped, blasted, and sculpted out of a sandstone cliff 15 miles south of Moab. It took Albert Christensen 20 years to hollow out his 5,000-square-foot residence, which includes a 65-foot chimney, a creepy taxidermy collection, and a portrait of F.D.R. cut into the outside wall. Albert is buried outside next to his wife Gladys, near the ostrich pen and concrete sculpture garden. Don't ask—just go. It's open daily 9 A.M.–6 P.M. (5 P.M. Labor Day–Memorial Day), $4 pp, with guided tours a few times per hour.

America's Most Scenic Dump, along the road up to the Slickrock Trail, offers unparalleled views of snow-capped mountains, red rock arches, and soaring eagles. Rumor has it that Juneau, Alaska, may have an even prettier setting for its garbage, but Moabites still claim their landfill is the most picturesque. At the apocalyptic ghost town of **Cisco,** near where U.S. 128 meets I-70, over 100,000 sheep once grazed in the shadows of the Book Cliffs before being shipped out by train. Founded in 1883, Cisco was abandoned (more or less—a few holdouts remain) when the interstate was built far enough away that passing traffic just kept passing. It's a strange place to visit, especially when overcast skies make the abandoned buildings, including the one-room Cisco post office, even spookier than normal.

Center St., 435/259-7985. Exhibits on geology, paleontology, and the town's human history include dinosaur bones and a 1907 Moab kitchen. It's across from the courthouse, open Mon.–Sat. 1–8 P.M. in summer (shorter hours in winter). **Moab's Skyway,** 985 W. Kane Creek Blvd., 435/259-7799, brings the incongruous sight of a ski lift to the cliff face southwest of town. The 12-minute ride carries you 1,000 feet up to the top of the Moab Rim, where there's a viewing deck and access to bike and hiking trails that would otherwise require hours of pain and suffering to summit.

The lift can carry bikes too. It operates daily 9 A.M.–9 P.M. Feb.–Dec. (weekends only 9 A.M.–7 P.M. the rest of the year) for $9 adults, $7 children under 13. (Another lift was built on the north end of town near the water park, but money matters—and perhaps the whims of taste—had kept it immobile into 2002.)

ACCOMMODATIONS

In Town

Bear in mind that in this tourist town, hotel prices can fall by as much as half off-season (Nov.–Feb.). Aside from camping, Moab's cheapest lodging is at the **Lazy Lizard International Hostel,** 1213 S. U.S. 191, 435/259-6057, www.gj.net/~lazylzrd, Lazylzrd@lasal.net. Chock full of character, it boasts a full kitchen, laundry, hot tub, and showers ($2 for non-guests). Dorm rooms are $8 pp, and they also have private rooms ($22 d) and log cabins ($27–29 d). Campsites are available for $6 pp with full use of the facilities.

While he was in town filming *Rio Bravo,* John Wayne stayed at the **Apache Motel,** 166 S. 400 East, 435/259-5727, fax 435/259-8989. Today their rooms go for $85 in season, as do the rooms at the **Big Horn Lodge,** 550 S. Main St. 435/259-6171 or 800/325-6171, fax 435/259-6144, www.moabbighorn.com. The **Virginian Motel,** 70 E. 200 South, 435/259-5951, fax 435/259-5468, is slightly less expensive at $75 d, and for the same price you can enjoy the hot tub and shaded back yard of the **Kokopelli Lodge,** 72 S. 100 East, 435/259-7615 or 888/530-3134, www.kokopellilodge.com, kokopeli@lasal.net, which offers eight rooms a block from Main Street.

It's easy to see how the **Adobe Abode,** 778 W. Kane Creek Blvd., 435/259-7716, www.adobeabodemoab.com, adobeabode@lasal.net, got its name. Located next to the wetland preserve, the distinctive building boasts tile floors, a hot tub, and rooms for $110. The attitude of many Moab visitors is summed up in the name of the **Gonzo Inn,** 100 W. 200 South, 435/259-2515 or 800/791-4044, fax 435/259-6992, www.gonzoinn.com, gonzoinn@gonzoinn.com, a more luxurious place with an outdoor pool. Rooms are $125, and the well-appointed suites start at $163 and range up to $300 for ones with espresso bars and private whirlpool baths.

A late-1800s Victorian home houses the **Cali Cochitta House of Dreams B&B,** 110 S. 200 East, 435/259-4961 or 888/429-8112, fax 435/259-4964, www.moabdreaminn.com, calicochitta@lasal.net. Three rooms and a suite ($90–150) share a wide front porch. Jim and Kathy Kempa have done a good job of making the **Dream Keeper Inn,** 191 S. 200 East, 435/259-5998 or 888/230-3247, www.dreamkeeperinn.com, info@dreamkeeperinn.com, a relaxing place. It's tastefully decorated with a pool, hot tub, and rose garden. Rooms are $90–115, and the two cottages go for $135 each. Moab's only AAA four-star lodging is the **Sunflower Hill B&B Inn,** 185 N. 300 East, 435/259-2974 or 800/MOAB-SUN, fax 435/259-3065, www.sunflowerhill.com, innkeeper@sunflowerhill.com. Twelve rooms in two buildings have antique beds (some have private balconies); wooded pathways lead to an outdoor hot tub. Rates: $140–200.

Outside of Town

Actor Robert Duvall and author Edward Abbey are just two of the notables to grace the **Pack Creek Ranch,** 435/259-5505, fax 435/259-8879, www.packcreekranch.com, pcr@packcreekranch.com, with their presence. Although it dates to the 19th century, this place is still a working ranch, said to have been named after an incident when a pair of prospectors ditched their gear by a nearby stream to escape Indians. The 300-acre ranch has a wide variety of lodging options, including rooms in the ranch house, bunk houses, and fully renovated cabins with full kitchens and rock fireplaces—but emphatically *no* phones or TVs. There's also a sauna and hot tub. Rates are $180–300 for up to four people in season ($90–150 in July and Sept.), and the two-person orchard house is $125 ($65). The ranch is in the foothills of the La Sals southeast of Moab; turn off at milepost 118 on U.S. 191 (8 miles south of town), then take a right onto the La Sal Mountain Loop Road and go six miles to Pack Creek Road on your right.

Even larger is the 9,000-acre **La Sal Mountain Guest Ranch,** 435/686-2223 or 888/870-1088, fax 435/686-2223, www.moab-canyonlands.com/mtranch, mtpeale@moab-canyonlands.com, run by the Redd family since 1914. Also still in operation as a working cattle ranch, it offers accommodations in hand-hewn log cabins, 19th-century wooden frame houses, and the 1938 Redd family home ($90–120). This one is 32 miles southeast of Moab in the La Sal foothills; call for directions.

Camping

All of these commercial campgrounds are open year-round. Sites at the **Canyonlands Campground and RV Park,** 555 S. Main St., 435/259-6848 or 800/522-6848, www.canyonlandsrv.com, info@canyonlandsrv.com, are $16 for tents, $23 for all hookups, and cabins are $32. The **Portal RV Park,** 1261 N. U.S. 191, 435/259-6108 or 800/574-2028, www.portalrvpark.com, camp@portalrvpark.com, is north of town on U.S. 191. They also offer tent sites ($17), RV sites ($23–26) and cabins ($35–39). A heated pool and hot tubs are a few of the many amenities of the **Slickrock Campground,** 1301 1/2 N. U.S. 191, 435/259-7660 or 800/448-8873, www.slickrockcampground.com, info@slickrockcampground.com. Tents are $16–26, RV sites are $22, and cabins with a/c are $27.

In addition to the campground at **Arches National Park, Canyonlands National Park,** and **Dead Horse Point State Park,** many primitive campsites are available on BLM and Forest Service land near Moab. All are open year-round; contact the Moab District Office for more details. There are nine campgrounds up U.S. 128 along the Colorado River, from Goose Island (1.4 mi) to Dewey Bridge (28.7 mi), ranging from $5–10 per site per night. Four more can be found down Kane Creek Road, from Kings Bottom (2.8 mi) to Echo (8 mi), all of which are $5. **The Sand Flats Recreation Area** near the Slickrock Trail has 143 sites ($8); along U.S. 279 south along the Colorado River are two more campgrounds: Jaycee Park (7 sites, $10) and the Goldbar campground (10.2 mi, 10 sites, $5). Finally, there are two campgrounds up the La Sal Mountain Loop Road: Ken's Lake (31 sites, $10) and Warner Lake (20 sites, $7).

FOOD

Breakfast and Coffee

Maybe it's all the physical exertion that goes on around here, but Moab has more than its fair share of places to gas up and refuel your internal engines. The **Jailhouse Cafe,** 101 N. Main St., 435/259-3900, occupies a turn-of-the-century courthouse with two-foot adobe walls, serving up justifiably famous Grand Marnier French toast and Southwest-style eggs Benedict for breakfast daily ($7–8). The outdoor porch at the **Eklecticafe,** 352 N. Main St., 435/259-6896, is a great place to enjoy some banana nut pancakes when it's sunny out, which it almost always is. Breakfast is served daily, and lunches, like Indonesian satay and curry wraps ($6–8) are served Mon.–Sat.

Homemade breads, pastries, and desserts are the specialty of the **Knave of Hearts Bakery,** 84 W. 200 North, 435/259-4116, open Tues.–Sun. The java is always fresh and flowing at the **Mondo Cafe,** 59 S. Main St., #6, 435/259-5551, which serves breakfast and baked goods daily until 6 P.M. **Dave's Corner Market & Cafe,** 401 Mill Creek Dr. at 400 East, is another standby for good coffee. Breakfast is served anytime at the throwback **Moab Diner,** 189 S. Main St., 435/259-4006, starting at $4, and they serve inexpensive lunches and dinners as well (open daily).

More Substantial

Satisfy your post-trail protein craving in a few juicy bites at the **Fat City Smokehouse,** 36 S. 100 West, 435/259-4302, serving excellent Texas-style pit BBQ for lunch and dinner Mon.–Sat. The **Poplar Place Pub and Eatery,** 11 E. 100 North, 435/259-6018, specializes in custom pizzas and offers Guinness on draft as well as a dozen microbrews (open daily for lunch and dinner). On that note, Moab has two true brew-pubs. The **Moab Brewery,** 686 S. Main St., 435/259-6333, has pool tables and separate restaurant and bar areas, where they serve steaks, seafood, pasta, and vegetarian dishes daily for lunch and dinner. Their brews include Dead Horse Ale and Raven Stout. **Eddie McStiff's,** 57 S. Main St., 435/259-2337, is Moab's oldest (dating all the way back to 1991), with a similar

menu but better food on average. Their brick-oven pizza and pasta dishes are especially good.

One of southern Utah's best restaurants is the **Center Cafe,** 92 E. Center St., 435/259-4295, with a Zagat's award of excellence and a secluded courtyard to its credit. Their "classical and globally inspired" menu lists dishes like Maine lump crab cakes and pan-seared lamb loin for lunch (up to $18) and dinner ($32), with homemade ice cream to top it off. Open daily for all meals.

More Unusual

Uranium millionaire Charlie Steen built his dream home on a hillside overlooking Moab. Today it goes by the name of the **Sunset Grill,** 900 N. U.S. 191, 435/259-7146, serving steaks and seafood (entrees $14–21) with a wonderful view thrown in for free. Open Mon.–Sat. for dinner. Families favor the Wild West show and cowboy supper cookout at the **Bar-M Chuckwagon,** 7000 N. U.S. 191, 435/259-2276, served "trail style" on metal plates. It all starts at 7 P.M. daily, faux gunfight and all, four miles north of Arches National Park ($20 adults, $10 children).

NIGHTLIFE

As a tourist epicenter, Moab has more nightlife than any three other towns in southern Utah combined. Eddie McStiff's and the Moab Brewery are the usual starting points, followed by **Club Rio,** 2 S. 100 West, 435/259-666, with live music Fridays and Saturday and karaoke Wednesdays and Thursdays. The **Outlaw Saloon,** 44 W. 200 North, 435/259-2654, set in what looks like an airplane hangar, has pool tables, cheap beer, and a rather startling painting behind the bar. **Woody's Tavern,** 221 S. Main St., 435/259-9323, is another rougher-edged place on Main Street.

SHOPPING

You'll find one of the best collections of books on all things Southwest *in* the Southwest at **Back of Beyond Books,** 83 N. Main St., 435/259-5154 or 800/700-2859. The **Tom Till Gallery,** 61 N.

Main St., 435/259-9808 or 888/479-9808, showcases the panoramic work of a local photographer, and the **Hogan Trading Co.,** 10 S. Main St., 435/259-8118, sells Indian art, sculpture, jewelry, baskets, kachinas, and pottery. (Main Street is full of interchangeable souvenir stores specializing in T-shirts, shot glasses, and sunscreen.) Even if you're not a geology buff, you should still drop by the **Moab Rock Shop,** 600 N. Main St., 435/259-7312, which is full of amazing (and often quite pricey) fossils, dinosaur bones, mining relics, and minerals.

Bike Shops

For obvious reasons, Moab has no shortage of these either. You can buy or rent bikes, browse gear, and have your bike repaired at the **Chile Pepper Bike Shop,** 702 S. Main St., 435/259-4688 or 888/677-4688, the **Moab Cyclery,** 391 S. Main St., 435/259-7423, or **Poison Spider Bicycles,** 497 N. Main St., 435/259-7882 or 800/635-1792, www.poisonspiderbicycles.com, which also has showers and a free repair stand out back. The **Rim Cyclery,** 94 W. 100 North, 435/259-5333 or 888/304-8219, www.rimcyclery.com, does all of the above and also sells camping gear.

Outdoor Gear

Gearheads, 59 S. Main St., 435/259-3633 and 471 S. Main St., 435/259-4327, has two locations crammed with camping and general outdoor gear, including maps, guidebooks, tents, clothes, and hydration systems. Get your climbing gear at **Pagan Mountaineering,** 88 E. Center St., 435/259-1117, www.paganmountaineering.com, which has more cams than you've probably ever seen together in one place. For topo maps and more guidebooks, head to **Times Independent Maps,** 29 E. Center St., 435/259-5529.

RECREATION
Mountain Biking

Moab has enough mountain bike trails to fill a series of guidebooks, so those below represent just a sample of the best. Don't underestimate this landscape—these trails can be highly difficult and even deadly in spots—and *always* bring enough food and water in case things don't go according to plan in the backcountry.

The granddaddy of all mountain bike routes, the **Slickrock Trail,** actually began as a motorcycle path. Mountain bikers have since taken over, with over 100,000 riders per year attempting the

MOAB CLIMATE

Month	Average High	Average Low	Mean	Average Precipitation
January	43°F	20°F	32°F	0.67 inches
February	53°F	26°F	39°F	0.50 inches
March	64°F	35°F	50°F	0.90 inches
April	73°F	42°F	58°F	0.99 inches
May	84°F	50°F	67°F	0.81 inches
June	95°F	58°F	76°F	0.37 inches
July	101°F	64°F	82°F	0.91 inches
August	98°F	63°F	81°F	0.83 inches
September	89°F	53°F	71°F	0.75 inches
October	75°F	41°F	58°F	1.26 inches
November	57°F	30°F	43°F	0.77 inches
December	46°F	21°F	34°F	0.63 inches

12-mile loop up, down, and around the petrified sand dunes northeast of town. This is a difficult trail, with sand traps, sheer drop-offs, few rest spots, and nothing but bare rock to cushion a fall. It's also some of the most fun you can have on two wheels—the pedaled equivalent of a roller coaster, with great views, to boot. If this is your first time, try the two-mile practice loop first. (**Bartlett Wash** northwest of town is another good slickrock area, albeit smaller, that sees much less traffic).

To reach the Slickrock trailhead, take 100 South toward the mountains from Main Street, then follow the signs to Tusher Street and Sand Flat Road, where you'll have to pay a fee ($5 per car or $2 per bike) to enter the **Sand Flats Recreation Area,** 435/259-2444. Keep going 6.4 miles past the Slickrock parking lot to reach the trailhead for the **Porcupine Rim** trail, an exhausting but exhilarating ride that climbs 1,000 feet up into the La Sal Mountains before peaking at a stunning view of Castle Valley from the southern rim. From here it's almost 3,000 feet downhill to U.S. 128. A car shuttle is a good idea for the 15-mile ride.

Another relentless climbs awaits at the **Moab Rim,** but thankfully this one is shorter: almost 1,000 vertical feet in less than a mile. (One biking guidebook says this "may well be the toughest mile in the world.") The top of the climb, 1.6 miles from the trailhead along Kane Creek Boulevard, is reward enough (feel free to give the chair lift riders a disdainful sniff), but you can also continue another six technical miles to Hidden Valley and a downhill bike portage to rejoin U.S. 191 south of Moab. Across the canyon is the **Poison Spider Mesa** trail, overlooking the Colorado above U.S. 279. A more moderate ride, this one starts near the dinosaur track and climbs 1,000 feet to the top of the mesa. Drink in the view, all the way to Arches National Park, before deciding if you're up for the Portal Trail, where you are highly advised to dismount and walk your bike down a narrow

The granddaddy of all mountain bike routes, the Slickrock Trail, actually began as a motorcycle path. Mountain bikers have since taken over, with over 100,000 riders per year attempting the 12-mile loop up, down, and around the petrified sand dunes northeast of Moab.

trail with a sheer drop to one side to avoid a possibly deadly fall. Via the Portal Trail this is a 12.7-mile one-way ride, rejoining U.S. 279 closer to Moab. Otherwise you can turn around to make it a 12-mile round trip.

On BLM land near the Island in the Sky are two good easy-to-moderate rides that should take about half a day each. The **Gemini Bridges** are a pair of arches at the edge of a mesa that you can walk out onto. The trail leaves U.S. 313 on its way out to the Island in the Sky, then coasts steadily downhill for 13.7 miles, passing the bridges and one small uphill en route, to U.S. 191 just south of the U.S. 313 turnoff. You'll need a car shuttle to do the one-way ride. Another trail takes you close to **Monitor and Merrimac Buttes** in roughly the same area. Turn off U.S. 191 to the left (west) just north of milepost 141, cross the train tracks, and park after another half a mile. The 13.2-mile loop trail (take the right fork initially) leads you past the buttes as well as Determination Towers and the Mill Canyon Dinosaur Trail (also accessed off U.S. 279). Farther up U.S. 191 from Moab (16.5 mi) is a trailhead on the right (east) leading to the **Klondike Bluffs,** a steady climb 800 feet up slickrock and dirt to an amazing view over the northern part of Arches National Park. This is a medium-difficulty trail that's 15.2 miles r/t.

Several longer trails await riders who are willing to spend a night or more outdoors (and carry everything they need during the day). While more of an undertaking, these really let you venture far into the backcountry, far from the day-pedal crowds. You'll need a set of racks and panniers or a bike trailer to carry your gear. The 100-mile **White Rim Trail** around Canyonlands' Island in the Sky is a three- to four-day ride, and one of the most incredible mountain bike trips in the country. **Kokopelli's Trail** is a 142-mile odyssey from the Colorado mountains to the Moab slickrock. It starts just over the border near Loma, Colorado, 15 miles west of Grand Junction, and roughly follows the Colorado River southwest before climbing into the foothills of the La Sals and descending to Moab. Most people take six days to do the entire ride, which covers everything from fire roads to singletrack, but it's possible to resupply, start, or stop at several points along the way. Various maps and guides to this epic journey are available.

Recommended companies for bike tours in Moab include **Rim Mountain Bike Tours,** 1233 S. U.S. 191, 800/626-7335, www.rimtours.com, info@rimtours.com; **Nichols Expeditions** out of the Chile Pepper bike shop, 497 N. Main St., 435/259-3999 or 800/648-8488, www.nichols-expeditions.com, info@nicholsexpeditions.com; **Western Spirit Cycling,** 476 Millcreek Dr., 435/259-8732 or 800/845-2453, www.western-spirit.com, biking@westernspirit.com; and **Kaibab Mountain Bike Tours,** 391 S. Main St., 435/259-7423 or 800/451-1133, www.kaibabtours.com, kaibabtour@aol.com. Prices start at $80 pp for half-day trips including bike rental, and a few, such as Nichols Expeditions, have a long roster of adventure trips around the world.

Hiking

Though most people around here hit the backcountry on two wheels (or four), dozens of hiking trails snake through the desert and hills around Moab. From Potash Road (U.S. 279), it's possible to hike two steep miles up to the **Portal Overlook** from the Jaycee Park Recreation Site and, six miles farther down the road, up to **Corona Arch** (1.5 mi o/w). Across the Colorado River on Kane Creek Boulevard, another steep trail leads up to the **Moab Rim,** at the top of the chair lift, and into the area known as **Behind the Rocks,** a maze of sandstone fins similar to the Fiery Furnace in Arches National Park. Farther down Kane Creek Boulevard, the Jeep road up **Pritchett Canyon** leads past (and sometimes through) small pools to a natural bridge, and a trail up **Hunters Canyon** passes Hunter Arch high on the right-hand side above cottonwood trees and pools. (The trailheads for these hikes are 2.6, 3.1, and 7.5 miles from U.S. 191/Main Street, respectively.)

From U.S. 128 upstream along the Colorado River, look for the turnoff for **Negro Bill Canyon** on the right after three miles. This slickrock gorge leads to Morning Glory Natural Bridge, the sixth-longest in the country at 243 feet, in a side canyon to the right, two miles up. You can keep hiking up the main canyon past the bridge for a few more miles. This was the site of a skirmish in the so-called "Sagebrush Rebellion" in 1979, when anti-government locals used a county bulldozer to break through a dirt barrier—twice—that the BLM had erected to protect the canyon while it was being considered as a wilderness area.

Off-Road Driving

Hundreds of miles of dirt roads crisscross the rough country of southeast Utah, and Moab sits at the center of it all. Blazed by ranchers and uranium prospectors, many are still popular with 4WD enthusiasts, who flock to town for the **Easter Jeep Safari. Farabees Adventures,** 401 N. Main St., 435/259-7494, runs three Jeep tours daily in season in six-person vehicles. **Tag-a-Long Expeditions,** 452 N. Main St., 800/453-3292, fax 435/259-8990, www.tagalong.com, tagalong@tagalong.com, has tours into Canyonlands National Park, including jetboat/Jeep combination day trips.

Climbing and Canyoneering

Although the Wingate sandstone layer is the only one really worth climbing around here, there are still plenty of options for climbers within a quick trip of Moab. **Wall Street** along Kane Creek Boulevard is frighteningly close to traffic but is a good place to experience desert climbing for the first time. **Castle Valley** up U.S. 128 is a broad, flat valley punctuated by towers the size of office buildings with names like the Nuns, the Priest, and the Rectory. Castleton Tower itself is the home of the one of the country's classic tower climbs, the Korr-Ingalls route (5.9, 4 pitches), leading to a flat peak the size of a studio apartment—an incredible spot. There are a few routes in Arches and Canyonlands National Parks, including Washer Woman Arch off the Island in the Sky and Owl Rock in Arches, but be warned that climbing regulations are more restrictive in the parks than outside (no chalk and no new bolts, for starters). **Indian Creek** on the way to the Needles district of Canyonlands is another world-famous climbing area; see "Canyonlands National Park," below.

Canyoneering is an exciting, relatively new sport that involves minor rock climbing and rappelling to access canyons that would otherwise be too difficult or dangerous to enter. This is not for the uninitiated or faint of heart, but if you know what you're doing—or are with someone who does—it can provide a feeling of adventure and discovery like few other pursuits.

Stock up on climbing gear (repeat after me: "cams, cams, cams") at Pagan Mountaineering, and book climbing trips and instruction through **Moab Cliffs & Canyons,** 63 E. Center St., 435/259-3317, www.cliffsandcanyons.com, or **Moab Desert Adventures,** 801 E. Oak St., 435/260-2404, www.moabdesertadventures.com. Prices start at $85 for a half-day trip for two people, and all three guide services also offer canyoneering trips. **Desert Highlights,** 50 E. Center St., 435/259-4433 or 800/747-1342, www.deserthighlights.com, info@deserthighlights.com, specializes in canyoneering for $80 pp per day.

Rafting

Moab's location near the confluence of the two biggest rivers in the Four Corners means that outdoor enthusiasts aren't limited to just dry land. Trips range from easy afternoon floats to serious, multi-day whitewater. Permits are necessary whether you're floating through Canyonlands National Park or BLM land outside of it. (For information on Labyrinth and Stillwater Canyons of the Green River, see "Floating Labyrinth and Stillwater Canyons" under Green River, below.)

Between Grand Junction, Colorado, and Moab, the Colorado River provides a great introduction to desert rafting. Rapids ranging from Class II to Class IV have names like Sock-It-to-Me, Last Chance, and Room-of-Doom. In all it's 131 river miles from the border to Moab. **Westwater Canyon,** from the Westwater Ranger Station (4.5 miles from the border) to the landing at Cisco, does require permits, which are available from the BLM office in Moab (82 E. Dogwood Ave., 435/259-7012, www.blm.gov/utah/moab/ww-info.html). Permittees are chosen by lottery. This

trip takes one to two days. From Dewey Bridge to the boat ramp below the Potash Plant along U.S. 279 is 46 miles, and takes two to three days. You don't need a permit for this stretch, but check with the BLM for camping rules.

The Potash ramp is the last takeout before Hite Marina on Lake Powell, 118 miles downriver. After two days of leisurely floating through deep canyons, the Colorado River joins with the Green and explodes into **Cataract Canyon,** where 26 rapids have names like Hell-to-Pay and the Big Drops. This stretch provides some of the best white-water thrills in the country from May to June, its spring surge unfettered by any dam. The still waters of Lake Powell mark the end of the trip. Boating permits ($20–30) are required to cross through Canyonlands National Park.

Moab is full of experienced rafting companies, which run trips from May to September. Prices start at $35 for a half day on The Daily to around $800 pp on a five-day Cataract Canyon adventure. Westwater Canyon will run you about $350 pp for two days or $500 for three.

One of the oldest companies in town is **Tex's Riverways,** 691 N. 500 West, 435/259-5101, www.texsriverways.com, info@texsriverways.com, which has been operating since 1958 on the Green and Colorado Rivers. They run a jetboat down to the confluence and back on a regular basis that can pick you up if you're doing your own trip. **Tag-a-Long,** 452 N. Main St., 800/453-3292, fax 435/259-8990, www.tagalong.com, tagalong@tagalong.com, in business since 1964, can help you organize self-guided trips. **Sheri Griffith Expeditions,** 2231 S. U.S. 191, 435/259-8229 or 800/332-2439, fax 435/259-2226, www.griffithexp.com, info@griffithexp.com, organizes women-only raft trips, among many others. **Adrift Adventures,** 378 N. Main St., 435/259-8594 or 800/874-4483, www.adrift.net, info@adrift.net, does horseback and 4WD excursions as well as raft trips.

Other good rafting companies in town are **World Wide River Expeditions,** 625 N. Riversands Rd., 435/259-7515 or 800/231-2769, fax 435/259-7512, www.worldwideriver.com, info@worldwideriver.com, and **Canyon Voyages,** 211 N. Main St., 435/259-6007 or

800/733-6007, fax 435/259-9391, www.canyonvoyages.com, info@canyonvoyages.com.

Other Tours

Local paleontology maven **Lin Ottinger,** who has a dinosaur named after him (*Iguanadon Ottingeri*), has been guiding geology, fossil, and rock hunting tours since the 1960s. Ask at the Moab Rock Shop. The **Camelot Lodge,** 435/260-1783, www.camelotlodge.com, camelot@camelotlodge.com, near Hurrah Pass south of town, offers half- and full-day trips on camelback for $70–140 pp, in addition to accommodations at their five-room lodge ($95 pp).

EVENTS

In late March, runners in the **Canyonlands Half Marathon** thank their guardian angels the desert heat hasn't ramped up to full intensity yet. The **Easter Jeep Safari** in April crams the streets and nearby 4WD trails with gleaming off-road trucks and their boisterous drivers. The **Green River–Moab Friendship Cruise** on Memorial Day weekend brings a flotilla drifting downstream from the city of Green River. June sees an influx of classic roadsters for the **Rod Benders Car Show** and is also the month to catch a rodeo, either the **PCRA Rodeo** or the **Canyonlands Rodeo,** both of which are held at the fairgrounds.

The **Grand County Fair** arrives at the fairgrounds in August, and the **Moab Music Festival** brings the strains of chamber music to Spanish Valley in early September. In October the **Canyonlands Fat Tire Festival** welcomes as many out-of-state bikers as the Jeep Safari does Jeepers. Later that same month the **Moab Film Festival** showcases the works of independent filmmakers.

GETTING THERE AND AROUND

Shuttle Services

If you're not up to tacking on a 10-mile pedal to each end of your exhausting mountain bike ride, ring up one of Moab's many shuttle services, which can drop you off and/or pick you up at either end. They're also handy for raft trips and getting to and from the airport. Prices start at

$25 per vehicle for trailhead runs. Options include **Atomic Transfer,** 438 N. Castle Valley Dr., 435/259-7062, atomic@moab-canyonlands.com; **Acme Bike Shuttle,** 702 S. Main St., 435/260-2534, kymears@yahoo.com; **Coyote Shuttle,** 435/259-8656; and, perhaps inevitably, **Roadrunner Shuttle,** 435/259-9402.

Bighorn Express, 801/328-9920 or 888/655-7433, www.bighornexpress.com, runs a daily shuttle to and from Salt Lake City via Price and Green River (and continuing to Monticello). The 4.5-hour trip costs $50 pp o/w (Fridays and Saturdays only in January and February).

Airlines

Great Lakes Airlines, 800/554.5111, www.greatlakesav.com, reservations@greatlakesav.com, flies to Denver and back twice daily for $116 pp o/w. They also have a daily flight to Page, Arizona, ($90 o/w), continuing on to Phoenix. Tickets can be booked through Frontier Airlines at 800/432-1359.

Car Rental

You can rent cars in Moab from **Thrifty,** 711 S. Main St. (at the Moab Valley Inn), 435/259-7317, and **Budget,** 401 N. Main St., 435/259-4274. **Farabees Adventures,** 435/259-7494, rents 4WD trucks at the same address. **Slickrock Jeep Rentals** is located at 284 N. Main St., 435/259-5678.

Information

While each federal land management agency has an office in town, they've turned over everything tourist-related to the **Moab Information Center,** Main and Center Streets, 435/259-1370 or 800/635-MOAB, open daily in season from 8 A.M.–8 P.M. "The Mic" is the place to go for just about any question you might have; if they don't have the answer, they know who does. They also sell maps and books. Public **Internet access** is available at the Lazy Lizard hostel, Red Rock Bakery, Slickrock Cafe, Mondo Cafe, and the Moab Public Library (25 S. 100 East).

More information on Moab and its environs can be obtained from the **Moab Area Travel Council,** 435/259-8825 or 800/635-6622,

www.discovermoab.com, info@discovermoab
.com, as well as from websites such as www
.moab-utah.com, www.moab.net, www.moab-
happenings.com, and www.canyonlands-utah.com.

ARCHES NATIONAL PARK

The Four Corners' most famous park is, in the
minds of many, synonymous with the Southwest itself; the image of Delicate Arch (only one
of over 2,000 found within the park) has been
emblazoned on everything from license plates
to shot glasses. Although arches occur around
the world, there are more here than anywhere
else, along with spires, fins, pinnacles, and balanced boulders, and more of these geological
oddities are almost surely waiting to be discovered
even inside the park itself.

To say the least, Arches is a popular park. Besides mountain biking, it's the other reason more
visitors come to Moab. Its wonders are for the
most part easily accessible (i.e., close to a paved
road) and the park is just the right size to "do" in
a day, making it popular with families and RV
drivers. Expect crowds and a full campground
in the spring and summer, especially around
popular weekends like the Jeep Safari and Fat
Tire Festival.

The Setting

Like most of the Moab region, Arches sits on
top of an ancient underground salt bed left over
from the sea that once covered the Colorado
Plateau. Over time layers of rock laid down on
top of the salt were thrust upward and cracked as
the salt shifted and flowed. Wind, water, and ice
gradually ate away at the exposed cracks to form
free-standing fins still visible throughout the area;
think of them as proto-arches or arch building
blocks. These in turn were undermined by erosion until the relatively soft sandstone collapsed.

Sometimes, though, the interplay of weight
and balance was just right so that an **arch** remained even after its supporting stone was swept
away. The physics of arch formation are complex, but in a nutshell it takes the least energy for
a chunk of rock to drop away in a curve, rather
than a straight line. Horizontal **pothole arches**

can also be cut through by the chemical reaction
of rainwater collecting in natural depressions.

Today the park's sandstone ranges in size from
three feet—the minimum for something to be
considered an arch—to 306 feet, in the case of
Landscape Arch. Most of them are formed from
salmon-colored Entrada sandstone, with a few
made from lighter Navajo sandstone.

Scenic Drive and Hikes

Arches National Park **visitor center,** 435/719-
2299, www.nps.gov/arch, is five miles north of
Moab on U.S. 191. Entrance is $5 pp or $10
per vehicle and good for a week. (The $25
Southeast Utah Group passport gives access to
Arches and Canyonlands National Parks, and
Hovenweep and Natural Bridges National
Monuments for a year.) Arches is open daily
year-round from 8 A.M.–4:30 P.M. (7:30 A.M.–
6:30 P.M. from Mar.–Oct.) There are books and
maps for sale, rangers to question, and exhibits
on the park's geology and human history, as
well as an orientation film shown every half
hour. Ask about guided hikes and campfire talks
programs at the campground.

From here the park's 18-mile **scenic drive**
zigzags up the steep side of the Moab Fault to
climb up onto the mesa where most of the park is
located. If this is your first taste of the local
scenery, be prepared to be impressed: the high-altitude desert in every direction is littered with
rock towers and formations of every shape imaginable, and the La Sal Mountains stand on the
horizon. It's truly an amazing sight, especially in
the early morning or late afternoon when the
sunlight sets the stone on fire.

The first turnoff is for **Park Avenue** through the
Courthouse Towers, a set of giant stone formations reminiscent of a row of skyscrapers. A moderate trail descends into a small canyon and leads
for a mile through the towers to rejoin the scenic
drive, so you can hike it in either direction or
arrange for a pickup. At the **Courthouse Towers
Viewpoint** at the far end of the trail, look for rock
formations with names like the Organ, the Three
Gossips, Sheep Rock, and the Tower of Babel.

The scenic drive continues between a set of
petrified sand dunes to the right (east) and the

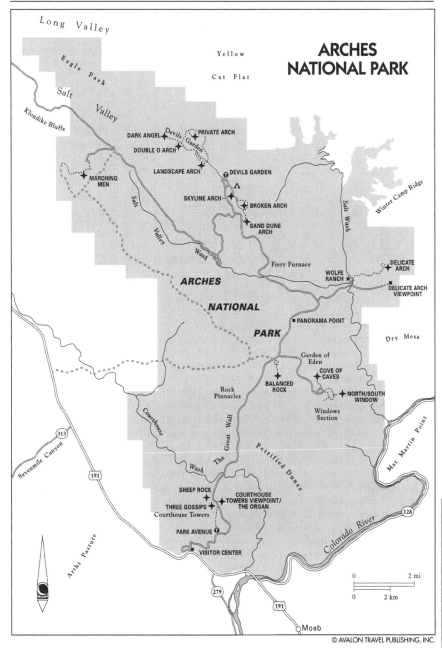

ARCHES
NATIONAL PARK

Long Valley

Eagle Park

Salt

Valley

Klondike Bluffs

Yellow

Cat Flat

DARK ANGEL
DOUBLE O ARCH
LANDSCAPE ARCH
MARCHING
MEN

Devils Garden
PRIVATE ARCH
DEVILS GARDEN
SKYLINE ARCH
BROKEN ARCH
SAND DUNE
ARCH

Salt

Valley

Wash

Salt Wash

Winter Camp Ridge

Fiery Furnace

ARCHES

NATIONAL

PARK

WOLFE
RANCH

DELICATE
ARCH

DELICATE ARCH
VIEWPOINT

PANORAMA POINT

Dry Mesa

Garden of
Eden

Rock
Pinnacles

BALANCED
ROCK

COVE OF
CAVES

NORTH/SOUTH
WINDOW

Windows
Section

Mat Martin Point

Courthouse

The Great Wall

Petrified Dunes

313

191

Sevenmile Canyon

Wash

SHEEP ROCK

THREE GOSSIPS
Courthouse Towers

PARK AVENUE

VISITOR CENTER

COURTHOUSE
TOWERS VIEWPOINT/
THE ORGAN

128

Colorado River

Arches Pasture

MOON

0   2 mi

0   2 km

279

191

Moab

Great Wall to the west, where you can sometimes spot climbers tackling cracks in the sandstone. A little over nine miles down the road from the entrance is one of the park's most famous formations: **Balanced Rock,** a 3,600-ton boulder that looks like a gentle breeze could knock it over. A short, paved trail leads around the rock. The park's original entrance road, now called Willow Flats Road, joins the scenic drive from the west here. This is one of the few opportunities for decent mountain biking in the park; you can ride this road all the way back to U.S. 191, eight miles north of the visitor center.

Just past Balanced Rock is a side road to **The Windows,** a pair of huge arches that dwarf hikers brave enough to climb up into the openings. An easy trail leads to the North and South Windows and Turret Arch, and a primitive loop trail heads behind them and back to the parking area. A second trail leads to the **Cove of Caves** and **Double Arch,** near a complex of standing rocks called the **Garden of Eden.**

Return to the main road and keep going for another 2.5 miles to reach a second side road. Civil War veteran John Wesley Wolfe built **Wolfe Ranch** near the turn of the century, where he lived with his family for two decades before moving back to Ohio. A nearby petroglyph panel that includes images of men on horseback is thought to be the handiwork of the Ute tribe. From the ranch a three-mile trail leads up across slickrock to the base of **Delicate Arch,** probably the most famous arch in the world. It takes a few hours at least to make the trip out and back, so bring water. Despite its size, Delicate Arch really does look fragile and imbalanced, as if a touch could send it toppling. (Early settlers had more descriptive names for it, including Cowboy's Chaps and Old Lady's Bloomers.) If you're content with the view from afar, keep driving a mile past the ranch to a parking area where a very short trail leads to a viewpoint, with a slightly longer trail climbing closer.

Back on the main road once again, head down into the crazy pastel colors of Salt Valley and back out again to the pullover for the **Fiery Furnace,** a maze of stone fins and canyons that are actually cooler in summer than the surrounding desert. There aren't any marked trails here, so the best (and safest) way to explore this fascinating corner of the park is on a ranger-led hike. Moderately strenuous three-hour excursions happen twice daily in season and cost $6 pp ($3 children). They're very popular and often fill up a day or two before; make reservations at the visitor center up to a week in advance.

Three more miles brings you to the turnoff for the unpaved **Salt Valley Road** that heads northwest to **Klondike Bluffs,** a striking and little-visited corner of Arches that is also accessible via a moderate mountain bike trail from U.S. 191. Out here you'll also find **Tower Arch** near the park border, accessed by a trail that begins eight miles from the scenic drive.

Only another mile of scenic drive remains, ending at the campground and a trailhead for **Devils Garden.** This is one of the park's arch hotspots, with no fewer than seven major arches along a 3.6-mile trail. Pass **Tunnel Arch** and **Pine Tree Arch** to where the trail splits. To the right it quickly becomes primitive (i.e., unmaintained) and loops past **Private Arch** to rejoin the main trail at **Double O Arch.** If you chose to go left you'll pass **Landscape Arch,** the park's largest, an impossibly thin span (only six feet across at one point) that dropped a large piece of rock in 1991. (It's an easy two-mile r/t hike here from the trailhead.) The trail becomes more difficult past this point as it leads to the aptly named **Dark Angel** formation.

The **Devils Garden campground,** open year-round, has 52 sites ($10) available on a first-come, first-served basis. It fills quickly in spring and fall, so preregister your site at the entrance station or visitor center early in the morning. There are tables, grills, toilets, and potable water, but no showers. **Skyline Arch,** a half-mile hike from the campground, doubled in size in November 1940 when a huge chunk fell from underneath.

NEAR MOAB

Highway 279: Potash Road

This beautiful drive snakes along the bank of the Colorado River after leaving U.S. 191 north of the bridge. It's paved for the 16 miles it runs within

© JULIAN SMITH

Castleton Tower, in Castle Valley north of Moab, is a favorite for climbing.

touching distance of the canyon's north wall. Look for a **rock art** panel five miles from the turnoff from U.S. 191, near a popular rock climbing spot called Wall Street (watch out for parked vehicles and climbers). More petroglyphs and a set of **dinosaur tracks** are signposted at 6.2 miles, and at 13.6 miles is **Jug Handle Arch** on the right-hand side. The pavement ends at the large evaporation ponds of the **Moab Salt Plant** (also known as the Potash Plant). From here the dirt road continues to the White Rim Road and the Schaefer Trail inside Canyonlands National Park.

Highway 128

Another Scenic Byway heads northeast along the Colorado River from the south side of the U.S. 191 bridge, paved all the way to I-70. It's a longer route that U.S. 279 and an even prettier drive. At the turnoff is a picnic area and, just upriver, a natural spring gushing from the canyon wall where you can fill water bottles for hikes up **Negro Bill Canyon.** The turnoff for **Castle Valley** is on the right at 15.5 miles, where huge sandstone towers jut towards the sky against the backdrop of the La Sal Mountains. Head up the wide valley, crosshatched by dirt roads and fields,

to access the **La Sal Mountain Loop Road,** a 62-mile paved road that climbs the mountains' flanks before looping back to Moab south of town. (It's closed by snow from early fall to late spring.) Back on U.S. 128, the weird muddy spires of the **Fisher Towers** rise above **Professor Valley** near milepost 21. These darker towers are much less photogenic than their cousins in Castle Valley, but they have also been climbed, despite the poor quality of the rock.

The road crosses the river at **Dewey Bridge,** where a one-lane suspension bridge of wood and steel built in 1916 was replaced by a concrete span in the 1980s. The old bridge is still there, near a picnic and boat-launching area. (Look for the abandoned gas station covered with biblical paintings nearby.) The landscape opens up into barren rolling flatland as the road nears I-70. If you have the time, don't miss the turnoff to the ghost town of **Cisco.**

La Sal Mountains

The second-highest range in Utah rises above the high desert east of Moab, tantalizing sweltering visitors with visions of snow-capped peaks well into summer. In fact, the name La Sal ("the

SOUTHEAST UTAH

salt" in Spanish) is said to have come from Spanish missionaries who couldn't believe there was snow in the midst of such a furnace.

Six peaks above 12,000 feet are capped by Mt. Peale (12,721 ft), and mountain lakes sparkle amid fir and aspen forests throughout. Plenty of trails tempt hikers, bikers, and horseback riders in the summer, and skiers and snowshoers in the winter. The 60-mile **La Sal Mountain Scenic Route** climbs the mountains' flanks between Castle Valley and U.S. 191 south of Moab. It's a gorgeous drive punctuated by picnic areas, viewpoints, and unpaved spur roads its entire length. (It's closed by snow from late fall to early spring.)

Over 60 miles of trails cross the mountains. Mountain bikers get a good lung workout at these elevations; the two most popular rides each cover about 3,700 feet of elevation change. The **Burro Pass** trail, an eight-mile loop that's half dirt road and half singletrack, passes two mountain lakes and viewpoints of Arches and Canyonlands National Parks. Another good ride is the **Three Lake Trail,** a 14-mile figure eight of faint singletrack past Oowah, Clark, and Warner Lakes. Many hikers try to summit **Mt. Tukuhnikivatz,** a five-mile endeavor up and back that starts at 10,000 feet and climbs another 2,400.

Canyonlands National Park

If one place encapsulates the heart of the Colorado Plateau, it is Canyonlands, the largest of southern Utah's five national parks. From lightning-swept mesa tops to the roiling depths of the Colorado and Green River gorges, Canyonlands encompasses rock art, prehistoric dwellings, sheer-walled ravines, lush riverside thickets, raging rivers, and abundant desert life. And for all there is to see and do, there are almost as many ways to go about it: scenic drives, easy hikes, placid floats, and sweeping vistas give way to 4WD tracks, steep trails, frothing white water, and claustrophobic slot canyons the farther you push in to the backcountry. Covering 527 square miles and ranging from 3,700 to 7,200 feet in elevation, Canyonlands is big enough to offer something for just about everyone. If, by some terrible turns of events, you had to pick only one park to visit on the Colorado Plateau, make it this one.

The Y formed by the confluence of the two rivers neatly divides the park into three sections (four, actually, counting the **River District** itself). The **Island in the Sky District,** north of both the rivers and closest to Moab, is a wide-

> *If one place encapsulates the heart of the Colorado Plateau, it is Canyonlands, the largest of southern Utah's five national parks. Canyonlands encompasses rock art, prehistoric dwellings, sheer-walled ravines, lush riverside thickets, raging rivers, and abundant desert life.*

open tableland far above the rivers themselves. Connected to the rest of southern Utah by only a narrow causeway, the Island has many viewpoints looking across thousands of square miles of canyon country. Most are easily accessible by a paved scenic drive, along with short trails and the longer White Rim Trail around the mesa's base. Dead Horse Point State Park gives a taste of the Island in miniature.

The **Needles District**, southeast of the Colorado River, takes its name from distinctive red and white spires of Cedar Mesa sandstone, jumbled like the skyline of an alien city. This is more of a backcountry district, with plenty of excellent trails and 4WD roads perfect for overnight trips. West of the rivers, the remote **Maze District** is almost a world in itself. Accessed by river or off of U.S. 24, it's by far the least visited and least accessible part of the park. It includes the separate **Horseshoe Canyon** section, rich with rock art. The Maze has plenty of opportunity for isolation and adventure, and is detailed in the South-Central Utah chapter.

One $10 fee (per vehicle) gives access to all

© JULIAN SMITH

Canyonlands National Park

districts of the park for a week. (A $25 passport to the Southeast Utah Group gives access to Canyonlands and Arches, and Hovenweep and Natural Bridges National Monuments for a year.) Backpacking permits are $15, and 4WD and mountain bike camping permits are $30; both are good for 14 days. Some 4WD roads in the Needles require permits for day use. For more information, contact the park office in Moab at 435/719-2313 (backcountry reservations 435/259-4351), www .nps.gov/cany. You can also get information on the park and the surrounding area from the **Canyonlands Natural History Association,** 3031 S. U.S. 191, Moab, 435/259-6003 or 800/840-8978, www.cnha.org, info@cnha.org. They stock a truckload of books, posters, and other goodies related to the Colorado Plateau.

THE SETTING

Canyonlands owes its stunning topography to the usual culprits of layered deposits, dramatic uplift, and gradual erosion. From the Paradox Formation at the bottom of Cataract Canyon to the Navajo sandstone on top of the Island in the Sky, the park's geologic history spans hundreds of

millions of years. Many of its most outstanding features occur in the Cutler Formation, dating to the Permian Period (245–286 million years ago). The unmistakable White Rim around the Island in the Sky, 200 feet thick and flat as a pancake, and the Cedar Mesa sandstone formations in the Needles and Maze Districts are both part of the Cutler Formation.

Above the White Rim, in order, are the brownish, silty Moenkopi Formation, the uranium-rich shale of the Chinle Formation, the soaring vertical cliffs of Wingate sandstone topped by the harder protective layer of the Kayenta Formation, and the creamy curves of Navajo sandstone, the youngest layer in the park. Another 140 million years of geology above all this is now gone, swept away by the rivers.

HISTORY

For such an inhospitable-looking place, Canyonlands has had many inhabitants over the years. The Fremont people left spectacular pictographs and petroglyphs in Horseshoe Canyon near the Maze and Salt Canyon in the Needles. Not to be outdone, the Anasazi left their own share of rock

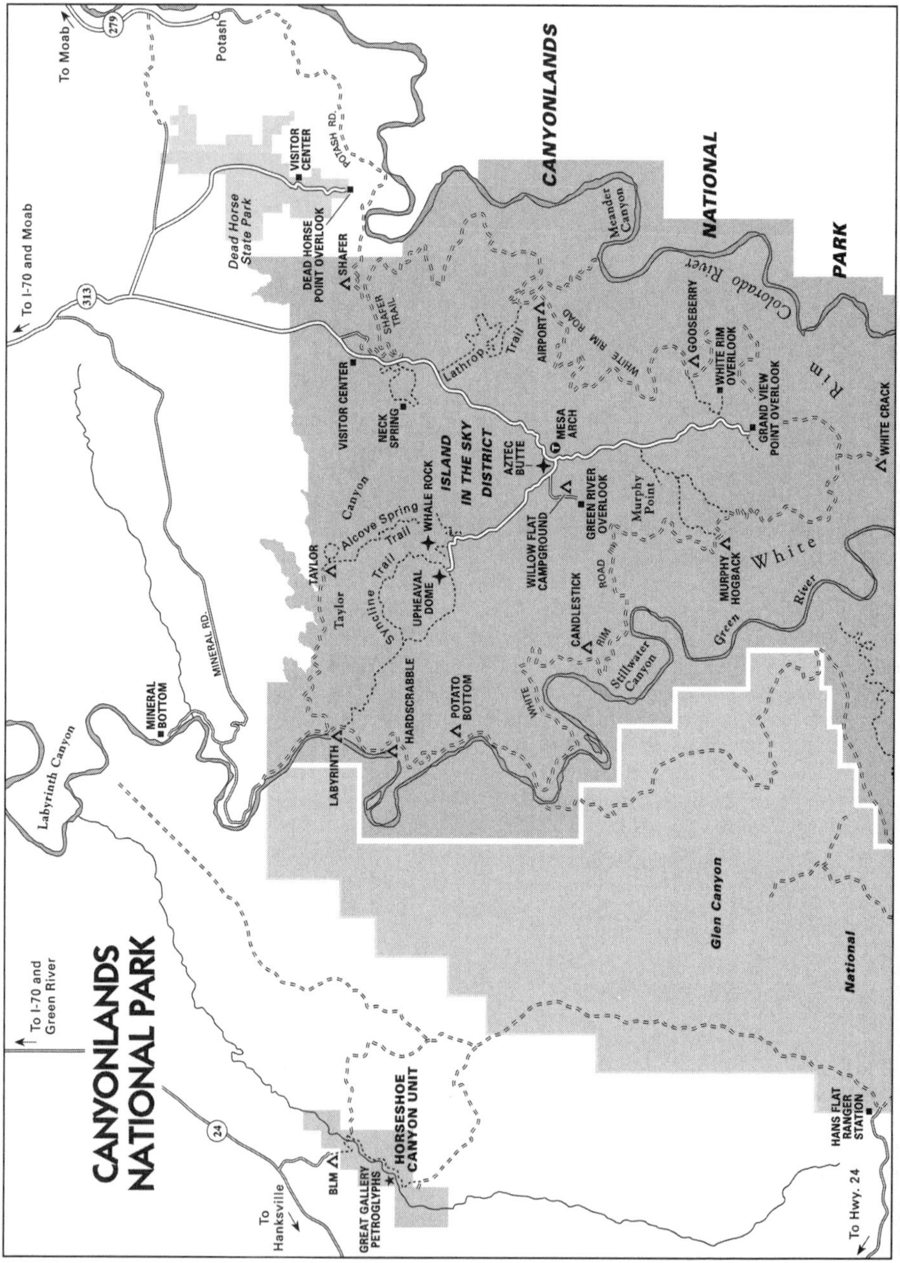

CANYONLANDS NATIONAL PARK
To I-70 and Green River
To Hanksville
24
BLM
GREAT GALLERY PETROGLYPHS
HORSESHOE CANYON UNIT
HANS FLAT RANGER STATION
To Hwy. 24
Glen Canyon
National
Labyrinth Canyon
MINERAL BOTTOM
MINERAL RD.
LABYRINTH
HARDSCRABBLE
POTATO BOTTOM
TAYLOR
Taylor
Canyon
Alcove Spring
Trail
Syncline
Trail
UPHEAVAL DOME
WHALE ROCK
ISLAND IN THE SKY DISTRICT
VISITOR CENTER
NECK SPRING
AZTEC BUTTE
MESA ARCH
WILLOW FLAT CAMPGROUND
GREEN RIVER OVERLOOK
CANDLESTICK
RIM
ROAD
WHITE
Stillwater Canyon
Murphy Point
MURPHY HOGBACK
White
Rim
Green
River
GRAND VIEW POINT OVERLOOK
WHITE CRACK
WHITE RIM OVERLOOK
GOOSEBERRY
AIRPORT
WHITE RIM ROAD
Lathrop
Trail
SHAFER TRAIL
SHAFER
DEAD HORSE POINT OVERLOOK
Dead Horse State Park
VISITOR CENTER
POTASH RD.
Potash
279
To Moab
To I-70 and Moab
313
Meander Canyon
Colorado River
CANYONLANDS
NATIONAL
PARK

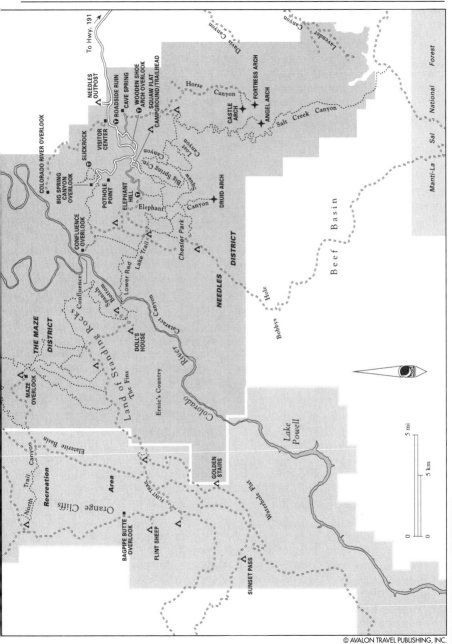

NEEDLES OUTPOST

ROADSIDE RUIN
CAVE SPRING
WOODEN SHOE
ARCH OVERLOOK
SQUAW FLAT
CAMPGROUND/TRAILHEAD

Horse Canyon

FORTRESS ARCH
CASTLE ARCH
ANGEL ARCH

Salt Creek Canyon

Davis Canyon

Lavender Canyon

COLORADO RIVER OVERLOOK

SLICKROCK
VISITOR CENTER

Lost Canyon
Squaw Canyon
Big Spring Cyn.

BIG SPRING
CANYON OVERLOOK

POTHOLE POINT
ELEPHANT HILL

Elephant Canyon

DRUID ARCH

CONFLUENCE OVERLOOK

Chesler Park

Lower Red Lake Trail

Lake Trail

NEEDLES DISTRICT

Beef Basin

THE MAZE DISTRICT

Confluence

Spanish Bottom

Land of Standing Rocks

DOLLS HOUSE

Cataract Canyon

Bobby's Hole

Hole

MAZE OVERLOOK

The Fins

Ernie's Country

Colorado River

Lake Powell

Elaterite Basin

North Trail Canyon

Orange Cliffs

Recreation Area

FLINT TRAIL

GOLDEN STAIRS

Waterhole Flat

BAGPIPE BUTTE OVERLOOK

FLINT SHEEP

SUNSET PASS

To Hwy. 191

5 mi
5 km
0
0

Manti-La Sal National Forest

SOUTHEAST UTAH

© AVALON TRAVEL PUBLISHING, INC.

EVERETT RUESS:
LOST WANDERER OF CANYON COUNTRY

Poet, artist, nomad, naturalist: these terms and more applied to Everett Ruess, who saw more of the Southwest in his teens than most do in a lifetime. The young man eventually vanished into the very canyons that had captured his vivid imagination. Born in Los Angeles in 1914, Everett grew up in a heady household. His mother was a noted art patron and his father a graduate of Harvard Divinity School. After graduating from Hollywood High School, the slim, baby-faced boy set out for the Southwest. He bought a burro from a Navajo and led it throughout northern Arizona and southern Utah, exploring alone for months on end in the remote reaches of the Grand Canyon, Zion, the Painted Desert, and the Escalante, Monument Valley, and Canyon de Chelly.

Flush with artistic zeal and the idealism of youth, Everett captured the wonders he saw in fervent journal entries and lyrical letters to his family and friends. "The wind is in my hair," he wrote, "there's a fire in my heels, and I shall always be a rover." In the days before the parks and monuments, few places were out of bounds. His mother cringed to read of him climbing cliffs to remote ruins and trudging alone across the desert for weeks. "There is a splendid freedom in solitude," Everett re-sponded, "and after all, it is for solitude that I go to the mountains and deserts, not for companionship. In solitude I can bare my soul to the mountains unabashed . . . and nothing stands between me and the Wild."

Everett quickly won over those he met along the way with his enthusiasm and openness. The Hopi granted him the rare honor of participating in their Antelope Dance, and he taught himself enough Navajo to sing with a medicine man at a sick girl's bedside. He supported himself by selling paintings and woodblock prints of the landscapes he traveled through, and spent the winters in California, where artists like Edward Weston, Dorothea Lange, Maynard Dixon, and Ansel Adams recognized his potential and encouraged him to continue.

His writings grew more impassioned with every season. "I have loved the red rocks, the twisted trees, the red sand blowing in the wind, the slow sunny clouds crossing the sky, the shafts of moonlight on my bed at night. I have seemed to be at one with the world. . . . I have really lived." His journey became more like a spiritual quest, and Everett began taking greater and greater risks. "I have been flirting pretty heavily with death, the old clown," he wrote, describing premonitions of vanishing into

art and stone dwellings, including dozens of small granaries and more impressive structures like Tower Ruin in the Needles.

Trapper Denis Julien carved his named along the canyons of the Green and Colorado in the 1830s, and on an 1859 expedition to the Confluence, Captain John N. Macob wrote while overlooking the Needles, "I cannot conceive of a more worthless and impracticable region than the one we now found ourselves in." Undeterred (or perhaps inspired) by this, Captain John Wesley Powell led two celebrated and nearly fatal expeditions down the Green and the Colorado in 1869 and 1871.

Utes and Navajos lived in the canyons until the late 19th century, when cowboys and their cattle crowded them out. At one point, tens of thousands of cattle were grazed in the region, including many in the lower canyons and up on the Island. Remains of cowboy camps are preserved in the Needles District, and Butch Cassidy and his Wild Bunch hid from the law in Robber's Roost Canyon near the Maze. In 1964, despite considerable opposition from within the state, Canyonlands National Park was signed into existence by President Lyndon Johnson.

Island in the Sky District

The park's lofty district is the closest to Moab and thus sees the most visitors. The Island is a plateau that soars 2,000 feet above the river canyons in two giant steps: one from the plateau top, at over 6,000 feet, down to the White Rim, and another from the White Rim to the rivers themselves.

To reach the Island, take U.S. 191 from Moab and turn left (west) on U.S. 313, 6.5 miles north the wild. "I shall go on some last wilderness trip to a place I have known and loved. I shall not return. When I go I leave no trace."

In November 1934, Everett rode into the town of Escalante, where he stocked up on provisions and talked with townsfolk in the dusty streets. Intending to spend the winter in Arizona, he then set off down the Hole-in-the-Rock Trail as an early blizzard moved in across the Kaiparowits Plateau. A week later he camped with a pair of sheepherders, and may have bumped into a party of cattlemen soon after. If so, they were the last to ever see Everett alive. In February, his two burros were found in Davis Gulch near what was thought to be his last campsite. Everett had vanished.

Search parties organized by his parents and friends from his travels combed the canyons of the Escalante, to no avail. An expert tracker, a half-Navajo half-Ute Indian named Dougeye, led one party across the Colorado into Davis Canyon, where he wandered stymied for days. Everett had entered the canyon, he agreed, but there was no sign that he had ever left. As reports came in of supposed sightings from Moab to Florida, theories flew around the canyon country: Everett had orchestrated his own disappearance; he had been killed in a flood or fell from a cliff; he had been killed by Indians and his scalp used in squaw dances. He appeared in the visions of Navajo medicine men and his signature inscription "NEMO"—meaning "no one" in Latin, and probably a reference to the fated submarine captain in Jules Verne's *Twenty Thousand Leagues Under the Sea*—kept turning up in caves and canyon walls. (Many are still visible today.)

As time passed, Everett's disappearance became a canyon country legend. In the early 1960s, archaeologists found his canteen and a box of razor blades from the Owl Drug Company of Los Angeles. The most widely accepted theory is that he was killed for his gear, and his body hidden in one of the countless nooks in the country he loved so much. His older brother Waldo eventually oversaw the installation of a plaque high on the wall of Davis Canyon, bearing a quote from Everett's journals:

Oh but the desert is glorious now, with marching clouds in the blue sky and cool winds blowing. The smell of the sage is sweet in my nostrils, and the luring trail leads onwards.

of the Colorado River bridge. This road winds southwest up onto the plateau. Just over 14 miles from the turnoff, a side road leads to **Dead Horse Point State Park,** which offers similar panoramic views as the Island but in a smaller package. The name supposedly came from a herd of horses left to graze at the end of the mesa, which became confused about the way down and died of thirst within sight of the river far below. There's a visitor center, 435/259-2614, http://parks.state.ut.us/parks/www1/dead.htm, open 8 A.M.–6 P.M. (9 A.M.–5 P.M. in winter). You can reserve sites at the campground (21 sites, $11) by calling 800/322-3770. Entrance is $7 per vehicle. Ask rangers to point you toward "Thelma and Louise Point," where the movie heroines (actually, stunt dummies) drove off into what was supposed to be the Grand Canyon. The climbing sequence at the beginning of *Mission: Impossible II* was also filmed here.

Back on U.S. 313, another six miles brings you to the park boundary and, after crossing a neck of rock barely wide enough for the road, the district **visitor center,** 435/259-4712, open daily 8 A.M.–4:30 P.M. Exhibits and an orientation video give introductory information on this section of the park, and books and maps are for sale. It's a good idea to get a weather report, even in summer: lightning is a real danger out in the open this high up. The road continues another six miles across the top of the plateau and forks near the **Willow Flat Campground,** with 12 sites open all year ($5). In spring and fall all the sites fill early and for good reason: the views from here, particularly at sunset, are dazzling. Head right (northwest) five miles to the road's end at

SOUTHEAST UTAH

Whale Rock and the edge of **Upheaval Dome,** a two-mile-wide crater whose origins geologists have debated for decades. Most think it is a collapsed salt dome, but some still hold that it is an eroded astrobleme (meteorite crater).

In the opposite direction at the fork, a six-mile drive brings you to the true edge of things: **Grandview Point,** one of the great views of the American West. Over 10,000 square miles of canyon country are on magnificent display, including the La Sal and Abajo Mountains, the Needles, Thousand Lake and Boulder Mountains, Ekker and Elaterite Buttes in the Maze, and the Orange Cliffs. It's a vista to lose yourself in, but be careful near the edge: it's a long way down.

The Island has fewer **hiking trails** than the park's other districts. **Short trails** (under 2 miles r/t) lead to the very tip of the mesa at Grandview Point, to an overlook over Upheaval Dome, up on top of the stone domes of Whale Rock and Aztec Butte, and to Mesa Arch, perched right on the edge of the precipice. (Sunrise through Mesa Arch is worth rising early for.) **Longer trails** lead down off the mesa to the White Rim and even the rivers. If you tackle one of these, remember that you'll have to climb back up whatever you descend, and there is very little water along the way. These include the Syncline Loop around Upheaval Dome, Lathrop Canyon, Taylor Canyon, and Murphy Loop. You can stop at Murphy Point for the night, but the rest of the overnight routes all involve at least a thousand-foot descent and steep switchbacks that are often very rough.

It's hard to miss the **White Rim,** a broad geologic layer midway between the Island and the rivers. A dirt track snakes across this mostly level plain, giving the adventurous the opportunity to enter the scenery so many others just look upon. The **White Rim Trail** is a 100-mile route gaining fame as one of the best multi-day mountain bike rides in the country. It's also popular with 4WD drivers and motorcyclists. There are eight campgrounds along the way, and you must reserve sites ahead of time for this popular trip. If you go clockwise, as most people do, you'll head down the gradually descending Mineral Bottom Road off U.S. 313 outside the park boundary,

and at the other end ascend the merciless switchbacks of the Schafer Trail, visible near the visitor center. The entire trail can be driven in a day, but mountain bikers typically take three to four days depending on whether they're self-supported or have a support vehicle. Many companies in Moab organize trips.

The Needles District and Vicinity

Multicolored Church Rock marks the turnoff to the Needles from U.S. 191, 40 miles south of Moab and 14 miles north of Monticello. From here, U.S. 211 snakes west across the flats before dropping steeply into the valley cut by Indian Creek. This marks the beginning of one of Utah's prettiest drives, a winding route around the feet of looming mesas. Ten miles in is **Newspaper Rock,** where ancient passers-by carved everything from bear tracks to mounted warriors into the dark desert varnish up to 4,000 years ago. There's a BLM campsite under the cottonwoods by the water, and more petroglyphs in nearby

hiking among the Needles

© JULIAN SMITH

canyons. The soaring red cliffs of Wingate sandstone along Indian Creek boast the best **crack climbing** in the world, with legendary routes like the Supercrack of the Desert (5.10) slicing upwards for hundreds of flawless feet. Keep your eyes out for climbers on the blank-looking walls, and if you're climbing bring plenty of medium cams and tape up your hands—these are tough, sustained routes.

A few miles farther at the mouth of Cottonwood Creek sits the **Dugout Ranch,** a private spread established in 1885. After the S&S Cattle Company bought it up in 1919, it became part of the largest cattle operation in Utah, with over 10,000 cows grazing on 1.8 million acres. The Redd family, who bought the spread in 1967, handed it over to The Nature Conservancy in the late 1990s to manage on the condition that it continue as a working, conservation-minded ranch. From here you can see the unmistakable North and South Six-Shooter Peaks that mark the entrance to the Needles. From the right (north) comes the dirt road into Lockhart Basin (and eventually the Shaefer Trail), where there's another BLM campsite about a mile down. Just past the park boundary is a turnoff to the **Needles Outpost,** 435/979-4007, cno@sanjuan.net, www.canyonlandsneedlesoutpost.com, a privately owned camp store, cafe, gas station, and campground ($15 per night) that's open more or less regularly from spring to fall.

Thirty-five miles from U.S. 191 is the Needles **visitor center,** 435/259-4711, open 8 A.M.–6 P.M. (9 A.M.–5 P.M. in winter). Get your hiking and 4WD permits here, and look over the scale model of the entire park. The pavement soon peters out at the **Squaw Flat Campground,** with 26 sites for $10 per night (this one also fills quickly in spring and fall), continuing a short way to the Big Spring Canyon Overlook.

Most visitors come to the Needles for the easily accessible backcountry, and they are seldom disappointed. Four short self-guided **hiking trails** leave the paved main road for Anasazi ruins and an old cowboy camp in a cave. Over 60 miles of longer trails snake over the slickrock and down into canyon bottoms, easily connected into challenging day hikes or overnight trips. The trail to

Chessler Park is one of the most popular, leading to an open grassy area surrounded by slickrock. It can easily be extended to include the **Joint Trail** through narrow, deep cracks in the rock. For more hikes of about 10 miles, try the Big Spring to Squaw Canyon Loop, Squaw Canyon to Lost Canyon, Elephant Canyon to Druid Arch, the Peekaboo Trail, and the "Lost Hiker" loop (rangers know which one this is). Lower Red Lake Canyon leads down to the Colorado River just across from Spanish Bottom and the Doll's House in the Maze (and just above Cataract Canyon, for anyone thinking to paddle across). You'll have to reserve a spot at one of over a dozen backcountry campsites. (Four vehicles campsites are set aside for drivers.)

Mountain bikers are limited to roads, but you can still ride seven miles to the **Confluence Overlook,** where you'll notice than the Green River is actually brown and the Colorado flows green. **Elephant Hill,** a short but ridiculously difficult climb in the heart of the district, is also popular with 4WD enthusiasts, who descend on the park in droves during Easter Jeep Week. (The back side, even worse than the front, includes a section with such tight corners that vehicles have to shift into reverse and back down part of the way.) Elephant Hill leads to a loop road through the **grabens,** an area of straight-sided, flat-bottomed valleys like city streets.

Salt Creek Canyon, once one of the most popular drives in the park, was closed to vehicles after research showed that its delicate riparian ecosystem—growing around the most extensive perennial water source in the entire park—could be damaged by 4WD traffic. It's here that the Needle's rich archaeology reaches its apex. Ancient granaries and rock art fill the upper canyon, including the famous red-white-and-blue "All-American Man" pictograph. (The blue is actually thought to be a faded brown.) The entire canyon takes two to four days to hike. Vehicles can still drive up **Horse Canyon** to the east, which leads to Tower Ruin and a horizontal larch called Paul Bunyan's Potty, as well as **Davis** and **Lavender Canyons** off of U.S. 211. (Lavender and Horse Canyons require a $5 permit for day use.)

Highway 24: Green River to Torrey

Leaving I-40 west of the town of Green River (not to be confused with Green River, Wyoming, which is also on the waterway of the same name), U.S. 24 heads bravely south across the San Rafael Desert. To the west rises the San Rafael Swell, a stone bulge carved by narrow canyons and protected by the serrated barricade of the San Rafael Reef. Goblin Valley State Park and Horseshoe Canyon, a detached portion of the Maze District of Canyonlands National Park, offer two versions of the fantastic on either side of the roadway, but past Hanksville the scenery really starts to get strange. A sickly expanse of badlands makes up the western San Rafael Desert, a gorgeous but forbidding wilderness of purples, grays, mustards, and tans. This lunar landscape is dominated by Factory Butte, a massive wedge of dark Mancos shale topped with tougher Mesa Verde sandstone. The topography gets older as you continue west along the Fremont River, through the huge monocline of the Waterpocket Fold, the backbone of Capitol Reef National Park (covered in the next chapter).

GREEN RIVER

An easy river crossing is a rarity in canyon country, so this valley south of the Book Cliffs, between Gray and Labyrinth Canyons, has been known since prehistoric times. During the Mexican occupation, the Spanish Trail forded the river just upstream on its way from Santa Fe to Los Angeles. Americans began to arrive from the east in the late 1870s, and in 1883 the Denver & Rio Grande Western Railway first dropped off mining supplies and carried away livestock. This ended when the railroad moved to Helper, Utah, and began a pattern of booms and busts that continued through eras of oil exploration, fruit growing, and the establishment of the Utah Launch Complex of the White Sands Missile Base in 1963. Test rockets were fired from along the river to land in White Sands Missile Range in New Mexico until 1979.

Today the town survives on farming, ranching, and, above all, the traffic off I-70, whose 105-mile run west to Salina is the longest stretch of interstate without services in the country. Green River (pop. 1,000) has been an obvious supply and staging point for river travel since Powell and his men floated through town. Hot summers, little winter frost, and just the right elevation (4,000 feet) give Green River the ideal climate for growing, of all things, melons. The town's justifiably famous cantaloupe and watermelons are sold from roadside stands in the summer and celebrated during a fall festival.

Sights

The **John Wesley Powell River History Museum,** 885 E. Main St., 435/564-3427, celebrates the career of the man whose descent of the Green River put much of this part of the country on the map. Exhibits on the geological and human history of the Green and Colorado Rivers includes the fascinating River Runner's Hall of Fame and models of the various boats that have made (or attempted) the difficult descents. It all leads to a mockup of the man himself in a chair on the bow of the *Emma Dean.* Open daily 8 A.M.–8 P.M. (to 5 P.M. Nov–Mar.) for $2 pp. The **Grand Country Travel Office,** 435/564-3526, is in the same building. (Another good source of local information is the website www.greenriver-utah.com.)

Towering cottonwoods shade green lawns on the east bank of the river at the **Green River State Park,** 450 S. Green River Blvd., 435/564-3633, http://parks.state.ut.us/parks/www1/gree.htm. It's a popular put-in place for trips down Labyrinth and Stillwater Canyons, and has 42 RV or tent campsites ($14), hot showers, and a nine-hole golf course. There is a $5 day use fee.

Accommodations

Two of Green River's least expensive lodgings are known by their classic neon signs: the reclining woman at the **Robber's Roost,** 225 W. Main St., 435/564-3452, and the flower and arrow of the **Sleepy Hollow Motel,** 93 E. Main St., 435/564-8189, which welcomes "Hip Cats and Kittens." Both are under $50 per night.

© JULIAN SMITH

pictographs, Canyonlands National Park

In the $50–100 range, the **Best Western River Terrace,** 880 E. Main St., 435/564-3401, fax 435/564-3403, has rooms with views of the river and the **Tamarisk Restaurant,** serving all meals, downstairs near the pool. The **Bookcliff Lodge,** 365 E. Main St., 435/564-3406 or 800/493-4699, is one of the newer places in town, with an outdoor pool and a restaurant serving all meals. The **Rodeway Inn,** 525 E. Main St., 435/564-8162, is part of the huge West Winds Truck Stop, which has a 24-hour restaurant, Greyhound stop, and gift store (rooms are $70).

Beautiful antique furniture fills the **Bankurz Hatt Bed & Breakfast,** 214 Farrer St., 435/564-3382, www.bankurzhatt.com, built in the late 1890s by the town's first banker with wood shipped from St. Louis. Owners Ben and Lana Coomer are full of information on things to do in the area. Rates are in the $100–150 range.

Next to the state park, the **Shady Acres RV Park,** 360 E. Main St., 435/563-3695 or 800/537-8674, fax 435/564-8838, www.shady-acresrv.com, shadya@etv.net, has 101 sites as well as a Blimpie restaurant and an Amoco station. Tent sites are $10–14, and RV sites are $17–22. Green River also hosts a **KOA Kampground,**

550 S. Green River Blvd., 435/564-3651, and the **United Campground,** 910 E. Main St., 435/564-8195, with sites in the same price range.

Food

Ray's Tavern, 25 S. Broadway, 435/564-3511, is a classic roadhouse with excellent burgers and other meaty delights, which are even better paired with a microbrew and a few rounds of pool or pinball. Mexican and American dishes start at $6 at **Ben's Cafe,** 115 W. Main, 435/564-3352, whose diner atmosphere comes from countertop jukeboxes and orange vinyl upholstery. Open daily for all meals.

Events

If you're in the area the third weekend in September, keep your eye out for a 25-foot watermelon that's rolled out to help celebrate **Melon Days,** accompanied by music, games, a parade, canoe races and, of course, lots and lots of melons.

Tour Companies

River running is the main diversion in Green River, and trips are run both up- and downstream: through Desolation and Gray Canyons to

SOUTHEAST UTAH

the north, and Labyrinth and Stillwater Canyons to the south. **Moki-Mac River Expeditions,** 100 S. Silliman Ln., 435/564-3361 or 800/284-7280, www.mokimac.com, mokimac@mokimac.com, runs river trips on both the Green and the Colorado Rivers, including the Grand Canyon. Their voyages last from three to 14 days, and include one-day excursions through Westwater Canyon of the Colorado ($150) and Gray Canyon ($50). If you want to do Labyrinth and Stillwater Canyons on your own, they'll rent you canoes for $17 per day and retrieve up to four people from Mineral Canyon for $250. **Way Out West Tours,** 63 N. Long St., 435/564-3611 or 866/894-8608, www.wayoutwesttours.com, tours@wayoutwesttours.com, specialize in land-based expeditions which start at $45 pp for day trips and range up to $1,500 pp for 10-day adventures. They also do river shuttles.

Getting There and Around

To arrange vehicle pickup from Mineral Bottom or elsewhere along the river, contact **Bobbie's Shuttle Service,** 435/564-3345, **Fluckey Shuttle Service,** 435/564-3246, or **Green River Shuttle Service,** 435/564-8292. **Bighorn Express,** 801/328-9920 or 888/655-7433, www.bighornexpress.com, runs a daily bus to and from Salt Lake City via Price (and continuing to Moab and Monticello). The 3.5-hour trip costs $42 pp each way (Friday and Saturday only in January and February). Green River's **Greyhound** stop, 435/564-3421, is at the West Winds Truck Stop at 525 E. Main St.

Crystal Geyser

An unsuccessful petroleum test well drilled in the 1930s concentrated bubbling, mineral-rich waters into a cold-water gusher that shoots up to 100 feet in the air two to four times per day. On the east bank of the river, 4.5 river miles south of the state park, it is surrounded by maroon deposits of travertine. To drive there, turn south onto Frontage Road off Main Street near milepost 4 and head south for three miles until you pass under a railroad overpass. Turn right and go six miles west to the river, on a road that quickly turns to dirt and passes under I-70.

Floating Labyrinth and Stillwater Canyons

If you've cut your teeth on day-long river trips and want to try something a little longer, this float just might be the perfect step up. It's a calm, winding journey downstream from Green River, with plenty of side canyons to explore and historic artifacts to puzzle over. You probably won't have it to yourself—powerboats zoom past pretty regularly, and it's popular with the canoe-and-kayak crowd—but for a relaxing, scenic trip that doesn't take all that much planning or expertise, these canyons are hard to beat.

The trip can be done year-round, but try to avoid Memorial Day Weekend, when the Annual Friendship Cruise fills the wide canyon with boaters. You'll need a free permit available from the BLM, the Park Service, the state park or museum in Green River, or the Moab Information Center, and you must be completely self-contained, with toilets and a keen eye for collecting all your own garbage.

Labyrinth Canyon begins south of Green River and winds for 68 miles to Mineral Bottom just north of Canyonlands National Park. Along the way you'll pass an old cabin at Doc Bishop Bottom, the privately owned Ruby Ranch, and the names of early river runners chiseled into the stone at Register Rock and the Post Office at the Bow Knot. The trip takes three to four days, leaving time to explore side canyons. You can arrange a vehicle pickup at Mineral Bottom through rafting or shuttle companies in Green River or Moab. The rafting companies can also arrange guided trips down this section of the Green. For more information check out the website www.blm.gov/utah/price/labyrinth.htm.

Stillwater Canyon continues another 53 miles from Mineral Bottom to the confluence of the Green and Colorado Rivers. You'll need an NPS permit for this section, since it crosses Canyonlands National Park, and you'll also have to arrange a pickup from one of the jetboats that descend to the confluence daily in season.

SAN RAFAEL SWELL

This kidney-shaped anticline covers 900 square miles on either side of I-70, stretching for 80 miles from north to south. Its southeastern edge along U.S. 24 is marked by the **San Rafael Reef,** a jagged line of thousand-foot hills like the teeth of some gigantic monster. Two perennial streams cut through this imposing wall, revealing 250-million-year-old Coconino Sandstone—one of the area's oldest exposed rocks layers—on their way east toward the Green River.

Pictographs found here, similar to those in Horseshoe Canyon, have been estimated to be at least 2,000 years old. In 1853, the head of a railroad survey team charting a route for the transcontinental railroad wrote,

As we approached the [Green] river yesterday, the ridges on either side of its banks to the west appeared broken into a thousand forms—columns, shafts, temples, buildings, and ruined cities could be seen, or imagined, from the high points along our route.

A member of Powell's second expedition down the Green River wrote in his journal that local Indians called the formations of the Reef "Sauauger-towip," or the "Stone House Lands," and conductors on the Denver & Rio Grande Western Railroad pointed out the "silent city" to passengers. Butch Cassidy is only one of dozens of outlaws who have sought refuge among the tortured canyons after various misdeeds.

Dozens of canyons and hundreds of side canyons lace through the Reef as well, making it a canyoneer's playground. Flood debris hangs 50 feet high between the walls of slot canyons. Others are filled with water for most of the year, meaning that if you're truly prepared, you'll find yourself hiking across the desert carrying a wetsuit and inner tube.

You probably won't be alone in the Swell. With the construction of I-70, the once remote area was made suddenly more accessible, and ORV use continues to be a contentious issue. A population of bighorn sheep has been established by the Utah Department of Wildlife Resources (at last count it was some 70 strong), and hundreds of pronghorn antelope live in the desert to the east and occasionally venture into the Swell itself.

Originally the San Rafael Swell was considered for national park status, but mineral development interests kept that from happening. There has been a growing push to have 600,000 acres of it declared a national monument, a proposal even Utah's Republican politicians have endorsed. This would be an especially welcome move to opponents of ORVs, whose tire marks scar hillsides on both sides of the highway.

Direct questions to the BLM offices in Richfield (150 E. 900 North, 435/896-1500) or Hanksville.

Exploring the Swell

Always take a topographical map; it's possible to get lost even among the slot canyons, which empty out into a confusing landscape beyond the Reef. By far the most detailed guide to the Swell is Steve Allen's *Canyoneering I* (see "Suggested Reading" in the "Resources" section).

Aside from I-70, the easiest way into the southern Reef is the road that leads to Goblin Valley State Park from U.S. 24. Instead of turning south toward the park, keep going west. Seven miles from U.S. 24 is a parking area on the right for the trail around **Temple Mountain,** a colorful pointed peak north of the road. The seven-mile mining road around its base makes a good ramble or mountain bike ride. Keep an eye out for open mineshafts.

Just past the Temple Mountain turnoff, head left (southwest) to reach a series of short but spectacular slot canyons cutting through the Reef. First is **Wild Horse Canyon,** an easy walk past a number of pictographs, which eventually intersects with the Temple Mountain road. (Sheepherders discovered uranium and vanadium, a mineral used to harden steel, here in 1903.) Keep going down the road past the turnoff for Goblin Valley to reach **Chute** and **Crack Canyons,** which are slightly more narrow and difficult, with some scrambling required. This is a longer hike, but can still be done in a day. The hike starts by heading up Chute Canyon, 6.5 miles from the Temple Mountain road.

Just over five miles past the Goblin Valley turnoff is the parking area for **Little Wild Horse Canyon,** the Reef's most popular hike, which joins with **Bell Canyon** into a relatively easy loop hike that can be done in a day. It's narrow and beautiful, and will coax a smile out of even

SOUTHEAST UTAH

veteran slot canyoneers. Just under a mile farther (6.5 miles past Goblin Valley) is a wash coming from the north. Head up here about 20 minutes to reach the mouths of **Ding** and **Dang Canyons,** a challenging (and less traveled) pair of slots. Look for pointy Ding Dang Dome at the top of the Ding Canyon, which is your signal to head left (west) and return via Dang Canyon.

This is just a taste of what the San Rafael Swell has to offer. Some of the other choices are serious undertakings, and every year some people underestimate them and have to be rescued. West of the Reef, via the road past Temple Mountain, is **Muddy Creek,** with a sinuous, deep section of narrows called simply **The Chute.** One of the best canyon hikes in the Southwest, this involves going down a deep sinuous chasm beneath logs jammed high overhead by raging spring floodwaters. The hike from Hondoo Arch to the Hidden Splendor Mine can be done, with a two-car shuttle, in a long day. Aside from spring, the water shouldn't be more than knee deep.

North of I-70, a section of the San Rafael River known as the **Black Box** has 400-foot-high walls that are sometimes only 10 feet apart. The problem is that it's full of water, and thus requires a wetsuit and inner tubes to avoid hypothermia and drowning. Also north of the interstate (turn off just west of mile market 145) is a dirt road to **Black Dragon Wash,** where an amazing panel of Barrier Canyon Style pictographs is half a mile up.

GOBLIN VALLEY STATE PARK

About 20 miles north of Hanksville on U.S. 24 is a signed turnoff to the west that leads, after another 12 miles and one more left turn, to one of the odder sights in this landscape of visual extremes. Imagine an amphitheater of house-high chocolate mushrooms left out in the sun, and you'll have a general idea of the crazily eroded sandstone formations that fill this small but detour-worthy park.

You can admire the stubby formations from a picnic area overlook or hike down among them; best of all, you're even allowed to climb them. (Movie buffs might recognize this place from a scene in the comedy *Galaxy Quest.* During the filming, some friends of mine unwittingly stumbled on a fake spaceship and nearly weightless fake boulders among the formations and were, let's just say, briefly but intensely confused.)

© JULIAN SMITH

Goblin Valley State Park

BUTCH CASSIDY AND THE WILD BUNCH

One of the West's most famous outlaws, Butch Cassidy is remembered as much for his wit, charm, and outright benevolence as for his utter disregard for the law. He was born Robert LeRoy Parker on April 13, 1866, to Mormon parents in Beaver, Utah. Raised on a ranch near Circleville, he fell under the wing of an old rustler named Mike Cassidy before leaving home to seek his fortune by any means necessary. Two years as a cowboy was followed by a stint as a butcher in Rock Springs, Wyoming. By adding his mentor's last name to his profession, Parker came up with the nickname that he would ride to worldwide fame: Butch Cassidy.

In Telluride, Colorado, Cassidy joined forced with another Utahn, Matt Warner, and in 1899 they staged their first major bank robbery in the mountain mining town. Butch served two years in a Wyoming jail for cattle rustling before finding his true calling as the leader of the "Wild Bunch," a loosely knit gang that kept the peacekeepers of the Intermountain West on their toes for the better part of a decade. Several famous outlaws belonged to the Wild Bunch at one time or another, including Ben Kilpatrick (the "Tall Texan"), Harvey Logan (a.k.a. "Kid Curry"), and Butch's best friend Elzy Lay. When Lay was captured and jailed in 1899, Butch teamed up with Harry Longabaugh, a gunslinger from Pennsylvania better known as the Sundance Kid.

Led by Butch and Sundance, the Wild Bunch embarked on one of the most successful crime sprees in the history of the West. They robbed banks and trains and rustled horses and cattle throughout Colorado, Utah, Wyoming, and the surrounding territories. The gang had a number of hideouts to retreat to when the heat was on, each with its own corrals for rustled livestock. There were inaccessible canyons like the grassy Hole in the Wall in northern Wyoming, and the remote Robber's Roost in south-central Utah, south of the San Rafael Swell. Brown's Hole (now called Brown's Park), a valley along the Green River where Utah, Colorado, and Wyoming come together, was another favorite lair.

Most of the Wild Bunch eventually found themselves in jail or pine boxes by the turn of the century, but Butch and Sundance kept going. Cassidy's gentleman charm no doubt helped, earning him the reputation of a fearless outlaw who never killed anyone and was polite to the ladies. Stories have him helping those in need, including a lost priest whom he helped back home, and ejecting a member from his gang who had stolen a horse from a young boy. He split up his crimes with interludes as a legitimate rancher, but the straight-and-narrow lifestyle never seemed to stick.

As the West filled with settlers and police, the once-easy life of an outlaw became more of an effort. The Pinkerton Agency, hired by the railroads, pursued the pair relentlessly. Butch sought an amnesty first from the governor of Utah, then from the Union Pacific Railroad, but neither worked. Along with Sundance and his girlfriend, Etta Place, Cassidy fled to New York City, where on February 20, 1902 he departed on a steamer for Buenos Aires, Argentina. The trio took aliases and bought a ranch in Patagonia, where for four years they tried to make a go at an honest living. When Etta returned to the United States in 1907, though, Butch and Sundance reverted to their old ways, robbing trains, banks, and rich mine stations in several countries.

The events surrounding the supposed death of Butch Cassidy and the Sundance Kid are still debated. On November 4, 1908, the pair found themselves at the Concordia Tin Mines near San Vicente, Bolivia. What happened there remains a mystery. According to an official document signed by the mayor, a pair of gringos who had robbed a mine payroll holed up in a local house, where they exchanged gunfire with a number of soldiers. When the troops approached the house the next morning, they found both men dead inside, one apparently from a self-inflicted gunshot. The men were quickly buried.

But were they Butch and Sundance? Many say they were actually another pair of outlaws, and that it would be just like Butch to spread the word that it had been him and his partner instead. According to this version, the pair returned to the United States and lived out the rest of their lives in peaceful anonymity. Some have sworn they spotted or even met with Butch in the 1920s and 1930s, including his sister Lula and Matt Warner's daughter Joyce. The myth got a boost with the 1969 hit movie starring Paul Newman and Robert Redford, although that had them meet their end at the hands of half the Bolivian army. It seems that no one knows for sure but Butch himself, and he probably would have wanted it that way.

Entrance is $5 per vehicle, and there's a 21-site campground ($14) with showers. You can reserve sites ahead of time by calling Utah State Parks and Recreation, 801/322-3770 or 800/322-3770, Mon.–Fri. 8 A.M.–5 P.M. For more information contact the park offices at 435/564-3633 or www.stateparks.utah.gov/parks/www1/gobl.htm.

HANKSVILLE

Established in 1882 on the bank of the Fremont River, Hanksville was named for one of its original settlers, Ebenezer Hanks. The only remnant of a string of Mormon communities along the river decimated by floods near the turn of the century, Hanksville has always been a remote town. Mail was once carried by horse from Green River three times a week, with riders making the 110-mile round trip in two days. Electricity only arrived in 1960. Today Hanksville, with a population of about 400, survives on mining, farming, ranching, and, increasingly, the tourist traffic to Lake Powell and parks to the west.

At the intersection of U.S. 24 and 95 is the **Hollow Mountain Gas & Grocery,** 435/542-3298, a filling station that has been hollowed out of a sandstone hillside. Next door, **Blondie's Eatery & Gift,** 435/542-3255, has a restaurant/deli serving all meals, including ice cream, vegetarian burgers, and platters starting at $6. There's a nice view from the picnic tables on the front patio. (Open daily year-round.)

Also near the intersection is the **Redrock Restaurant,** 435/542-3235 or 800/452-7971, probably the best eatery in town, with sandwiches from $3 and chicken, steak, and seafood entrees from $7. (Open for all meals in season.) They also offer campsites in back for tents ($10) and RVs ($16), and showers for $3. The rib-eyes are tasty at **Duke's Slickrock Grill,** 435/542-3441, which also offers authentic Dutch oven cooking nightly from $8. Open Mon.–Fri. for breakfast and dinner.

Joy's B&B, 296 S. Center St. 435/542-3252, fax 435/542-3858, is a cozy place with great breakfasts and three rooms for $50. Other lodging options in town include **Fern's Place,** 435/542-3251, on U.S. 24, the **Whispering Sands Motel,** 435/542-3238, on U.S. 95, and the **Best Value Inn,** 435/542-3471, at 322 E. 100 North. You can't miss the **Desert Inn Motel,** 197 E. 100 North, 435/542-3241; just look for

© JULIAN SMITH

Hollow Mountain Gas & Grocery in Hanksville is actually carved into the side of a cliff.

the scrap-metal dinosaur skeletons out front, especially the one with the hood and trunk lid of a Volkswagen Beetle for a skull. None of these places charges over $50 per night.

Stock up on groceries and sundries at **Johnson's,** 44 E. 100 North, 435/542-3249. For information on the surrounding landscape stop by the **BLM Station,** 435/542-3461, about half a mile south on 100 West from U.S. 24.

CAINEVILLE

A struggling town surrounded by otherworldly scenery, Caineville is the kind of place that makes you wonder who thought, way back when, that this would be a good place for a settlement. Many local businesses have closed, ATV scars mark the barren hillsides, and local kids have to endure hours of busing to get to school and back. Business hours are strictly seasonal, and it's still often a hit-or-miss proposition finding them open.

RV and tent sites at the **Sleepy Hollow Campground,** 435/456-9130, will run you $12–15. Located at milepost 95 at the Fremont River bridge, they have full RV services and showers. At milepost 99 is the **Caineville Cove Inn,** 435/456-9900, with 16 rooms with microwaves and refrigerators for $50, and a pool and hot tub to boot.

Look for the offbeat **Luna Mesa Cafe,** 435/456-9122 or 9141, a movie-worthy desert oasis that serves Mexican and American food behind a porch covered with rose vines. Burgers and tacos start at $3, and they're open daily from 9 A.M.–9 P.M. ("more or less") in season. The owners also offer motel rooms ($35), teepees ($25), and a campground with sites for RVs ($12) and tents ($8), and can organize 4WD tours of the surrounding area for $75 pp. A mile east, the coffee at the **Mesa Farm Market,** 435/979-8467, is proclaimed by its brewers to be the best in the state (it is pretty good), and goes well with their organic produce, fresh salads, and baked goods.

South-Central Utah

South-central Utah is big, beautiful, remote, and nearly empty. Garfield and Wayne Counties combined are larger than five entire U.S. states, but count fewer than 7,000 residents between them. That's more than a square mile for every inhabitant, and not just any square mile, either. On your winding way across the state's emptiest quarter, you'll cross through some of the country's wildest topography.

Southern Utah is defined by geographical features on a monumental scale. Start with the San Rafael Swell, a gigantic blister on the earth's skin worn away over millennia to a jagged outline laced with slot canyons. I-70 slices through its center, but the Swell still contains enough wilderness that in 2002 it was seriously being considered for national monument status. The outlandish cliffs of the Waterpocket Fold in Capitol Reef National Park are evidence of an even larger uplift.

Passing over the cool evergreen slopes of Boulder Mountain and the Aquarius Plateau, you'll be riding yet another geologic bulge, this one not yet eroded away. From here the tortuous canyons of the Escalante River drain southeast to Lake Powell, and the vast sweep of the Grand Staircase–Escalante National Monument, littered with the leftovers of ancient cultures, spreads south and west. The vividly named steps of the

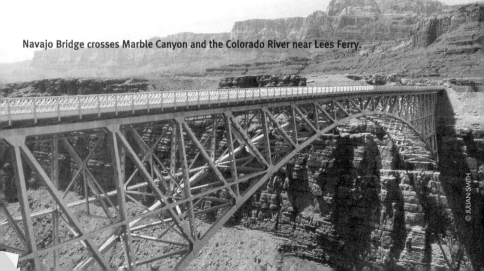

Navajo Bridge crosses Marble Canyon and the Colorado River near Lees Ferry.

© JULIAN SMITH

SOUTH-CENTRAL UTAH HIGHLIGHTS

Capitol Reef National Park: Surreal, overwhelming scenery along the Waterpocket Fold, this includes the historic oasis of Fruita (page 183)

Utah Highway 12: One of the most amazing roads in the country, it winds across narrow ridges through the Grand Staircase–Escalante National Monument (page 190)

Grand Staircase–Escalante National Monument: Vast and empty, this new monument protects desert plateaus, river canyons, and archaeological treasures (page 196)

Paria Canyon: A 38-mile hike down one of the Southwest's premiere canyons requires a permit, a good pair of legs, and a lot of film (page 217)

Grand Staircase march from north to south in the monument's western reaches. Along the way, isolated towns such as Boulder and Escalante are just beginning to see an influx of visitors and new residents drawn by the landscape and seclusion.

For all intents and purposes, the city of Page, Arizona, and the **Paria Plateau** to the west can be considered part of south-central Utah, and so they are included in this chapter. Built to house workers on the Glen Canyon Dam, the tidy little tourist town of Page sits at the southern end of Lake Powell, the region's water-sport Mecca, and offers plenty of budget accommodations. Canyon hikers flock to the Paria Plateau, where the multiday hike down Paria Canyon, including the leg-endary Buckskin Gulch narrows, is one of the best in the Four Corners.

Each of these features would be worth a trip in itself, but luckily you can get a tantalizing but substantial taste of them all in a few days' drive along the meandering byways of U.S. 24 and 12, which connect I-70 with U.S. 89 near Bryce Canyon National Park. Page is connected to Kanab, Utah, and Flagstaff, Arizona, by U.S. 89, whose spur 89A crosses south of the Paria Plateau and offers access to the North Rim of the Grand Canyon. The paved road is only the beginning, however. Most of this area is back-country—*way* back country—and can be explored only by 4WD, horse, mountain bike, or sweat and boot leather.

Capitol Reef National Park and Vicinity

Word is starting to leak out about Utah's least-known national park, but Capitol Reef still gets only a fraction as many visitors as its more famous neighbors. The long, narrow park—the second-largest in the state—follows the Waterpocket Fold, a gigantic north-south wrinkle in the earth's crust that stretches over 100 miles. U.S. 24 bisects the northern end of the park along the Fremont River, but those who venture south past the startling green oasis of the historic Fruita settlement will find a world of dreamlike rock formations, narrow slot canyons, and silent battlements of stone. The best part, at least for the moment, is that you still stand a very good chance of having it all to yourself, at least a sizeable chunk of it.

The Setting

Geology is the language of the Reef. In all, almost 10,000 feet of sedimentary layers are on display here, ranging from the Permian Period (270 million years ago) to the late Cretaceous (80 million years ago). The park's main feature, the **Waterpocket Fold,** is a classic monocline (a single-step fold) and all that remains of a huge bulge in the planet's surface thrust skyward 65 million years ago. After the fold was exposed to the elements 15 to 20 million years ago, it eroded away until only jagged ranks of stone remained along what was once its base.

Since the Waterpocket Fold tilted up to the west, the rock layers are in order of age, with younger layers to the east and older (once deeper)

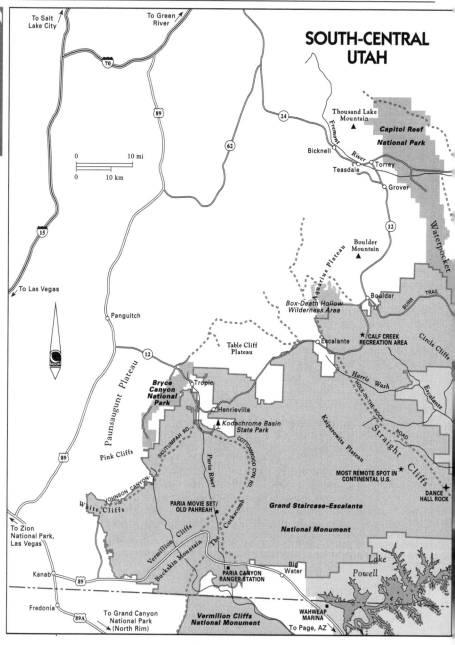

SOUTH-CENTRAL UTAH

SOUTH-CENTRAL UTAH

To Salt Lake City

To Green River

70

89

62

24

15

Thousand Lake Mountain ▲

Capitol Reef National Park

Bicknell

Fremont River

Torrey

Teasdale

Grover

12

Boulder Mountain ▲

Aquarius Plateau

Waterpocket

To Las Vegas

Panguitch

Box-Death Hollow Wilderness Area

Boulder

BURR TRAIL

Escalante

★ CALF CREEK RECREATION AREA

Circle Cliffs

12

Table Cliff Plateau

Harris Wash

HOLE-IN-THE-ROCK

Escalante

Bryce Canyon National Park

Tropic

Paunsaugunt Plateau

Henrieville

Kaiparowits Plateau

Straight Cliffs

ROAD

▲ Kodachrome Basin State Park

Pink Cliffs

89

SKUTUMPAH RD.

COTTONWOOD CYN. RD.

Paria River

MOST REMOTE SPOT IN CONTINENTAL U.S. ★

DANCE HALL ROCK ★

JOHNSON CANYON

White Cliffs

PARIA MOVIE SET/ OLD PAHREAH ■

Grand Staircase–Escalante

National Monument

Vermilion Cliffs

Buckskin Mountain

The Cockscomb

Big Water

Lake Powell

To Zion National Park, Las Vegas

Kanab

89

PARIA CANYON RANGER STATION ■

Fredonia

89A

To Grand Canyon National Park (North Rim)

Vermilion Cliffs National Monument

WAHWEAP MARINA ■

To Page, AZ

0   10 mi

0   10 km

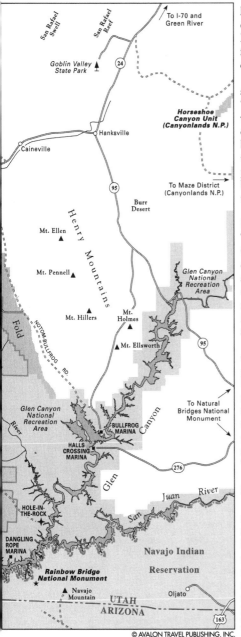

To I-70 and
Green River

San Rafael
Swell

San Rafael
Reef

Goblin Valley
State Park 24

Horseshoe
Canyon Unit
(Canyonlands N.P.)

Hanksville

Caineville

To Maze District
(Canyonlands N.P.)

95

Burr
Desert

Henry Mountains

Mt. Ellen ▲

Mt. Pennell ▲

Glen Canyon
National
Recreation
Area

Waterpocket Fold

NOTOM-BULLFROG RD.

Mt. Hillers ▲

Mt.
Holmes ▲

▲ Mt. Ellsworth

95

Glen Canyon
National
Recreation
Area

River

BULLFROG
MARINA

Glen Canyon

To Natural
Bridges National
Monument

HALLS
CROSSING
MARINA

276

Glen Canyon

Juan River

San

HOLE-IN-
THE-ROCK

DANGLING
ROPE
MARINA

Navajo Indian

Reservation

Rainbow Bridge
National Monument

▲ Navajo
Mountain

Oljato

UTAH
ARIZONA

163

© AVALON TRAVEL PUBLISHING, INC.

layers to the west. It's easy to recognize the domes of light-colored Navajo sandstone, like Capitol Dome and the Golden Throne. Cathedral Valley's formations in the north end of the park are of darker Entrada sandstone.

The term "Waterpocket" refers to natural sandstone basins that collect rainwater, and "Capitol" came about because the huge round white domes of sandstone concentrated in Cathedral Valley reminded early settlers of the capitol building in Washington, D.C. The other half of the park's name has its roots in the high-seas experiences of early pioneers, so that anything that blocked travel—such as a huge ridge of rock—they called a "reef."

Fruita Historic District

The first stop after turning off U.S. 24 is the Capitol Reef **visitor center,** 435/425-3791, open daily 8 A.M.–4:30 P.M. with extended hours in summer. Various exhibits explain the park's geology, history, and archaeology, and books and maps are for sale. Pick up free backcountry camping permits here, and check on the weather before setting off down any of the park's dirt roads.

Keep going south into the **historic district,** where Mormon settlers planted orchards on the green banks of the Fremont River in the 1880s. Originally called Junction, as it stood at the intersection of the Fremont River and Sulphur Creek, the settlement quickly became known as the "Eden of Wayne County" about around the time when Butch Cassidy and his Wild Bunch are said to have hidden out in the nearby canyons. The settlement changed its name to Fruita in 1902 after the apple, cherry, peach, apricot, mulberry, and pear trees started bearing fruit.

In the early 1900s the population hovered around 10 families, who raised sorghum, alfalfa, and vegetables. Fruit still provided most of the income, though, and only rough tracks connected Fruita with the rest of the world. A mainly barter economy helped the tiny community weather the Great Depression, and the first tractor didn't arrive until WWII. Visitors began to arrive with the declaration of Capitol Reef National Monument in 1937, and the National Park Service eventually purchased most of

© JULIAN SMITH

Capitol Reef National Park

the land peacefully by the late 1960s. The last resident moved away in 1969.

Today all that remains of the original settlement are the historic **school** on U.S. 24, the Gifford farmhouse and barn, a few minor outbuildings, and the famous Fruita **orchards.** The Park Service maintains about 2,700 trees with year-round irrigation and care, and in season each fruit crop is available to visitors on a pick-your-own basis for a small fee. Fruits are ready for harvest anywhere between late June (cherries) and early October (apples); contact the visitor center for a schedule. Follow the **Fremont River Trail** through the orchards to an overlook 800 feet above the valley. Just over a mile long, it's easy for the first half mile but starts to climb steeply after that.

Another, steeper trail leaves the road to the east just before the campground, climbing up to **Cohab Canyon,** named after the

> *Capitol Gorge used to be the only way vehicles could cross the Waterpocket Fold before U.S. 24 was built. Look for Fremont petroglyphs and the "Pioneer Register," where passing settlers carved their names on the canyon wall near the turn of the 20th century.*

Mormon polygamists who sought refuge from the law in this classic "hanging" canyon that's hard to see from below. Climbing steeply at first, the 1.5-mile trail has short side spurs leading to various overlooks.

There's a pleasantly shady picnic area among the cottonwood and willows by the river, and interpreters at the Gifford farmhouse explain and demonstrate various aspects of pioneer life. The **Fruita Campground** just down the road has 71 sites for $10, open year-round. The park is free up to this point, but to continue down the scenic drive you'll have to pay a $5 **entrance fee** per car.

Scenic Drive

The Reef's main thoroughfare, relatively speaking, starts at the visitor center and heads south for 12.5 paved miles. Past Fruita, the first major point of interest is the short dirt spur into **Grand Wash,** which is good enough for 2WD vehicles in dry weather. Butch Cassidy was said to have a hideout in this narrow, sheer-sided canyon. True or not, there's an arch named after him today. The trail to **Cassidy Arch** (1.75 mi) climbs steeply to a spot above it.

Keep driving south past the **Egyptian Temple** and the **Golden Throne,** two of the park's more unusual landmarks. The Temple looks like a vertical accordion of dark Moenkopi sandstone topped by the harder Shinarump layer, and the Throne is an unmistakable dome of gleaming Navajo sandstone. A tough two-mile trail climbs to the top of the cliffs to a view over the Golden Throne and the surrounding landscape.

A short distance farther down the road another dirt spur heads east into **Capitol Gorge,** which is just as deep and narrow as Grand Wash. This used to be the only way vehicles could cross the Waterpocket Fold before U.S. 24 was built. It's probably the closest you'll ever come to driving through a slot canyon, weather permitting. Look for Fremont petroglyphs and the "Pioneer Register,"

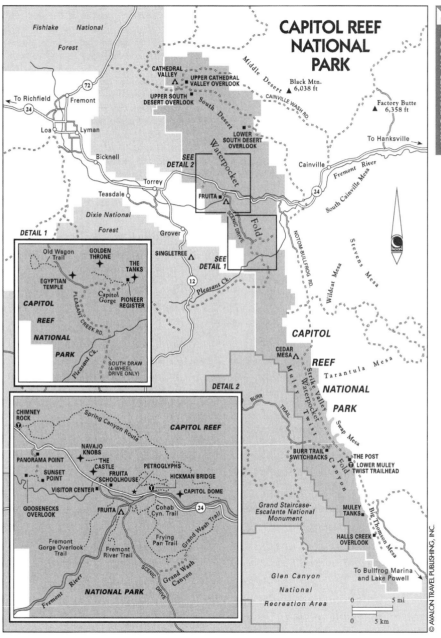

© AVALON TRAVEL PUBLISHING, INC.

where passing settlers carved their names on the canyon wall near the turn of the 20th century.

Beyond Capitol Gorge the pavement ends and the scenic drive crosses Pleasant Creek to become the **South Draw Road,** a rougher track that curves around to the southwest to join UT-12 near the Pleasant Creek and Oak Creek Campgrounds up on Boulder Mountain.

Cathedral Valley

North of U.S. 24 lies some of the Reef's most unusual landscapes—and by now you should know that's saying a lot. It's a 4WD-only adventure past stone formations jutting abruptly from a nearly level plain, formed by a layer of Curtis sandstone capping softer Entrada sandstone. Check with the visitor center for current weather conditions before setting out on this or any other dirt roads in the park.

Most visitors see Cathedral Valley from a 60-mile loop that starts at the **Fremont River Ford** 12 miles east of the visitor center on U.S. 24. (It's a good idea to start here to make sure you can make the crossing, which can be flooded after thunderstorms or during spring runoff.) Please close the gate behind you, and don't park or camp on private property along the road.

The loop follows the **Hartnet Road** past sweeping views over the stark South Desert. Turn off onto the **Caineville Wash Road** at **Hartnet Junction,** 28 miles from the ford, which is near the primitive **Cathedral Valley** campsite (six sites) at 7,000 feet on the base of **Thousand Lake Mountain.** Notice the changes in the landscape as the road's elevation rises. Heading east on the Caineville Wash Road, the loop passes innumerable volcanic dikes and plugs in **Cathedral Valley** proper, of which the sharp spires of the **Temple of the Moon** and the **Temple of the Sun** are the two most striking examples. Eventually the road rejoins U.S. 24 just west of Caineville.

Highway 24 Through the Park

East of the **Fruita schoolhouse,** built in 1896 and used until 1941, are a set of beautifully made **pictographs** chipped into the canyon wall by the Fremont people, a stone's throw above the river. (The Fremont culture was actually named after

sites found along the river in 1929.) You can't approach the stone carvings, but the view through binoculars or the telescopes provided is still impressive. Deer like to congregate in the grass below and in the orchards across the road. Keep going east past **Hickman Bridge** and **Capitol Dome**— short, steep trails lead up to both—to reach the pioneer-era **Behunin Cabin** and eventually to leave the park for the Caineville badlands.

West of the visitor center, U.S. 24 passes **The Castle,** formed of angular Wingate sandstone, and a turnoff to **Panorama Point** and a very short dirt track leading to the **Goosenecks Overlook** over Sulphur Creek. The bulbous **Twin Rocks** are the last formation of note before you leave the park to the west.

Notom-Bullfrog Road

A little over nine miles east of the visitor center on U.S. 24 is a turnoff to the south for another popular Capitol Reef back road. The 65-mile route, paved only on either end, runs down the east side of the Waterpocket Fold. About 17 miles south of U.S. 24 it passes the primitive **Cedar Mesa Campground** (five sites) and then enters Strike Valley to intersect the Burr Trail from Boulder after 29 miles.

Past the Burr Trail switchbacks is the entrance to **Lower Muley Twist,** a popular narrows hike through a canyon so sinuous they say it could tie a mule in knots. If you hike the canyon south of the road, you can exit east to Halls Creek after four miles and climb a cut-off trail back to the road at a parking area on the Notom-Bullfrog Road called The Post. This six-mile hike can be done in a day. Otherwise, keep heading south down the canyon, which becomes more interesting after it joins Halls Creek. Keep an eye out for pourovers, pools, huge undercuts, and a cowboy camp, and imagine being a Mormon pioneer hauling wagons and cattle through here in the 1880s.

The Notom-Bullfrog Road leaves the park just south of The Post. It becomes paved once again as it nears Bullfrog Marina and Glen Canyon National Recreation Area. A side (dirt) loop off the paved southern end leads across Big Thompson Mesa to the **Halls Creek Overlook** and the trailhead to another outstanding narrows hike: the

Halls Creek Narrows. The narrows themselves, three miles long and 100 meters deep, are 10 miles south of the overlook, so getting there and back is an overnight trip or a long day hike, but deep shade and a trickling perennial stream help make it worth the effort. An old wagon trail to Halls Crossing on the Colorado River once ran down this canyon, still visible in many stretches.

Another trail leads west from the overlook to **Brimhall Bridge,** a moderately challenging route that's five miles round-trip. Head up-canyon for three miles to **Hamburger Rocks,** dark hoodoos of stone that look like burgers on a white stone grill.

More Information

Direct your questions to the park's visitor center, above, or its website at www.nps.gov/care. Another good source of info on the park and its surroundings is the **Capitol Reef Country Travel Council,** 435/425-3365 or 800/858-7951, info@capitolreef.org, www.capitolreef.org.

TORREY

Capitol Reef's gateway town stretches for a half mile or so along U.S. 24 near its intersection with UT-12, west of the park. Large cottonwoods and a canal follow the road, along with a growing handful of hotels, restaurants, and other businesses.

Everything tourist-related closes down from late fall through spring. The listings below are ordered from west to east along U.S. 24.

Accommodations and Food

Starting from the west end of town on U.S. 24 (a.k.a. Main Street), the **Thousand Lake RV Park,** 1050 W. Main St., 435/425-3500 or 800/355-8995, has tent and RV sites ($12.50–18.50) open Apr.–Oct., as well as a heated pool, grocery store, showers, and Western cookouts five nights a week. They also rent 4WD Geo Trackers for $75 per day. The **Cafe Diablo,** 599 W. Main St., 435/425-3070, www.cafediablo.net, may not look that fancy from the outside, but their nouveaux Southwestern dishes, like pumpkin seed trout and pecan chicken, are outstanding. (Open daily for dinner in season.) They have an

outdoor patio that's lovely once it starts to cool off at night. Sites at the **Sand Creek RV Park,** 520 W. Main St., 435/425-3577, are $9 for tents and $15–18 for full hookups. They also offer hostel rooms ($10–12 pp), a laundry, showers ($2.50, open to the public), and an espresso bar.

Another hidden gem of the southern Utah dining scene (there are more than you'd think!) is the restaurant at the **Capitol Reef Inn & Cafe,** 360 W. Main, 435/425-3271, cri@capitolreefinn .com, www.capitolreefinn.com. Fresh local produce goes into their healthy creations spanning the spectrum from 10-vegetable salads to lemon hickory chicken dinners. Dinner entrees at $8–18, and lunch sandwiches run $6–7. (Open daily for all meals in season.) Southwest-style rooms with handmade furniture are $48, complete with satellite movies and a shared hot tub. Elm trees, a waterfall, and a desert garden decorate the grounds, and in 2001 the owners were building an Anasazi-style kiva next door.

Motel rooms are $35 at the **Torrey Trading Post & Cabins,** 75 W. Main, 435/425-3716, tuentinc@gbasin.net, and their cabins cost $30. **Austin's Chuck Wagon Motel,** 12 W. Main, 435/425-3335 or 800/863-3288, info@austins-chuckwagonmotel.com, www.austinschuck-wagonmotel.com, offers rooms for $60 and two-bedroom log cabins, with full kitchens and enough room for six people, for $100. Outdoors is a large heated pool, and the general store on the premises has a full selection of groceries and a bakery.

The UT-12 intersection is dominated by the Taft Travel Plaza, centered around a **Days Inn,** 801/425-3111. Rooms are $50–60, featuring an indoor pool and a hot tub. There's a Subway sandwich shop in the Chevron station next to the **Torrey Visitors Center,** 435/425-3365, open noon–7 P.M. daily in season. In the same building, you'll also find the goodies-stocked **Castle Rock Coffee & Candy,** open daily 7 A.M.–7 P.M. in season, with Internet access (30 minutes for $5) and local art on the walls.

Atop a mesa at the same intersection, above the Texaco station, is the **Wonderland Inn,** 435/425-3775 or 877/854-0184, www.capitol-reefwonderland.com. This sprawling complex boasts 50 rooms ($50–60), a heated pool, a Jacuzzi, and a sauna, as well as a 39-space RV park and a restaurant serving all meals (entrees $9–14). A much more intimate experience awaits at the **Sky Ridge B&B**, 435/425-3222, skyridge@color-country.net, www.bbiu.org/skyridge, a AAA four-diamond property that's also above the intersection. Six rooms with names like Juniper and Tumbleweed are eclectically decorated; the $104–172 rate includes a full, tasty breakfast. The views up here are great.

Two miles east of Torrey towards the park are two chain hotels: the **Best Western Capitol Reef Resort**, 435/425-3761, fax 435/425-3300 ($100–140), and the **Holiday Inn Express** at the Hidden Falls Resort, 435/425-FUNN, 888/232-4082, www.holidayinncapitolreef.com ($70–90). Continue east another mile to find the **Rim Rock Inn**, 435/425-3388 or 888/447-4676, www.therimrock.com, set on a cliff in the middle of a 120-acre ranch. Ten large windows overlook the Waterpocket Fold and Boulder Mountain, and two stone fireplaces keep things snug in colder weather. Rooms are $50–80, and a restaurant serves all meals. (Open Mar.–Nov.)

Shopping and Services

Anglers who swoon at the potential of a place called Thousand Lake Mountain should head for the **Alpine Anglers Flyshop and Boulder**

Mountain Adventures, 310 W. Main St., 435/425-3660 or 888/484-3331, www.fly-fishing-utah.net. Southern Utah's only full-service fly shop and fishing guide service offers trips into the mountains and the nearby Fremont River starting at $175 pp and lasting up to a week in length. Fly-fishing horse pack trips start at $650 for two days.

For a dose of caffeine and/or literature, look for the conical roof of **Robber's Roost Books & Beverages**, 185 W. Main St., 435/425-3265. It's a great place to lounge and sip, with couches and a wood-burning stove inside and a glassed-in porch out back. They have a small but well-chosen assortment of titles, including many works by local authors. **The Old Cedar Tree**, 135 W. Main St., 435/425-3992, sells rocks, fossils, and gifts made from natural products.

Wild Hare Expeditions, 116 W. Main, 435/425-3999 or 888/304-4273, thehare@color-country.net, http://members.color-country.net/~thehare, organizes half-, full-, and multi-day trips all over the area. Choose from hiking, biking, backpacking, and 4WD ventures, with gear for rent and well-trained guides available. They can also shuttle you to a trailhead and/or pick you up after a hike. Their "Hare Lair" headquarters is a combination gift shop and gear store, stocking maps and guidebooks.

The **Teasdale Ranger Station** of the Dixie National Forest, 435/425-3702, is at 138 E. Main St.

Highway 12 Scenic Byway

The most spectacular drive in a land of superlatives, this road takes the cake by a wide margin. It's one of the most beautiful routes in the country, the kind that can make you swerve in awe—a definite problem when it's the 500-foot drop off the shoulder that's making you gasp. Take turns at the wheel or, if you're alone, stop often to admire the views. This is a drive not to be missed.

Starting at Torrey, UT-12 climbs to almost 10,000 feet at the top of the Aquarius Plateau before dropping down to skewer two of the most remote towns in the Lower 48, Boulder and Escalante. Meandering unhurriedly across

the slickrock expanses of the northern edge of the Grand Staircase–Escalante National Monument, the road passes livestock grazing in green fields near Henrieville. It continues west for the neon spires of Bryce Canyon National Park and climbs the Paunsaugunt Plateau to U.S. 89 just south of Panguitch.

You can drive it in an afternoon or spend a lifetime exploring the canyons visible from just one of the overlooks. Well worth at least a few days' meandering, UT-12 showcases the amazing diversity of what was one of the last blank spots on the map of the United States.

WEST ON HIGHWAY 12

On its way up over the flank of **Boulder Mountain,** UT-12 cuts across the eastern edge of the Aquarius Plateau and the Dixie National Forest, the largest in Utah. Peaking at 11,322 feet, Boulder Mountain forms one of the largest high-elevation plateaus in the country. It is home to hundreds of small lakes above 10,000 feet elevation. (The mountains around here seem to be deliberately misnamed: most of the lakes are on Boulder Mountain, and most of the boulders are on Thousand Lake Mountain.) As the road climbs, piñon and juniper gradually give way to aspen, pine, fir, and spruce. Pullouts lead to stupendous overlooks wide enough to encompass entire eastern states. Paving on this stretch of UT-12 was not completed until 1985.

About 25 miles east of Boulder is the **Singletree Campground** (26 units, $10), followed five miles later by the **Oak Creek Campground,** with eight units for $9. A spur road after another mile leads to **Pleasant Creek Campground** (16 units, $9), near the **Wildcat Ranger Station,** open in summer only. Highway 12 tops out at 9,400 feet at Roundtop Flat before dropping down to Boulder, 39 miles from Torrey.

BOULDER

A cattle ranching community settled in 1889, Boulder is little more than a wide spot on UT-12. The tiny community is so isolated by the canyons of the Escalante River and its tributaries that it was the last community to receive its mail by mule in the country. It did so until 1935, when the river was finally bridged, making Boulder one of the last towns in the country to gain automobile access.

Ranches spread to the south and west, and Boulder Mountain rises to the north. Huge, glowing domes of Navajo sandstone surround the town, cracked into regular patterns like the hide of some huge desert creature. Boulder itself is a pretty, green oasis that's seen land values rise significantly since the declaration of the Grand Staircase–Escalante National Monument.

Sights

Part of an 87-room Anasazi village has been excavated and partially reconstructed on the grounds of the **Anasazi State Park Museum,** 435/335-7308, parks.state.ut.us/parks/www1/anas.htm. There's a newly remodeled indoor museum and a six-room replica of an ancient dwelling inside the museum building. Open year-round 9 A.M.–5 P.M. and May–Sept. 8 A.M.–6 P.M., $5 per vehicle.

Accommodations and Food

Just down the road from the state park is the **Boulder Mountain Lodge,** 435/335-7460 or 800/556-3446, fax 435/335-7461, bmlut@color-country.net, www.boulder-utah.com, one of the Four Corner's most enticing getaways. The timber lodge combines Western coziness with first-class comfort. Tapestries and local artists' works decorate the tasteful interior, and the whole thing is set around an 11-acre private waterfowl sanctuary complete with pond and marsh. There's also a library and a sandstone fireplace for lounging. The Tibetan Buddhist–inspired food at the lodge's **Hell's Backbone Grill,** 435/335-7464, www.hellsbackbonegrill.com, is good enough to make the drive here just for dinner. Some of the best cooking in southern Utah combines local meats and organically grown veggies into Southwest delicacies like chipotle meatloaf and pecan skillet trout. The Grill is also the only place in the city you can buy wine and microbrewed beer, after a fight against the town government that went all the way to the Utah Supreme Court in 2002. Entrees are $10–20, and they'll make you a picnic lunch to go for $6–8 (order the night before). Open daily for all meals in season. Rooms at the lodge are $80–140.

Across from the state park, **Poles Place,** 435/355-7422 or 800/730-7422, polesplace@boulderutah.com, www.boulderutah.com/polesplace, is a motel with 12 guest rooms ($50–60), and a cafe with good burgers and shakes at their walk-up window. Two more Boulder dining options are along the Burr Trail. The **Burr Trail Trading Post & Grill** 435/335-7500 or 877/633-8012, at the turnoff for the trail, has outdoor dining, pizza, and sandwiches for $6–7 and steaks up to $15 for dinner, along with the best selection of

Native American crafts around in their gift shop. The **Boulder Mesa Restaurant,** 435/335-7447, located in a log building a few hundred yards down the trail, features homemade pies, soups, and salads. Both are open for all meals in season.

For snacks and sundries there's the **Hills & Hollows Mini-Mart,** 435/335-7349, a 24-hour gas station just west of town on UT-12, which offers bunkhouse rooms for rent. Campers can find a spot at the **Deer Creek Campground** 6.7 miles down the Burr Trail for $4 per night.

Activities

There is definitely something about this scenery that makes you want to ride off into it, so luckily the **Boulder Mountain Ranch,** 435/335-7480, fax 435/335-7352, www.boulderutah.com/bmr, offers multi-day horse pack trips from their working cattle ranch 3.5 miles out Hell's Backbone Road. Their fully supported trips range from half-day rides ($60 pp) through full-day "No Pansy Rides" ($150) to a six-day "Long in the Saddle" adventure for experienced riders ($856). They'll even let you participate in an honest-to-gosh cattle roundup. Their log cabins sleep two to six people for $55–83.

Red Rock 'n Llamas, 435/559-7325 or 877/955-2627, rllama@color-country.net, www.redrocknllamas.com, has four- to five-day guided hikes to Glen Canyon, Rainbow Bridge, and the Escalante and Colorado Rivers starting at $725. Llamas, easier on the scenery than horses or mules, carry most of the gear. Other guide services operating out of Boulder include **Escalante Canyon Outfitters,** 435/335-7311 or 888/326-4453, ecohike@color-country.net, www.ecohike.com, with 10 different trips starting at five days for $1,000 pp. **Earth Tours,** 435/691-1241, info@earth-tours.com, www.earth-tours.com, starts with half- and full-day trips for $50 and $75 pp, respectively, and goes from there.

Local fishing guide Steve Stoner runs **Boulder Mountain Fly Fishing,** 110 W. 300 N., 435/335-7306 or 435/691-0368, stevestoner@color-country.net, www.bouldermountainfly-fishing.com, offering trips in search of the cutthroat and brook trout that fill the many lakes up on Boulder Mountain. He provides all the equip-

ment and can guide two people for a full day for $300. If you happen to see a bedraggled group limp into town and head straight for the burgers at Pole's Place, they're probably with the **Boulder Outdoor Survival School,** 303/444-9779, info@boss-inc.com, www.boss-inc.com, which is actually based in Boulder, Colorado. Their desert survival courses are only a few of the many educational trips they offer.

Information

More details about the area's attractions and businesses can be found at the website of the **Boulder Business Alliance,** info@boulderutah.com, www.boulderutah.com. The Escalante Chamber of Commerce website, www.escalante-cc.com, also has information on services in Boulder.

Burr Trail

This old cattle trail winds east from Boulder, crosses the Circle Cliffs and the southern end of Capitol Reef National Park, and joins the Notom-Bullfrog Road to reach Bullfrog Marina on Lake Powell. One John Atlantic Burr constructed the trail in the late 1800s to move cattle between winter and summer ranges and to market. In 1882, a pioneer wrote in her journal:

> *It is the most God-forsaken and wild looking country that was ever traveled . . . It is mostly uphill and sandy knee and then sheets of solid rock for the poor animals to pull over and slide down. I never saw the poor horses pull and paw as they done today.*

After the trail was improved by the Atomic Energy Commission to help uranium prospectors access the backcountry, controversy erupted in the 1970s over whether it should be paved its entire length. Garfield County officials held that paving would boost the local economy and improve transportation, while conservationists argued that ORV damage would increase. Acrimony reached a bitter peak in the 1980s when directors of the Southern Utah Wilderness Association were hanged in effigy in Escalante, and four county bulldozers were sabotaged near the switchbacks.

The Burr Trail is paved for a few dozen miles on either end, but through the Waterpocket

Fold and the park it remains unpaved, and things can get bad quickly in inclement weather. Steep winding switchbacks in the park make RVs a poor choice. There are no services the entire 68-mile length, so carry all the water and gasoline you think you'll need, plus some extra. Intermittent posts along the road serve as reference markers for some of the more major turnoffs. Find more information on the Internet at www.nps.gov/glca/burrtr.htm.

Dozens of side roads and trails branch off from the main route. After passing the Deer Creek Campground at mile 6.5, you'll cross The Gulch at 10.7 miles, a very popular trailhead from which you can reach the Escalante River in about two days. The Burr Trail then follows Long Canyon, a colorful gorge reminiscent of Zion Canyon, for about seven miles. Twenty-five miles from Boulder is the intersection with the west end of the Wolverine Road, a 28-mile loop through remote, rugged terrain that rejoins the Burr Trail 11 miles west near Long Canyon. The Wolverine Road is a rougher route that passes an area of petrified logs on BLM land (collecting any is illegal).

Once inside Capitol Reef National Park, the Burr Trail turns to dirt and is recommended for 4WD vehicles only. Soon you'll cross Muley Twist Canyon. From Muley Twist, the Burr Trail climbs a daunting series of switchbacks—gaining 800 feet in half a mile—and intersects with Notom-Bullfrog Road. The view to the east is outstanding. From here Notom-Bullfrog Road leaves the park and parallels the Waterpocket Fold north and south. Head south to join UT-276 after 65.3 miles from Boulder; Bullfrog is only a short distance ahead.

Boulder to Escalante

The most scenic stretch of UT-12 runs for less than 30 miles between Boulder and Escalante. Finished by the Civilian Conservation Corps in 1940, the "Million-Dollar Highway to Boulder" allowed the first year-round vehicular access to the towns cut off from the rest of the world by the Escalante canyons. It wasn't fully paved until 1971.

Drive it and you'll agree the nickname refers to the views as much as the cost: blonde and rosy

slickrock undulates toward the horizon, with green lines of cottonwoods following invisible watercourses down in the brown canyon bottoms and the Henry Mountains, Navajo Mountain, and the Straight Cliffs standing above it all. Try to do this drive in the morning or late afternoon to fully appreciate the three-dimensionality of the landscape. Few roads interact with their scenery as spectacularly as this one, and it's worth doing it right.

Heading west from Boulder, **Hell's Backbone Road** soon joins the highway from the right. UT-12 crosses a winding section called the **Hogback,** a rocky spine just wide enough for the two-lane road, a narrow shoulder, and a few small pullouts. It then descends the Haymaker Bench to Calf Creek. Just over 11 miles west of Boulder is the popular **Calf Creek Canyon Recreation Area,** run by the BLM, with 13 campsites for $7 per night (day use is $2 per car). From here a trail heads up Calf Canyon for just under three miles to the beautiful **Lower Calf Creek Falls,** which plunge 126 feet into a sandy pool. Look for ruins and pictographs along the way as you pass beaver-dammed pools lined with reeds. The trail is a moderate walk and offers an easy taste of the Escalante canyons, so it can get relatively crowded. Fewer people take the one-mile trail to the 90-foot **Upper Calf Creek Falls,** starting at a dirt road between mileposts 81 and 82 on UT-12, just uphill toward Boulder.

Continuing toward Escalante, you'll cross the Escalante River at another popular trailhead for hikes down the canyon. Next comes Boynton Overlook, offering a glimpse of the Escalante River and Calf Creek. (Get out your binoculars and look for a pictograph panel of handprints on the opposite canyon wall, just above the mouth of Calf Creek.) Head of the Rocks four miles later offers more great views, and beyond that farmland replaces bare rock as you pass the turnoff for the **Hole-In-The-Rock Road.** Escalante is 27 miles from Boulder.

ESCALANTE

For some reason the Mormon pioneers who founded this town in 1875 decided to name it after the Spanish priest Francisco Silvestre Vélez de Escalante, who didn't come within 150 miles of the place during his 1776 wanderings. Drawn to the area's mild climate, 6,000 feet high between the Kaiparowits and Aquarius Plateaus, the settlers nicknamed their new home "Potato Valley" for a local variety of wild tuber and set about exploring the grazing potential of the nearby canyons and benches. Families drew numbers from a hat to decide who got which 1.25-acre lot, logs houses went up, and the new town was off and running. When the Centennial rolled around in July 1876, no one had an American flag yet, so a striped Navajo blanket was proudly hoisted instead. Piped drinking water didn't arrive until 1937.

Today the economy of tiny Escalante (pop. 900) remains based on farming and livestock, but change began to stampede across the horizon with the declaration of the national monument next door. As the main gateway to the wonders of the Grand Staircase and the Escalante canyons, the town is also at the center of controversy, since government restrictions on grazing could deeply affect local ranchers. Among the pioneer homes and barns you'll see signs demanding the government give locals back their backyard, and for every "Wild Utah" bumper sticker you'll see one proclaiming "Wilderness: Land of No Use." The local old guard is slowly coming round, grudgingly admitting the monument's economic potential, as real estate prices seem to rise with every SUV that rolls into town. In 2002 a Main Street beautification project was in the works, but a number of beautiful old wooden pioneer homes still stood empty in the center of town.

Sights

If you need a break from the unending swells of slickrock, the **Escalante Petrified Forest State Park,** 435/826-4466, parks.state.ut.us/parks/ www1/esca.htm, offers a 130-acre reservoir for fishing and swimming, as well as two short self-guided trails past rainbow-colored chunks of petrified wood and fossilized dinosaur bones. The park is a mile and a half west of Escalante on UT-12, and has a 22-site campground for $14 per night (call 800/322-3770 for reservations). Day use is $5 per vehicle.

Accommodations

Escalante has a number of modest motels with room for under $50, including the **Circle D Motel,** 475 W. Main St., 435/826-4297, fax 435/826-4402, www.utahcanyons.com/circled .htm, circledmotel@color-country.net, and the **Padre Motel,** 20 E. Main St., 435/826-4276. The 50 rooms at the **Prospector Inn,** 380 W. Main St., 435/826-4653, fax 435/826-4285, www.prospectorinn.com, start at $50. A night at **Escalante's Grand Staircase B&B/Inn,** 280 W. Main St., 866/826-4890, www.escalantebnb.com, escalbnb@color-country.net, starts at $65 from Mar.–Oct., and they have a two-night package including guided sunset hike and slot canyon adventure for $270 pp. The Old West–style place also offers mountain bike rentals and shuttle service. In the same price range is the **Rainbow Country Bed & Breakfast Inn,** 300 S. 586 East, 435/826-4567 or 800/252-8824, fax 435/826-4557, www.color-country.net/~rainbow, rainbow@color-country.net, with a great view from the large sun deck. Four guest rooms include a hearty breakfast and access to the pool table and outdoor hot tub.

The **Serenidad Retreat,** 435/826-4720 or 888/826-4577, www.escalanteretreat.com, hpriska@juno.com, takes its name from the Spanish word for (you guessed it) "serenity," and has the secluded location and views to back it up. Three bedrooms, two baths, and a complete kitchen can accommodate 10 people year-round. There's a wood-burning stove and large deck, and pets are welcome. Rates are $95. The owners of **Escalante's Wild West Retreat,** 300 S. 200 E., 866/292-3043 or 435/826-4849, www.wildwestretreat.com, yahoo@wildwestretreat.com, took a 1930s barn and completely restored it. Now it's a luxury-rustic getaway with a full kitchen, hot tub, covered porches, and a star-gazing upper deck. Rates start at $100, and horses and mules are boarded free. Another private building for rent for the same price is the **Southwestern Retreat,** 877/777-7988 or 435/826-4967, www .utahcanyons.com/swretreat.htm, retreat@utahcanyons.com. It sleeps seven people in three bedrooms and comes complete with kitchen, laundry, deck, and entertainment center.

Camping

The **Broken Bow RV Camp,** 495 W. Main St., 435/826-4959 or 888/241-8785, has 28 full hookup sites, cabins, hot showers, and a laundry room. You can also pitch a tent on BLM land at the Escalante Petrified Forest State Park, in the campgrounds at the Calf Creek Recreation Area, and up in the Dixie National Forest, accessed via the Hell's Backbone Road.

Food

All restaurants in Escalante (there aren't many) are open daily for all meals. The Prospector Inn's **Ponderosa Restaurant,** 435/826-4658, is probably the nicest of the bunch, serving American and European dishes from Apr.–Nov. Burgers at the **Golden Loop Cafe,** 39 W. Main St., 435/826-4433, start at $3, and they also serve sandwiches, tacos, and steaks topping out at $10. There's a similar menu at the **Cowboy Blues Restaurant,** 530 W. Main St., 435/826-4577. For outfitting yourself stop by the Mom-and-Pop **Griffin Grocery,** 30 W. Main St., 435/826-4226, for groceries, ice, and a deli.

Shopping and Activities

An espresso bar isn't the rarity it once was in southern Utah, but the "Esca-Latté" sign at **Escalante Outfitters,** 310 W. Main St., 435/826-4266, fax 435/826-4388, www.aros.ent/~slickroc/escout, is still a welcome sight to road-tripping caffeine hounds. Along with a small wine shop and pizza parlor, this all-inclusive place stocks gear, guidebooks, and microbrews. The Spartan but clean log bunkhouses next door go for $25 d.

Right across the street, **Utah Canyons,** 325 W. Main St., 877/777-7988 or 435/826-4967, www.utahcanyons.com, offers maps, gear, guidebooks, water, and a wealth of friendly advice about the surrounding countryside. Day hikes and trailhead shuttle service are only two of the services they offer in the guise of **Escalante Outback Adventures,** www.escalante-utah.com, tours@utahcanyons.com. Guided tours to slot canyons and waterfalls run $50–160 for two people.

Rick Green's **Excursions of Escalante,** 800/839-7567, www.excursions-escalante.com, outdoor@excursions-escalante.com, operating

out of the Trail Head Cafe at 100 East and Main Street, advertises canyoneering, fishing, mountain biking, and backpacking trips starting at $45 pp for a half day. For more camping supplies and hardware, try the Griffin Grocery.

Pick up the "Escalante Arts & Crafts Guide" pamphlet anywhere in town for information on local artists like Ruthanne Oliver and Susan Kay and their galleries. **Brigitte Delthony,** 435/826-4631, www.sculpturedfurnitureartandceramics.com, ddelth@color-country.net, has a gallery half a mile west of town on UT-12 where she exhibits pit-fired pottery and ceramics inspired by the area's prehistoric cultures. Her husband **David** sculpts beautiful, organically inspired wooden furniture.

Information

The U.S. National Park Service, National Forest Service, and Bureau of Land Management have set aside their differences long enough to establish the **Escalante Interagency Visitor Center,** 435/826-5499, escalant@ut.blm.gov, on the western edge of town. It's open year-round, Mon.–Fri. 8 A.M.–4:30 P.M., and Mar.–Oct. daily 7:30 A.M.–5:30 P.M. Individual numbers for the agencies are: Park Service, 435/826-5651; Dixie National Forest, 435/826-5400; and BLM 435/825-5600.

Direct any other questions to the **Escalante Chamber of Commerce,** 435/826-4810, www.escalante-cc.com, escalante@escalante-cc.com.

Near Escalante

The name would be reason enough to recommend it, but **Hell's Backbone Road** goes one better: this 40-mile loop takes you up into the 25,000-acre **Box-Death Hollow Wilderness Area** north of Escalante. The 4WD track follows sheer ridge tops and crossed gorges lined with orange-gray walls of Navajo sandstone. Along the way it passes **Posey Lake Campground** at 8,700 feet (23 sites, $5 per night) and the **Blue Spruce Campground** at 7,800 feet (6 sites, $5). The eastern end of the road meets UT-12 at mile 60.2 east of Escalante (head east and north past the cemetery and the old garbage dump).

This end of the road is the terminus of a number of popular **hikes** in the canyons that flow into the upper reaches of the Escalante River. Pine Creek, which parallels Hell's Backbone Road initially, offers a stretch of narrow, tree-lined streambed called the **Pine Creek Box.** Most people drive up the road about eight miles, descend to the streambed, and follow it back to Escalante in a day. **Death Hollow** itself, east of Pine Creek, is much more of an undertaking. You'll need up to five days to do the entire canyon from the trailhead, which is 22.5 miles up Hell's Backbone Road, back down to Escalante. Along the way you'll thread about three miles of high-quality narrows and encounter pools that may require some swimming to cross. This is a serious hike, but one of the best in southern Utah. This should

not be your first canyoneering trip, and some climbing experience wouldn't hurt either. Both of these hikes are easier with a two-car shuttle.

One way out of Death Hollow is via the **Boulder Mail Trail,** which, until 1935, was just that—the only way the U.S. Postal Service could reach the remote town. This 16-mile route cuts across the Pine Creek, Death Hollow, and Sand Creek Canyons and the exposed slickrock in between. You can do it in a day, but take two to fully enjoy it. You'll need some cross-country route-finding ability, but look for sporadic rock cairns and old telegraph wire. Its eastern end intersects UT-12 near where Hell's Backbone Road rejoins it, near milepost 84.

Grand Staircase–Escalante National Monument

At 1.9 million acres—almost 3,000 square miles—the latest addition to Utah's protected lands dwarfs the surrounding national parks. It's almost as big as Delaware and Rhode Island put together, yet few people outside of the Four Corners could place it on a map, and even fewer have been lucky enough to venture inside. Word is starting to get out, however, and thousands of visitors are already arriving each year to explore this little-known wonderland of cliffs, canyons, rivers and desert plateaus. Whatever your interest—archaeology, geology, history, biology, paleontology, desert scenery, or just escaping into the wild—the monument is more than big enough to accommodate.

THE SETTING

The monument can be roughly divided into three regions from west to east: Grand Staircase, Kaiparowits Plateau, and Escalante Canyons.

Grand Staircase

The southwest corner of the monument is the kind of landscape that makes geologists drool. First described by geologist Clarence Dutton in his *Report of the Geology of the High Plateaus of Utah* (1880), it consists of a series of huge geological steps rising 3,500 feet from the North Rim of the Grand Canyon to Bryce Canyon National Park,

150 miles to the north. Over 250 million years of uplift and erosion are on stark display in five major terraces named for their gaudy colors: the Chocolate Cliffs, the Vermilion Cliffs, the White Cliffs, the Gray Cliffs, and the Pink Cliffs. Five distinct life zones, from Sonoran Desert to coniferous forests, shelter a wide variety of plant and animal life, including bald eagles and peregrine falcons.

Kaiparowits Plateau

The monument's middle section is the most rugged, one of the largest remaining blank spots on a road map of the Four Corners. Some have likened this region of canyons and mesas to an "American Outback," and if it's solitude you're after—and you can handle yourself in the desert—this is the place to go. Desert bighorn sheep and mountain lions roam among rare plants and remnants of the Fremont and Anasazi cultures. Kaiparowits means "Big Mountain's Little Brother" in the Paiute language, referring to the point near its north end the region was named after. Many prehistoric human sites have been recorded here, and it has recently been recognized as a world hotspot for late-Cretaceous paleontology.

Escalante Canyons

Dinosaur tracks and historic pioneer routes converge along the spider web of the Escalante River,

Devils Garden at Grand Staircase–Escalante National Monument

the last major river to be "discovered" by Anglo settlers in the contiguous United States. The runoff from the southern edge of the Aquarius Plateau has created a thousand-mile labyrinth of converging canyons that eventually drain into the upper reaches of Lake Powell. Many of the monument's 200 or so bird species congregate here along the leafy drainages, including some from the Neotropics. This is the easiest part of the monument to access (relatively speaking, of course) and thus sees the most visitors. It was named after Spanish priest Francisco Silvestre Vélez de Escalante by the Powell survey team in 1872, although the Father never saw the river himself.

> *Dinosaur tracks and historic pioneer routes converge along the spider web of the Escalante River, the last major river to be "discovered" by Anglo settlers in the contiguous United States.*

HISTORY
Early Inhabitants
It goes to show how remote this region is that humans didn't settle more or less permanently here

until about A.D. 500 during the late Basketmaker period. Both the Fremont and Kayenta Anasazi took advantage of the wide climatic range to co-exist peacefully. While the Anasazi farmed in the Escalante canyons and up on the Kaiparowits Plateau, the Fremont tended to hunt and gather below the plateau and near the Escalante Valley. Both groups grew corn, beans, and squash, and built brush-roofed pithouses or took advantage of natural rock shelters. The largest Kayenta settlements were scattered across the Kaiparowits Plateau near the present town of Boulder, while the Fremont lived in Calf Creek Canyon, Harris Wash, and near the town of Escalante.

Today it's hard to find a corner of the monument without some evidence of early human use, whether it's ruins, carefully chipped Moqui steps up a rock wall, or rock art with characteristic trapezoidal bodies, animals figures, and abstract designs. Once these groups left or were absorbed into other cultures that arrived around A.D. 1300, the canyons were quiet, aside from Navajo hunting deer and sheep and herding livestock into the east reaches of what would one day be declared the monument.

European Settlement
The first record of Anglo settlers in the region dates to 1866, when Captain James Andrus led a group of cavalry to the headwaters of the Escalante River. Five years later, Jacob Hamblin of Kanab, on his way to the Colorado River to re-supply the second Powell Expedition, mistook the Escalante for the Dirty Devil River and thus became the first European to travel the length of the canyon. The unforgiving topography was never demonstrated more clearly than during the 1879-80 Hole-in-the-Rock Expedition. To this day, the canyons of the Escalante remain a major barrier to east-west vehicle travel, and the river is only bridged at its upper end.

Recent News
Although the Department of the Interior had proposed the creation of a national monument as

early as 1936, it took another 60 years for reality to catch up. In September 1996, President Bill Clinton declared the creation of the Grand Staircase–Escalante National Monument, and sparks immediately began to fly. Utah politicians, no big fans of Washington to begin with, were enraged they weren't consulted in the transfer of such a huge chunk of their state to federal jurisdiction. The fact that the declaration was made from the rim of the Grand Canyon, in *Arizona,* just added fuel to the fire.

Tensions have sprouted between local ranchers, miners, and farmers, who feel that their land and way of life is being legislated out of existence, and newly arrived environmentalists and government workers scrambling to protect the huge area. Many of the latter camp see tourism and tourist dollars as inevitable (and point out that many of the former have quietly stuck their fingers in the tourism pot already). Land values and visitation are already rising.

The monument's proclamation was vague enough on what is and isn't allowed within the boundaries to ensure years of land-use controversies. In 1991, the Dutch mining company Andalex applied for a state permit to mine the estimated 62 billion tons of coal under the surface of the Kaiparowits Plateau, the largest deposit of its kind in the country. While the proclamation didn't specifically prohibit the development of existing mining leases, the roads, traffic, and construction that mining would bring conflict enough with the monument's stated purpose to preserve the "unspoiled natural area" that the company eventually withdrew the proposal. They've since begun negotiating land exchanges with the federal government for the leases. As of 2002, legal and political battles were still being fought over the future of grazing within the monument.

VISITING THE MONUMENT
Information and Permits

In 2002, new federal money was earmarked to expand the network of BLM visitor centers that surround the monument. The **Escalante Interagency Visitors Center,** 755 W. Main St.,

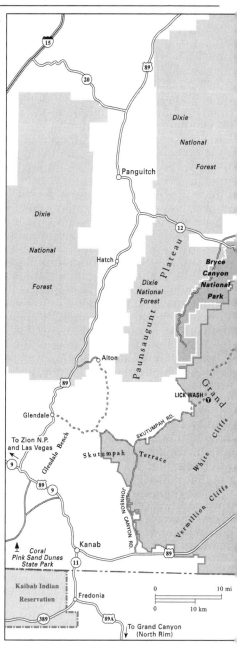

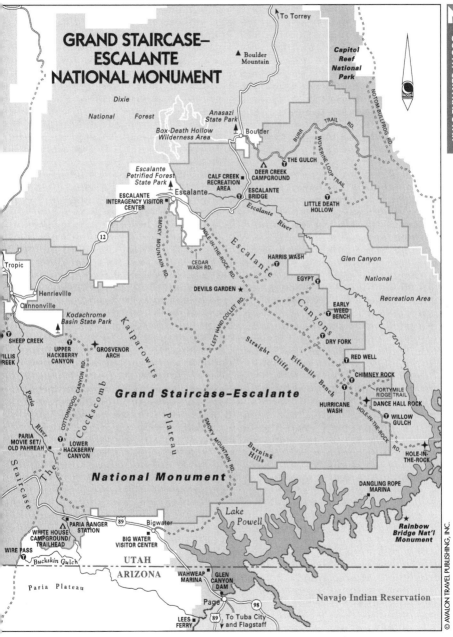

GRAND STAIRCASE–
ESCALANTE
NATIONAL MONUMENT

To Torrey

Capitol
Reef
National
Park

Boulder
Mountain

Dixie

National   Forest   Anasazi
State Park

Box-Death Hollow
Wilderness Area   Boulder

Escalante
Petrified Forest
State Park

THE GULCH

DEER CREEK
CAMPGROUND

CALF CREEK
RECREATION
AREA

Escalante

ESCALANTE
INTERAGENCY VISITOR
CENTER

ESCALANTE
BRIDGE

LITTLE DEATH
HOLLOW

Escalante River

12

SMOKY MOUNTAIN RD.

HOLE-IN-THE-ROCK RD.

CEDAR
WASH RD.

HARRIS WASH

Glen Canyon

EGYPT

National

Tropic

DEVILS GARDEN

Recreation Area

LEFT HAND COLLET RD.

EARLY
WEED
BENCH

Henrieville

Cannonville

Kodachrome
Basin State Park

DRY FORK

SHEEP CREEK

Kaiparowits

Straight Cliffs

Fiftymile Bench

RED WELL

ILLIS
REEK

UPPER
HACKBERRY
CANYON

GROSVENOR
ARCH

CHIMNEY ROCK

COTTONWOOD CANYON RD.

FORTYMILE
RIDGE TRAIL

Paria

Cockscomb

Grand Staircase-Escalante

Plateau

HURRICANE
WASH

DANCE HALL ROCK

HOLE-IN-THE-ROCK RD.

WILLOW
GULCH

PARIA
MOVIE SET/
OLD PAHREAH

LOWER
HACKBERRY
CANYON

SMOKY MOUNTAIN RD.

Burning
Hills

HOLE-IN-
THE-ROCK

National Monument

DANGLING ROPE
MARINA

Staircase

The

Lake
Powell

Rainbow
Bridge Nat'l
Monument

PARIA RANGER
STATION

89

Bigwater

WHITE HOUSE
CAMPGROUND/
TRAILHEAD

BIG WATER
VISITOR CENTER

WIRE PASS

Buckskin Gulch

UTAH

ARIZONA

WAHWEAP
MARINA

GLEN
CANYON
DAM

Paria Plateau

Navajo Indian Reservation

Page

98

LEES
FERRY

89

To Tuba City
and Flagstaff

THE HOLE-IN-THE-ROCK EXPEDITION

It was 1879, and Mormon Church President John Taylor had called on a group of believers to colonize Montezuma Creek in southeast Utah to secure a remote corner of the rapidly expanding Mormon empire and "breed goodwill among the Indians." And so they set out—236 people, many recent arrivals to the western desert, in 82 wagons surrounded by hundreds of horses and cattle, embarking on one of the most arduous journeys in the history of the American West.

From the start they knew the trip would not be easy. Leader Silas Smith had chosen to cut straight across the barren Escalante Desert to save 250 miles over alternate routes to the north and south. Cattle could find hardly any forage in the wasteland, and resourceful Mormon wives, lacking wood, had to burn weeds and sagebrush to cook the food.

In December, with snow blocking any hope of retreat through the mountains behind, the ragged party reached the edge of Glen Canyon,

took one look over the 1,800-foot drop, and immediately sent Smith and two boys back to Salt Lake for blasting powder, mining equipment, and food. When they returned, the pioneers sat down to figure out how to get everything down to the river in one piece.

Plagued by bitter cold and dwindling food, 60 men set about building a road where, as author Wallace Stegner writes, "God certainly never intended a road to be." While one team hung from the cliff edge in barrels, chiseling blasting holes to widen and level an existing crack, another group essentially began tacking a road onto the sheer rock face below it. First they blasted a small ledge just wide enough for the uphill wagon wheels, then drove two-foot cottonwood stakes into a row of holes gouged every 18 inches into the sandstone. Rocks, dirt, and vegetation were piled on top of the stakes, and gradually a makeshift road began to take shape. At an average angle of 50 degrees, the dizzying route was named Uncle Ben's Dugout for its de-

---

435/826-5499, is still the main source of information. It will eventually be enlarged to hold 70 employees, who will steer their energies toward studying and protecting the biological riches of the monument. Open daily 7:30 A.M.–5:30 P.M. (Mon.–Fri. 8 A.M.–4:30 P.M. in winter). The **Cannonville Contact Station,** 435/679-8981, in the northwest corner near Bryce Canyon National Park, will also be expanded, with a focus on Mormon history. (Open daily 8 A.M.–4:30 P.M., mid-Mar.–mid-Nov.) A third visitor center in **Big Water,** on U.S. 89 along the southern edge of the monument, slated to open in 2003, will focus on paleontology.

The **Kanab Resource Area Office,** 318 N. 100 East, 435/644-4600, in Kanab on the western edge, is open daily 7:30 A.M.–5:30 P.M. mid-Mar.–mid-Nov. (Mon.–Fri. 8 A.M.–4:30 P.M. in winter). The **Paria Contact Station** on U.S. 89, 44 miles east of Kanab. For maps and books on the Escalante area contact the **Dixie Interpretive Association** at 435/826-5499; for the Kanab

(western) area contact the **Arizona Strip Interpretive Association** at 435/688-3246, www.ut.blm.gov/monument.

Backcountry visitors currently need free **backcountry permits** to spend the night in the monument. These are available at any of the contact stations listed above, and in register boxes at major trailheads. They're required as much to find you if something goes wrong as for any other reason, so it's a good idea to fill one out.

Access

Most access from the north branches off of UT-12 between Bryce Canyon National Park and Boulder. A few of these run all the way through the monument to U.S. 89, on the southwest side between Kanab, Utah, and Page, Arizona. Both highways are paved, but the rest of the monument's graded and/or gravel roads can quickly become impassible when wet. Even when dry, they're often rough enough to loosen the bolts on most 2WD vehicles.

The **Johnson Canyon/Skutumpah Road**

signer, engineer Benjamin Perkins. Far below, a third party was busy building a ferryboat to cross the river. On weekends everyone returned to camp to nurse their bruises, and still found enough energy to fill the icy nights with fiddle music and singing.

On January 25, after six weeks of backbreaking labor, the Hole-in-the-Rock Road was finished. Perkins went first, his horses rearing and shying away from the drop-off. (Other accounts say he had to use horses blinded by pinkeye.) The settlers tried everything they could think of to slow the wagons—holding ropes and chains wrapped around the wheels, tying large juniper trees to the frames, rigging a pulley system from the top. Each wagon smoothed the passage more, making it harder and harder to hold the vehicles back. The women and children walked.

By February 10, everyone was down with all their possessions. Amazingly, no lives had been lost, human or otherwise, but many had been injured and all were exhausted. In passing they had worn the road down to almost nothing, so once again there would be no going back. It took a week to get across the river and up the equally steep wall on the other side. There they met a Ute Indian who, on hearing their story, called them liars and rode away insulted.

After that, things got even worse. Scouts almost died of thirst and starvation trying to find the route ahead, which they only stumbled on by following a herd of mountain sheep. The remaining distance, some 150 miles, took almost four months—an average of just two miles a day—as they pulled, pushed, and dragged the wagons over slickrock and through sandy wash bottoms. By the time they reached the banks of the San Juan River, everyone had had enough. The six-week trip has taken six months, and nobody had the strength or will to push on another mile. Instead, they settled the town of Bluff, which faltered over the years but always managed to pull through, perhaps drawing strength from the echoes of its founders.

---

connects Kodachrome Basin State Park with U.S. 89 about 10 miles east of Kanab. The 46-mile graded dirt road offers glimpses of the Grand Staircase and access to trailheads at Sheep Creek, Willis Creek, and Lick Wash. It's paved for its southernmost half. The **Cottonwood Canyon Road** runs for 46 miles along the Cockscomb (a.k.a. the East Kaibab Monocline), a huge north-south fold in the earth that divides the Grand Staircase from the Kaiparowits Plateau. Along this road, which heads southeast from Kodachrome Basin, are trailheads for Upper and Lower Hackberry Canyon and Grosvenor Arch, 17 miles south of UT-12. From Escalante, the **Smoky Mountain Road** winds for 78 rough miles across the Kaiparowits Plateau, providing the best access to the remote area. It eventually hits U.S. 89 at Big Water.

Perhaps the most popular way to access the eastern half of the monument is via **Hole-in-the-Rock Road,** blazed by a courageous band of Mormon pioneers on their way to the Col-

orado River. This official Scenic Backway runs for 57 miles parallel to the Straight Cliffs, from UT-12 just east of Escalante to the Hole-in-the-Rock itself, overlooking Lake Powell. In good weather, passenger cars can usually negotiate most of the graded dirt road, except for the last six or so miles that require high-clearance 4WD. At 10.4 miles from UT-12, a side road leaves to the east for Harris Wash and a large primitive campsite near a corral. Devil's Garden is on the right at 12.1 miles, a small but beautiful area of rock hoodoos. There's a picnic area but no overnight camping allowed.

More turnoffs from Hole-in-the-Rock Road lead to side tracks and trailheads. All of the following are to the east (left). At 16.5 miles is the turnoff to the Egypt area, followed by ones for Early Weed Bench (23.6 mi), Dry Fork (25.9 mi), and Fortymile Ridge (36.1 mi). Half a mile past Fortymile Ridge is a natural redrock amphitheater knows as Dance Hall Rock, where the original pioneer group held dances. At 50 miles from UT-12 are the access points to

Llewelyn, Cottonwood, and David Canyons. Finally, after 56 miles, rise great views of Lake Powell from the Hole in the Rock overlook, the true end of the road. A steep ravine trail leads downward a third of a mile to the lakeshore, but the remnants of the pioneer track itself have been drowned by Lake Powell.

For details on the **Burr Trail** in the northern tip of the monument, see "Near Boulder," above.

Hiking

Entire books have been written about hiking in the monument, so this is just a taste. Most of the more popular trails are concentrated in the Escalante River drainage, accessed via Hole-in-the-Rock Road. Trails descend side canyons to the Escalante Canyon itself; they either ascend via the same route or else form a loop using the Escalante River or an overland trail as a connector. These include pastoral **Harris Wash,** a relatively easy two- to three-day hike that starts 10.5 miles down the road from UT-12. The **Egypt 3** slot, down the next turnoff from Hole-in-the-Rock Road, is legendarily long and tight, not for beginners or claustrophobes. Return overland to the east of the north-south slot. Also from the Egypt trailhead, the triangular route down **Fence Canyon,** then down the Escalante River (some wading required) and back up **Twentyfive Mile Canyon** is an excellent, moderate canyon trip that can be done in two or three days. Don't miss the Golden Cathedral at the end of pretty little Neon Canyon.

Spooky, Peek-a-Boo, and **Brimstone** are three small gulches off the Dry Fork of Coyote Gulch, accessed from the Early Weed Bench Road or the Dry Fork Coyote trailhead, 26 miles down Hole-in-the-Rock Road. Along with Egypt, these are three of the best slot canyons in the Four Corners. The names only hint at the ambiance, but slot aficionados will be in heaven. Again, this is *not* a place for those afraid of tight spaces. All three can be done in a day.

Coyote Gulch is probably the most popular canyon in the Escalante drainage. Tree-lined and wet, it can be hiked down to the Escalante River

in a day, but take two or three to explore all the side canyons. At 50 miles from UT-12—almost all the way to the Hole-in-the-Rock itself—are the access points to **Llewelyn and Cottonwood Canyons,** two difficult slots that lead southeast to Lake Powell. These will require three to five days and some climbing experience. **Davis Gulch** heads north from the same trailhead and is too narrow for large packs. This is a strenuous day hike. Keep an eye open near the end of the slot for a memorial plaque to Everett Ruess, high on the wall to the right.

Near UT-12 between Escalante and Boulder are the **Lower Calf Creek Falls** trail and the **Boulder Mail Trail,** and **Death Hollow,** described in "Near Escalante," above. From the UT-12 bridge over the Escalante River, an easy two-mile trails leads upstream to **Escalante Natural Bridge** on the south side of the canyon. Many people hike down this section of the river from the town of Escalante to the bridge, taking three to four days to cover the 27 miles. Be prepared from some scrambling and plenty of wading and bushwhacking. **Phipps Wash,** about a mile and half downstream from the bridge, has a natural bridge in a west side drainage and an arch in an east side drainage.

In the western part of the monument you can find **Bull Valley Gorge** and **Willis Creek** off the Skutumpah Road about 10 miles south of Cannonville. Good narrows in the upper parts of both can be explored in a day, or you can connect them via Sheep Creek for a good overnight hike. (In 1954, three people were killed when their pickup ran off the road at the bridge over Bull Valley Gorge—the truck is still visible, wedged into the slot.) Farther down the Skutumpah Road toward Kanab is **Lick Wash,** an easy day hike southeast toward No Mans Mesa.

About 13 miles down the Cottonwood Canyon Road from Cannonville is **Round Valley Draw,** a tributary of upper Hackberry Canyon. Explore the upper slots in a day, or else continue down narrow **Hackberry Canyon** on a multi-day adventure. It eventually rejoins the Cottonwood Canyon Road after 22 miles. You can explore the side canyons Booker, Stone Donkey, and

THE MOST REMOTE SPOT

Choosing the most remote spot in the continental United States depends on your definition of "remote." If you mean the farthest point from a paved road or town, then take your pick between the southeast corner of Wyoming's Yellowstone National Park, up in the Absaroka Mountains near the Thorofare Ranger Station, or somewhere in the lava beds in northern Nevada's Black Rock Desert.

If, on the other hand, you simply go by the farthest distance from any human dwelling, then dig out the census data and head the other way. Cartographic Technologies, a geographic consulting company, did just this and came up with a spot on the Kaiparowits Plateau in the Grand Staircase–Escalante National Monument. To be exact: 111° 16' 47.03" W. Longitude, 37° 24' 49.5" N. Latitude, at the head of Basin Canyon, on the Fiftymile Bench and west of the Straight Cliffs, opposite Brimstone Gulch on Hole-in-the-Rock Road. It's only 30 miles from Escalante, but it feels like a million miles from nowhere.

geological kaleidoscope, particularly at sunset. Keep going down the road to the river for a dose of the real thing: the foundations of the actual **Pahreah Town Site,** abandoned in the 1930s after nearby gold mines played out and the river kept flooding. The town's graveyard is on the near side of the river, which can often be easily waded, while the town itself is across the water. Hike upriver to **Starlight Arch,** a scenic trip that can be done in a day.

Camping

There are only two developed campgrounds in the monument: Calf Creek and Deer Creek. Beyond that, and the campgrounds in nearby parks, you're on your own—which is exactly how most visitors to the Escalante like it. Free backcountry permits are required for overnight trips, and minimum-impact camping techniques are crucial to keeping this delicate area as pristine as possible.

Mountain Biking

With all this backcountry available, mountain bikers may cringe to learn that bikes must stay on roads inside the monument. This still leaves hundreds of miles of remote riding, though. Any of the access roads described above are fair game, although some—particularly Hole-in-the-Rock Road—see a good bit of dust-raising vehicle traffic. Try to aim for lesser-used routes like the **Cedar Wash Loop,** a 20-mile back road connecting Escalante to Hole-in-the-Rock Road, or the **Wolverine Loop Road** off the Burr Trail. Roads to trailheads, some of which get pretty rough, are also recommended. The **Egypt** road (10 mi o/w) is one, as is the one up to **Fiftymile Bench** (27 mi r/t), which leaves Hole-in-the-Rock Road at the Willow Tank slide and rejoins it down the Sooner Slide.

Nipple Creek Wash and **Tibbet Canyon** near Big Water on U.S. 89 are good, steep rides, as is the **Smokey Hollow Loop** off of the Smoky Mountain Road. **Sand Gulch** is an alternate way to get to the Paria Movie Set, leaving U.S. 89 from a corral one mile west of the obelisk. It's 12 mostly level miles round-trip.

Pollock (which contains an arch), and look for the old Watson Cabin near the bottom. Keep going down the road from Round Valley Draw to reach the turnoff to the east for **Grosvenor Arch**—actually a cluster of cream and gold arches—and adjoining picnic area. It's another three miles south to **Cottonwood Creek,** a short slot canyon that runs parallel to the road on the west side for half a mile.

Ten miles west of the Paria Contact Station on U.S. 89 is a sandstone obelisk marking the turnoff for a post-post-modern blend of fantasy and reality, in the shadows of one of most colorful hillsides in the hemisphere. Six miles down the graded dirt road is the **Paria Movie Set,** where parts of *The Outlaw Josie Wales* and episodes of *Gunsmoke* were filmed—well, kind of. The original weathered buildings had become so rickety that they were torn down and replaced by replicas, so the faux town is really a copy of a copy. The eroded hillsides above are a

NEAR THE MONUMENT

Bryce Canyon National Park

The Paiute Indians told of the "Legend People" who lived in a beautiful city, but misbehaved and were turned to stone as punishment. They remain standing to this day, filling the gigantic amphitheater of Bryce Canyon National Park with peculiar limestone hoodoos in every imaginable shade of white, yellow, pink, and brown. This section of the Pink Cliffs (remember your Grand Staircase geology?) has eroded out of the eastern edge of the Paunsaugunt Plateau, so it lights up best at sunrise. The park was named for Mormon pioneer Ebenezer Bryce, who lived here in the late 19th century. Leaving for Arizona after only a few years, all he had to say of the beautiful amphitheater was that it was "a hell of a place to lose a cow."

A 17-mile scenic drive follows the rim (shuttle bus service was begun in 2002 to ease congestion), and hikers can choose from 61 miles of trails ranging from 9,100 feet elevation at the rim to 6,500 down in the fantasyland of rock. Cross-country skiing along the rim is popular in winter, when the park is practically deserted. The main **visitor center,** 435/834-5322, www.nps.gov/brca, is open daily from 8 A.M.–8 P.M. (shorter hours out of season). Entrance fees are $20 per car; back-country permits are $5.

While you're here you can stay at the **Bryce Canyon Lodge** 435/834-5361, fax 435/834-5464, info-bryce@xanterra.com, www.bryce-canyonlodge.com, built near the rim by the Union Pacific Railroad Company in the 1920s, or at the **Best Western Ruby's Inn** 435/834-5341, www.rubysinn.com, a monstrous resort-style spread just north of the park boundary. Both have rooms starting at $100. Cheaper accommodations and more food choices can be found in the nearby towns of Tropic and Panguitch.

For complete coverage of Bryce Canyon, see *Moon Handbooks Zion & Bryce* by W. C. McRae.

Kodachrome Basin State Park

In 1949, photographers from *National Geographic* used a new type of film to shoot the colorful sandstone arches and chimneys just south of Cannonville on UT-12. Since then, the area has been set aside as **Kodachrome Basin State Park** 435/679-8562, http://parks.state.ut.us/parks/www1/koda.htm, which offers a 27-unit year-round campground ($14), short hiking trails, and horseback and stagecoach rides. The day-use fee is $5.

Lake Powell and Glen Canyon

Coming on Lake Powell unprepared is like stumbling on a mirage. Wavering between red rock and blue sky, the lake's turquoise waters seem outrageously out of place, yet at the same time are undeniably inviting in the heart of the desert. Whether or not you agree with its existence, it's hard to deny that Lake Powell is an impressive piece of engineering, and seems to be here to stay. One of the largest manmade lakes in the country, it stretches for 186 miles from Glen Canyon Dam up what used to be the Colorado and San Juan Rivers to its upper end at Hite Marina.

In between is nearly 2,000 miles of convoluted shoreline—more than the entire West Coast—that is perforated by 96 major canyons. When it's full the reservoir can hold enough water to cover 27 million acres a foot deep.

Around the lake's northern shore, the Glen Canyon National Recreation Area protects the upper reaches of canyons that once took weeks to reach by horseback. Countless secluded beaches dot the shoreline, and fish now swim where eagles soared.

In the process, opponents of the dam will point out, one of the most beautiful canyons in the Southwest was drowned, along with countless sites of historical and archaeological value. At least two places sacred to the Navajo were affected. One was at the confluence of the San Juan and the Colorado, where the two deities embodied in the rivers met to create children from the clouds and rain. The other, Rainbow Bridge, now stands at the very edge of the water within easy reach of day boaters. By

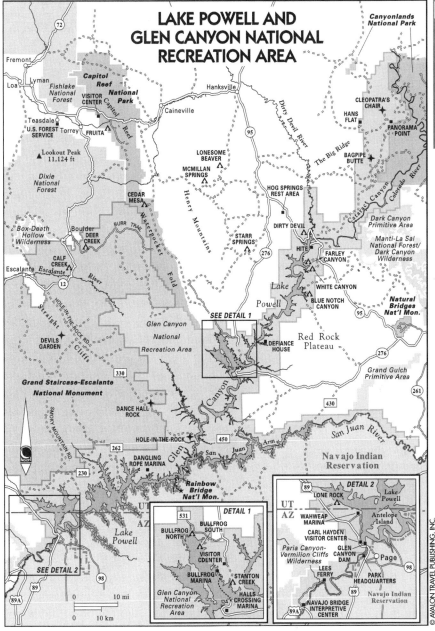

LAKE POWELL AND GLEN CANYON NATIONAL RECREATION AREA

Canyonlands National Park

Fremont
Loa
Lyman
Teasdale
Fishlake National Forest
Capitol Reef National Park
VISITOR CENTER
U.S. FOREST SERVICE Torrey FRUITA
Lookout Peak 11,124 ft
Dixie National Forest
Box-Death Hollow Wilderness
Boulder DEER CREEK
CALF CREEK
Escalante Escalante River
DEVILS GARDEN
Straight Cliffs
HOLE-IN-THE-ROCK RD.
Grand Staircase-Escalante National Monument
SMOKY MOUNTAIN RD.
DANCE HALL ROCK
HOLE-IN-THE-ROCK
DANGLING ROPE MARINA
Rainbow Bridge Nat'l Mon.
Lake Powell
SEE DETAIL 2

Hanksville
Caineville
Dirty Devil River
Henry Mountains
LONESOME BEAVER
MCMILLAN SPRINGS
CEDAR MESA
BURR TRAIL
STARR SPRINGS
Waterpocket Fold
Glen Canyon National Recreation Area
Glen Canyon
San Juan Arm

The Big Ridge
HOG SPRINGS REST AREA
DIRTY DEVIL
HITE
FARLEY CANYON
WHITE CANYON
BLUE NOTCH CANYON
Lake Powell
DEFIANCE HOUSE
SEE DETAIL 1
San Juan River

CLEOPATRA'S CHAIR
HANS FLAT
PANORAMA POINT
BAGPIPE BUTTE
Cataract Canyon
Colorado River
Dark Canyon Primitive Area
Manti-La Sal National Forest/ Dark Canyon Wilderness
Natural Bridges Nat'l Mon.
Red Rock Plateau
Grand Gulch Primitive Area
Navajo Indian Reservation

DETAIL 1
531
BULLFROG SOUTH
BULLFROG NORTH
VISITOR CENTER
BULLFROG MARINA
STANTON CREEK
HALLS CROSSING MARINA
Glen Canyon National Recreation Area

DETAIL 2
89
LONE ROCK
Lake Powell
WAHWEAP MARINA
Antelope Island
CARL HAYDEN VISITOR CENTER
Paria Canyon- Vermilion Cliffs Wilderness
GLEN CANYON DAM
LEES FERRY
Page
PARK HEADQUARTERS
NAVAJO BRIDGE INTERPRETIVE CENTER
Navajo Indian Reservation

0   10 mi
0   10 km

JOHN WESLEY POWELL

We are now ready to start on our way down the Great Unknown.

John Wesley Powell, starting down the Green and Colorado Rivers

Opening up the last unknown region of the continental United States was just one item on John Wesley Powell's long resume. The one-armed Civil War veteran also laid the groundwork for some of the fundamental principles of geology. Additionally, he raised a firm but ultimately futile voice for the wise development of the American West and the principled treatment of its natural resources and native tribes.

Powell was born on March 24, 1834, in western New York, the son of a Methodist preacher. He picked up his interest in natural history while being tutored by George Crookham, a farmer and amateur naturalist, who encouraged him to go out and get his hands dirty collecting specimens of plants, rocks, and animals. Powell defied his father's wishes to follow him into the clergy, instead working as a teacher and attending college at Wheaton and Oberlin. He collected geologic samples along the rivers of the Midwest, but when the Civil War erupted in 1861, he dropped his studies and enlisted in the Union Army.

In April 1862, one month after he had married his cousin Emma Dean, Powell was struck by a rifle ball in the right forearm during the battle of Shiloh. Hasty surgery saved his life but not his arm, which was amputated above the elbow. Nonetheless, he returned to service, was promoted to Major, and took part in the siege of Vicksburg, where he collected fossils in the trenches. Discharged in 1865, Powell taught geology and curated museums at colleges in Illinois.

Two years later, Powell began a series of scientific expeditions into the little-known country of the West. With the help of the Smithsonian, he led a group of students and his wife (cousin Emma Dean) into the Rocky Mountains in the Colorado Territory to collect museum specimens. In 1868 he returned with a similar group and climbed 14,255-foot Long's Peak. Gazing down on the headwaters of the Grand River, as the Colorado was then called, Powell decided that he would descend the river in small boats, despite stories of earlier explorers who had never emerged from the canyon country into which the rushing waters plunged.

The country the Colorado River passed through was probably the least-known land remaining in the Lower 48. Powell did some research, talked with mountain men and Indians, and studied the few documents on the region that existed. The first expedition set off from Green River Station in the Wyoming Territory on May 24, 1869. The money came from private sources and the Illinois State Natural History Society. A crew of nine, including his brother Walter, packed into four small boats of Powell's design. They had no idea what lay ahead. "What falls there are," wrote Powell, "we know not; what rocks beset the channel, we know not; what walls rise over the river, we know not." His headstrong nature, insatiable curiosity, and his ability to inspire others were about to be put to the supreme test.

The thousand-mile journey took only three months, as opposed to the six to nine they had planned for. Raging rapids tossed the wooden dories like corks, equipment sank as the boats overturned repeatedly, and muddy water worked its way into precious stores of food. One crew member had enough and left after a month. After weeks in the dark depths of the Grand Canyon, three others left to find an overland route home. They were killed soon after they emerged from the canyon, different theories pointing the finger at local Indians or Mormon settlers. Two days later, the remaining five emerged at the mouth of the Virgin River, in Arizona, to the astonishment of the nation and local Indian tribes, all of whom had thought the plan was certain suicide.

Frustrated by how little scientific data he had been able to collect while trying to keep his party alive, Powell lost no time in readying a second expedition. Securing $10,000 from Congress, he planned supply caches along the route and improved the design of his boats. On May 22, 1871, the second expedition set out from Green River Station in three boats, with Powell perched in a chair tied to the deck of the lead vessel. The roster included surveyor and professor Amon Thompson, Powell's brother-in-law, and photographer E. O. Beaman. During the initial easy miles, Powell spent much of the time on land, studying the local tribes and traveling back east to find more funding. He also became a father on September 8, naming his only child Mary Dean.

In the spring of 1872 the expedition discovered the last unknown river in the country while trying to get supplies to the riverbank. They named it the Escalante and continued to Lees Ferry, where the river, fed with heavy snowmelt and spring rains, raged through Marble Canyon. The ride got so rough that Powell ended it at Kanab Canyon in the Grand Canyon. Although abbreviated, the second expedition was a scientific success. Thompson had finished his topographic maps of the Grand Canyon and the surrounding region, and hundred of photographs recorded the group's progress and captured the canyon's majesty for eager Eastern audiences. The Smithsonian published Powell's *Exploration of the Colorado River of the West and Its Tributaries* (revised as *Canyons of Colorado* in 1895), which is still required reading for anyone who runs the rapids or dreams of it.

As a result of his courageous leadership, Powell had become a national figure. Despite his exploits, he always maintained that he was a scientist first and foremost, not an adventurer, and he was eager to get back to his true calling. In 1873, Powell was appointed special commissioner to the Indians in Utah and eastern Nevada, where he worked to improve native tribes' education and economic situation. His *Introduction to the Study of Indian Languages* was published in 1877, cementing his reputation as an anthropologist. Powell's true landmark work, however, was his *Report on the Lands of the Arid Region of the United States* (1878).

In this weighty tome, produced for Congress, he addressed the problem of settling the arid West. He knew firsthand how unsuited the region was for unplanned settlement, huge populations, and Eastern-style agriculture. With wisdom and remarkable foresight, he advised classifying the land according to physical characteristics—chiefly rainfall—as well as its economic potential. Counties should be demarked by watershed boundaries, he said, not arbitrary political lines. The Homestead Act's 160-acre homestead was far too small to graze animals, he added, recommending a farm of at least 2,560 acres for adequate pasturage. Most of his advice was ignored in the country's rush to achieve Manifest Destiny, but today it is recognized as a watershed document, whose prescience and predictions make it a milestone of conservation literature.

In 1879, Powell founded and became the first director of the Smithsonian Institution's Bureau of Ethnology. Here he continued his work on the languages of the tribes of the Intermountain West, which he had studied in person on his various journeys. (At one point he was adopted into a Hopi clan.) A year later, Powell became director of the newly organized U.S. Geological Survey, where he continued with his mapping and helped plan irrigation projects for settlers pouring toward the California coast. He held the post until 1892. He died September 23, 1902, in Haven, Maine, and was buried in the officer's section of Arlington National Cemetery.

some estimates, the dam's benefits—flood prevention, water for irrigation, hydroelectric power, and recreation—will be moot in 400 years anyway, when the tons of silt dropped in the basin every year finally fill it to the rim and turn Glen Canyon Dam into a waterfall.

The National Park Service charges fees for using Lake Powell and the Glen Canyon National Recreation Area, which surrounds it to the north: individuals pay $3, vehicles $7, and boats $10 (all are good for a week). Annual boat and vehicle passes are $20.

LAKE FACILITIES

Wahweap Marina

Just about anything you could do on, under, or near the surface of Lake Powell is available at the main marina just west of Glen Canyon Dam on Lakeshore Drive. Wahweap, which means "bitter water" in the Ute language, is the largest marina west of the Mississippi. Hundreds of boats bob at anchor in front of the **Wahweap Lodge,** 928/645-2433, fax 928/645-1031. Many of the hotel's 350 units ($100–160) have patios or balconies overlooking Wahweap Basin, while the **Rainbow Room** provides fine dining with a panoramic view of the water. They serve all meals daily, with buffets for breakfast and lunch in the Navajo Room and a cafe for snacks.

Marina services are offered by ARAMARK's **Lake Powell Resorts & Marinas,** 928/645-1070 or 800/528-6154, www.lakepowell.com. Boat rentals and tours are offered at the front desk, ranging from a short cruise to Antelope Canyon to all-day tours to Rainbow Bridge. You can also enjoy breakfast or a sunset dinner aboard the *Canyon King* paddle wheeler. Advance reservations are recommended; call or visit their website for the latest prices.

The **Wahweap Campground** is open all year, with sites ($15) available on a first-come, first-served basis. The **Wahweap RV Park,** also open year-round, has full hookup sites for $28 ($20 in winter). Primitive camping at **Lone Rock,** six miles northwest on U.S. 89, costs $6 per vehicle. Free camping is also permitted anywhere along the lakeshore beyond the developed areas.

Dangling Rope Marina

This outpost, 40 miles east of Wahweap, accessible only by boat, is the closest to Rainbow Bridge National Monument. There's a ranger station, restrooms, a boat fueling station (the only one between Wahweap and Bullfrog), and limited marina facilities.

Halls Crossing Marina

The south side of a popular river crossing dating back centuries, Halls Crossing, 435/684-2261 or 435/684-7460, is named for Charles Hall, one of the founders of Escalante and the builder of a ferry he operated here 1881-84. Highway 276 connects Halls Crossing with U.S. 95 at Natural Bridges National Monument, 48 miles to the east. Ninety-five miles upriver from Wahweap, Halls Crossing has a ranger station, campground ($18), RV park ($30), and a marina. Boat rentals, lake tours, and a camp store are also available. The ferries *John Atlantic Burr* and *Charles Hall* cross between Halls Crossing and Bullfrog four to 11 times a day from mid-Apr. to late Oct., depending on the time of year. (They leave every hour on the hour from mid-May to mid-Sept.). Rates are $12–50 (vehicles) or $3 pp on foot.

Bullfrog Marina

Glen Canyon's second-largest marina is opposite Halls Crossing. Here you'll find the obligatory ranger station/visitor center, 435/684-7400, along with a marina, a campground ($18), and an RV park ($30). The luxury **Defiance House Lodge** ($83–128) has a restaurant that serves all meals. Primitive camping is also available nearby for $6 per vehicle (call 435/684-7400 for information on the developed campsites). You can rent boats and arrange tours here as well. U.S. 276 heads north to meet U.S. 95, 20 miles west of Hite.

Hite Marina

Lake Powell's northernmost marina, Hite, 435/684-2457, caters to boaters and anglers with boat rentals, a launching ramp, camp store, ranger station, and an undeveloped campground ($6). It's off U.S. 95, 57 miles west of Natural Bridges

National Monument, near a pair of bridges over the flooded mouths of the Dirty Devil and San Juan River canyons.

RAINBOW BRIDGE NATIONAL MONUMENT

The largest natural bridge in the world (275 feet across), once one of the most remote spots in the Lower 48, now stands at the very edge of Lake Powell. If you don't have access to a boat, the only other way to see the multihued sandstone span, 50 miles from Wahweap, is via the hike from the end of Navajo Mountain Road west of Kayenta, Arizona.

Rainbow Bridge sits within a 160-acre national monument, www.nps.gov/rabr, surrounded by the Navajo Reservation. Soaring 290 feet above Bridge Creek, the salmon-pink bridge is only 32 feet across at its narrowest point. It's an extraordinary sight that inspired Zane Gray to write a novel about it. Theodore Roosevelt woke several times during a 1913 visit to gaze on it by moonlight.

Long known to local tribes, the bridge symbolizes rainfall and fertility to the Navajo. It was formally "discovered" by white men in August 1909, when two Paiutes guided two expeditions that joined forces and surveyed the scene. A BLM report in 1985 found no measurable effect of the nearby water on the stability of the bridge, but the effect of hundreds of thousands of visitors annually is another story. The filling of Lake Powell has brought Rainbow Bridge within easy access of anyone with a power boat, but the National Park Service has prohibited walking or swimming under the bridge out of respect for Navajo religious beliefs.

RECREATION

Michael Kelsey's *Boater's Guide to Lake Powell* is the best resource for exploring the lake and its environs by foot, wheel, or water. Life jackets are highly recommended out on the water, and there's no boating after dark. Cliff diving into the lake isn't smart, since it's usually impossible to tell how deep the murky water is.

Boating

The incongruous sight of an SUV towing a boat across the San Rafael Desert starts to make sense at any one of Lake Powell's marinas, where houseboats, fishing boats, and Jet-skis vie for space. A houseboat is one of the most popular ways to explore the lake, with many visitors renting one for a week or more and finding their own private canyon to hole up in.

Boat rentals are available from Lake Powell Resorts & Marinas, 928/645-1070 or 800/528-6154, www.lakepowell.com, based out of Wahweap Marina near Page. Four classes of houseboats range from 36–59 feet and start at $1,350 for three days. Powerboats, fishing boats, kayaks, and Jet-skis are also available. Boaters must be aware of all state boating regulations, as well as those imposed by the National Park Service.

Kayaking

A quieter way to reach the lakeside backcountry is by paddling a sea kayak. From Sept.–May the weather is at its mildest and the power boaters are fewer. The possibilities are almost limitless; you can take an afternoon to explore the crannies of Wahweap Bay, one of the biggest in the lake, or take a day or two to ascend long, narrow Navajo Canyon east of Page. Crosby and Antelope Canyons, also popular, are both within a day of Wahweap, while the lower Escalante and San Juan Rivers are good for multi-day trips.

Fishing

The Colorado River's native catfish, carp, suckers, and squawfish have been largely supplanted by introduced species such as bluegill sunfish, black crappie, walleye, and bass (striped, largemouth, and smallmouth). Hook and line is the only permitted fishing technique, and if you're over 14 years old a license will cost you $12 for a day, $26 for five days, or $42 for a season. (Trout require their own additional license: $8 per day, $21 per week, or $46 for a season.) The lake's now-endangered native fish, including the Colorado squawfish, humpback and bonytail chub, and the razorback sucker, are off-limits.

GLEN CANYON DAMMED

When Interior Secretary Bruce Babbit brought a sledgehammer down on McPherrin Dam near Chico, California, in 1998, the symbolic blow—ostensibly for the good of spawning salmon—struck more than the dam itself. In recent years cracks have appeared in an entire ideology begun over a century ago when settlers first began using dams and irrigation to feed crops and cities in the deserts of the American West. Nowhere is the controversy more heated than over the 710-foot face of Glen Canyon Dam.

Water has always been the limiting factor in the settlement of the West, and it's a problem whose solutions are, at best, temporary. Dam supporters include ranchers, farmers, developers, and anyone else who benefits from water where it doesn't occur naturally (i.e., most of the country between Colorado and California). Government agencies like the Bureau of Reclamation and the U.S. Army Corps of Engineers that built dams by the hundreds in the early and middle 20th century remain committed to dams as emblems of scientific and technological prowess. These groups espouse benefits like pollution-free power, irrigation, flood control, and smooth waterways to transport goods.

On the other side are scientists, conservation groups, and fish and river lovers who cite growing evidence of the catastrophic effects dams have on river ecosystems—fish runs decimated, fertile banks turned barren—and who question the integrity of values behind golf courses in Phoenix and the Colorado River drying to a trickle before it even reaches the Gulf of California.

Many dam opponents look at Glen Canyon Dam as environmental author Edward Abbey did: as the ultimate symbol of the bulldozing of the West by overeager engineers and shortsighted developers. From the moment the last spillway closed on March 13, 1963, the dam's opponents have mourned the loss of one of the West's most beautiful canyons. They point out that the river ecosystem is so altered that trout—cold, clear-water fish, mountain fish—now thrive in the once warm and muddy river, that sediment has filled one seventh of the lake, and that pollutants have become so concentrated that pregnant women are warned to stay out of the water. They're in for a fight from the three million tourists who enjoy the lake every year, as well as anyone who pulls in part of the $400 million they spend, or who still draws water from the lake or power from the dam.

Abbey advocated the dam's destruction for decades in his novels and essays, but only recently has the idea begun to seem possible. The environmental group Earth First! kicked off its career in 1981 by unfurling a gigantic plastic "crack" down the face of the dam, and in 1996 the Sierra Club, which had let the dam be built unopposed in the first place in a Faustian bargain to keep two more out of Dinosaur National Monument, passed a resolution calling for the drain-

Getting There and Around

Lake Powell and the Glen Canyon National Recreation Area are only accessible by 2WD vehicle at Wahweap Marina near Page, and at Bullfrog and Halls Crossing, both on U.S. 276 off U.S. 95 west of Natural Bridges National Monument. 4WD vehicles can use Hole-in-the-Rock Road from UT-12 at Escalante, or a dirt road that leaves U.S. 89A at Big Water and heads up onto the Kaiparowits Plateau.

Frog Air (American Aviation), 801/537-1537 or 800/628-1137, flies from Salt Lake City daily to Bullfrog ($140 pp o/w), Halls Crossing ($150), and Page ($160), leaving at noon and returning between 1:30 and 2 P.M.

ing of Lake Powell. The proposal was heard before a subcommittee of the House Committee on Resources in September 1997.

Five years later, the worst drought in a quarter century gripped the Four Corners. At its peak, three inches of Lake Powell was evaporating away every day, until the upper part of the long-drowned Cathedral in the Desert came into view. As water levels dropped 15 percent, the idea of keeping the lake half full suddenly didn't seem so crazy. In a normal year, a full Lake Powell loses 163 billion gallons to evaporation. This is wasted water, according to the lake's original purpose of providing a steady supply to states downriver. Dropping the level by even one quarter, reducing surface area and eliminating shallows, could eliminate up to half the loss to evaporation. And out here, water is money—that's about $100 million saved.

Proponents present it as a win-win situation—more water is available for irrigation and thirsty cities, and at least some of the lake remains—and they are starting to gain the ear of California politicians. Opponents such as the local Friends of Lake Powell see this as the first step to draining the lake completely, the doomed end of electricity generated by the Glen Canyon Dam, and the catastrophic elimination of a recreation industry that brings in $500 million per year to Page alone.

The battle lines have been drawn, with groups like the Sierra Club, the Glen Canyon Institute, and

© JULIAN SMITH

Glen Canyon Dam

the Glen Canyon Action Network lobbying for the dam's removal, while the Friends of Lake Powell (and just about everyone employed in Page and south-central Utah) fight to keep it in place.

Over it all hangs the irony of naming a dam after the canyon it covered, and an artificial lake after the explorer and scientist who spent much of his life campaigning against the unwise use of the West's most precious resource.

Page and the Paria Plateau

PAGE, ARIZONA

This tidy little town (pop. 9,000) was built from scratch in 1957 for workers on the Glen Canyon Dam, at the time one of the largest construction projects in the world. Since then it's become the tourist center of northernmost Arizona, and has kept most of its prefab, company-town atmosphere. Every other vehicle seems to be towing some kind of watercraft, which together with marinas and swimwear shops give Page an odd beach-town-in-the-desert feel. It's sandwiched between the dam and the Navajo Power Plant,

two of the most important revenue-generators (and worst environmental insults, according to many) in the Four Corners.

About two-thirds of Page's workforce is Navajo, and most of the town's economy comes from tourism and the power plant, squatting like a smoking spaceport on the desert plain to the east. Built in 1974, this coal-fired station can produce up to 2,250 megawatts of power for cities such as Tucson, Las Vegas, and Los Angeles. This takes 1,000 tons of coal per hour—coal brought in by electric train from the controversial mines at Black Mesa, 70 miles south on the Hopi Reservation.

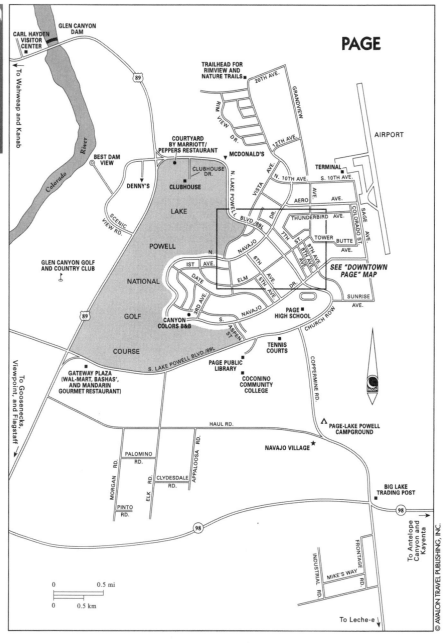

PAGE

GLEN CANYON DAM

CARL HAYDEN VISITOR CENTER

To Wahweap and Kanab

Colorado River

89

TRAILHEAD FOR RIMVIEW AND NATURE TRAILS

20TH AVE.

GRANDVIEW

RIM VIEW DR.

12TH AVE.

AIRPORT

COURTYARD BY MARRIOTT/ PEPPERS RESTAURANT

VISTA AVE.

N. LAKE POWELL

McDONALD'S

TERMINAL

N. 10TH AVE.

S. 10TH AVE.

BEST DAM VIEW

CLUBHOUSE DR.

CLUBHOUSE

AERO

AVE.

AVE.

COLORADO ST.

SAGE AVE.

DENNY'S

CLUBHOUSE

LAKE

BLVD./89L

DR.

THUNDERBIRD AVE.

SCENIC VIEW RD.

POWELL

NAVAJO

7TH ST.

TOWER

BUTTE AVE.

9TH AVE.

8TH AVE.

SEE "DOWNTOWN PAGE" MAP

GLEN CANYON GOLF AND COUNTRY CLUB

NATIONAL

N.

1ST AVE.

DATE

6TH AVE.

ELM

6TH AVE.

DR.

SUNRISE AVE.

89

GOLF

3RD AVE.

S.

NAVAJO

PAGE HIGH SCHOOL

CHURCH ROW

COURSE

CANYON COLORS B&B

S. ASPEN ST.

TENNIS COURTS

COPPERMINE RD.

GATEWAY PLAZA (WAL-MART, BASHAS', AND MANDARIN GOURMET RESTAURANT)

S. LAKE POWELL BLVD./89L

PAGE PUBLIC LIBRARY

COCONINO COMMUNITY COLLEGE

To Goosenecks, Viewpoint, and Flagstaff

HAUL RD.

PAGE-LAKE POWELL CAMPGROUND

PALOMINO RD.

APPALOOSA RD.

NAVAJO VILLAGE

MORGAN RD.

ELK RD.

CLYDESDALE RD.

BIG LAKE TRADING POST

PINTO RD.

98

98

To Antelope Canyon and Kayenta

INDUSTRIAL RD.

MIKE'S WAY

FRONTAGE RD.

0   0.5 mi

0   0.5 km

To Leche-e

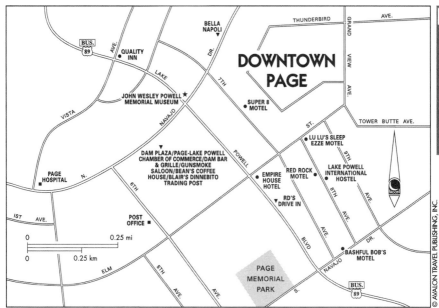

The process creates a haze of nitrogen oxides and other gases, which can obscure visibility as far away as the South Rim of the Grand Canyon.

With a good museum and plenty of outdoor activities within easy range, Page is a good base for visiting the Paria Plateau, Glen Canyon and Lake Powell, the northern Navajo Nation, and the southern Grand Staircase–Escalante National Monument. (For information on Wahweap Marina, seven miles northwest on U.S. 89, see "Glen Canyon National Recreation Area" in the South-Central Utah chapter.)

Sights

The **John Wesley Powell Memorial Museum,** 6 N. Lake Powell Blvd., 928/645-9496, www.powellmuseum.org, houses an excellent collection covering early cultures, river runners, and natural history. Displays on Powell's life and explorations include an interesting set of photos from his expeditions, paired with pictures taken a century later to show the environmental changes. Kids can grind corn amid the exhibits on native cultures and early explorers. Nearby are displays by local artists and a pictorial history of the dam

and Lake Powell. The museum is also the local information center, and you can make reservations for tours of the lake and Antelope Canyon here as well. Open daily 8 A.M.–6 P.M. in summer (off-season Mon.–Fri. to 5 P.M.) for $1 adult pp.

Get a taste of Navajo culture through programs held at **Navajo Village,** 928/660-0304, www.navajovillage.net, a living museum open Apr.–Oct. You can take a guided tour of a traditional Navajo home during the day (9 A.M.–3 P.M., $10 adults, $5 children 6-13) or opt for the full four-hour evening program, which includes demonstrations of weaving and silversmithing, a traditional dinner, and singing, dancing, and stories around the campfire ($50 adults, $35 children). Shorter evening programs are also available; get tickets at the Powell Museum or the Chamber of Commerce visitor center. It's a little hard to find, off Haul Road near the intersection with Coppermine Road.

Accommodations

Since Page is such a busy tourist hub, it's a good idea to call ahead for reservations, particularly in the summer. The summer rates listed here drop dramatically in winter. Plenty of inexpensive accommodations line 8th Avenue, Page's "Street of Little Motels," which originally housed supervisors during the construction of the dam. The **Lake Powell International Hostel,** 141 8th Ave., 928/645-3898, www.iplex.com/montys/hostel/lkpowell.htm, has beds for $12–15 and rooms with shared bath for $30–35. Clean, comfortable rooms for under $50 d can be found nearby at **Lu Lu's Sleep Ezzze Motel,** 105 8th Ave., 928/608-0273; **Bashful Bob's Motel,** 750 S. Navajo Dr., 928/645-3919; and the **Red Rock Motel,** 114 8th Ave., 928/645-0062.

Chain hotels galore are sprinkled throughout the rest of the town. In the $50–100 category are a **Super 8,** 75 S. 7th Ave., 928/645-2858, fax 645-2890, and a **Quality Inn,** 287 N. Lake Powell Blvd., 928/645-8851, fax 645-2523. A pool, patio, dog, and cat await at the **Canyon Colors B&B,** 225 S. Navajo Dr., 928/645-5979 or 800/536-2530, www.pagehost.com/lakepowell/color.htm, whose owners can book tours and lend you beach towels and coolers for a day on the lake ($75–85).

On a hillside overlooking the dam and the lake is the **Courtyard by Marriott,** 600 Clubhouse Dr., 928/645-5000, fax 645-5004, with a golf course, heated outdoor pool, and Peppers restaurant, voted one of Arizona's 100 best in 1995. (Rooms are $140.) The **Page-Lake Powell Campground,** 849 S. Coppermine Rd., 928/645-374, http://campground.page-lakepowell.com, is southeast of downtown. Full hookup sites are $26, and tent sites are $17. (Showers are $4.) More campsites are available west of the dam at Wahweap Marina.

Food

With a few exceptions, Page's eating options tend toward the generic. **Peppers,** 928/645-1347, at the Courtyard by Marriott, is probably the best restaurant in town, serving Southwest fare daily for all meals (dinner runs $15–20), with a good lunch buffet. On the other end, the **Empire House Hotel,** 107 S. Lake Powell Blvd., 928/645-2406, has a $1.89 all-you-can-eat pancake special for the thrifty or impecunious. **RD's Drive In,** 143 Lake Powell Blvd., 928/645-2791, was the first in

town when Glen Canyon Dam was only a dream on paper. It's a local hangout for burgers and ice cream, especially for high schoolers around lunchtime. Hardly anything costs over $4.

Bella Napoli, 810 N. Navajo Dr., 928/645-2706, does a good Italian dinner, with pasta, fish, and seafood entrees around $10. In the Dam Plaza shopping center is the **Dam Bar & Grille,** 644 N. Navajo Dr., 928/645-2161, serving BBQ ribs and steaks ($15–20) for dinner Mon.–Sat. It includes the Gunsmoke Saloon, a sports bar with live music (most country) Wed.–Sat. Next door, **Bean's Coffee House,** 928/645-6858, offers breakfast and lunch ($3–5) on weekdays, and coffee and Internet access during all hours (Mon.–Fri. 6 A.M.–5 P.M., Sat. 7 A.M.–5 P.M., Sun. 8 A.M.–noon).

Shopping

Also in the Dam Plaza is **Blair's Dinnebito Trading Post,** 626 N. Navajo Dr. (928/645-3008 or 800/644-3008, www.blairstradingpost.com, blairs@blairstradingpost.com, which evolved from a remote trading post deep in the Navajo Reservation. Along with a large selection of rugs, kachinas, pottery, baskets, and paintings, they also stock raw wool, saddle leather, and pawned jewelry. Ask to see the private collection upstairs, collected over half a century by patriarch Elijah Blair, who helped create the black-background Dinnebito style of Navajo weaving. The old cash registers, guns, historical photos, jewelry, and rugs are not for sale, but worth a peek nonetheless.

Recreation

The **Rim Trail** is an eight-mile bike and foot path around the edge of Manson Mesa, with great views of the lake and desert. One access point is via the nature trail at the north end of town near the Lake View School at N. Navajo Drive and 20th Avenue. Another short trail (1.5 mi r/t) leads to an overlook above the impressive **Horseshoe Bend** of the Colorado, from a parking area just south of milepost 545 on U.S. 89 South. Watch your footing here—there are no guardrails—and try to come at sunset, when flocks of birds swarm after insects above the abyss. The trail to **Wiregrass Canyon,** a steep wash down to Lake Powell, begins

PAGE CLIMATE

Month	Average High	Average Low	Mean	Average Precipitation
January	43°F	26°F	35°F	0.61 inches
February	50°F	30°F	41°F	0.48 inches
March	59°F	37°F	48°F	0.65 inches
April	69°F	44°F	56°F	0.50 inches
May	78°F	53°F	66°F	0.40 inches
June	90°F	62°F	76°F	0.14 inches
July	95°F	68°F	82°F	0.58 inches
August	92°F	66°F	79°F	0.69 inches
September	84°F	58°F	71°F	0.66 inches
October	70°F	47°F	58°F	0.99 inches
November	54°F	35°F	44°F	0.56 inches
December	44°F	27°F	35°F	0.48 inches

off U.S. 89 between mileposts 7 and 8 toward Big Water. Turn right and go about five miles down a dirt road to a parking area. The hike follows the unmarked wash about three miles to the lake, and involves some scrambling around pouroffs. Keep an eye out for arches, balanced rocks, and a natural bridge.

In addition to the ARAMARK tours of Lake Powell, you can explore the waters in a kayak with **Glen Canyon Kayak Guides,** 888/854-7862, www.kayakpowell.com, kyle@hawaiicity.com. Captain Ray Leese, who has been teaching kayaking since 1979, offers full-day trips starting at $125 pp including lunch, as well as overnighters ($200 pp per day) and rentals for $35–45 per day. The **Twin Finn Dive Center,** 811 Vista Ave., 928/645-3114, www.twinfinn.com, also rents kayaks year-round starting at $35/day.

Rent a Jet-ski, boat, or kayak at **Bill & Toni's Marine,** 803 Vista Ave., 928/645-5990, and take a half- or full-day raft trip down the Colorado to Lees Ferry with **Wilderness River Adventures,** 50 S. Lake Powell Blvd., 928/645-3279 or 800/528-6154, www.riveradventures.com. Sign up for raft trips through the Grand Canyon with **Wilderness River Adventures,** 928/645-3296 or 800/992-8022, choosing from either the whole thing or just the placid, winding stretch

of the Colorado through Marble Canyon to Lees Ferry. Pick up a game of pool or bowling at **The Bowl,** 24 N. Lake Powell Blvd., 928/645-2682, which also has a bistro and a bar.

Getting There

Great Lakes Airlines, 800/554-5111, reservations@greatlakesav.com, www.greatlakesav.com, flies to Moab once a day ($90 pp o/w), and to Phoenix once a day ($109 pp). Tickets can be purchased through Frontier Airlines at 800/432-1359. **Frog Air,** 801/537-1537 or 800/628-1137, flies to Salt Lake City daily for $160 pp o/w.

Information

The **Page/Lake Powell Chamber of Commerce,** 928/645-2741 or 888/261-7243, www.pagelakepowellchamber.org, chamber@pagelakepowellchamber.org, operates a visitor center in the Dam Plaza shopping center, next to the Dam Bar and Grill. They dispense plenty of information about the area and offer reservations for local tours. Open Mon.–Sat. 8 A.M.–8 P.M., Sun. 9 A.M.–6 P.M. in season, Mon.–Fri. 9 A.M.–5 P.M. the rest of the year.

Find more information on the area, especially its natural and human history, from the **Glen Canyon Natural History Association,** 32 N.

10th Ave., Suite 9, 928/645-3532 or 877/453-6296, fax 928/645-5409, www.pagelakepowell.org, vistas@pagelakepowell.org. They fund research projects, help staff park visitor centers, and sell books and maps by mail order.

Visitors can access the Internet at the **Page Public Library,** 479 S. Lake Powell Blvd., 928/645-4270.

NEAR PAGE
Glen Canyon Dam

Page's raison d'être plugs Marble Canyon a few miles west of town with nearly five million cubic yards of concrete, poured around the clock for three years. It was built between 1960 and 1963, stands 710 feet high, and holds back 27 million acre-feet of water when the reservoir is full. Free tours of the dam's cave-cool innards are given at the National Park Service's **Carl Hayden Visitor Center,** 928/608-6404, on the west side of the U.S. 89 bridge. These occur four times daily with a maximum of 20 people per tour, and take you from the gigantic turbines and transformers to an incongruous patch of green grass at the base. Open Memorial Day–Labor Day 7 A.M.–7 P.M., otherwise 8 A.M.–5 P.M.

The **best dam view** in Page can be found behind the Denny's off U.S. 89. Go down Scenic View Drive to the sign for the overlook. To take in the entire sweep of this end of the lake, head west about a mile past the visitor center, then climb the steep but short hill to your right (north). The sight is startling, bizarre, and undeniably beautiful—the blue of the lake, the green oasis of Page, the monolithic dam, and Navajo Mountain, all in one grand panorama.

Antelope Canyon Navajo Tribal Park

Discovered in 1931 by a 13-year-old girl, this world-famous slot canyon is 120 feet deep and only a few yards wide in spots. The rosily lit sandstone curves are a photographer's dream—bring a tripod and cable release, and try to shoot near noon. It's an easy hike, but you should be able to climb ladders and walk in deep sand for about a quarter mile. The canyon gets very warm in the summer months.

Many companies in Page offer tours (the only way to see the canyon), including **Roger Ekis' Antelope Canyon Tours,** 18 N. Lake Powell Blvd., 928/645-9102, www.antelopecanyon.com, starting at $20 pp ($10 children 6–13) for a 90-minute visit to the upper canyon. Longer photography tours are also possible. **Overland Canyon Tours,** 928/608-4072, www.overland-canyon.com, info@overlandtours.com, takes visitors to Antelope Canyon and the less-visited "Canyon X" five or so times daily. (Add a $5 tribal permit to the prices.)

Antelope Canyon is a mile east on U.S. 98 from the Big Lake Trading Post. Like any slot, Antelope is prone to flash flooding from storms upstream, even if the sky is blue overhead. If your Navajo guide says get out, listen to him—something 11 European tourists didn't do in 1997. It took months to dig their bodies out of the mud and debris. Call the park office, 928/698-2808, for more information.

PARIA PLATEAU

As the steps of the Grand Staircase march down to the Colorado River, this plateau between the Kaibab Mountains and the Vermilion Cliffs forms one of its bottom steps. Outlined by U.S. 89 and U.S. 89A, the Paria Plateau forms the eastern end of the Arizona Strip, the isolated piece of the state north of the Grand Canyon. Centering on the Big Knoll (6,844 ft), it is sliced neatly in two by the lower reaches of the Paria River, which offers one of the Four Corners' great canyon hikes. If you're going to do just one river-narrows hike in the Four Corners, make it this one.

The canyon constricts in its upper reaches into some of the longest and tightest slot canyons in the world, before opening up into a majestic gorge with thousand-foot walls that empties into the Colorado at Lees Ferry. To keep a handle on the canyon's growing popularity, 112,500 acres have been set aside as the **Paria Canyon–Vermilion Cliffs Wilderness,** https://paria.az.blm.gov, which is enclosed by the little-known, 293,000-acre **Vermilion Cliffs National Monument.**

Hiking the Canyons

You have a few different options for hikes. The easiest access is off U.S. 89, 43 miles east of Kanab and just under 14 miles west of Big Water. Here, near the Paria River Bridge, is the **Paria Contact Station,** open daily 8:30 A.M.–4:15 P.M. mid-Mar.–mid-Nov. You can pick up permits, ask advice, and buy maps and guidebooks, including the BLM's "Hiker's Guide to Paria Canyon." Just down the gravel road is the **White House Campground,** where primitive sites are $10. The **Paria River Trailhead** is two miles farther down the road. A trail meanders along the riverbanks, which are wide for four miles before closing in sharply and rising to about 200 feet. The play of light and shadow and the gurgle of water make the seven miles to the Buckskin Gulch confluence an enchanting hike that can be done in one long day.

THE CONDOR SOARS AGAIN

If you see a huge silhouette gliding across the sun near the Vermilion Cliffs, it might be one of six California condors *(Gymnogyps californianus)* released near here in 1996. The gigantic birds, which can reach 10 feet from wing to wing, hadn't been seen in Arizona in 75 years. By 1982, there were only 22 condors left in the mountains of California, making them one of the most endangered vertebrates in the world. In a last-ditch effort, all the wild California condors were rounded up and placed in captivity, where it was hoped they could breed themselves back from the brink.

The program has seen some success, but also some setbacks. Of the 35 condors released so far in Arizona, 14 have been killed by predators, power lines, or people. In 2000, five died from lead poisoning, probably from eating a carcass contaminated by buckshot. The recovery plan calls for three self-supporting populations, two in the wild and one in captivity, with at least 150 birds in each. So far, so good, but keep your fingers crossed.

Your best chance of seeing a condor is near the release site at the intersection of U.S. 89A and House Rock Valley Road, about 15 miles east of Jacob Lake.

Keep going west on U.S. 89 five miles past the contact station until the road curves sharply north at the Cockscomb, an unmistakable monocline. A reasonably good dirt road heads south here parallel to the gigantic ridge; follow it south to the **Buckskin Trailhead** (4.5 miles) or the **Wire Pass Trailhead** (8.5 miles). (The road continues all the way to U.S. 89A near Jacob Lake.) There is good at-large camping nearby—just don't sleep in your car at the trailhead. Wire Pass offers the quickest access to the narrows—less than two miles—which are on most desert rats' lists of the best slot canyons in the Southwest. Deep, dark, and drop-dead gorgeous, Buckskin Gulch gives even slot veterans goosebumps. At points the canyon walls are barely shoulder width apart. From Wire Pass it's 14 miles downstream to the confluence with Paria Canyon (it's 16 miles from the Buckskin trailhead). The Buckskin-to-Wire Pass loop is good for a day hike, but you can make it to White House in a long day. To descend all the way down to Lees Ferry (38 mi) takes four to five days.

About three miles farther south is the access point to **Coyote Buttes,** another popular spot. By now you've seen the amazing postcard photos of red and white rock layers swirling like ice cream frozen in an ocean wave. Day-use permits are required here as well.

Permits and Details

Since this is such a popular hiking area, the BLM has instituted a permit system. You can get these at the contact station or, since they fill up months in advance, secure them up to seven months ahead of time from the BLM's **Arizona Strip Field Office,** 345 E. Riverside Dr., St. George, UT 84790, 435/688-3230, www.az.blm.gov/paria, azafoweb @blm.gov (permits are also available online). The fee is $5 pp per day, and you can pay this at the trailheads for day use. Get permits at the contact station for Coyote Buttes early in the morning the day before you want to go; a maximum of 20 people are allowed per day.

Campfires are prohibited in the canyons, toilet paper must be packed out, and you should pay particular attention to the weather. Precipitation is highest July–Sept., peaking in August, and a cloudburst can fill the narrows much faster than you can get out—notice the logs jammed between the canyon walls high overhead.

Car shuttles can be arranged through **End of the Trail Shuttles,** 928/355-2252, and **Happy Trails,** 928/355-2295, both based out of Marble Canyon.

Paria Canyon Adventure Ranch

This friendly, sprawling operation, 435/689-0398, www.pariacampground.com, easton@pariacampground.com, is between mileposts 21 and 22 on U.S. 89. They offer a wide range of services; trail rides in the Grand Staircase, volleyball, horseshoes, horseback riding ($20 per hour), and a climbing wall are a few of the options. To spend the night you can choose between the bunkhouse hostel ($12 pp), tent spaces ($15 d), RV sites, or a spot in a teepee. They also have a shuttle service for hiking the Paria canyons. Next door is the **Paria Outpost Restaurant,** 928/691-1047, with great BBQ, delicious cinnamon rolls, and a big wrap-around porch to enjoy the scenery. Food, drinks, maps, and guidebooks are available in the general store.

LEES FERRY AND VICINITY

Driving north on U.S. 89A from Flagstaff, past Cameron and the turnoff for Tuba City, you'll pass along the base of the Echo Cliffs until the road splits. U.S. 89 heads right, climbing the cliffs via Antelope Pass (6,533 ft), and arrowing for Page. U.S. 89A continues north across a flat plain toward the Vermilion Cliffs. Before you know it, up rise two shining metal arches across the Colorado, deep in a canyon that remains invisible until you reach its edge.

Marble Canyon

Navajo Bridge crosses the river at an area of spectacular scenery and intriguing history. When it was opened in 1929, the original bridge was the highest cantilevered steel arch in the world, soaring 467 feet above the river, and the only place to cross between Moab and the Hoover Dam. During its construction, the two cantilevered halves were gradually extended across

the abyss until they met in the middle. Parts had to be shipped from one side to the other all the way though Needles, California—an 800 mile trip to travel 800 feet across the river. The road wasn't paved until 1937.

The bridge was replaced in 1995 by a stronger, wider twin—still one of only seven river crossings in 750 miles—and the original is now open only to pedestrians. It's worth a walk across to gaze down at the Colorado River, colored a Caribbean turquoise from its source at the base of the Glen Canyon Dam. You'll often see rafters heading downstream from Lees Ferry. There is a National Park Service **interpretive center** at the western end, open mid-Apr.–Oct. daily from 9 A.M.–5 P.M. (weekends only in early April and November, 10 A.M.–4 P.M.) The Civilian Conservation Corps built the rustic stone observation structure in the 1930s; now you can listen to Charlton Heston narrate a documentary video in a kiosk outside, next to a memorial plaque to John Doyle Lee, a "man of great faith, sound judgment, and indomitable courage" (more on him soon).

Just up the road is the **Marble Canyon Lodge,** 928/355-2225 or 800/726-1789, fax 928/355-2227, built in 1926 in anticipation of the bridge's construction. It was owned and operated by Lorenzo Hubbell's trading company 1937–1950, and the master trader's influence still shows in the excellent crafts shop, offering a large selection of books as well. It's a comfortable, rustic place of stone and logs, with wide porches and cottonwoods for shade. Rooms are $70, with cottages for $90 and apartments for $143. They also offer a full service fly shop (www.mcg-leesferry.com), convenience store, gas station, general store, and post office. The restaurant, decorated with photos of river runners, serves entrees like pan-fried trout ($10–21) and veggie melts ($6).

Lees Ferry

Descend to the river's edge past house-size rocks balanced on pedestals of compressed earth. Six miles down the paved road, where the Paria River empties into the Colorado, is a small historic district and the major put-in spot for raft trips heading into the Grand Canyon. Before the era of pavement and suspension bridges, Lees Ferry was an important passage from Utah to Arizona and New Mexico.

The area was named for John D. Lee, who is most well known as the engineer—or scapegoat—behind the Mountain Meadows Massacre, one of the darkest chapters in the history of the Mormon pioneers. In 1857, a party of 137 Arkansas emigrants was crossing southern Utah on their way to California. In early September, they were ambushed near Cedar City, Utah, by a group of Paiute Indians and Mormons, angered by U.S. government interference in what they saw as their territory. Led by Lee, the group promised the emigrants safe passage, convinced them to lay down their arms, and then killed everyone except the young children.

Details of the crime were slow in leaking out (and are still being debated today), but Lee was worried enough to seek refuge here in 1871. He built the Lonely Dell Ranch with the help of Emma, his 17th wife out of 19. (The name comes from her exclamation upon seeing her new home: "Oh, what a lonely dell!"). The Lees saw a good bit of traffic, in part because their home was on Honeymoon Trail for newly married Mormons traveling by wagon from new settlements in Arizona to have their marriages officially sanctioned in St. George, Utah. Lee was eventually tracked down and arrested in 1875, but the trial resulted in a hung jury. He was re-arrested the next year, convicted of first-degree murder, and in 1877 was shot at the site of the massacre, standing in front of his own grave.

Lonely or not, it's hard to imagine a more spectacular setting, with green cottonwoods and fruit trees contrasting with red and gold cliffs and surging blue water. The Lees' log cabin, built in the 1870s, stands near an orchard of peach, pear, apricot, and plum trees and a stone building built in 1916 for the Bar Z Ranch. Maintained by the National Park Service, it is open to the public.

Apr.–Oct. chances are you will see a raft trip packing up at the boat launch ramp. Over 20,000 people brave the rapids and drink in the scenery (and some of the river) every year. About 100 yards upriver are the remains of a few stone buildings that served as trading post and post office, near the sunken carcass of a steamboat brought here in the early 1900s in an unsuccessful attempt to extract gold from the Chinle shale. The old ferry crossing, in operation from 1873–1928, is another mile upstream, reachable via the old wagon road from the ruins. A campground ($10/night) is on the hillside overlooking the river.

Along the Vermilion Cliffs

U.S. 89A continues west through a wild landscape at the foot of the cliffs, with huge tumbled boulders and condors soaring overhead. Nine miles west of Marble Canyon is the **Cliff Dwellers Lodge,** 928/355-2228 or 800/433-2542, with rooms for around $70 in season, a gas station, and a small store. The spread includes **Lees Ferry Anglers** 928/355-2261, or 800/962-9755, www.leesferry.com, anglers@leesferry.com, with a fly shop, guiding services, and gear rental. A few hundred yards away are the ruins of the original Cliff Dwellers Lodge, built by a Zigfield Follies dancer and her tubercular husband during the Great Depression.

Resources

Suggested Reading

OUTDOORS

Falcon Publishing is the undisputed leader in Western outdoor guides. All of their books have detailed route descriptions, elevation charts, and background information. Other companies are edging in on their territory, though, including **Michael Kelsey's** guides. If you can get past their somewhat petulant tone, you'll find that this line of self-published hiking guidebooks are full of information on front- and backcountry destinations throughout the Four Corners. (Take the time estimates with a grain of salt, too— this guy practically jogs his trails.) Some are getting out of date, but they're all as comprehensive as they come. The list includes *Boater's Guide to Lake Powell* (2001), *Canyon Hiking Guide to the Colorado Plateau* (1999), *Hiking, Biking and Exploring Canyonlands National Park and Vicinity* (1992), *Hiking and Exploring the Paria River* (1998), *Hiking and Exploring Utah's San Rafael Swell* (1999), *Hiking and Exploring Utah's Henry Mountains and Robbers Roost: The Life and Legend of Butch Cassidy* (1990), and *River Guide to Canyonlands National Park and Vicinity* (1991). They're available at bookstores in the area and from Amazon.com. **The Mountain Bike America** series is particularly good, with topographic maps and elevation charts for every ride.

Hiking

Adkinson, Ron. *Best Easy Day Hikes Grand Staircase–Escalante & the Glen Canyon Region.* Helena, MT: Falcon, 1998. A pocket-sized guidebook listing 19 hikes on Cedar Mesa, the Escalante, and the Paria Plateau.

Adkinson, Ron. *Hiking Grand Staircase–Escalante & the Glen Canyon Region.* Helena, MT: Falcon, 1998. Meticulous trail descriptions of nearly 60 hikes across the monument and its surrounding area, with elevation maps and mileage charts.

Grubbs, Bruce. *Hiking Northern Arizona.* Helena, MT: Falcon, 2001. Includes descriptions of dozens of trails in the mountains and national monuments near Flagstaff.

Grubbs, Bruce and Aitchison, Stewart. *Hiking Arizona.* Helena, MT: Falcon, 2001. More than 100 of the state's best trails, with many (of course) in and around the Grand Canyon.

Hall, Dave. *Hiking Utah.* Helena, MT: Falcon, 1991. Includes about two dozen hikes in south-central and southeast Utah.

Hinchman, Sandra. *Hiking the Southwest's Canyon Country.* Seattle: The Mountaineers, 1997. Six itineraries through the Four Corners region, each of which takes two to three weeks. Emphasizing outdoor recreation, it's written in an easy style. A fun book for planning your next venture.

Lambrechtse, Rudi. *Hiking the Escalante.* Tucson, AZ: Treasure Chest Publications, 1999. Accurate coverage of many of the monument's best trails.

Parent, Lawrence. *Hiking New Mexico.* Helena, MT: Falcon, 1998. Includes four hikes in northeast New Mexico, such as Angel Peak and the Bisti Badlands.

Urmann, David. *Trail Guide to Grand Staircase–Escalante National Monument.* Salt Lake City: Gibbs Smith, 1999. This small book, slim enough to fit in your pack, details 52 hikes throughout the monument.

Wilson, Dave. *Hiking Ruins Seldom Seen.* Helena, MT: Falcon, 1999. Cultural background and detailed directions to ruins and rock art throughout the Four Corners states, mostly concentrated in central Arizona but also five in southeast Utah.

Mountain Biking

Alley, Sarah Bennett. *Mountain Biking New Mexico*. Helena, MT: Falcon, 2001. Covers the whole state, including six rides near Farmington and Chaco Canyon.

Beakley, Paul. *Mountain Bike America: Arizona*. Guilford, CT: Globe Pequot Press, 2002. Includes half a dozen trails near Flagstaff, a few more in the Grand Canyon area and one near Page.

Bennett, Sarah. *Mountain Biking Arizona*. Helena, MT: Falcon, 1993. Many trails near Flagstaff and up on the Kaibab Plateau, as well as the Monument Valley loop, with maps and trail information.

Bridgers, Lee. *Mountain Bike America: Moab*. Charlottesville, VA: Beachway Press, 2000. Fifty rides from easy to punishing, plus superb maps and trail details.

Bromka, Greg. *Mountain Biking Utah*. Helena, MT: Falcon, 1999. About half the trails in this all-inclusive guide are located in the southern half of the state, from Hovenweep to the Hole-in-the-Rock.

Campbell, Todd. *Above and Beyond Slickrock*. Salt Lake City: University of Utah Press, 1999. The original comprehensive guide to the Moab area's mountain biking wonders.

Gong, Linda and Bromka, Gregg. *Mountain Biking Colorado*. Helena, MT: Falcon, 1994. Sixty-six mountain bike trails throughout the state, including seven near Durango and Flagstaff.

Grubbs, Bruce. *Mountain Biking Flagstaff & Sedona*. Helena, MT: Falcon, 1999. A pocket-sized guide with 25 rides near Flagstaff and 10 more around Sedona, featuring the typical Falcon attention to detail.

McCoy, Michael. *Mountain Bike! Southern Utah*. Birmingham: Menasha Ridge Press, 2000. About half of the 75 rides in this slim but detailed volume are in southeast and south-central Utah.

Rock Climbing

Bjørnstad, Eric. *Desert Rock: Rock Climbs in the National Parks*. Helena, MT: Falcon, 1996. Routes in Arches, Canyonlands, Capitol Reef, Zion, and Glen Canyon National Recreation Area.

Bjørnstad, Eric. *Desert Rock II: Wall Street to the San Rafael Swell*. Helena, MT: Falcon, 1998. Covers short crack routes in the San Rafael area as well as some spots near Moab.

Bjørnstad, Eric. *Desert Rock III: Moab to Colorado National Monument*. Helena, MT: Falcon, 1999. Authoritative and detailed, this guide covers over 500 routes in all the climbing spots near Moab, from the Fisher Towers to the Island in the Sky.

Bjørnstad, Eric. *Desert Rock IV: Remote Areas of the Colorado Plateau*. Helena, MT: Falcon, 2002. Includes the Valley of the Gods and other even more isolated spots.

Macdonald, Dougald and McNamara, Chris. *Desert Towers Select*. SuperTopo, 2002. This incredibly detailed guide to 15 tower routes in Arches, Castle Valley, Colorado National Monument, Canyonlands, and Indian Creek is available for download in PDF format for $9.95 from www.supertopo.com, and includes free updates for three years.

Canyoneering

Allen, Steve. *Canyoneering: The San Rafael Swell*. Salt Lake City: University of Utah Press, 1992. The definitive guide to exploring the canyons of south-central Utah. Incredibly detailed and comprehensive.

Allen, Steve. *Canyoneering 2: Technical Loop Hikes in Southern Utah*. Salt Lake City: University of Utah Press, 1995. Seven weeklong routes in south-central Utah, all covered with Allen's typical thoroughness.

Allen, Steve. *Canyoneering 3: Loop Hikes in Utah's Escalante.* Salt Lake City: University of Utah Press, 1997. Descriptions of 37 hikes and 14 roads, mostly in Grand Staircase–Escalante National Monument.

Other Guides

Eddington, Patrick and Makov, Susan. *The Trading Post Guidebook.* Flagstaff, AZ: Northland Publishing, 1995. Although somewhat out of date, this is a beautiful book listing trading posts, galleries, museums, auctions, and individual artists throughout the Four Corners region, illustrated with maps and hand-tinted photos.

Kosik, Fran. *Native Roads: The Complete Motoring Guide to the Navajo and Hopi Nations.* Tucson, AZ: Rio Nuevo, 1996. Bursting with fascinating details, this guide takes you down all the major roads on the reservations.

NATURAL HISTORY

The **Western National Parks Association,** 12880 North Vistoso Village Dr., Tucson, AZ 85737, 520/622-1999, fax 520/623-9519, www.wnpa.org, info@wnpa.org, offers many excellent natural history guidebooks to the Four Corners and the greater Southwest. These are available from them or at bookstores in the area, and include *Shrubs and Trees of the Southwest Uplands, Flowers of the Southwest Deserts, 50 Common Amphibians and Reptiles of the Southwest, 70 Common Cacti of the Southwest, 50 Common Mammals of the Southwest, 50 Common Reptiles of the Southwest, 100 Desert Wildflowers of the Southwest, 100 Roadside Wildflowers of the Southwest,* and *Flowers of the Southwest Mountains.*

Another good line is the **"The Story Behind the Scenery"** series produced by KC Publications, 3245 E. Patrick Ln., Suite A, Las Vegas, NV 89120, 888/KCBOOKS, www.kcpublica-

tions.com, kcp@kcpublications.com. These large-format publications (part book, part glossy magazine) treat the natural and human history of a specific Southwest location. A good way to get an overview of an area or topic, they're sold at bookstores and gift shops in parks and major towns. *Arches: The Story Behind the Scenery* is a good example of the series. The rest of the Four Corners list includes *Canyonlands, Canyon de Chelly Landforms: Heart of the Colorado Plateau, Capitol Reef, Glen Canyon/Lake Powell, Grand Canyon, Grand Circle Adventure, Monument Valley, Petrified Forest, Mesa Verde,* and *Rainbow Bridge.* KC Publications also produces, in a similar format, *Southwestern Indian Tribes, Southwestern Indian Ceremonials, Southwestern Indian Pottery, Southwestern Indian Weaving, Southwestern Indian Arts and Crafts,* and two volumes subtitled "Voyages of Discovery": *Major John Wesley Powell* and *Mormon Trail.*

Flora and Fauna

Arizona Birds: An Introduction to Familiar Species. Blain, WA: Waterford Press, 2001. A folding, plastic-coated sheet with dozens of illustrations of common species.

Fagan, Damian. *Canyon Country Wildflowers.* Helena, MT: Falcon, 1998. Look up that pretty blossom by color in this photo-rich guide covering the central Colorado Plateau.

McIvor, D. E. *Birding Utah.* Helena, MT: Falcon, 1998. Detailed route descriptions and species lists, with over a dozen in the Colorado Plateau region.

Peterson, Roger Tory. *Western Birds.* Boston: Houghton Mifflin, 1990. "The Birder's Bible" includes full-color paintings and range maps of over 1,000 birds from 700 species.

Stuckey, Maggie and Palmer, George. *Western Trees: A Field Guide.* Helena, MT: Falcon, 1998. Identification information on common trees from Colorado to Washington state and Northern California.

Utah Birds: An Introduction to Familiar Species. Blain, WA: Waterford Press, 2001. A folding, plastic-coated sheet with dozens of illustrations of common species.

Williams, David. *A Naturalist's Guide to Canyon Country.* Helena, MT: Falcon, 2002. Covers the geology, flora, and fauna of the canyonlands in one handy volume. If you buy only one natural-history guide, make it this one.

Geology

Baars, Donald. *A Traveler's Guide to the Geology of the Colorado Plateau.* Salt Lake City: University of Utah Press, 2002. Organized by route, this guide takes you from the Paradox Basin to the High Plateaus and explains everything you see along the way.

Baars, Donald. *Navajo Country: A Geology and Natural History of the Four Corners Region.* Albuquerque: University of New Mexico Press, 1995. If you've ever giggled at terms like "Shinarump Member," this book will tell you what it really means. An in-depth exploration of the amazing scenery on the reservation and surrounding lands.

Blair, Gerry. *Rockhounding Arizona.* Helena, MT: Falcon, 1992. Seventy-five sites throughout the state, including Petrified Forest National Park, the Navajo Reservation, and the Grand Canyon area.

Kappele, William A. *Rockhounding Utah.* Helena, MT: Falcon, 1996. What to look for and where to look for it, from agate in the San Rafael Swell to petrified wood in Fry Canyon.

Land Use, Development, and Water Issues

Farmer, Jared. *Glen Canyon Dammed: Inventing Lake Powell and the Canyon Country.* Tucson, AZ: University of Arizona Press, 1999. Discusses the Glen Canyon Dam and its place in the economy and culture of the Southwest.

Fradkin, Philip. *A River No More: The Colorado River and the West.* University of California Press, 1996. The story of the Colorado River and its tributaries, and their impact on the ranches, towns, and cities of the region.

Fradkin, Philip. *Sagebrush Country: Land and the American West.* Tucson, AZ: University of Arizona Press, 1989. Examines the role of land issues in shaping the history of the West, from the perspectives of settlers, miners, scientists, ranchers, environmentalists, and Native Americans.

Martin, Russell. *A Story That Stands Like a Dam: Glen Canyon and the Struggle for the Soul of the West.* Salt Lake City: University of Utah Press, 1999. The colorful story of the construction of Glen Canyon Dam and the controversy that arose in its wake.

Porter, Eliot. *The Place No One Knew: Glen Canyon on the Colorado.* Salt Lake City: Gibbs Smith, 2000. The commemorative edition of the classic paean to the canyon that was drowned beneath Lake Powell. Evocative photographs accompany writings by Wallace Stegner, Joseph Wood Crutch, and others.

Reisner, Marc. *Cadillac Desert: The American West and Its Disappearing Water.* Penguin USA, 1993. The rollicking tale of water use, and misuse, in the West. Seldom has such a potentially dry topic been covered so entertainingly.

General Guides

Grubbs, Bruce. *Desert Hiking Tips.* Helena, MT: Falcon, 1998. A pocket-sized guide on staying safe and happy in the desert, whether you're driving or hiking.

MacMahon, James. *Deserts.* New York: Alfred A. Knopf, 1997. A National Audubon Society Guide to all the major North American deserts, this wide-ranging field manual includes photographs and descriptions of plants, animals, insects, and ecosystems.

Tweit, Susan. *The Great Southwest Nature Factbook*. Seattle: Alaska Northwest Books, 1992. Packed with tons of tidbits on the region's plants, animals, and natural features, this book is equally fascinating at home as on the trail.

Magazines

Subtitled "Land and Peoples of the Colorado Plateau", the *Plateau Journal* 928/774-5211, ext. 240, www.musnaz.org/Research/Publications.htm, publications@mna.mus.az.us, is a gorgeous magazine put out by the Museum of Northern Arizona. It covers the human and natural history of the Four Corners in vivid prose and photography, and can be found a bookstores and gift shops. *Inside Outside*, PO Drawer J, Durango, CO 81302, 970/247-3504, fax 970/259-5011, www .insideoutsidemag.com, is a tabloid-format magazine on recreation, health, entertainment, and the cultures of the Four Corners. It's put out eight times a year by the *Durango Herald*, and is available throughout the region for free.

NATIVE CULTURES

Anasazi

Frazier, Kendrick. *People of Chaco*. New York: W.W. Norton & Co., 1999. One of the best single-volume treatments of the ancient culture, its history, and descendants.

Lekson, Stephen. *The Chaco Meridian*. Walnut Creek, CA: Altamira Press, 1999. Explores the implications of the fact that the ruins at Aztec, Chaco, and Paquime, Mexico, are on almost the exact same longitude.

Roberts, David. *In Search of the Old Ones*. New York: Touchstone, 1996. The author's descriptions of his explorations of Anasazi ruins and history read like a good novel.

Archaeology

Gardner, A. Dudley and Brinkerhoff, Val. *Architecture of the Ancient Ones*. Salt Lake City: Gibbs Smith, 2000. A beautifully photographed book on the design of the Anasazi ruins.

Kelen, Leslie and Sucec, David. *Sacred Images: A Vision of Native American Rock Art*. Salt Lake City: Gibbs Smith, 1996. More great photos of Anasazi remnants, this time concentrating on their rock art, as well as that of the Fremont and the Ute.

Noble, David Grant. *Ancient Ruins of the Southwest: An Archeological Guide*. Flagstaff, AZ: Northland Publishing, 2000. Rich with background information, this guide covers the ruins of the Mogollon, Hohokam, Anasazi, Fremont, and other ancient cultures.

Slifer, Dennis. *Guide to Rock Art of the Utah Region*. Santa Fe: Ancient City Press, 2000. Background and location information on dozens of sites on public land in southern Utah, Colorado, New Mexico, Arizona, and Nevada.

Modern Tribes

Fergusson, Erna and Hillerman, Tony. *Dancing Gods: Indian Ceremonials of New Mexico and Arizona*. Albuquerque: University of New Mexico Press, 2001. Visiting details and background information on native ceremonies open to the public on the Navajo, Hopi, and Apache Reservations and the Zuñi and Rio Grande Pueblos.

Locke, Raymond. *The Book of the Navajo*. Los Angles: Mankind Publishing, 2002. Addresses the Navajo belief system and other aspects of traditional culture, as well as their history.

Pettit, Jan. *Utes: The Mountain People*. Boulder, CO: Johnson Books, 1990. The full tribal history, with rare historic photographs and extensive cultural detail.

Water, Frank. *Book of the Hopi*. New York: Penguin, 1977. The tribe's historical, spiritual, and cultural history, touching on creation stories, clan migrations, and the ceremonial cycle.

Crafts

Bassman, Theda. *Treasures of the Hopi*. Flagstaff, AZ: Northland Publishing, 1997. Covers all the tribe's major crafts, including jewelry, kachinas, pottery, and baskets.

Bassman, Theda. *Treasures of the Navajo*. Flagstaff, AZ: Northland Publishing, 1997. Covers all the tribe's major crafts, including jewelry, pottery, rugs, and sandpaintings.

Day, Jonathan. *Traditional Hopi Kachinas*. Flagstaff, AZ: Northland Publishing, 2000. Describes and depicts the work of a new generation of artisans and their relationship to older styles of carvers.

Hayes, Allan and Blom, John. *Southwestern Pottery: Anasazi to Zuni*. Flagstaff, AZ: Northland Publishing, 1996. A definitive guide to all major indigenous styles of pottery in the Southwest, with photos and interesting historical anecdotes.

Page, Jake. *Field Guide to Southwest Indian Arts and Crafts*. New York: Random House, 1998. Fully illustrated guide to crafts, with descriptions of techniques, cultural history, and information on hundreds of individual artisans.

Wright, Barton. *Hopi Kachinas: The Complete Guide to Collecting Kachina Dolls*. Flagstaff, AZ: Northland Publishing, 1977. A concise but comprehensive manual, with photographs and descriptions of most major kachina figures.

HISTORY

Bergera, Gary (Ed). *On Desert Trails with Everett Ruess*. Salt Lake City: Gibbs Smith, 2000. A selection of Everett's poems and letters, with commentary, photos, and woodcuts.

Clark, H. Jackson. *The Owl in Monument Canyon*. Salt Lake City: University of Utah Press, 1993. Fascinating stories and memories from the author's four decades as a trader on the Navajo Reservation during the mid-20th century.

Murray, John. *Cinema Southwest*. Flagstaff, AZ: Northland Publishing, 2000. The history of the Southwest as seen through the movie camera's lens. Describes movie locations and biographies of major Western stars.

Rusho, W. L. (Ed). *Everett Ruess: A Vagabond for Beauty & Wilderness Journals*. Salt Lake City: Gibbs Smith, 2002. The combined edition of both books about the teenage wanderer combines letters and journal entries from his all-too-brief life.

Taylor, Mark. *Sandstone Sunsets: In Search of Everett Ruess*. Salt Lake City: Gibbs Smith, 1997. The story of one man's obsession with one of the Southwest's most enduring mysteries.

Warner, Ted (Ed.) *The Dominguez-Escalante Journal*. Salt Lake City: University of Utah Press, 1995. The story of the incredible 1776 journey in the Padres' own words, with annotations and maps.

Scenery and Photography

Spring, Anselm. *Wild and Beautiful: Grand Staircase–Escalante National Monument*. Salt Lake City: Gibbs Smith, 1998. Striking photographs of the monument's many moods, with an essay by Mark Taylor.

Telford, John and Williams, Terry Tempest. *Coyote's Canyon*. Salt Lake City: Gibbs Smith, 1981. Telford's photographs and Williams' prose do a wonderful job of evoking the grandeur of the Four Corners' landscapes.

LITERATURE

Nonfiction

Abbey, Edward. *Beyond the Wall: Essays from the Outside*. New York: Henry Holt, 1984. A collection of essays on life in the West, in Abbey's trademark cantankerous, yet reverent style.

Abbey, Edward. *Desert Solitaire.* New York: Ballantine, 1968. The classic story of the author's sojourn at Arches before the crowds arrived. Should be required reading for all visitors.

Abbey, Edward. *The Journey Home: Some Words in Defense of the American West.* New York: E.P. Dutton, 1991. More essays, with a focus on the desert Southwest.

Dunaway, David King and Spurgeon, Sarah. *Writing the Southwest.* New York: Penguin, 1995. An excellent introduction to the regional literature with pieces by Edward Abbey, John Nichols, Barbara Kingsolver, Tony Hillerman, and others, as well as a selected bibliography.

Ellis, Reuben (Ed). *Stories and Stone: Writing the Anasazi Homeland.* An anthology of writing about the prehistoric Southwest, with contributions from Barry Lopez, Willa Cather, Robert Frost, Leslie Marmon Silko, and others.

Powell, John Wesley. *The Exploration of the Colorado River and Its Canyons.* Washington, D.C.: National Geographic, 2002. The exhilarating, first-hand account of one of the most incredible voyages of discovery in American history.

Shoumatoff, Alex. *Legends of the American Desert.* New York: HarperCollins, 1997. Subtitled "Sojourns in the Greater Southwest," this highly readable account covers the many diverging worlds that make up the region, from Mormons to drug traffickers.

Stegner, Wallace. *Beyond the Hundredth Meridian: John Wesley Powell and the Second Opening of the West.* New York: Penguin, 1992. Probably the best account of Powell's life, adventures, and struggles.

Stegner, Wallace. *Mormon Country.* Lincoln, NE: University of Nebraska Press, 1992. Essays on southern Utah, both historical and modern, in the author's gorgeous prose.

Fiction

Tony Hillerman's best-selling series of police mysteries, set on the Navajo reservation, give a fascinating glimpse into modern Navajo culture—and they're darn good reading as well. Titles include *A Thief of Time, First Eagle, Sacred Clowns, The Dark Wind, The Fallen Man, Listening Woman, Skinwalkers, Hunting Badger, Dance Hall of the Dead, Coyote Waits, The Blessing Way, Talking God, People of Darkness, The Ghost Way,* and *Wailing Wind.*

The other two best-known novels set in the Four Corners are **Edward Abbey's** hilarious *The Monkey Wrench Gang* (New York: Avon, 1985) and *Hayduke Lives!* (New York: Little Brown & Co., 1991), both detailing the exploits of a band of eco-saboteurs fighting against the industrialization of the Colorado Plateau. The first (the better of the two) was partly responsible for the creation of Earth First!, the confrontational environmental group.

Internet Resources

www.recreation.gov

This government website provides information on federal recreation areas, including many in the Four Corners. Searchable by state and activity, as of 2002 it was being expanded to include data on state, tribal, and local recreation areas.

www.desertusa.com

An excellent online resource for information on the deserts of the American Southwest, with everything from cultural history to shopping. Regularly updated with new articles, it includes maps, wildflower reports, current festivals, and a message board.

www.canyonlands-utah.com

A joint venture of the Moab Area Travel Council (www.discovermoab.com) and San Juan County Visitor Services (www.southeastutah.com), this site provides links to attractions, activities, tour operators, accommodations, and other online travel resources.

www.cpluhna.nau.edu/index.htm

Titled "Land Use History of the Colorado Plateau," this website is full of information on the natural and human history of the Four Corners. It's produced by NASA, the USGS, and Northern Arizona University, so you know it's accurate, covering everything from uranium mining to endangered species.

http://ourworld.compuserve.com/home pages/larry_dilucchio/homepage.htm

Computer systems analyst Larry DiLucchio has compiled an extensive collection of information on the Navajo tribe and reservation. Having lived in Chinle for over 15 years, he has assembled an excellent list of questions and answers on daily life on the Res from an outsider's perspective.

www.infozona.com

Virtual Arizona is a one-stop site for links to nearly everything related to visiting Arizona, including (but definitely not limited to) travel, recreation, food, entertainment, and lodging.

http://archive.li.suu.edu/voices

This online archive compiled by Southern Utah University features photographs and oral history recordings of life on the Colorado Plateau. You'll need the Flash player to view the recordings, but it's worth it to be able to hear the voices of native elders and settlers.

www.go-utah.com

Over 10,000 pages of information on the Beehive State, covering 100 cities and towns as well as parks, activities, and lodging. Basically an online travel guide, this rivals many print versions and even includes an online bookstore.

www.gorp.com

The Great Outdoor Resource Page is the place to go for details on anything and everything in outdoor recreation. You can browse by state (Arizona, for example, is at http://gorp.com/gorp/location/az/az.htm) or other destination, as well as by activity. It even book trips online—just be ready for plenty of advertisements.

www.americansouthwest.net

This well-organized site covers the parks and scenic spots of Arizona, California, Colorado, Nevada, New Mexico, Texas, and Utah. Articles feature excellent photography and detailed visiting instructions, and there's a particularly good section on slot canyons.

**www.nau.edu/library/speccoll/exhibits/trad
ers/index.html**

A series of interviews with the owners and operators of trading posts in the Four Corners is presented in this well-designed site from Northern Arizona University. It's part of the legacy of the United Indian Traders Association, which disbanded in 1997. The oral histories are a fascinating window into life on the reservations through the 20th century. There is also a slideshow of historic images and descriptions of trade goods and philosophies.

Index

Camping

Index

Hiking

Scenic Drives

Acknowledgments

I am grateful to everyone who helped me see this guide through or appreciate the Four Corners in a new way, including Alison Flynn, Jamie Jensen, Clifton Koontz, Kellie McBee, Chris McNamara, Seth Plunkett, Zane Sadler-holl, Tony Semallie, Mara Shurgot, Adam Switalski, Catherine Woolley, and Patti Zink. This book is dedicated to everyone fighting to protect the beauty, culture, and history of the Colorado Plateau.

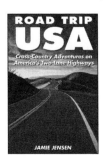

U.S.~Metric Conversion

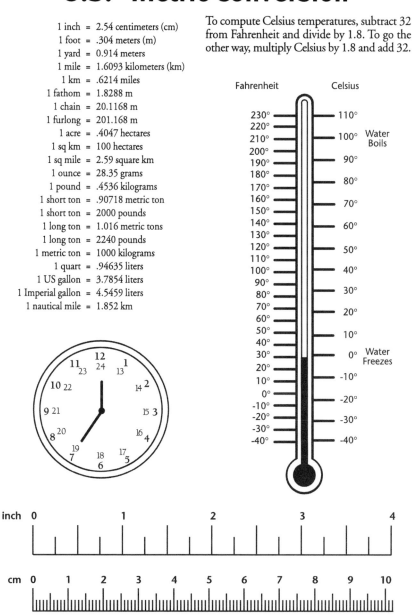

1 inch	=	2.54 centimeters (cm)
1 foot	=	.304 meters (m)
1 yard	=	0.914 meters
1 mile	=	1.6093 kilometers (km)
1 km	=	.6214 miles
1 fathom	=	1.8288 m
1 chain	=	20.1168 m
1 furlong	=	201.168 m
1 acre	=	.4047 hectares
1 sq km	=	100 hectares
1 sq mile	=	2.59 square km
1 ounce	=	28.35 grams
1 pound	=	.4536 kilograms
1 short ton	=	.90718 metric ton
1 short ton	=	2000 pounds
1 long ton	=	1.016 metric tons
1 long ton	=	2240 pounds
1 metric ton	=	1000 kilograms
1 quart	=	.94635 liters
1 US gallon	=	3.7854 liters
1 Imperial gallon	=	4.5459 liters
1 nautical mile	=	1.852 km

To compute Celsius temperatures, subtract 32 from Fahrenheit and divide by 1.8. To go the other way, multiply Celsius by 1.8 and add 32.

Fahrenheit   Celsius

230° — 110°
220°
210° — 100° Water Boils
200°
190° — 90°
180°
170° — 80°
160°
150° — 70°
140° — 60°
130°
120° — 50°
110°
100° — 40°
90°
80° — 30°
70°
60° — 20°
50°
40° — 10°
30°
20° — 0° Water Freezes
10° — -10°
0°
-10° — -20°
-20°
-30° — -30°
-40° — -40°

inch 0   1   2   3   4

cm 0 1 2 3 4 5 6 7 8 9 10

Keeping Current

Although we strive to produce the most up-to-date guidebook humanly possible, change is unavoidable. Between the time this book goes to print and the moment you read it, a handful of the businesses noted in these pages will undoubtedly change prices, move, or even close their doors forever. Other worthy attractions will open for the first time. If you have a favorite gem you'd like to see included in the next edition, or see anything that needs updating, clarification, or correction, please drop us a line. Send your comments via email to atpfeedback@avalonpub.com, or use the address below.

Moon Handbooks Four Corners
Avalon Travel Publishing
1400 65th Street, Suite 250
Emeryville, CA 94608, USA
www.moon.com

Editor and Series Manager: Kevin McLain
Copy Editor: Elizabeth Wolf
Graphics Coordinator: Justin Marler
Production Coordinator: Amber Pirker
Cover Designer: Kari Gim
Interior Designers: Amber Pirker, Alvaro
    Villanueva, Kelly Pendragon
Map Editor: Olivia Solís
Cartographers: Mike Morgenfeld, Kat
    Kalamaras, Suzanne Service, Tim Lohnes
Indexer: Rachel Kuhn

ISBN: 1-56691-581-3
ISSN: 1543-7000

Printing History
1st edition—October 2003

Some photos and illustrations are used by permission and are the property of the original copyright owners.

Front cover photo: Monument Valley, © John Elk
Table of Contents photos: © Julian Smith

Printed in the United States by Malloy Inc.